Castles and Fortifications in Ireland

1485 – 1945

Paul M. Kerrigan

Castles and Fortifications in Ireland

1485 – 1945

Paul M. Kerrigan

The Collins Press
Careys Lane, Huguenot Quarter, Cork

First published in 1995 by
The Collins Press, Carey's Lane, Cork.
© Paul M. Kerrigan, 1995.

British Library cataloguing in publication data.

A CIP catalogue record for this book is available from the
British Library.

Printed in Ireland by Colour Books Ltd., Dublin, Ireland.

Typeset by Upper Case Ltd., Cork.

ISBN-1898256128

The main function and justification of a defensive work, be it of earth, wood or stone, is to enable relatively few defenders to withstand with success the attacks of greater numbers.

H. C. Leask, Irish Castles and Castellated Houses (1941).

Fortification is the art of strengthening, by works of defence, positions in which it is proposed to place troops so as to render them secure from the attack of an enemy. Such positions may contain within them towns, dockyards, arsenals, and ports, or may serve merely for shelter for an army in the field; but the object to be obtained is always the same, and the works of defence are so disposed round the position that, while they offer the greatest obstacles to the advance of their assailants, they afford the utmost shelter to their defenders. Fortification is, in short, the art of enabling the weak to resist the strong.

J. E. Portlock and C. H. Nugent, 'Fortification', in Encyclopaedia Britannica (1879).

The transformation of the styles in which churches and palaces were built during the Renaissance was accompanied by a revolution in the design of fortifications. The explosive mine and gunpowder artillery led to the supplanting of the 'picturesque' castle by the sterner fortress or citadel of the towered wall by the squat bastioned trace.... Yet in the mainstream of architectural history fortifications are accorded but a fitful or embarrassed attention.

J. R. Hale, Renaissance Fortification: Art or Engineering? (1977)

To Eóin and Hugh

Contents

List of Illustrations and Maps

CASTLES AND FORTIFICATIONS IN IRELAND 1485 – 1945

LIST OF MAPS

Foreword

By Dr. Maurice Craig

WHETHER WE LOOK THROUGH the large-scale Ordnance Survey maps, or drive, ride or walk through the Irish countryside, we cannot help noticing features which arouse our interest but do not come under the heading of archaeology as it used to be understood by most people. Most antiquities are either ecclesiastical, military or sepulchral. The traces of early industry are not very conspicuous to the untrained eye. But with the beginning of what we loosely call the 'modern world' all this changes. From the numerous 'tower houses' onwards the physical evidence of attack and defence become more and more noticeable.

The dialectic of challenge and response is the same whether the field is chess, tax-avoidance, espionage (military or industrial), or in the new art of 'hacking' (which presumably elicits that of 'counterhacking'). Most obviously this is so in the art of fortification. As soon as a new method of defence is devised someone invents a method of penetrating it, which in turn provokes counter-innovation, and so it goes on, always under the influence of technological change.

Our island has been much fought over. But even more to the present purpose, the preparations for fights that never happened have left their traces, from the bawn walls and pistol loops of the 17th century through such massive artillery fortifications as Charles Fort, Shannonbridge and the Martello towers, to the concrete pill-boxes left over from the 'Emergency' of 1939-45, not to mention more recent conflict.

Till now these monuments – for so we must call them – have received much less attention than the ruins from the medieval period. There is much overlap, of course, because not only were such early castles as Athlone, Carrickfergus and Limerick adapted for artillery defence, but, owing to the difficulty of using cannon where there no roads, the earlier, 'vertical' type of fortification lasted in Ireland much longer than in most other countries. We hear much today of 'networks'. It is worth remembering that the rapid transmission of information is a vital part of defence, and that the signal towers and coast-guard stations of the 19th century are sometimes as conspicuous, though seldom as solidly built, as the batteries and emplacements which embody defence.

All these monuments receive their due in Paul Kerrigan's pages, set in their context described in detail, and illustrated. Those who have enjoyed and profited by his articles in *An Cosantóir* and *The Irish Sword* will welcome this book, and for a wider public it will be an introduction to a new world of pleasure in exploration, discovery and recognition.

Preface

This outline of the development of fortifications in Ireland in the age of artillery and firearms starts with the introduction of these weapons in the fifteenth century. The increasing effectiveness of artillery was paralleled by the increasing power of the state, in the form of the Tudor monarchy, represented in Ireland by the lord deputy, his officials and military forces. A distinction gradually emerged between the castles and new forts garrisoned by forces of the lord deputy and the castles of the landowners and chieftains, which were usually unable to offer any effective resistance to attack by the government forces when these were equipped with artillery.

The form of artillery fortification based on the angled bastion, which developed in Italy in the early sixteenth century, was well established in Ireland by the end of the Elizabethan wars, both as fieldworks or earthwork campaign forts and permanent masonry works. The new forts played an important part in the subjugation of Ulster and in coastal defence. Following the plantations of the early seventeenth century, with their distinctive fortified houses and bawns and the construction of the larger defensible settlements such as Coleraine and Derry, the rising of 1641 heralded more than a decade of warfare, which included numerous sieges of towns and castles. As many of those in command of the various forces in Ireland at this time were veterans of the Thirty Years' War, the fortifications reflected contemporary European ideas in design and construction. The Cromwellian period resulted in the construction of new forts and citadels for coastal defence and internal security.

The later seventeenth century, which might be termed the classical period of bastioned artillery fortification—the age of Vauban—is represented in Ireland by Charles Fort, constructed to defend the harbour of Kinsale. The war between James II and William of Orange was notable for the sieges of several towns and forts, while fieldworks were constructed by both armies at strategic locations and as outworks to earlier defences. The Williamite settlement was accompanied by a network of barracks constructed throughout the country, some of which were small defensible works known as redoubts, sited at strategic positions.

For most of the eighteenth century there was little activity in the construction of new fortifications. Towards the end of the century defences were erected at Cork Harbour: some ten years later the outbreak of war with France in 1793 was to lead to more than twenty years of conflict. From 1803 onwards an extensive scheme of coastal defence works, including the Martello towers, was under construction, with additional fortifications inland on the Shannon and elsewhere. This building programme was on a larger scale than that of any previous defence works undertaken in the country, and shows that invasion was considered a serious threat.

The next important programme of construction followed the development of armoured warships and the introduction of rifled ordnance, with a much-increased range and effectiveness, in the second half of the nineteenth century. As artillery became more powerful at the end of the century there was a move towards siting the guns in open concrete emplacements, with little protection for the gun crews. These forts and batteries defended ports and anchorages which, after the Anglo-Irish Treaty of 1921, became known as the Treaty Ports. These remained under British control until 1938, when, under the Anglo-Irish Agreement, they were handed over to the Irish Government, and detachments of the Irish army replaced the British garrisons. During the 1939-45 period these coastal defences were added to by the construction of a new fort in the Shannon estuary.

Some fortifications have been dealt with at length, others much more briefly, partly reflecting the number of surviving structures of each period and the availability of documentary evidence. For many sites, particularly those of the sixteenth and seventeenth centuries, the only evidence apart from that which might emerge from archaeological excavations is in the form of contemporary documents, maps or plans. In some instances contemporary plans, with the aid of large-scale modern maps and site investigation, have enabled the size and extent of fortifications to be determined. Sometimes fragmentary remains of town defences may be identified in this way. A large number of seventeenth-century fieldworks must remain to be identified at various places throughout the country. A great deal of documentary material survives on the Napoleonic period, including records of building operations and costs with, in some instances, plans and maps. However, there must be a considerable amount of material awaiting discovery in record offices and libraries. The fortifications of the later part of the nineteenth century and the opening years of the present century have been dealt with in outline only, in an attempt to bring the story of defence works in Ireland up to the present day. Much more space is required

than is available within the confines of this book to describe the complex of late nineteenth-century works and batteries at the harbour entrance forts of Camden and Carlisle defending Cork Harbour. The later batteries and forts at Berehaven and Lough Swilly also require investigation and description.

An attempt was made to visit as many as possible of the fortifications described or noted in this account. Where this has not been possible, the evidence of contemporary documents, plans, maps or published work has been used where available. The topic of artillery fortifications in Ireland has not previously been dealt with in any detail, with a few exceptions, such as a number of articles by the present writer in *An Cosantóir* and *The Irish Sword*. Dr Rolf Loeber has carried out pioneering work on seventeenth-century engineers and architects in Ireland, many of whom were involved in the design and construction of fortifications. A certain amount has been published on the plantation castles and bawns, particularly in the *Ulster Journal of Archaeology*; while Dr Maurice Craig has discussed tower houses and the early seventeenth-century fortified houses in detail in *The Architecture of Ireland from the Earliest Times to 1880*. Of particular importance is *Ulster and Other Irish Maps c. 1600* edited by the late G.A. Hayes-McCoy, for contemporary plans of forts in Ulster and elsewhere. This survey of fortifications in Ireland over the last five centuries is offered as an introduction to the subject. Further investigation - both fieldwork and research - will fill in a number of gaps in the story.

Acknowledgements

THIS BOOK IS THE result of many years of research and fieldwork: assistance, advice and information from a large number of people has enlarged the scope and detail of the work considerably. Among those who have helped in a variety of ways are Con Costello, former editor of *An Cosantóir*, who first encouraged me to write on fortifications in Ireland, Dr. Harman Murtagh, editor of *The Irish Sword*, Dr Rolf Loeber for information on seventeenth-century fortifications in Ireland and Dr. Kenneth Ferguson on various aspects from the late sixteenth century to the Napoleonic Wars. Dr. John de Courcy Ireland provided information on Martello and signal towers, and the late N.W. English encouraged my research on the Shannon fortifications near Athlone.

Niall Brunicardi showed me around Hawlbowline Island many years ago; the late Tony Bishop conducted me around Fort Camden, while subsequent visits to Camden and Fort Carlisle were arranged by Commandant Michael Verling, Walter McGrath, formerly of *Cork Examiner*, provided information on the Cork Harbour Martello towers and the Cork signal towers. The late Stan Carroll and Ben Murtagh introduced me to the town wall fortifications of Waterford. Among those concerned with various aspects of Irish history, help and information has come from Dr. Maurice Craig, Dr. John Andrews formerly of the Department of Geography, Trinity College, Dublin, Commandant Peter Young, Army Archives, Dublin and Ruth Delany for information on the Shannon defence works.

I am grateful for the help from the staff of a number of libraries and other institutions where I was able to see maps, plans and contemporary manuscripts. in particular the National Library of Ireland, the library of Trinity College, Dublin, the Royal Irish Academy, the Ordnance Survey, Phoenix Park, Dublin and Army Archives, Dublin.

Paul Gosling provided information on the Galway bay Martellos towers and west coast signal towers; Tim Robinson also produced information on the western signal towers and the Aran Islands garrison at Arkin. With Hugh Dixon and Brian Williams I visited a number of sites in the north of Ireland and Ian Gailey has provided information on Greypoint Battery. Local historians in various parts of the country have drawn my attention to particular sites - Ireland is fortunate in having a number of very active local history societies.

In England, Andrew Saunders and Dr. Alan Guy have introduced me to material on Irish fortifications in the Public Record Office and elsewhere.

Finally, I would like to thank my sons Eóin and Hugh, who have explored many Irish castles and fortifications with me, often assisting with surveying and measurements; they have also had to live with the preparation of this book for a considerable time.

Illustration Credits

Fig 3 KLM Aerophoto NV Schipo, figs.16, 22, 25, 44, 46, 47, 80, 127, 140, 141, the library, Trinity College Dublin; 18, 19, 20, 73, 74, 98 and 125; Public Record Office, London; fig.23 the Hunt Museum, the University of Limerick; figs, 26, 27, 52, 55, 59, 62, 68, 71, 75 and142, the National Library of Ireland; figs. 30, 31, 34, 48 and 25, the British Library; fig. 45 Cambridge University Collection of Air Photographs; fig.50 Worcester College Oxford; fig.55 Staffordshire County Library; fig.64. National Gallery of Ireland; fig.95. National Library of Scotland; fig.97 the Irish Air Corps; fig.126. Simmons of Athlone; figs 160 and 161, Historic Monuments and Buildings Branch, Department of the Environment, Northern Ireland; fig.162. Dr. Daphne Pochin Mould; fig.163 Dr Colin Rynne.

Chapter 1
Artillery Fortifications in Europe and Ireland

BY THE SECOND HALF of the fifteenth century, the increasing effectiveness of artillery was bringing about a change in the design and construction of fortifications. The tall medieval walls and towers of towns and castles were unable to withstand a constant battering by well-placed siege guns. Turkish artillery at the capture of Constantinople in 1453 heralded the end of the siege warfare of battering rams and stone-throwing catapults of the middle ages. Some years earlier the French were taking English-held towns in France with the aid of cannon. Only the central authority of the state or the more wealthy cities and towns could afford to equip and maintain a train of artillery, a development that was to contribute considerably to the consolidation of state power in the early modern period.

Castles and town defences were modified to allow for the mounting of artillery on platforms or behind embrasures in walls or towers; but these limited alterations were ineffective in countering the fire of siege batteries. Defences were strengthened with earthworks, either behind existing walls or in the form of a protective embankment of earth on the exterior, while gun platforms and outworks were placed outside gateways and at salient angles of the defences. Some of these outworks took the form of circular or semicircular bastions in front of the earlier towers or gatehouses, low earthwork and timber structures mounting artillery.[1] However, these modifications were soon to give way to a new, scientific approach to the design of fortifications, which evolved in the late fifteenth century in Italy, becoming well established by the early decades of the following century. With further elaborations, this system of low, broad bastions

and ramparts with triangular outworks was to last for some three hundred years, until the close of the eighteenth century. During these three centuries the weapons that determined this defensive system remained essentially unchanged in effectiveness and range: the muzzle-loading smooth-bore cannon, and the musket of the infantryman. The development of the square-rigged sailing ship, carrying a broadside armament of heavy cannon, in the early years of the sixteenth century, emphasised the importance of fortifications equipped with artillery for defending ports and anchorages.

In 1494 King Charles VIII of France invaded Italy with a mobile train of siege artillery: bronze guns on field carriages, firing iron shot. The French successes in taking fortresses with their cannon had a considerable impact, causing many places to surrender without resistance and this campaign may be considered a turning-point in military history.

The art of fortification and siege-craft developed rapidly in Italy during the first three decades of the sixteenth century. Designs of 1487 attributed to Giuliano Sangallo had included the angle-bastion; his brother Antonio built a fortress including the new type of bastion in 1494. This was followed by other bastioned works, including one of a regular pentagonal plan, a form that was to reappear frequently over the next three centuries, particularly for citadels and larger detached forts. The first large-scale use of the bastion for town fortifications was at Verona, where Michele di Sanmicheli added large angle-bastions to the defences between 1525 and 1530; he also carried out work at Brescia, Padua and elsewhere for the Venetian

1

Republic. The bastioned system of artillery fortification gradually spread to other European countries and to their overseas colonies, aided by the translation of illustrated Italian works on fortification into French, English and other languages.

In the north of England, works of a transitional nature were carried out at Berwick-upon-Tweed to strengthen the medieval defences against Scottish attack; in 1522-23 earthen bulwarks or gun platforms were built in several places outside the walls, and an earth backing was provided inside the curtain wall to reinforce it against artillery fire. Works in 1539-42 included a large circular bastion at a salient angle for artillery, and smaller towers in which guns were mounted.[2] The large circular bastion here, and the circular coastal forts built at this time by King Henry VIII, reflected to some extent the large semi-circular bastions for artillery proposed by Albrecht Dürer in his publication of 1527. However, by the end of Henry's reign English engineers were becoming familiar with the new Italian system, when Sir Richard Lee designed the first bastioned town fortifications in England, for Portsmouth in 1545.

In Ireland, the first recorded use of artillery in siege work was the attack on Balrath Castle, Co. Westmeath in 1488 by Garret Mór Fitzgerald, Eighth Earl of Kildare, lord deputy to King Henry VII (Fig.1). Kildare controlled the only artillery in Ireland except for that of the walled towns; he used the king's ordnance for his own purposes, attacking the castles of his opponents. Large guns were used at the siege of Waterford in 1495, when the city was attacked by the supporters of Perkin Warbeck.

After the death of Garret Mór in 1513 his son, Garret Óg, Ninth Earl of Kildare, succeeded him as lord deputy, but he did not remain in the position with the same continuity as his father. He was called to London in 1534, and one of the charges laid against him was the use of the royal

ordnance for his personal advantage. On the false report of his death, his son, Lord Offaly, who had been appointed vice-deputy in his absence, broke out in rebellion and attempted to capture Dublin Castle, where ammunition and gunpowder for the king's artillery were stored. Most of the guns were at Maynooth and other Kildare castles.

In 1535 Maynooth Castle was besieged by Sir William Skeffington. The castle was defended by artillery and new defence works: there is a contemporary reference to a bulwark or bastion newly constructed. The English artillery breached the defences after five days and the

Fig. 1. The ruins of Balrath Castle, Co. Westmeath. The castle was taken in 1488 by the Eight Earl of Kildare, using artillery, the first recorded use of cannon in siege warfare in Ireland.

castle was taken. The attack on Maynooth and the fall of the house of Kildare marks a point of departure in Irish history: the control of Ireland by the great families such as the Fitzgeralds and Butlers was ended, and the new policy of Henry VIII put into effect. The English government was to rule Ireland from Dublin Castle, through English viceroys and government officials.

The capture of Maynooth was followed by attacks on several other castles by Skeffington and his successor, Lord Deputy Grey, demonstrating an equally effective use of artillery. In 1538 Grey sent guns by sea to Galway, avoiding the problems of transporting them overland, with the lack of adequate roads and the danger of ambush. Guns could be unloaded anywhere within reach of ships' boats in estuaries and rivers; control of the sea was to be a decisive factor in military affairs in Tudor Ireland and throughout the following centuries.

There is some evidence for the use of artillery at Irish castles and town defences during the late fifteenth and early sixteenth centuries. At Aughnanure there are small circular openings near ground level in the bawn wall; at Woodstock, Athy—a Fitzgerald castle—two gun-embrasures at high level are in an extension to the earlier castle; Cahir Castle and the castle at Leighlinbridge have gun-embrasures of a different form.

During the brief reign of Edward VI two new defence works, Fort Governor and Fort Protector, were constructed in the midlands, later to be named Philipstown (Daingean) and Maryborough (Portlaoise), after Philip of Spain and Mary Tudor, respectively. These towns were to become the strong-points of the plantations of King's County (Offaly) and Queen's County (Laois). Contemporary plans of Maryborough Fort depict a square structure at one corner of a rectangular enclosure, with a round tower or bastion diagonally opposite; the layout does not reflect the new ideas of the angle-bastion form of artillery fortification. The square enclosure of Philipstown Fort is perhaps essentially the perimeter of the O'Connor fort or castle of Daingean, which contained a tower house in the centre.

Concern for coastal defence in 1548 was repeated in 1551 with proposals to fortify ports on the south and north-east coasts, because of fears of intervention in Ireland by France or Scotland. Sir James Croft was to inspect the harbours and ports from Berehaven along the south coast to Waterford; in the north he was to see to the defence of Strangford, Carrickfergus, Olderfleet, and the estuary of the Bann. There is little evidence that much work was carried out, although the English engineer, John Rogers, was sent to Ireland early in 1551 and presumably the plans sent to London of Baltimore, Kinsale and Cork were prepared by him; and it is recorded that Rogers made a plan of a new castle at Olderfleet, near Larne. It seems probable that the fort of Corkbeg at the eastern side of the entrance to Cork Harbour, depicted on Elizabethan and later maps as the 'King's Work,' was constructed at this time. A plan of c. 1569, when the fort was still not completed, depicts an irregular work with two acute-angled bastions and a demi-bastion; the shape and size of the bastions is similar to those of the citadel under construction at Berwick-upon-Tweed between 1550 and 1557. Work was under way at Berwick between 1560 and 1569 on extensive, large-scale bastioned defences, the costliest fortification programme undertaken in England during the reign of Queen Elizabeth.

Other coastal defence works in Ireland that may have originated from the 1551 survey were at Waterford, Kinsale and Youghal. There was a proposal for a blockhouse for the defence of Waterford Harbour and town in 1560; sixteenth and seventeenth-century plans of Waterford depict a gun battery at the riverside attached to Reginald's Tower. Alternatively, it is possible that the work referred to in 1560 was the block-house at Passage East on the eastern side of Waterford Harbour, which was constructed by the citizens of Waterford by 1568, a low, broad round tower mounting ordnance. Some years later, funds were provided for a similar structure at Kinsale, with a tower projecting into the harbour from the town wall, while seventeenth-century views of Youghal show a low blockhouse with three cannon ports on the side overlooking the harbour. At Galway there had been proposals for fortifying the port in 1548, and in 1550 bulwarks or bastions were to be set out. But it appears that in most places finance was not available, either locally or from the government, for artillery works proposed for coastal defence.

Plans for plantations in eastern Ulster between 1566 and 1573 included the construction of fortifications at strategic points, and conditions were set out to ensure that the new colonists would build castles and defensible settlements, similar to those that were eventually to be constructed in the early seventeenth-century Ulster plantation. Similar proposals for fortified settlements for the Munster coast did not materialise. However, in Ulster, one of the few English garrisons, that at Carrickfergus Castle, was provided with gun-embrasures between 1561 and 1567, and a ditch and rampart were built around the town by 1574; a town wall was under construction some years later, but was still not completed in 1596.[3]

Spanish attempts to control the Netherlands led to intensive warfare there, resulting in new developments in fortification and siege-craft during the last three decades of the sixteenth century. In 1567 work began on a Spanish citadel at Antwerp, a regular pentagonal fort designed by the Italian architect Paciotto, who had built a similar citadel at Turin five years earlier. The citadel was to be a principal element in fortification design for the next three centuries. Often of pentagonal plan, like that at Antwerp, it provided a strong-point for a town or city: a place of last resort in time of siege, like the keep of a medieval castle, and a place of refuge for the garrison in the event of a local uprising. The Dutch developed their own approach to the design of fortifications, with the extensive use of water defences and earthworks, and began to some extent to replace the Italians as leaders in the field of military engineering.

The late sixteenth century also saw the increasing involvement of Spain in Irish affairs, giving aid to those in revolt against Queen Elizabeth. In 1580 a force of Spanish and Italian soldiers occupied an old promontory fort, Dún an Óir at Smerwick, Co. Kerry. On the landward side of the fort they constructed an earthwork parapet and two demi-bastions, traces of which still remain. The position was attacked by English naval and land forces and after a short resistance the garrison surrendered. Earlier that year the English use of sea power had been demonstrated at the capture of Carrigafoyle Castle on the Shannon Estuary, when the guns of the besieging force had been landed from ships, a tactic to be repeated in the Elizabethan wars in Ireland.

The defences of harbours and estuaries assumed greater importance as regular sea warfare developed with Spain in the years leading up to the sailing of the Spanish Armada in 1588, with the increasing risk of a large-scale Spanish landing in Ireland. At Duncannon, Co. Wexford, a castle formed the nucleus for the later artillery fortifications; towards the end of 1587 works were started here for the protection of Waterford Harbour, but in 1589 Lord Deputy Fitzwilliam was against the proposal to complete the fort, as it was commanded by high ground inland. In 1590 extensive earthwork defences were under construction outside the medieval walls of Waterford, while across the estuary from Duncannon Fort the earlier blockhouse at Passage was surrounded by a star-shaped *tenaille trace*: at Limerick and Cork fortifications were also to be built, evidently similar to those at Waterford. It is clear from contemporary documents that fear of a Spanish landing was the reason for the rapid construction of these defence works at the principal southern ports. Captain Edmund Yorke supervised the works at Waterford and Duncannon, and with Sir George Carew was involved in those at Limerick and Cork.

The last decade of the sixteenth century was remarkable for the resistance of Gaelic Ireland to the completion of the Tudor conquest. It was in Ulster that the Gaelic order, under the leadership of Hugh O'Neill, Earl of Tyrone, was to prove most difficult to defeat. After a degree of authority had been established by the English government in Connacht and Munster, attention was turned to the north; the Maguire castle at Enniskillen was taken in 1594, adding a further garrison to those of Carrickfergus, Newry, Monaghan, and the new fort of the Blackwater built in 1575. O'Neill destroyed the Blackwater Fort in 1595, while a new fort built to replace it in 1597 brought about the Battle of the Yellow Ford a year later. In an attempt to relieve the English garrison, a force of some three thousand men was attacked on the march, and O'Neill and his Ulster allies won the greatest victory ever achieved by an Irish army up to that time. For several years the Blackwater river was one of the frontiers of O'Neill's territory, on which attacks were made from Newry and Armagh, and movements into Ulster were attempted from Ballyshannon and from Carrickfergus. Of particular significance was a landing at Lough Foyle under Sir Henry Docwra, who established fortified posts at Derry and Dunalong, farther upstream.

A key element of the warfare in Ulster between 1595 and 1603 was the construction of forts: earthworks with timber palisades constructed by the soldiers to hold key strategic points. The forts were laid out on the principles of artillery fortification, with bastions or demi-bastions at the salient angles; at the fort of Mount Norris an earlier Irish ring-fort formed part of the defences, while in several instances castles were strengthened with earthen outworks. As Lord Deputy Mountjoy was maintaining a continuous pressure on O'Neill in Ulster in 1601, news arrived of the Spanish landing in Kinsale, where the force under del Aguila held the walled town and the outposts of Castle Park and Ringcurran Castle, preventing the use of the harbour by the English fleet. Towards the end of the year the army of O'Neill and O'Donnell marched south to join with the Spaniards in Kinsale; the English victory there at the battle outside the town forecast the end of the Gaelic order in Ireland.[4]

A further Spanish landing in Ireland was widely expected, so plans were made for new forts at Kinsale and at Haulbowline Island in Cork Harbour, while at Galway a rectangular bastioned fort was completed. The engineer for the works at Kinsale and Haulbowline was Paul Ive or Ivye. Work began at Castle Park, Kinsale, early in 1602, a regular pentagonal earthwork fort completed in 1604. Proposals for forts at Berehaven and Baltimore were not carried out. Paul Ive had designed an outer line of defences at Castle Cornet, Guernsey, and carried out other works in the Channel Islands. At Pendennis Castle, Falmouth, he planned a new fortification in 1598-99 around the earlier castle built by Henry VIII, an irregular layout with bastions, adapted to the narrow headland.

With the defeat of the Irish at Kinsale, Mountjoy's attention was again turned to Ulster. O'Neill's castle of Dungannon was taken and more new forts were constructed. Negotiations were opened with Mountjoy, resulting in O'Neill's surrender at Mellifont early in 1603. The war ended with a network of forts in strategic locations across Ulster, their design reflecting the contemporary approaches to fortification design on the Continent. It is known that Dutch engineers were involved in the design of some of them.[5]

Some of the temporary campaign forts were developed into permanent masonry works, such as Charlemont Fort, while temporary earthworks at Derry were replaced between 1614 and 1618 with masonry defences of ramparts and nine bastions. At Coleraine the earthwork defences were in a poor condition when they were surveyed in 1625, the ramparts too narrow and the bastions too small. Many of the forts formed the nucleus of new plantation towns and settlements, while the plantation of Ulster with English and Scottish settlers included conditions for the building of castles and fortified houses or bawns, and most of the smaller settlements were built adjacent to these defensible strong-points. It was believed at the time that it was preferable to build a larger number of fortified towns, such as Derry, in order to control adequately the planted territory; many of the small fortifications of the new settlements were not completed and little resistance could be made when the rising of 1641 broke out.

The opening decades of the seventeenth century saw the development of the fortified house or 'stronghouse,' a transitional type of residence between the tower-house and the undefended mansion of the late seventeenth and eighteenth centuries; examples include Kanturk and Portumna. The house was provided with musket and pistol loops at windows and doorways, while the bawn wall and corner turrets or flankers were also provided with loops for firearms. Similar houses were constructed in Ulster and other plantation areas such as parts of the midlands, often forming one side of a defensive enclosure of courtyard walls and flanking corner towers.

War with Spain in 1625, and later with France, renewed concern for coastal defence. Galway was considered vulnerable, and a new fort was soon constructed, built outside the town at the opposite end of the bridge over the Corrib. The fort had the rectangular plan with corner bastions typical of so many seventeenth-century forts in Ireland. Elizabeth Fort in Cork, built outside the walls to the south of the city in the opening years of the century, was rebuilt. At Waterford a bastioned citadel known as St Patrick's Fort, originally proposed more than ten years earlier, was built as an extension to the walls of the city on the west side. Castle Park Fort at Kinsale and the fort on Haulbowline Island in Cork Harbour were reported as being in a neglected state in 1625. There were frequent reports throughout the seventeenth century in Ireland of the poor condition of fortifications; only the rumours of war, or the outbreak of war, provided the impetus to repair ramparts and parapets and to mount serviceable ordnance. Fortifications both of town defences and individual forts were generally on a small scale, and lacked the elaborate outworks of the continental fortresses.

Warfare in the Netherlands in the late sixteenth-century struggle against Spain had led to the development of new elements of fortification. The Italian triangular outwork, the ravelin, originally developed as a form of barbican or outer defence to protect a gateway, had subsequently been used extensively to protect the main rampart of a fortress between each pair of flanking bastions. On a flat site permitting a regular geometrical layout the ravelin came to be used opposite each length of rampart, providing for flank fire across the faces of the adjacent bastions. Another Italian development of the mid-sixteenth century had been the 'covered way,' a broad pathway on the counterscarp or outer retaining wall of the ditch. The covered way was protected by the artificial embankment of the glacis, a gradual slope down to the surrounding countryside. With the effective range of musketry at some two hundred yards, musketeers stationed in the covered way provided an important extension of the defence.

To these defensive elements were now added the demi-lune or 'half-moon,' a triangular work in front of the bastion, and the hornwork, a more spacious outwork with two demi-bastions joined by a short length of rampart facing the enemy. All these outworks, while extending the defence and the range of the musketry and cannon of the garrison, were open-backed and commanded from the bastions and ramparts of the main fortress. Extensive outworks, however, while increasing the difficulties of the besieging force, required a larger garrison to defend them. A characteristic of the sieges in the Netherlands in the opening years of the seventeenth century was the increasing size of the forces involved: the outcome of a campaign often depended on the successful siege of one or two strongholds, and warfare became increasingly a succession of sieges, as armies became dependent on fortified posts. The outworks at the principal strongholds led to elaborate siegeworks, and the besiegers constructed in addition a line of earthwork forts and trenches in their rear, to protect them against attack from a force coming to the aid of the besieged fortress (Fig.2).

The sixteenth-century leadership of the Italians in fortification design gradually declined in the early decades of the following century, as the Dutch, Spanish, French and Swedish forces in the Thirty Years' War gained experience in siege-craft and in the design and construction of fortifications. In most countries the absence of an effective organisation for military engineering contributed to the lack of progress in siegecraft and fortification; however, by 1641, the engineer officers of the Swedish army had been formed into an engineer corps, a pattern to be followed by other countries in the second half of the seventeenth century.[6]

In Ireland the rising of 1641 in Ulster developed into an alliance with the 'Old English' or Anglo-Irish of the Pale. With the outbreak of civil war in England in the following year the isolated English garrisons in Ireland were soon divided in their loyalty between king and parliament, while the Scottish settlers in Ulster provided another political and military element, at first in alliance with the forces of the English parliament. Owen Roe O'Neill, a veteran soldier in the service of Spain in the Netherlands, landed in Ulster in 1642, bringing with him other Irishmen experienced in the Continental wars: his Army of Ulster was to be the most effective of the several armies of the Catholic Confederacy, which was based in the city of Kilkenny. O'Neill defeated the Scots under Munro at Benburb on the Blackwater in 1646, but the advantage was not followed by the capture of Dublin, which was the key position in several centuries of warfare in Ireland.

The Irish cause was weakened by a truce with James Butler, First Duke of Ormond, the royalist viceroy; and eventually, when Cromwell landed at Dublin in 1649, the forces of the Confederation were in alliance with the remnants of the English royalist garrisons under Ormond. O'Neill died before he could meet Cromwell in battle. The capture of Drogheda and Wexford by Cromwell's forces, and the slaughter that followed at those towns, encouraged many garrisons to surrender at the approach of the parliamentary forces, but must also have stiffened the resolve of many to fight on. The war was to last until 1652, when Galway surrendered, to be followed by some smaller garrisons still holding out.

Those fighting in Ireland between 1641 and 1652 included many who had seen service in the Continental wars of the previous decades and who would have been familiar with the latest ideas on artillery fortification. Many castles were strengthened by outworks of earth; at Trim Castle the curtain wall was reinforced with an inner earth-embankment, providing a gun platform, and several of the towers were filled in to form artillery bastions. An illustration of

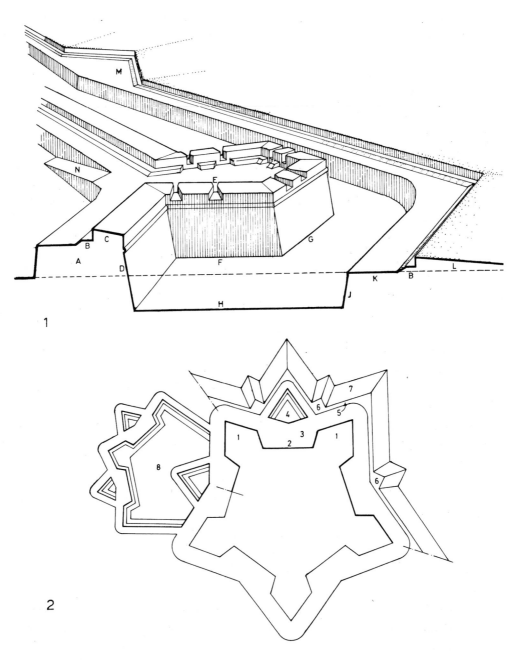

Fig. 2. Elements of artillery fortification, seventeenth century.
1. A rampart; B banquette or firing step; C parapet; D scarp; E gun-embrasure; F bastion flank; G bastion face; H ditch or moat; J counterscarp; K chemin-couvert or covered way; L glacis M place d'armes; N ramp for artillery.
2. Pentagonal bastioned fort with ravelin and crownwork. 1 bastion; 2 curtain; 3 ditch or moat; 4 ravelin; 5 covered way; 6 place d'armes; 7 glacis; 8 crownwork

Ballyshannon Castle in 1650 depicts the place under attack by parliamentary forces: a tower house with the usual bawn wall and flankers is enclosed by a square-bastioned outer line of defence, in a water-filled moat. Many castles were fortified at this time by the addition of earthen defences and detached works, and there are numerous references to works defending such strategic places as river crossings.

At Duncannon Fort the Confederates conducted a regular siege, with trenches on the landward approaches, while at Bunratty Castle, another English garrison, earthworks and a fort constructed by the defenders helped prolong the resistance for several months. At Galway the medieval walls were strengthened by the addition of artillery bastions between 1645 and 1650. Clonmel and Kilkenny were medieval walled towns modified as much as possible to resist artillery. Clonmel was taken with considerable losses by Cromwell; he had been unable to take Waterford the previous year.

The Cromwellian Protectorate was a period of considerable activity in fortifications in Ireland. Town walls were repaired, citadels were constructed at Galway, Limerick, Clonmel and Derry, and forts were built for coastal defence, to protect settlements and at strategic positions inland. Existing castles were in some instances occupied as garrisons or citadels. The new forts were generally rectangular or square enclosures with bastions at the corners, such as the fort at Newtown, near Bantry and 'Fort Cromwell' at Bellahy, all of similar size and plan.

Extensive works were carried out at Athlone, where it appears that masonry bastions were added to the town wall on the Leinster side, and earthwork ramparts and bastions were erected on the west bank of the river, to enclose that part of the town surrounding the castle.

At the restoration of King Charles II in 1660 many of the garrisons of the Protectorate were retained, but reports indicate that many were neglected, much of the ordnance at the coastal forts being unmounted. Inland garrisons were continued at the principal crossing-places of the Shannon and other strategic places. During this period of relative prosperity a considerable number of large country houses was built, their only defensive elements being high walls, usually surrounding the house and outbuildings.[7] The cities and towns expanded, and fortifications were now for the most part related to the defence of the coast.

The Dutch descent on the Medway and their blockade of the Thames in 1667 led to the rapid construction of extra fortifications at Kinsale, in the form of fieldworks to complement Castle Park Fort and the adjacent blockhouse. On the site of Ringcurran Castle a new earthwork fortification was laid out, to be replaced with a permanent work some ten years later, which was to be named Charles Fort in 1680.[8] The lack of defence works at Dublin caused plans to be drawn up by Sir Bernard de Gomme, chief engineer to Charles II, of a scheme for a large citadel at Ringsend in 1673. Plymouth citadel, the new fort at Tilbury in the Thames Estuary and the remodelling of the fortifications of Portsmouth were other projects for which de Gomme was responsible at this time. In 1685 the engineer, Captain Thomas Phillips, was sent to Ireland to carry out a military survey; he reported on the condition of the fortified towns, harbours and forts in the country. With the exception of Athlone and Charlemont Fort, seaports and harbours liable to attack constitute the main part of his report, with his own proposals and estimates for improvements.[9] He described the recently completed Charles Fort at Kinsale, constructed between 1678 and 1680, as the best-equipped town or fort, both in the number and calibre of guns, but he considered the work badly sited, overlooked by high ground inland. He proposed an extensive outwork to occupy this position, and it was here that one of the siege batteries was sited during the successful attack on the fort by Marlborough in 1690.

Phillips' proposals for Dublin included a citadel on higher ground than that proposed by de Gomme, approximately on the present site of St Stephen's Green. He recommended the strengthening and fortifying of six principal places in the country, each strong enough to resist an invading army. The report emphasised the concern with possible external aggression rather than with internal insurrection, reflecting the maritime strength of Holland and the growing naval power of France. Phillips was well qualified to comment on Irish defence works, having visited Luxembourg and other European fortresses in 1684, where he had met Marshal Vauban, the most outstanding military engineer of the seventeenth century (Fig.3).

Sebastien le Prêstre de Vauban, chief engineer to King Louis XIV of France, was engaged in constructing fortresses and fortified towns on the French frontiers until the early years of the eighteenth century. Like the other military engineers of the time, he both designed and besieged fortifications, the methods of attack that he developed being followed for over a century after his death. Vauban began his career as a soldier in 1650 and a few years later was in charge of sieges of Spanish fortifications on the northern frontier of France. In 1678 he was made Commissaire General of the fortifications of France; his most well-known works were the town and citadel of Lille, begun in 1668, Mauberge and Neuf-Brisach. He refortified Lille and constructed a large pentagonal citadel. Mont Louis in the Pyrenees, Briançon, Mont Dauphin and Chateau Queyras are examples of his work in mountainous districts, the defences following the contours of the site. In 1678 Vauban prepared a plan for the fortification of Dunkerque; in 1681 he produced a plan for Strasbourg. Other works included the pentagonal fort of Mont-Royal on an island in the Moselle; Landau, a new octagonal fortress; Namur, which he besieged in 1692, taking it in thirty days and afterwards repairing the defences; Pignerol and many other places. Over ninety forts and fortified towns were designed or reconstructed to some degree by Vauban or by engineers under his supervision and he was involved in some fifty sieges.[10]

Neuf-Brisach was constructed following the

Fig. 3. The seventeenth century fortified town of Naarden in the Netherlands. The fortifications include large angle-bastions and detached triangular ravelins in the moat.
(Copyright photograph KLM Aerocarto NV Schipol).

Peace of Ryswick in 1697 and completed in 1708. The flat site some distance from the Rhine permitted a regular geometrical design, in this case an octagonal fortress, the details illustrating the ultimate development of Vauban's method. It was to be later authors who classified his methods into various 'systems': Vauban always insisted that each fortification must be adapted to its site and he was quite prepared to produce an irregular layout to suit contours and natural features. He developed a system of attack by excavating a sequence of three parallel trenches, each subsequent trench closer to the defences under attack, linked by zigzag approach trenches; his scientific approach replaced the uncoordinated earlier methods and formed the basis for siegework up to the time of the Napoleonic wars and after (Figs. 4 and 5).

The war between the supporters of King James II and William of Orange brought into prominence many inland towns in Ireland that had not been surveyed by Phillips in 1685. The larger towns had medieval defences strengthened by artillery outworks, while the movements of the armies led to a number of places being defended with temporary fieldworks. On the Shannon, bridges and fords were fortified by fieldworks defended by the forces of James II after their defeat at the Battle of the Boyne in 1690, while their opponents strengthened their winter quarters in the midlands with temporary earthwork defences at Mullingar, Roscrea and Thurles. At the walled town of Clonmel they constructed earthen ravelins outside the gates and wall towers. The defences of the more important towns lacked the extensive outworks then regarded on the Continent as essential elements of fortification; however, many held out against prolonged

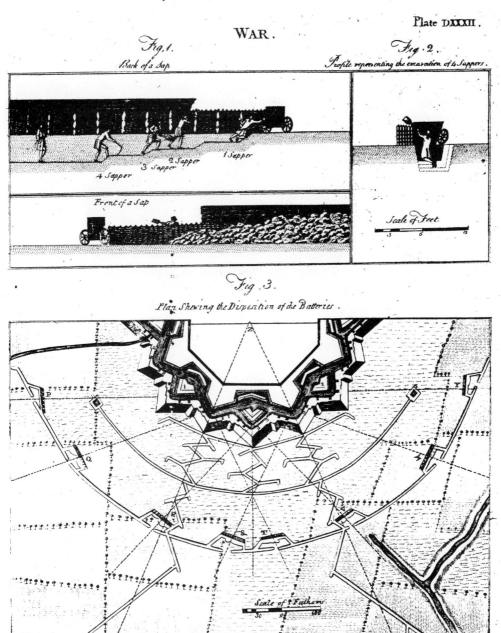

Fig. 4. An attack on a fortress, mid-eighteenth century, which appears to be a copy of plate VI and IX from The Attack and Defense of Fortify'd Places by John Muller (London 1747). It shows the excavation of a sap or approach trench and the layout of the three parallels and their zig-zag connection saps - the system of attack developed by Vauban.

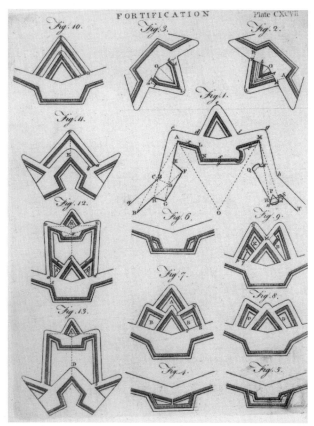

Fig. 5. Elements of fortification, seventeenth and eighteenth centuries. 1 setting out a bastioned fortification with a ravelin; 11 counterguard in advance of a bastion; 12 and 13 two forms of hornwork.

attack. The lack of outworks on the higher ground overlooking Charles Fort at Kinsale led to the capture of the fort. The surrender of Limerick after the second siege in 1691 ended the war in Ireland, the Treaty of Limerick resulting in the majority of the Irish army going overseas to serve James II, in the hope of returning to Ireland with the aid of the French. These troops were to form the basis of the Irish regiments in France, Spain and other countries in eighteenth-century Europe (Fig.6).

The Williamite settlement of Ireland was accompanied by the construction of a network of barracks across the country, sited for the most part in the cities and smaller towns, while smaller defensible barracks or redoubts were built in more isolated areas, at strategic positions such as

'passes' or river crossings. The establishment of these military posts in the last decade of the seventeenth century and the early years of the following century was part of the consolidation of English rule: for most of the following century the army detachments carried out a police function, except for short intervals when there was fear of foreign invasion. Apart from some small works for coastal defence proposed, and some evidently carried out, in the early years of the century, few new defences appear to have been executed in Ireland between the reign of Queen Anne and the French Revolution. An extensive work was begun in 1710 in the Phoenix Park, Dublin, intended as an arsenal, but it was not completed; nearby, the Magazine Fort, a rectangular demi-bastioned work was constructed by 1738. By the 1740s a fort had been built at Cove (Cobh), overlooking Cork Harbour, comprising batteries on three levels with virtually no landward defences. Existing fortifications were repaired in time of war, such as the new covered way at Charles Fort, Kinsale, where additional barracks were constructed by 1751. Many of the smaller seventeenth-century coastal forts were abandoned while the defences of most towns were neglected or demolished. In 1747 the town walls of Galway were in a ruinous condition, with many breaches and broken parapets, but no action appears to have been taken to remedy the defects, even though the town defences when equipped with artillery were capable of providing a degree of protection for the adjacent anchorage.

The most important fortification constructed in Britain in the mid-eighteenth century was Fort George near Inverness in the north of Scotland. Built following the Jacobite rising of 1745, the fort, on a promontory site, has bastions and a ravelin on the landward side considerably larger than most seventeenth-century works, with a covered way similar in its details to that rebuilt at this time at Charles Fort, Kinsale. Works at

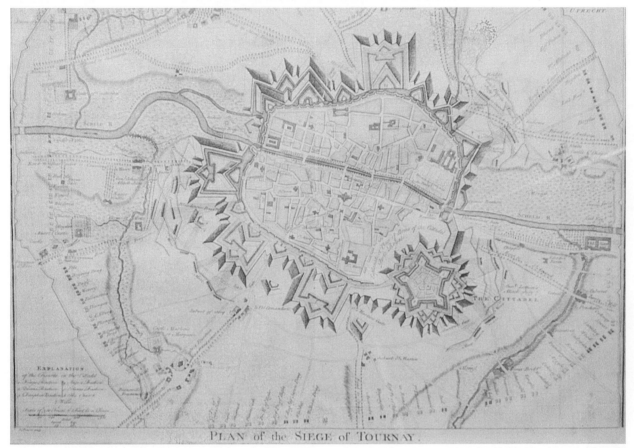

Fig. 6. Siege of Tournai 1709. Pentagonal citadel on right, and four hornworks with other outworks form defensive strongpoints to the city.

Plymouth from 1770 onwards also reflected the move towards larger bastions, and several detached redoubts—basically rectangular batteries—were constructed here, a new approach in place of the more usual continuous line of defence with bastions and ramparts. Other works to protect naval bases and dockyards were built at Chatham and Portsmouth, while in the Channel Islands round gun-towers were erected, some twenty years before the more well-known Martello towers of the Napoleonic period.

In 1776 the Marquis de Montalembert published a work critical of aspects of the bastioned system of fortification: he advocated the use of a *tenaille trace* in place of the bastion, the use of casemates to flank the ditch, and other ideas that influenced the development of the 'polygonal' system, which was to replace bastioned fortification in the nineteenth century.

During the American War of Independence, fortifications were constructed around Cork Harbour; these defences appear to have been mostly fieldworks, but were well equipped with artillery. They were maintained for the duration of the war only. A fort was constructed at the eastern end of Spike Island which, with Cove Fort, protected the harbour and the main channel for shipping, while forts were built on the two headlands at the narrow harbour entrance at Ramhead (later known as Fort Camden) and opposite, at Fort Carlisle.

War with the French Republic in 1793 revealed the lack of artillery defences in Ireland, both for coastal defence and at strategic inland centres such as Athlone. Colonel Tarrant of the Royal Engineers reported on the ruined state of

Athlone Castle and surveyed Carrickfergus Castle and the harbours at Cork and Waterford. In December 1796, a large French fleet transporting some 14,000 soldiers set out from Brest, evaded the British Channel Fleet and arrived at Bantry Bay a few days later.[11] The French were to join forces with the United Irishmen aiming to establish an Irish republic, but bad weather and indecision led to the French fleet returning to France without landing any of the troops. This expedition emphasised the need for coastal defence works and it is possible that fortifications then under construction at Cork Harbour influenced the choice of Bantry Bay as a landing-place. Charles Fort, Kinsale, Duncannon Fort, a battery at Tarbert Island in the Shannon Estuary and Carrickfergus Castle, overlooking Belfast Lough, which was equipped with some artillery, constituted the extent of coastal defence elsewhere.

In 1798 General Humbert landed on the west coast at Killala, Co. Mayo, with just over a thousand men, some two months after the suppression of the rising of that year. After some initial successes he marched eastwards, crossed the Shannon, and was defeated at Ballinamuck, Co. Longford. His expedition emphasised the difficulty of defending or patrolling the west coast and the importance of the Shannon as a line of defence. The renewal of the war against France in 1803 after the short period of the Peace of Amiens marked the start of the largest programme of defence works ever undertaken in Ireland. Martello towers, signal towers and batteries were constructed at various positions around the coast; work continued on the forts at Cork Harbour and circular redoubts were built on Whiddy Island in Bantry Bay. Inland, the Shannon for thirty-five miles south of Athlone was defended with fieldworks at fords and bridges, while further north defences were constructed to protect Lough Swilly. The towers in the Dublin area were under construction in 1804,

as were those in Wexford and Bantry Bay, a year earlier than the first Martellos in England. Also in 1804 the signal stations were established, the signal tower forming a defensible barrack for the naval signal crew and military guard. In the Shannon Estuary, batteries were constructed for from four to seven guns, having a rectangular 'bomb-proof' barrack at the rear of a semicircular enclosure. Galway Bay was defended by three Martello towers, while earlier temporary batteries at Lough Swilly were replaced with permanent works by 1812.

Inland, the crossing-places of the Shannon, defended by fieldworks in 1804 at Athlone, Shannonbridge, Banagher, and elsewhere, were strengthened by the construction of permanent works after 1810. The massive bridgehead defence at Shannonbridge, a Martello tower at Banagher and a large three-gun tower at Meelick were under construction between 1812 and 1814.

A military road was constructed from the southern edge of Dublin for some thirty miles through the Wicklow mountains between 1800 and 1808. At intervals along its length were defensible barracks. The road and barracks were built to counter the activities of Michael Dwyer and his followers, who held out in the mountains after the 1798 rising. The barracks were intended to accommodate a hundred soldiers each and were completed by 1803. At two diagonally opposite corners of the perimeter wall were bastion-shaped projections provided with musket loops for flank defence (similar barracks had been built in Scotland in the early eighteenth century).

The period of the Napoleonic wars was one of great activity in barrack building in Ireland. Many of the smaller barracks of the early and mid-eighteenth century were enlarged and a number of completely new barracks were established, particularly in the south, midlands and west of the country, to guard against invasion. Most of these had defensive arrangements at the gateways and provision for flank fire along the perimeter walls by means of small projections with loops for firearms. Many of the new barracks accommodated from one to three thousand troops, in contrast to the earlier barracks, most of which held a hundred men or less. The new accommodation was required for the greatly increased garrison of the country, both regular and militia regiments, which had to be prepared to act against both invasion and insurgency.

Defence works in England at this time included the line of Martello towers along the south-east and east coasts. A line of defence was proposed around London, and there were works at Dover, at the castle and the Western Heights,[12] and at Chatham. At Dover Castle, caponnières and galleries were built as defences to the ditch; on the Western Heights a citadel and redoubt were linked by defence lines, and there was provision for close defence by guns and firearms in casemates. The Chatham defences, improved during the American War of Independence, were remodelled, while at Portsmouth, Southsea Castle was partly reconstructed and a caponnière built, providing communication to new counterscarp galleries. In Portugal the lines of Torres Vedras were constructed in 1810 by Wellington, three lines of detached redoubts and earthworks some thirty miles long that prevented the French army from taking Lisbon, demonstrating the effectiveness of detached works backed by a large force able to provide support at any threatened point of the defence.

In Ireland, after the conclusion of the Napoleonic wars in 1815 most defence works were occupied by much smaller garrisons and most of the signal towers were abandoned. No new work appears to have been undertaken in the years up to the Crimean War, apart from some barracks with defensible perimeter walls. Just after the war the new pier-head battery at Kingstown (Dún Laoghaire) was completed in 1857.

By the mid-nineteenth century sail was giving way to steam in the navies and merchant fleets of the world, and naval forces, now almost independent of wind and tide, had iron-clad ships equipped with long-range rifled guns. After 1860, because of these improvements in artillery and the threat of the new French iron-clad steam warships, extensive fortifications were constructed at the naval bases of Portsmouth and Plymouth, including a ring of detached forts on the landward side. Designed on the 'polygonal' system, for close defence the forts had deep ditches defended by caponnières and counterscarp galleries, while guns on the ramparts provided long-range armament: there were no bastions. New work at Forts Camden and Carlisle in Cork Harbour reflected these approaches to fortification design, where new, deeper ditches were provided with caponnières, with gun-embrasures and loops for firearms. New gun positions were constructed overlooking the harbour entrance, including casemates protected by iron shields, sited near the water level.

The Franco-Prussian War in 1870 demonstrated the ineffectiveness of earlier fortresses designed in the age of the smooth-bore cannon and musket when attacked by modern long-range artillery: the elaborate outworks of such places as Strasbourg were of no use when siege artillery placed at a considerable distance was able to bombard the town. Improvements in ordnance, both in range and effectiveness, in the second half of the nineteenth century led to rapid changes in the design of fortifications; new methods of construction included the use of iron shields for casemated guns and the increasing use of concrete.

In the closing years of the century and the opening decade of the next, new batteries were constructed at Belfast Lough and Bere Island, Bantry Bay, while those at Lough Swilly were remodelled, to mount new breech-loading guns then coming into use. At Cork Harbour entrance, south of Fort Camden, Templebreedy battery was established by 1906. The outbreak of war in 1914 emphasised the importance of Lough Swilly, Berehaven and Cork Harbour as fortified anchorages for naval vessels protecting the merchant shipping lanes passing north and south of Ireland.

Following the 1916 rising and the Anglo-Irish war of 1919-21, the Irish Free State was established, the treaty of 1921 conceding dominion status to twenty-six counties; under the Government of Ireland Act, 1920, a separate parliament for six Ulster counties had come into existence. Lough Swilly, Berehaven and Cork Harbour with their forts and batteries were retained by Britain as the 'Treaty Ports' from 1921 to 1938. In 1938 British detachments marched out of the forts, to be replaced by units of the Irish army under the terms of the Anglo-Irish Agreement of that year. During the 1939-45 period Ireland remained neutral, while a new fort was constructed in the Shannon Estuary.

The story of artillery fortification in Ireland, starting with the mid-sixteenth-century proposals for the defence of harbours and anchorages, closes with reinforced-concrete gun emplacements on the Shannon, constructed to help ensure the neutrality of the Irish state.

Chapter 2

Castle to Fort: Tudor Ireland, 1485-1603

THE CLOSING YEARS OF the fifteenth century were a time of European exploration and expansion overseas. With the opening up of the New World the centre of gravity in Europe moved increasingly away from the Mediterranean towards the Atlantic, bringing into prominence in the following century the strategic position of Ireland and the need—from the standpoint of the English government—for a more complete control of the country by the English crown. Scotland, France and Spain were involved in varying degrees in Irish affairs during the Tudor period, and at times posed a threat to English rule. Proposals for coastal defence in Ireland and plans for coastal settlements and inland plantations by English colonists from as early as the middle of the sixteenth century must be seen in part as a reaction by the English government to the strategic position of Ireland. The possible occupation of the country or its principal ports by enemy forces in alliance with the Irish constituted a threat to England. The strategic importance of Ireland was to increase in the following centuries with the conflict between the principal maritime countries of Europe for mercantile and naval supremacy.

Defence against external aggression, and the conquest of Irish-held territory subsequently garrisoned against the threat of insurrection, were the main factors that determined the development and location of the principal new fortifications in Ireland from the middle of the sixteenth century onwards. In many instances these two factors combined to produce a fortification with the dual role of coastal defence and colonial garrison, a role exemplified in much earlier strongholds such as Carrickfergus Castle.

In the last decades of the fifteenth century the fortifications in Ireland consisted of the larger Norman castles, such as those at Carrickfergus, Roscommon, Athlone, and Limerick, many established as royal garrisons when they were constructed some three hundred years earlier; a variety of later castles; the defences of the walled towns, of which the most important were also seaports; and the tower-house castles, subsequently to be the most numerous type of castle in Ireland.

Several of the Norman castles, such as Dublin, Carrickfergus, and Limerick, continued as administrative and garrison centres, while many others, such as Athlone and Roscommon, became royal garrisons again as the sixteenth century advanced. The principal walled towns were Dublin, Galway, Limerick, Kilkenny, Cork, and Waterford; all except Kilkenny were important ports. In the second half of the fifteenth century part of the wall enclosing the Irish Town at Limerick was under construction, being finally completed in 1496. At this time work went on at Galway to strengthen the defences: in 1498 a considerable part of the waterfront fortifications were constructed. In 1505 a deep ditch or moat was excavated around the walls on the east side; the town had been invested and taken by de Burgo and O'Brien of Thomond the year before, before their defeat by the Eighth Earl of Kildare at the Battle of Knocktoe. In 1519 the town wall was extended and part of the quay built at the joint expense of the town and government. Other defended port towns were Dundalk, Drogheda, Wexford, and New Ross, enclosed like the other towns with curtain walls, towers, and gatehouses. At Drogheda, the barbican or outer gate of St

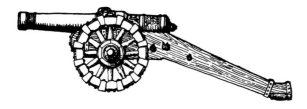

Fig. 7. Early sixteenth century muzzle-loading cannon.

Lawrence's Gate is a most impressive reminder of the strength of these medieval defences. Youghal and Kinsale were also walled towns with a considerable overseas trade, and with good harbours; by the middle of the sixteenth century, artillery defences were being proposed to protect these harbours and other ports.

The tower-house castle is one of the most prominent features of the Irish countryside, particularly in the south and west of the country: a tall four or five-storey tower usually square or rectangular in plan, enclosed within a bawn or courtyard, which has flanking corner towers or turrets and possibly a small gatehouse structure (Fig.8). These fortified residences of the Old English and Gaelic landowners or chiefs were not able to resist artillery, but because of the considerable problems of transporting heavy guns in difficult terrain, many retained a military importance well into the middle of the seventeenth century. The period of construction of the tower-house was from the fifteenth century, through the sixteenth century and into the early decades of the next, when they began to be superseded by the fortified house.

These were the fortifications in Ireland when in 1485 King Richard III was killed and his army defeated at Bosworth Field in the English midlands by the invading army of Henry Tudor, Earl of Richmond, who came to the throne of England as Henry VII. He confirmed Garret Mór Fitzgerald, Eighth Earl of Kildare, as the king's deputy in Ireland, a post he had held since 1479 and was to hold with one short interval until his death in 1513. His son Garret Óg, the Ninth Earl, was to be lord deputy for most of the fol-

lowing twenty years. In 1506 Henry VII had proposed a large-scale expedition to Ireland but was persuaded that it would require some 6,000 men, three large and sixty light cannon, and several hundred arquebuses and hand-guns.

For almost fifty years, apart from a few short intervals, the first Tudors had no choice but to allow the Fitzgeralds of Kildare to continue in their role as virtual rulers of Ireland. The principal reason for reliance on the earls was financial, as they were able to govern in the king's name without the need for funds from England. It was to be the second Tudor, Henry VIII, who was to begin what has been termed the 'Tudor reconquest of Ireland,' with the opportunity created by the downfall of the house of Kildare.

By the end of the fifteenth century two impor-

Fig.8. Rathmacknee Castle, Co. Wexford: a tower-house in a small rectangular bawn, typical of many of the fifteenth and sixteenth-century tower-houses in Ireland.

Fig. 9. Moorstown Castle, Co. Tipperary: a circular tower-house within a rectangular bawn.

tant improvements had been made in artillery: the addition of trunnions—projections serving as pivots at each side of the gun barrel near the balancing point of the gun, which allowed for elevating or depressing the piece—and the development of the wheeled gun-carriage with its trail, allowing for recoil when the gun was fired and for transport for both field and siege artillery by attaching the trail to a horse-drawn limber (Fig.7). However, well into the following century the more primitive gun mountings survived for some artillery aboard ship, and in castles and town defences where there was no space for a wheeled gun-carriage; these were usually built-up wrought-iron breech-loaders, not requiring to be run back to be reloaded, as was the case with the new bronze muzzle-loaders. The gun barrel was fixed to a wooden bed at ground or floor level (Fig.10), or in some defence works a form of timber trestle or swivel gun was used. From the surviving architectural evidence and some con-

temporary lists of ordnance it is apparent that these arrangements were used where a gun was mounted at an embrasure with a limited field of fire. These guns were often loaded with a variety of small shot, the equivalent of what was later to be known as canister or grape-shot, for short-range use. At new ground level outworks, on new ramparts and on top of the towers where new gun platforms were constructed there was room to handle the new longer-range cast-bronze and later cast-iron muzzle-loaders, which fired cast-iron shot.

While most of the artillery in Ireland at the opening of the sixteenth century was controlled by the Earls of Kildare, in their role as lords deputy, the walled towns also possessed guns. The O'Donnells received some ordnance from Scotland; in 1516 they captured the castle at Sligo with the assistance of the guns of a French ship. The first recorded date for the use of firearms in Ireland is 1487, but their widespread use in Europe by that time would suggest the use of hand-guns here well before then. English garrisons in Ireland in the first half of the sixteenth century are listed as having more archers than arquebus-men; the arquebus was later gradually replaced by the heavier musket and the lighter caliver. Firearms eventually replaced the longbow, as they required a much shorter period of training and less physical strength than was required for an archer.[1]

During the early Tudor period the relatively

Fig. 10. Late fifteenth or early sixteenth-century breech-loading cannon on a timber bed. A forged gun barrel; B and C breech chamber; D wedge; E timber bed.

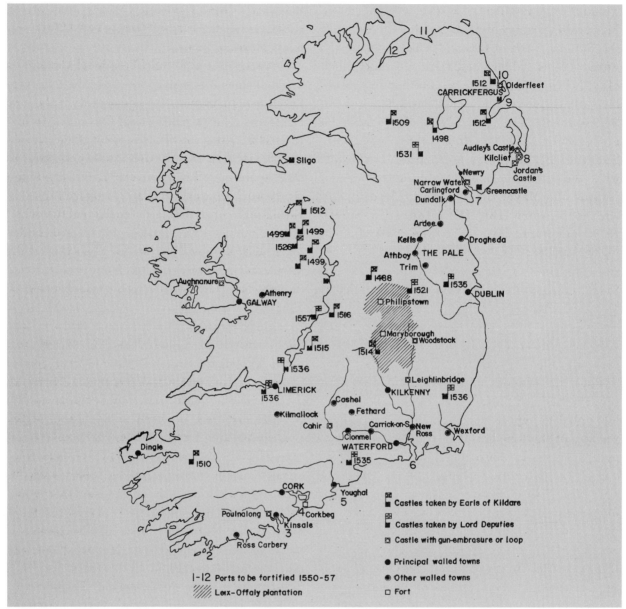

Map 1. *Ireland 1485-1558. Ports to be fortified 1550-1557:* **1** *Berehaven;* **2** *Baltimore;* **3** *Kinsale;* **4** *Cork;* **5** *Youghal;* **6** *Waterford;* **7** *Carlingford;* **8** *Strangford;* **9** *Carrickfergus;* **10** *Olderfleet;* **11** *The Bann (Coleraine)* **12** *Lough Foyle.*

small area of the country under English control was the Pale around Dublin, enclosed for much of the second half of the fifteenth century by a double earthwork or embankment six feet high, primarily intended, it seems, to prevent the theft of cattle, but acting also as a boundary and in a secondary sense as a fortified line. It was close to several walled towns, settlements, and castles. From Dundalk in the north, the boundary ran

south-west to Ardee, Kells, and Athboy, then southwards to Dangan, Kilcock, Clane, and along the Liffey to Kilcullen and Ballymore Eustace. From here the line ran north-east to Rathcoole and eastwards below the Dublin Mountains to the sea near Dalkey. The earthwork was evidently still in existence in 1515 (Map 1).

'Beyond the Pale, Ireland was divided into

numerous lordships. To the west was the Fitzgerald territory of Kildare, while to the south the Butlers, Earls of Ormond, chief rivals to the Fitzgeralds of Kildare and Desmond, held much of Kilkenny and Tipperary, another branch of the Butlers holding the strong castle at Cahir on the river Suir. The Earls of Desmond held much of Limerick, Kerry, and Cork; across the Shannon the O'Briens controlled Thomond; while the de Burgos or Burkes occupied parts of Galway and Mayo. Other powerful lordships in the west were the O'Connors in north Roscommon and the O'Rourkes of Breifne; in Fermanagh, with their castle at Enniskillen, were the Maguires; while to the north were the O'Donnells of Tyrconnell and the O'Neills of Tyrone.[2] These, and many less powerful lordships paying tribute to them, formed various alliances, with frequent changes of allegiance and constant raids and local warfare.

Onto this complex social and political structure the Earls of Kildare and other lords deputy attempted to impose some control. The frequent warfare of the time is reflected in the very large number of castles constructed during the second half of the fifteenth and much of the sixteenth centuries. Most of these were tower-houses, most numerous in the south and west, less numerous in the north midlands and Ulster. Much larger castles of the mid-fifteenth century include Bunratty, built by the MacNamaras but soon in the possession of the O'Briens of Thomond, and the MacCarthy castle at Blarney. Many earlier castles continued in use, such as those at Adare and Askeaton, Co. Limerick, the Butler castle of Kilkenny, and the principal stronghold of the Kildares at Maynooth.

The seaports and inland towns held out behind their medieval walls against the Gaelic countryside, where many of the Anglo-Normans or Old English were now allied by marriage to the principal Irish families. To the west of the Pale the lands of the Kildares acted as a buffer between the English-held territory and the Irish of the midlands, such as the O'Connors of Offaly and the O'Mores of Laois.

The Eighth Earl of Kildare used the king's artillery for his own purposes, attacking the castles of his opponents; he controlled the only guns in Ireland apart from those of the walled towns. In 1484 he was granted aid to strengthen his castle at Kildare; the baronies of Castleknock, Dunboyne and Ratoath were each to provide eighty workmen, evidently to be engaged in excavating and constructing defensive earthworks.[3] He also obtained a grant of labour towards building a castle at Castledermot, while another of the Fitzgeralds received a similar grant for erecting a castle at his town of Lackagh, five miles west of Kildare.

In 1488 Kildare attacked and captured the MacGeoghegan castle of Balrath, Co. Westmeath, using cannon: the first record we have of the use of siege artillery in Ireland (see Fig.1). Large guns were used at the siege of Waterford in 1495, when the city was attacked by the forces of the Earl of Desmond and Perkin Warbeck. Ships' guns fired on the city for eleven days and were answered by guns on Reginald's Tower, a prominent corner tower at the riverside, sinking one ship and driving off the others. At some time in the following century, perhaps resulting from the defence proposals of 1548-51, a gun battery was constructed here, below the tower. In 1498 Kildare took the O'Neill castle of Dungannon, and in 1499 he captured the castles of Roscommon, Athleague, Tulsk, and Castlereagh, no doubt using the royal ordnance. The following year he was again active in Ulster; in 1509 he destroyed Omagh Castle, while Pailis Castle near Beaufort, west of Killarney, was taken in 1510. Two years later Kildare placed a garrison in Roscommon Castle and captured Cavetown Castle near Boyle; then he marched into Ulster, where he took the castles of Belfast and Larne. Leap Castle in Offaly was attacked in 1513, but

his guns proved ineffective; he intended returning with heavier ordnance but was injured by
gunshot, and died later at Athy.

He was succeeded as lord deputy by his son,
Garret Óg, Ninth Earl of Kildare, who was also
active in military expeditions, taking the castle at
Abbeyleix in 1514, Leap Castle in 1515, and
another O'Carroll stronghold, Garrycastle, the
following year.

In 1520 the Earl of Surrey arrived in Ireland
to replace Garret Óg as lord deputy. Surrey recommended a permanent army of 500 men, and
stated that at least 6,000 were required for a conquest of the country. Fortresses must be constructed and, to succeed, military occupation
must be supported by a large-scale plan of
colonisation. In 1521 he took O'Connor's castle
at Monasteroris near Edenderry with the aid of
three large guns. He compared Monasteroris, as
a frontier post on the western edge of the Kildare
territory, to Berwick on the Scottish border,
proposing to hold it as a permanent garrison.
Daingean, nine miles to the west, another
O'Connor castle, was to be established as a permanent garrison some twenty-five years later,
subsequently renamed Philipstown. Recalled
from Ireland by Henry VIII, in 1523 Surrey
crossed the border into Scotland with a force of
2,000 men, three heavy siege guns, and eight
smaller pieces; as in Ireland, the castles attacked
could seldom resist siege artillery. Kildare was
reinstated as lord deputy in 1524; he campaigned
in the north, and in Connacht in 1526 he captured the castles of Castlereagh and Ballintober,
which were given to O'Connor Roe.

The Earl of Ossory replaced Kildare as deputy
in 1528, to be followed in 1530 by Sir William
Skeffington, who marched into Ulster, destroying
the castles of Portnelligan and Caledon to obtain
the submission of the O'Neills in 1531 and in the
following year he took Dungannon Castle. He
had for some time previously been master of the
ordnance in England, and it must be assumed

that he used artillery on these expeditions into
Ulster.

In 1532 Kildare was again appointed deputy,
but the following year he was called to London.
Before his departure he transferred the royal
ordnance from Dublin Castle to his Kildare castles. He was charged with using the king's
artillery for his own purposes and using it to fortify his own castles. On the marriage of Anne
Boleyn to Henry VIII, in 1533, the influence of
the Fitzgeralds of Kildare gave way to that of
their rivals, the Butlers of Kilkenny, who were
related to the Boleyns by marriage. On the false
report of the death of the Ninth Earl, his son,
Thomas Fitzgerald, Lord Offaly—known as
'Silken Thomas'—broke out in rebellion in June
1534 and attempted to capture Dublin Castle,
where ammunition and powder for the royal ordnance were stored (the guns were already at
Maynooth and other Kildare castles).

The Fitzgeralds and their allies held the castles
of Maynooth, Portlester, Rathangan, Lea, Athy,
Woodstock, Carlow, Kilkea and Castledermot.
The castle at Kildare was taken but regained by
the rebels; Lea castle was used for the storage of
supplies, ordnance and property removed from
Maynooth. The Earl of Ossory captured the castles of Carlow, Athy and Woodstock, but they
were retaken by the Fitzgeralds. The rebel cause
was linked to opposition to the Reformation in
England, soon to be attempted in Ireland, and
there appeared to be the prospect of Spanish aid
in July 1534 and early in 1535. Skeffington,
appointed lord deputy, arrived in Ireland late in
1534 and, after several months of inactivity, laid
siege to the principal Fitzgerald castle at
Maynooth the following March. The garrison of a
hundred men is recorded as including sixty 'gunners': presumably most of these were equipped
with hand-guns, while others worked the guns
mounted on the castle and on new defence works.
There is a reference to a bulwark or bastion constructed at the north-east end of the courtyard,

well equipped with ordnance.[4] It seems likely that the curtain wall of the castle was reinforced with an earth embankment, either inside or on the exterior to protect the masonry from gunfire.

Skeffington set up siege batteries to the north of the castle. After two days these were ready, and they fired on the castle for five days, first silencing the guns on the northern side of the massive Norman keep. Eventually a large breach was made in the perimeter defences and the courtyard taken by assault, and the survivors of the garrison in the keep surrendered. Of the thirty-seven prisoners, twenty-five were killed; one of the officers of the garrison was Fitzgerald's master of ordnance, Donagh O'Dogan.

After the fall of Maynooth the castles of Athy and Woodstock were abandoned by the rebels; the O'Mores who had garrisoned them destroyed the windows, doors, and battlements, and the bridge of Athy. It is recorded that Silken Thomas had a stronghold near Rathangan fortified with earthworks and wet ditches—a brief reference perhaps to a native Irish form of fortification. Daingean Castle in Offaly relied on these elements for its defence, while a pictorial plan of 1602 depicts Inisloughan, an Ulster stronghold of the O'Neills, as having two concentric lines of wet ditches and timber palisades.[5] Crannógs—timber-palisaded strongholds built on artificial islands in midland and Ulster lakes—were in use until the end of the sixteenth century, and similar structures are recorded in the midlands during the Cromwellian wars.

Thomas Fitzgerald surrendered in 1535 and was imprisoned in the Tower of London with five of his Kildare uncles, until they were all executed in 1537. The downfall of the Fitzgeralds of Kildare foreshadowed the exercise of centralised authority in Ireland and the control of the country by the great families such as the Fitzgeralds and Butlers was ended.

To the personal and political complexities of the Irish scene was now added the factor of religion. The Reformation in England, which was to be attempted now in Ireland, brought a new dimension to the conflict, with Irish leaders turning for assistance to the Catholic countries of Europe.

The year 1534 has been described as a turning-point in Irish history, its events bringing forward a demonstration of English power that was to be continued until Irish resistance was finally overcome at the close of the seventeenth century. After the surrender of Fitzgerald, Skeffington continued his campaign; he attacked Dungarvan Castle late in 1535 and, after spending two days placing his artillery, made an effective breach after six hours. In the following year the new lord deputy, Lord Leonard Grey, advanced on Ferns Castle, Co. Wexford, and after taking the gateway and outer works with his smaller guns he received the surrender of the garrison before his larger siege guns were placed in position. Also in 1536, Grey captured a fortified bridge on the Shannon above Limerick. At O'Brien's Bridge he used demi-culverins, six falcons, and a bronze saker; the Irish defenders had an iron gun of large calibre, a ship's gun, and a Portuguese piece, while the castles at each end of the bridge were strengthened with earthworks and timber.[6] The artillery did little damage to the castle at the east bank, and after two days' bombardment the besieging force had no ammunition left. The moat was filled in with brushwood and the castle carried by assault. The garrison of the other castle retreated and the timber bridge was destroyed by Grey's soldiers.

At Carrigogunell Castle, five miles west of Limerick, Grey first attacked the outer wall and then brought in his guns to fire on the keep; a siege gun was brought from Carrick-on-Suir for this attack. In 1537 he captured the new O'Connor castle at Daingean, described as built in a morass surrounded by great double ditches and waters. A causeway was made and the courtyard taken; with two falcons, two sakers and a siege gun he fired on the keep, but the heavy siege piece—the only gun of this type then in Ireland—was damaged. He wrote to Cromwell, Henry VIII's chief minister, asking for a replacement as soon as possible.

In 1538 Grey sent a demi-culverin, a saker and some falcons to Galway from Limerick by sea aboard an Irish galley, which was preferable to transporting them overland. The absence of adequate roads and the danger of ambush in the difficult terrain emphasised the importance of the sea in transporting artillery and ammunition: guns could be unloaded anywhere within reach of ships' boats in estuaries and rivers. It is probable that the siege gun used at Carrigogunell had been brought upriver to Carrick-on-Suir from Waterford. Control of the sea was to be a decisive factor in military affairs in Tudor Ireland and throughout the following centuries.

There are references to Irish leaders having guns at this time: the O'Connors of Offaly had some ordnance from the Ninth Earl of Kildare, the O'Carrolls had falcons captured from the Earl of Ormond, and the O'Donnells used artillery to capture Castlemore Costello in Mayo in 1527. Guns were used by the O'Donnells in 1536, while the O'Connors had guns at Sligo Castle in 1538. With the gradual improvement in artillery there was a corresponding improvement in and reliance on firearms in the warfare of sixteenth-century Ireland; a resolute defence of a castle or fortification by firearms might repel an assault at a time when the defenders' artillery had been silenced. The controlling factor in the spacing of artillery bastions in the new style of fortification then emerging in Italy was the range of the musket: a maximum spacing of about two hundred yards was recommended, so that each bastion was defended by flank fire from musketeers on adjacent bastions. As the sixteenth century advanced, loops for firearms became a more prominent feature of the Irish castle, and may in some instances assist in dating the structure,

where it is evident that they are not later insertions.

Several Irish castles have early gun-ports or embrasures for cannon. At Aughnanure Castle, Co. Galway, there are small circular openings in the bawn wall close to ground level; these were for cannon mounted on timber beds placed on the ground, probably built-up iron breech-loaders. Two of these circular gun-loops with splayed internal embrasures are sited to flank the wall where it makes a right-angled change of direction, while other openings have the addition of a vertical aperture some two to three inches wide and from sixteen to thirty inches in height immediately above the gunhole, forming a type of opening known as an 'inverted keyhole' loop. It is perhaps significant that the flanking close-range loops with a line of fire directly along the external face of the wall, requiring little or no traversing of the gun, are circular loops, while the openings for longer-range fire directly away from the castle have a sighting slit above, providing an improved view for the gunner.

A similar arrangement may be seen at the circular tower at the south-east corner of the bawn, originally the salient angle of the castle here but now enclosed by a later, outer line of defence. In this tower the two loops immediately flanking the bawn wall are simple circular openings, while the other loops for longer-range fire are the inverted-keyhole type. There is also a cross-shaped loop. In these tower loops the gun-hole is situated just above a broad, splayed internal cill some three to four feet above floor level, indicating the use of small cannon on timber trestles, or hand-guns. There is a similar inverted-keyhole loop in the tower-house, opening off the staircase, and another in part of the surviving structure of the gatehouse, providing for flank fire along the outer defences (Fig.11).

These loops, both circular and keyhole pattern, are found in defences in England from the time of the first use of artillery in castles and town walls in the late fourteenth century to the early sixteenth century, when they were being superseded by larger double-splayed rectangular openings. The many gun-loops at Aughnanure appear to be an integral part of the structure of the castle, which possibly dates from the second half of the fifteenth century or the early decades of the sixteenth.

Unusual gun-embrasures at Woodstock Castle, Athy, may be of similar date to those at Aughnanure, coinciding with the rule of the Earls of Kildare as lords deputy of Ireland between 1485 and 1534 (Fig.12). Attached to the principal rectangular tower of this Kildare castle is an extension some seventeen feet by fourteen feet wide on plan, with walls approximately three feet in thickness; the floors were of timber construction, supported on stone corbels. There are two gun-ports, one each at first and second-floor level; a circular opening some ten inches in diameter on the inner face of the wall opens into an external splayed embrasure with a sloping cill.

The guns positioned here at high level presumably had a field of fire over the outer walls of the castle, which no longer survive. The circular openings are placed a few inches above the original floor level; above and to one side of each gun-port is a tall, narrow loop on the external face of the wall with a wide, splayed internal embrasure, evidently intended to provide a field of view for the gunner stationed beside the gun. As at the low-level gun-loops at Aughnanure, these gun-ports were for use with cannon—probably iron breechloaders—secured to a timber bed placed on the floor.

Woodstock was a Fitzgerald castle, and it is known that the royal ordnance was stored and mounted at Maynooth and other castles under the control of the Earls of Kildare: it is quite likely therefore that these gun-embrasures are of Fitzgerald origin. However, it is possible that the extension containing the gun-ports was constructed by Lord Deputy Grey, who provided 'lime and masons intending to re-edify and forti-

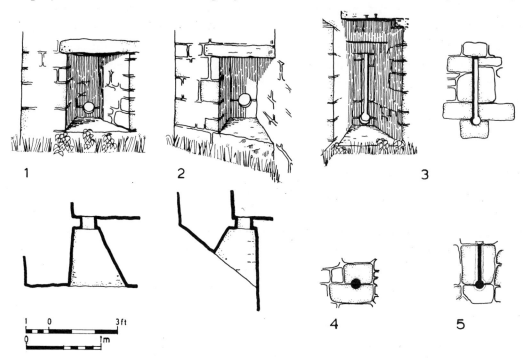

Fig. 11. Aughnanure Castle, Co. Galway. 1 and 2 interior view and plan of gun-ports in bawn wall; 3 interior and exterior of gun-loops in bawn wall; 4 and 5 gun-loops in circular tower.

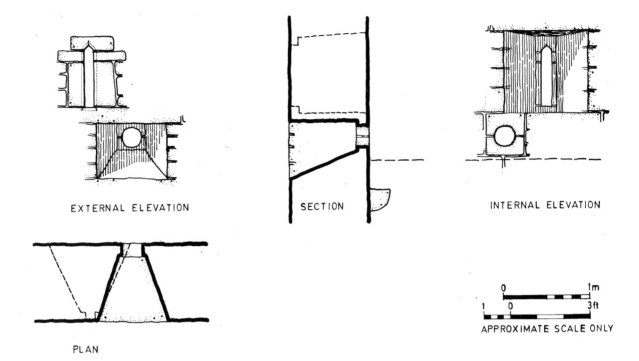

EXTERNAL ELEVATION   SECTION   INTERNAL ELEVATION

0   1m
1   0   3ft
APPROXIMATE SCALE ONLY

PLAN

Fig. 12. Gun-port at Woodstock Castle, Athy, Co. Kildare.

fy the castle and bridge of Athy and the Manor of Woodstock'—presumably Woodstock Castle—in June 1536. Two months later work was continuing here.

Gun-loops at Cahir Castle intended for small cannon or hand-guns are composed of a semicircular gun-hole at the base of a narrow vertical aperture—a type known as a 'stirrup-loop.' They are situated in the outer walls to the east and west, built outside the earlier castle perimeter, suggesting the fifteenth century as the date for their construction. However, much of the castle was restored in the 1840s, and some of these loops, some having in addition a short cross-slit, are in reconstructed parts of the walls, and may have been rebuilt or repositioned to some extent. Three similar loops are in the rear wall of the gatehouse at first-floor level, while in the adjacent round tower, projecting into the eastern or entrance courtyard, is a short cross-loop with a broad semi-circular opening at the base, the external cill of which is angled steeply down-

wards (Fig.13)

Of particular interest at Cahir are two double-splayed gun-embrasures in the northwest tower; the cill level of these openings is just above the level of the ground floor. Again as at Aughnanure and Woodstock, the guns here would have been secured to wooden beds on the floor. The narrow vertical opening of the embrasure positioned at the centre of the wall—which is over five feet thick—provided a view for the gunner. The probable date for these gun-embrasures is the first half of the sixteenth century; similar openings at Leighlinbridge may date from the late 1540s. Another double-splayed embrasure in the western wall at Cahir is most likely from the second half of the sixteenth century or later, having a much wider opening and a higher cill, suitable for a small field-piece on a wheeled gun-carriage.

The Black Castle at Leighlinbridge has two double-splayed gun-embrasures at ground floor level (Fig.14). Similar to those in the north-west tower at Cahir, there is a vertical opening, some

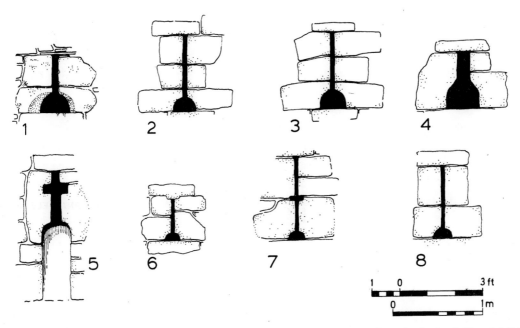

Fig. 13. Gun-loops: *1 Reginald's Tower, Waterford; 2 and 3 Watch Tower, Waterford; 4 Dundrum Castle, Co. Dublin; 5-8 Cahir Castle, Co. Tipperary.*

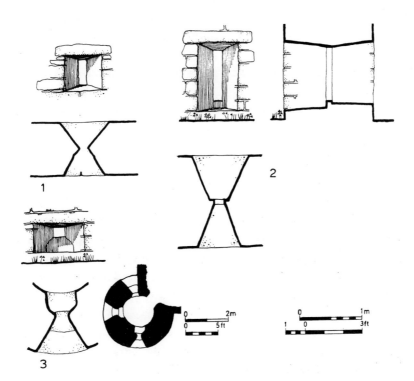

Fig. 14. Gun-ports: *1 Carlingford town walls; 2 Black Castle, Leighlinbridge; 3 Poulnalong.*

thirty-three inches high and six inches wide; the internal cill is ten inches above floor level. It is possible that there was a third embrasure here in part of the castle to the south that has collapsed. The two embrasures have a field of fire across the River Barrow to the west, just downstream of the bridge. Leighlinbridge was an important garrison in the middle of the sixteenth century, at the time of the establishment of the midlands forts of Philipstown and Maryborough, and it is possible that these gun-ports date from this period, 1546-48.

Gun-ports of a different form occur at Poulnalong Castle near Kinsale, overlooking the Bandon (Fig.14). Here at the landward side in a circular turret at one corner of the castle are three external splayed embrasures, each with an internal recess and a six-inch-square opening. The limited space of the interior suggests that only one small cannon may have been accommodated and positioned at the appropriate embrasure as required, a breech-loader being easier to reload here than a muzzle-loader. Above these ground-level gun-ports are six slots for firearms, angled steeply downwards towards the ground near the base of the turret wall. A date of 1543 has been given for this castle: it is recorded that one of the Roches of Kinsale built it at that time, while the form of the gun-ports reinforces the probability that it is from this period. Lewis, in his *Topographical Dictionary of Ireland* (1837), gives the date of construction of Poulnalong as 1496.

The double-splayed loop found at Cahir and Leighlinbridge, serving guns at floor level, is to be found in other castles but at a higher level, with the cill some three feet above the ground or floor. These were intended for small cannon or hand-guns, and are in castles dating from the fifteenth to the early or middle sixteenth century. Examples of these loops are to be found at Kilclief, Jordan's Castle, and Narrow Water Castle, all in Co. Down, and in part of

Carlingford town wall (Fig.14).

An example of an early gun-loop of the inverted-keyhole type is to be found in the wall of Irish Town, Limerick, which was under construction in the second half of the fifteenth century. This loop, no longer accessible, was illustrated by Leask.[7] It is most probable that at Limerick and other walled towns there were a number of these early gun-loops of the fifteenth or early sixteenth centuries. At Waterford there is a stirrup-loop in Reginald's Tower, close to the present pavement level, while other early gun-loops of this form— probably fifteenth-century in date—are at the Watch Tower, near the south-west corner of the walls (Fig.13).[8] Another stirrup-loop is to be found at Dundrum Castle in south Co. Dublin (Fig.13).

Proposals for suppression of the monasteries were put forward in 1536, and plans for reconquest and settlement included the scheme to fortify and garrison some of them. By the end of 1539 the monasteries in Leinster had been suppressed; no overall plan seems to have been implemented, but the conversion was carried out in some instances. At Leighlinbridge the buildings of the former Carmelite friary provided accommodation for the garrison, and there are frequent examples of the granting of monastic buildings to English settlers on condition that they be fortified. In the second half of the century the abbey buildings at Armagh were made defensible and garrisoned from time to time in the warfare against the O'Neills, and later the abbey at Boyle was converted into a government outpost, one of the garrisons of the Elizabethan settlement of Roscommon. In many areas, and in particular in the northern half of the country, abbeys and friaries were the only substantial stone buildings, while in the midlands and south many of the former monastic properties were on good land, attractive to English colonists. Granting these lands and buildings to settlers avoided in many instances a direct conflict with the Old English or Gaelic landowners, who were alarmed at the increasing policy of confiscation and plantation of their territory.

In 1536 Brabazon, vice-treasurer of Ireland, was building the castles of Powerscourt and Fassaroe outside the southern boundary of the Pale, as outposts against the O'Tooles and O'Byrnes of Wicklow. The fall of the Kildare Fitzgeralds had left the Pale without protection to the west and south-west, and English settlements were proposed at Rathangan, Woodstock, Castledermot, Leighlinbridge, and Carlow. In 1540 the constable of Athy Castle was granted Woodstock Castle and Manor. Further to the west, after Sir Anthony St Leger became lord deputy in 1541, garrisons were advocated at Kinnegad, Kishevan in Kildare, Castle Jordan in Meath and Ballinure in Offaly.

The O'Connor castle at Daingean, and Ballyadams in the O'More territory four miles from Athy, were taken by Brabazon in 1546, and both were garrisoned. The following year Sir Edward Bellingham arrived from England as captain-general of the forces in Ireland, to reinforce St Leger and to pursue a more active military policy. Fort Governor was constructed at Daingean on the site of the O'Connor stronghold; Bellingham became lord deputy in May 1548, and after a short campaign in Laois he established Fort Protector there. By this time Athlone Castle had been regained by the government forces, and garrisons had been established at Leighlinbridge and Nenagh. The Black Castle at Leighlinbridge on the east bank of the Barrow was possibly constructed at this time and combined with the former friary buildings to guard this important crossing-point of the river on the route from Dublin to Kilkenny. The castle, a rectangular tower at the east end of the bridge, perhaps formed the north-west angle of an enclosure approximately 300 by 250 feet (Fig.15). At the diagonally opposite corner to the castle is a ruined circular tower and part of a curtain wall some six feet thick, which formed the southern boundary. The tower, extensively overgrown with ivy, is some twenty-five feet in external diameter, the walls six feet thick. An internally splayed gun-loop intended for a gun on a timber bed has an irregular opening two feet high and some eight inches wide, the cill being about six inches above ground level. A similar loop at ground level, an irregular form of stirrup-loop—the opening being wider at the base—flanks the eastern curtain wall of the enclosure, with another loop positioned above this at first-floor level. The fortification complex originally included the former friary church and other buildings. The conjectured layout of the Leighlinbridge garrison, with the rectangular tower of the Black Castle at the north-west corner of the enclosure and a circular tower diagonally opposite at the south-east angle, is comparable in plan to the contemporary outpost at Fort Protector.

In the summer of 1548 construction work was progressing at Fort Protector, and at Fort Governor seventeen miles farther north. A plan

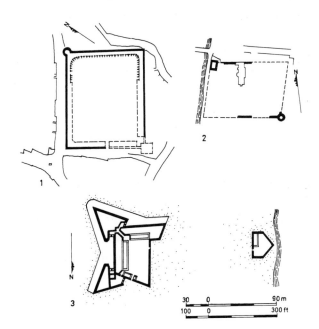

Fig. 15. Comparative plans of : 1 Maryborough Fort; 2 Leighlinbridge; 3 Corkbeg Fort.

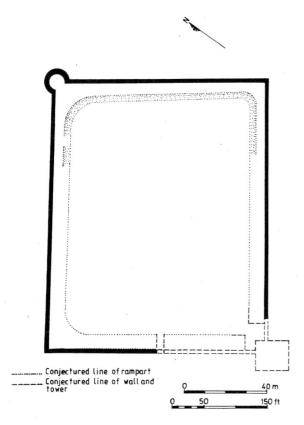

_____ Conjectured line of rampart
_____ Conjectured line of wall and
tower

0   40 m

0   50   150 ft

Fig. 16. Plan of Maryborough Fort, based on contemporary plan TCD Ms. 1209 (10), Ordnance Survey 1909 and surviving structures.

of Fort Protector drawn some years later, when it was known as the Fort of Maryborough, illustrates the layout of the defences.[9] A rectangular tower stands at one corner of a large rectangular enclosure, while at the diagonally opposite corner is a round tower or bastion. A long, narrow building occupies one side of the enclosure, and a gateway provides access to the fort. The round bastion and extensive parts of the perimeter wall remain today, but the site of the rectangular tower is occupied by later buildings (Fig.16). From the Ordnance Survey most of the outline of the fort may be traced, enclosing an area some 415 by 350 feet, dimensions that agree with those on the contemporary plan when allowance is made for the thickness of an earth rampart inside the curtain wall. The size of the enclosure is almost twice the conjectured size of the

Leighlinbridge garrison outlined above, and almost three times the size of Cahir Castle, one of the larger Irish castles.

The round bastion is some forty feet in diameter, the wall thickness at the base some five feet, reducing to about three feet at the top because of a pronounced batter on the external face. The remaining parts of the perimeter wall have a similar batter, the wall thickness reducing from some three or four feet at the base to about two feet at the top. The interior and exterior of the bastion provide no evidence for openings or floor levels, and local information suggests that the bastion was filled with earth until the 1940s. The 1909 Ordnance Survey 5 feet: 1 mile (1:1,056) of Maryborough depicts a rampart or embankment behind the curtain walls linking to the bastion. The rampart was some twenty-five feet broad, supported on the outside by the curtain wall, and must have been intended as a defence against artillery and also to provide a fighting platform for the garrison at the same level as the gun platform of the bastion. The bastion height today of some twenty feet is perhaps a few feet lower than the original structure: in size and profile it is comparable to a Martello tower.

Philipstown fort survives in outline, an enclosure some 250ft square, raised some six to eight feet above the adjacent ground level. In the centre was the O'Connor castle of Daingean. It seems the O'Connor castle of Daingean was garrisoned in 1546 with little alteration to the castle and the perimeter defences (Fig.15).

The two new forts, Fort Protector (Maryborough) and Fort Governor (Philipstown), were provided with relatively large garrisons, of a hundred men or more; the usual establishment at other strongpoints was considerably less. Among those listed in the 1550s were Athy, Monasterevan, Lea Castle, Carlow, Leighlinbridge, Enniscorthy, Ferns, St Mullins, Trim, Athlone, and Roscommon. In the north, Newry, Carlingford, Greencastle and

Carrickfergus were English garrisons.

As early as 1552 it was suggested that the two midlands forts should be expanded into market towns; the situation of the forts was uncertain, however, and they continued as fortified outposts in a hostile countryside. In 1556 large settlements were being proposed for the midlands plantations, in effect defensible villages, as smaller settlements were vulnerable to attack. This emphasis on the concentration of the colonists in towns or villages was to be continued in the various proposals for plantations in eastern Ulster at this time and over the following fifteen years. During the Ulster plantation in the early seventeenth

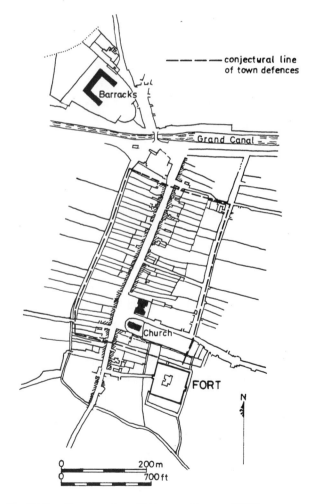

Fig. 17. Fort Governor, later Philipstown Fort, and Philipstown defences, based on 1st edition Ordnance Survey, 1838.

century the same point was made: that the colonists were safer from attack if they were in towns rather than scattered in small settlements, which offered little or no defence against an Irish uprising. The events of 1641 were to confirm the vulnerability of the plantation of Ulster.

Twelve defensible settlements were proposed for Laois in 1557, including Stradbally, Ballyadams and Abbeyleix. At some of these places, existing castles or former monastic buildings provided a strong-point around which the settlement or village developed; some may have been enclosed by a ditch and earthwork rampart. These concentrations of settlers gave support to the fort at Maryborough; in 1557 the districts known as Laois and Offaly were renamed Queen's County and King's County, respectively, and Forts Protector and Governor became Maryborough and Philipstown, named after Mary Tudor and her consort, Philip II of Spain. Ten years later permission was given for the settlements of Maryborough and Philipstown to become market towns. Outside these defensible towns the colonists were armed, and the larger landowners were obliged to provide a certain number of soldiers from among their tenants: a large proportion of the settlers were army officers or soldiers, while others were government officials, and a smaller proportion were Old English and native Irish.

Maryborough and Philipstown were enclosed by earthwork defences to protect the towns that had grown up outside the forts; proposals for these works are recorded in 1559 and by 1566 had evidently been completed. A plan of Maryborough not earlier than 1571 shows the fort with the same layout as the earlier plan but of somewhat different proportions; the town is also shown on three sides of the fort, with three gates and an enclosing rampart or wall, which has no flanking defences such as towers or bastions at the corners (Fig.18).[10] In 1570 charters were conferred on the two towns, and the corpo-

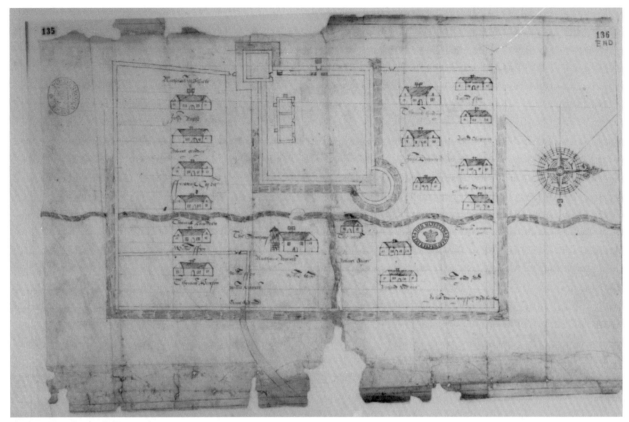

Fig. 18. Maryborough Fort and town.

rations were to fortify them with ditches and stone walls. Philipstown town defences enclosed a narrow rectangle of streets and buildings, the fort being at the south east corner (Fig.15).

Bellingham, who as lord deputy in 1548 had established the two new midlands forts, was also concerned with the defence of the coast against possible intervention or invasion from Scotland or France. In that year the mayor and corporation of Galway informed him that they were unable to make any fortifications on account of their poverty; some ten years earlier the south quay or new tower gate had been built and the walls had been repaired and provided with guns. Also in 1548 the sovereign and council of Kinsale promised Bellingham that they would make a strong fortress or bulwark for the defence of their town, while at Waterford some work appears to have been carried out under his direc-

tion.

In 1550 instructions to St Leger, reappointed lord deputy, included discussions with the port towns and any cities and towns near harbours on the means of fortifying them: the deputy and council were to advise on 'setting out bulwarks' or bastions. Articles for the expedition into Ireland of January 1551, for fortifying the havens in the south and north, specify the harbours of Baltimore, Berehaven, Olderfleet and the Bann (Coleraine); there were to be six ships and two or three rowing pinnaces, and 1,000 men, of whom 200 were to be pioneers, 100 artificers, and 200 seamen. Later that month the lord deputy was informed of these plans and was instructed to have a survey made of Cork, Kinsale, Baltimore, and Berehaven; there was fear of a French landing in Ireland, and the south-west coast was considered to be particularly vulnerable. In the following month the castles of Carrickfergus and Olderfleet were to be strengthened against the Scots.[11] Sir James Croft was now put in charge of the expedition that was to carry out the proposed fortification of the ports; two ships and a pinnace with ordnance and munitions were to be sent to Ireland, to Waterford and Cork. Croft was ordered to inspect the towns and harbours of Cork and Kinsale, to select sites for fortifications to protect them, and to give orders for works to be started as soon as possible. Baltimore and Berehaven were to be inspected and plans made of them and other harbours between them and Kinsale, and Croft was also to consider what was necessary for the defence of other ports along the coast, including Youghal and Waterford. It is likely that the situation at Dungarvan was to be investigated, where the castle overlooks the harbour. At Cork and Kinsale, Croft was to suggest ways of strengthening the fortifications of those towns and to have plans made of both places. In March 1551 St Leger was complaining that he had been provided with no funds for these proposed defence works.

Croft replaced St Leger as lord deputy three months later and was instructed to give special consideration to the southern ports of Waterford, Cork, Kinsale, Baltimore, Berehaven and 'Shepehaven' (presumably west of Bantry Bay), and also the northern ports of Strangford, Olderfleet, Carrickfergus and the Bann. In May plans of Cork, Kinsale and Baltimore were received by the government in London, evidently prepared by John Rogers, the English military engineer. Croft asked that Rogers be 'employed for furtherance of the fortifications', but there appears to be little surviving evidence that the proposals were carried out, with the possible exception of works at Kinsale, Youghal, and Waterford, and the probability that Corkbeg Fort at Cork Harbour originates from this defence scheme. Also in May 1551 St Leger and

Croft informed London of the arrival of 1,000 soldiers and 120 pioneers from Bristol, but they had no money to pay them. It was intended that work should be done that summer, the ships transporting the soldiers and pioneers to the ports that were to be fortified. In the north Rogers had prepared a plan of the new Olderfleet castle, as the Privy Council in London referred to the plan in correspondence with the lord deputy in 1552, stressing the importance of Olderfleet and Carrickfergus.

It is not clear which of the three castles in the district Rogers surveyed: Olderfleet is said to have been at the mouth of the River Larne; the other castles were Tchevet and Coraine. Coraine, now known as Olderfleet, is a sixteenth-century tower at the end of a narrow peninsula, in a good position to control access to the harbour; possibly this is the 'new Olderfleet Castle' of Rogers' plan. A mid-nineteenth-century description notes earthworks on the peninsula, 'an earthen fortification in the form of a ravelin or projecting bastion ... flanked by curtains extending on each side to the edge of the bay.' These were noted as then being some three to four feet high.[12]

The first edition of the Ordnance Survey map (Antrim, sheet 40) indicates a fort, a square structure a short distance north-west or to the landward side of the castle. It is depicted as a square some 110 feet in external dimensions, with an internal area 50 to 60 feet square. The shape suggests a small redoubt or battery of the eighteenth or early nineteenth century, although it is possible that it dates from the seventeenth. As it is shown sited diagonally on the peninsula, it is possibly the earthen fortification noted in 1855, by which time two sides of the work may have disappeared, leaving a triangular shape like a ravelin.

Coraine, like several of the Co. Down castles, has a number of double-splayed loops at ground-floor level. These loops, three to four feet above floor level, are arranged systematically at

Coraine; five survive, of which four are grouped in pairs at two corners of the tower. It seems probable that opposite the fifth loop, on the other side of the castle, where the wall is demolished, there was another loop, giving a symmetrical layout. These openings for small hand-guns or firearms suggest a date for the castle of the beginning or middle of the sixteenth century, or possibly earlier. It seems most likely that this structure is the Olderfleet Castle mentioned at intervals during the Elizabethan period as an important garrison.

In June 1549 Nicholas Bagenal was placed in charge of Carlingford and Greencastle, Co. Down, where both castles were in need of repair, together with Newry, where he was reconstructing defences around the settlement. Late in 1551 Bagenal was converting the church buildings at Armagh into a fortified post by blocking up the windows and doors, while in the following year it was recommended that the old castle at Belfast should be garrisoned. Carrickfergus continued to be the principal English garrison in Ulster, and was to be the base for expeditions by sea to the estuary of the Bann and to Lough Foyle; but it was not until the end of the century that permanent garrisons were to be established in Tyrone and Donegal, after several years of warfare against the O'Neills and O'Donnells.

It is not clear what resulted from the expedition of 1551 to fortify the southern and northern ports. A cylindrical tower projecting out from the town wall of Kinsale into the harbour, which was under repair in 1576, may have been constructed as part of the 1551 scheme; in 1548 the corporation of Kinsale had promised Bellingham that they would make a strong fortress or bulwark for the defence of their town, possibly a reference to this structure. The circular gun-tower was a typical form of harbour defence work in the first half of the sixteenth century. The harbour tower is shown on Elizabethan and seventeenth-century maps of Kinsale.

Seventeenth-century views of Youghal include a blockhouse or low tower with three cannon-embrasures on the side overlooking the harbour that may date from the mid-sixteenth-century coast defence proposals.[13] It is also shown, with somewhat taller proportions, on the *Pacata Hibernia* view of the town, with two guns projecting out at low level. This tower at the end of the quay at Youghal is referred to in 1627 as the 'old blockhouse,' when a new work was being proposed for this site.

At Waterford below Reginald's Tower a gun battery or blockhouse is depicted on late sixteenth and seventeenth-century plans and views, a semicircular-ended structure with eight gun-embrasures, which may have been constructed between 1548 and 1552. Some work was carried out under Bellingham's direction at Waterford. Early in 1552, when work on new fortifications was being reduced or stopped, it was agreed by the Privy Council that works must go on at Waterford, Baltimore, and other places in the south: harbour defence works that were intended to keep out the Spanish and French. At Baltimore, Croft had proposed a semi-military plantation, and the harbour was to be fortified, but there appears to be no evidence that any defence work was erected here.

In the north, Bagenal held Newry, Carlingford Castle and across Carlingford the castle of Greencastle in Co. Down. On a small rocky island at the entrance to the Lough is an artillery blockhouse, which may date from the time of the coast defence proposals of 1551, but the first documentary reference to a Carlingford blockhouse appears to be 1602, when Lord Deputy Mountjoy proposed a work here on the island.[14] The character of the work suggests a mid-sixteenth-century date; it is similar in style to Brownsea Castle, Poole Harbour, one of Henry VIII's coastal forts built in 1539-40. A semi-circular-ended tower originally of three storeys is joined to a gun platform; the gun-embrasures in

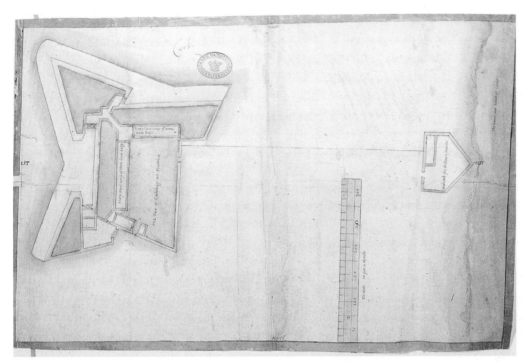

Fig. 19. The Fort of
Corkbeg by Robert
Lythe 1569, PRO
MPF 85.

the blockhouse while similar in external form to those at Calshot and Portland castles overlooking the Solent, do not have the double-splay plan of the English works. The Carlingford Lough blockhouse has unusual embrasures with internal splays. Further evidence for a seventeenth-century date for the blockhouse may be derived from a map of 1602-03 by Richard Bartlett.[15] This detailed map of the area between Dundalk and Newry depicts the walled town of Carlingford, Narrow Water Castle, Greencastle, and other castles, but nothing is indicated on the islands at the entrance to Carlingford Lough. A careful cartographer such as Bartlett would surely have indicated a structure such as the blockhouse if it were in existence when he prepared his map.

The most positive evidence for a work of harbour defence arising from the 1551 scheme is the plan of the fort of Corkbeg by the English engineer and surveyor, Robert Lythe, probably drawn in 1569 (Fig.19).[16] Late sixteenth and early seventeenth-century maps of Cork Harbour depict this fort as the 'King's Work,'

apparently a reference to King Edward Vl (1547-53). In the shape of the bastions and other details Corkbeg is remarkably similar to the forts constructed by the English in Scotland between 1548 and 1550, in particular Dunglass, south of Dunbar on the east coast, built in 1548.[17] The two acute-angled bastions on the landward front of Corkbeg, with their recessed flank gun emplacements, are very close in size and proportions to the bastion and demi-bastion at Dunglass: these and other features, such as the narrow ditch and the small chambers for the guns in the bastion flanks, would suggest a mid-sixteenth-century date for Corkbeg. The plan by Lythe shows a detached bastion-shaped work several hundred feet away to the west, overlooking the entrance to Cork Harbour, noted as a 'bulwarke for the haven mouthe.' In a sense the function of the fort was to protect this harbour-mouth gun battery from attack from the landward side. On the site of Corkbeg and its detached bastion today is the eighteenth- and nineteenth-century complex of Fort Carlisle, several hundred feet above sea level. The Lythe plan of Corkbeg and the later

Elizabethan and seventeenth-century maps, on which it is depicted with reasonable accuracy, appear to be the earliest documentary evidence for the fort, which must be the earliest bastioned work of the Italian style in Ireland. A further confirmation of a mid-sixteenth-century date is Sir George Carew's reference in 1602 to a fort at the harbour mouth 'begun in King Edward's time.'

In 1556 Sir Thomas Radcliffe, Lord Fitzwalter, later to be Earl of Sussex, replaced St Leger as deputy. In the following year, commenting on proposals for a settlement in eastern Ulster, he advocated the fortification of harbours from Carlingford to Lough Foyle, including Strangford, Carrickfergus, Olderfleet, the Bann (at Coleraine), and Lough Foyle.[18] Settlers were to be established at these places and at Belfast in fortified towns, and in other fortified towns inland, to resist both the Scots and the native Irish. A garrison was left in Culmore Castle at Lough Foyle, later to be the site of an important fort and garrison established in 1600, while Carrickfergus was reinforced. However, Sussex failed to exclude the Scots and made little impact on the power of the O'Neills in mid-Ulster.

In the midlands the policy of plantation was continued, and Sussex was authorised to grant to settlers land that had formerly been held by the O'Mores, O'Connors and other Irish chiefs. Also in 1557 Sussex marched across the midlands from Dublin to Meelick on the Shannon to attack the castle there, which was held by the O'Connors. Heavy cannon were brought down the Shannon from Athlone and placed in the grounds of Meelick Friary; the castle garrison refused a summons to surrender, and the following day, at the sixteenth shot, a large part of the courtyard wall collapsed, the O'Connors escaping by a postern gate. Sussex left a force at Meelick, which was to be a government garrison for several years, as it was to be again in the seventeenth century, when a fort was built on an island here. He marched back to the fort at Philipstown, where the outlying buildings of the settlement had been burnt by the Irish: driven out of their castles by English artillery, they retaliated with the tactics of raid and ambush, increasingly using firearms.

In 1557 there was again war with France and Scotland, and the English lost their last stronghold in France, the fortified town of Calais. On the death of Mary Tudor in November 1558, Mary Queen of Scots was recognised as ruler of England, Scotland and Ireland by Henry II of France. In a time of uncertainty for England, Elizabeth came to the throne to face an alliance of the Scottish crown with France, giving rise to the possibility of intervention in Ulster by Scotland. Peace was made with France in 1559, and for the remainder of the century, particularly after 1570, the greatest external threat to English rule in Ireland was to come from Spain.

Sussex was reappointed as lord deputy by Queen Elizabeth in 1559. In the following year there was still fear of invasion from France or Spain, and concern was expressed for the defence of the southern ports. In 1560 it was proposed that a blockhouse should be made at Waterford for the 'safety of the haven and town,' possibly a reference to the structure at Reginald's Tower, or perhaps the first proposal for the circular tower at Passage, which was built by 1568 (Map 2, see page 45).[19]

In the north, Carrickfergus Castle was provided with gun-ports—large brick-built arched gun-embrasures—between 1561 and 1567 [20] At Armagh the church buildings were again fortified as an English outpost, and a garrison of two hundred soldiers established there in 1561. The following year Sussex was proposing the establishment of walled towns at Carrickfergus, Lough Foyle, and Newry, and again the harbours were to be defended, existing castles garrisoned and new castles built where required to defend landing-places. Lands in Ulster were to be awarded to soldiers, who were to build castles to defend their settlements. The plantations in the midlands continued, centred around the garrisons at Maryborough and Philipstown. In 1563 fortifications, evidently earthworks, were almost completed at Armagh.

A large-scale project for plantation in Ulster was proposed in 1565; it was to be a joint venture between private individuals and the military and naval forces of Queen Elizabeth. In January 1566 Sir Henry Sidney became lord deputy, but it was not until September that year that Colonel Edward Randolph arrived at Lough Foyle, entrenched his force, and fortified the church buildings at Derry. Sidney marched across Ulster to join Randolph, then returned through Donegal, Roscommon and Athlone to Dublin. In Carrickfergus the friary was entrenched and the town defended by a ditch; at Armagh, Shane O'Neill had burnt the cathedral to prevent Sidney reoccupying it as a military post. At Derry, Randolph was short of food and supplies; he was killed in an action against the O'Neills, and in April 1567 an accidental fire destroyed the buildings, and the gunpowder exploded. The garrison was evacuated, but the landing at Lough Foyle had demonstrated the effectiveness of English sea power, and a similar amphibious operation was to be repeated with more success in 1600, when permanent garrisons were established at Culmore and Derry.

Garrisons proposed by Sidney for Ulster in 1567 included Newry—where fortifications had been made by Bagenal—Strangford, Coleraine, Toome, and Massarene, where the abbey buildings would provide a strong-point. Ten garrisons suggested by Sidney were increased to make a total of fourteen, including several at sites where forts were to be constructed in the opening years of the following century. At Strangford it was recommended that a blockhouse be built to guard the harbour. Belfast was another proposed site for a settlement, and Olderfleet was regarded as one of the best harbours. Landing-places along the Antrim coast were also to be fortified; but most of these proposals for garrisons and fortifications in Ulster were not carried out until the closing stages of Mountjoy's campaign against Hugh O'Neill more than thirty years later. Queen Elizabeth refused to provide funds for forts or garrisons in Ulster at this time, except on the coast, where fortifications at Carrickfergus and Olderfleet were approved.

At Passage, on the west side of Waterford Harbour, a coastal defence work had been constructed by 1568: built by the citizens of Waterford, a broad round tower mounting ordnance commanded the estuary and anchorage. It is depicted on Elizabethan and seventeenth-century maps and views and was similar to the circular towers overlooking the harbours at Kinsale and Youghal.[21] In 1576 Sir Henry Sidney provided funds for the repair of the tower at the pier at Kinsale, which he was hopeful would be completed that summer, but in 1586 the work was not yet finished.[22]

An important factor in the need for artillery defences at ports and anchorages was the prevalence of piracy, which was to continue as a feature of life along the Irish coast well into the seventeenth century. Contemporary accounts refer to problems of piracy at Kinsale, Waterford and other harbours, and to the lack of protection for fishing craft and merchant ships.

Fear of Spanish invasion was one of the arguments put forward for English settlements in Munster. The south west coast was felt to be particularly vulnerable, and the harbours at Valentia, Berehaven, Crookhaven and Baltimore were undefended—the coast was well known to the crews of Spanish fishing craft and trading vessels. Proposals for plantations were under way by 1569, and included in these schemes were fortified coastal settlements. Among those involved were Warham St Leger and Sir Richard Grenville. Lands to be planted by St Leger and

Grenville were attacked by James FitzMaurice Fitzgerald and MacCarthy Mór, who appeared outside the walls of Cork with a force of some three to four thousand men. In the midlands and south east they were joined by forces under Sir Edmund Butler, a brother of the Earl of Ormond. Both the Irish and Old English were alarmed at the confiscation of land by the Crown and the policy of plantation, and to some extent they united to resist the new English settlers.

James FitzMaurice Fitzgerald sacked the walled town of Kilmallock in 1570; the decision of the pope to excommunicate Queen Elizabeth early in that year helped to turn the revolt into a religious crusade, and foreign intervention from Spain was feared. Before Sidney gave way to his successor as lord deputy, Sir William Fitzwilliam, in March 1571, he had established 'lord presidents' in Munster and Connacht. Sir John Perrot was lord president in Munster, and in 1571 he attacked the castle of Castlemaine for five weeks without success. The following year the castle held out for several months, even though the besieging force under Perrot used artillery. A contemporary view reproduced in *Pacata Hibernia* illustrates the castle situated in the centre of the River Maine, linked to each bank by a bridge. James FitzMaurice Fitzgerald submitted in 1572 and went overseas in 1575; he was to return in four years' time at the head of a small invasion force.

In the years 1571-74 several attempts were made to set up colonies in eastern Ulster; one of these expeditions was led by Walter Devereux, Earl of Essex. Private 'adventurers' were to be granted lands, each estate was to be defended by a small castle with a bawn or courtyard, and new settlements were to be entrenched as fortified towns. A fortification that may possibly originate from this attempt by Essex to establish a colony in Antrim—in which he received little help from the lord deputy, Fitzwilliam—is the fort at Fortwilliam in north Belfast.[23] This is a square

earthwork fort with two square bastions at diagonally opposite corners; a similar fort is shown on a plan of the defences of Lifford of 1600-03.

In 1574 an earthwork rampart was built around Carrickfergus, after Brian MacPhelim O'Neill had attacked and burnt much of the town. A contemporary plan depicts rounded bastions at two positions on the rampart, one of which was later known as Essex Mount. An earlier plan by Lythe of 1567 that shows the town and buildings in some detail depicts an angular bastion at one corner of the earthworks enclosing the friary.[24] A fortification was also proposed in 1574 to enclose the settlement or garrison at Belfast, again an earthwork of ditch and rampart.

Earthwork defences had the advantage that they could be rapidly constructed by soldiers or labourers; the disadvantages were their need for continual rebuilding and maintenance, while heavy rainfall for a prolonged period tended to reduce their height and effectiveness. Timber palisades or retaining structures, and planks forming gun platforms, were liable to decay after a few years and had to be replaced. The programme of coastal defence for England in 1539-40 included the construction of temporary earthworks until the permanent masonry fortifications were completed. A possible reason for the lack of evidence for defence works built by Sir James Croft in his expedition to fortify the Irish coast in 1551 may be that they were, to a large extent, earthworks. Earthwork ramparts evidently enclosed the towns of Maryborough and Philipstown, with the earlier forts acting as strong-points or citadels. In 1574 the town of Loughrea in Co. Galway was described as 'well ditched and trenched.' Walls had been started, there were three gatehouses, and the place was recommended as convenient for a garrison. In 1576 what must have been earthwork ramparts were constructed around Wicklow and Arklow; the towns were 'walled' by Captain Francis

Agard on the recommendation of Sidney, who had returned to Ireland as lord deputy the year before.

The smaller midlands settlements were to be defended by ditch and earthwork, while the various proposals for Ulster included 'entrenching towns.' A plan of Roscommon of 1581 depicts what must be earthwork ramparts and bastions enclosing a settlement immediately to the east of the castle, which is shown with reasonable accuracy (Fig.20).[25] The bastions forming part of the defensive line around the settlement are not of the Italian angular form: they are round or semi-circular in plan, while a square tower is shown at the end of the town rampart south of the castle. In 1578 Sir Nicholas Malby had offered to build a wall around the town of Athlone and to build a walled town at Roscommon, where he inserted mullioned windows in the castle.

In the summer of 1579 James FitzMaurice Fitzgerald returned to Ireland, arriving at Smerwick in the Dingle Peninsula. Here the invasion force of some seven hundred men established a fortified post at Dún an Óir, the 'Fort of Gold,' an old promontory fort overlooking Smerwick Harbour.[26] The revolt was to receive little support outside Munster, apart from an uprising in Leinster by Viscount Baltinglass and the O'Byrnes of Wicklow. FitzMaurice was killed a month after his arrival, but his place was taken by the brother of the Earl of Desmond. Spanish and Italian reinforcements of about six hundred soldiers arrived at Dún an Óir in August 1580; attacked by English land and sea forces, the garrison surrendered after a short bombardment. Lord Grey de Wilton, the lord deputy—who had been defeated by the O'Byrnes in Wicklow earlier that year—ordered that the defenders be killed after they had given up their weapons.

On the landward side the garrison had constructed an earthwork parapet, flanked at each end by a demi-bastion. Remains of these works still survive on the site; the demi-bastions are

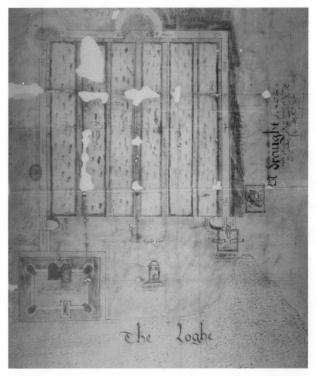

Fig. 20. The town and castle of Roscommon, 1581, PRO MPF 95.

about 80 feet apart, and their faces vary from 44 to 60 feet in length. These earthworks at Smerwick are amongst the earliest surviving angle-bastion fortifications in Ireland.

The affair emphasised the importance of the English control of the sea, as the small fort was under fire from naval vessels at the same time as it was attacked from the land. Earlier in 1580 the English use of sea power had been demonstrated by the capture of Carrigafoyle Castle on the Shannon Estuary, where the guns of the besieging force had been landed from ships.

In the same year concern for coastal defence again gave rise to the recommendation that the principal harbours be fortified, and a citadel was advocated for Galway, with the dual function of controlling the city and providing protection to the harbour. Fords over the Shannon, the bridge of Athlone, a ford below Clonmacnois (possibly Shannonbridge, where a massive early nineteenth-century bridgehead now stands), and

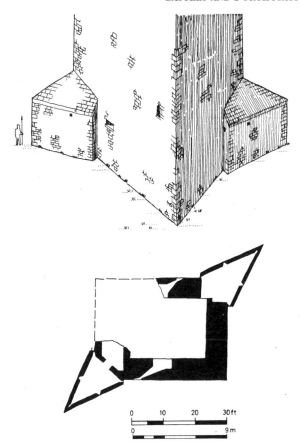

Fig. 21. Mashanaglas Castle, Co. Cork. Partly reconstructed axonometric view, with first floor plan (after Cork Hist, Soc. Jnl, 1, 1892, p234).

fords at Banagher and Meelick, were to be fortified.[27] All these places were to be important fortified posts in the seventeenth century and during the Napoleonic Wars. Fortifying the harbour towns was proposed as the best way to establish English rule in Munster; plantation schemes of ten years earlier that had included fortified coastal settlements had not materialised.

The influence of the new ideas of artillery fortification may be seen at Fiddaun Castle Co. Galway, where there is a triangular projection or redan on one side of the bawn wall.[28] Fiddaun is recorded as an O'Shaughnessy castle in 1567 and 1574. Defended to the east and west by small lakes, with a detached gatehouse to the north, the south wall, most open to attack, is the wall with the triangular work, flanked by loops for

firearms. Further south a stone wall that at first glance appears to be a field boundary is provided with musket loops; it forms an outer line of defence linking the two lakes. At Mashanaglas in west Cork, the MacSweeney castle of before 1585 has acute-angled spurs or redans at two diagonally opposite corners; these triangular projections at the corners are two-storey in height, solid at ground level, and contain a stone-roofed room at first-floor level, loopholed for musketry.[29] Loops in the tower-house flank the faces of the spurs (Fig.21). At both Fiddaun and Mashanaglas the triangular projections are an integral part of the structure, not additions.

The Irish tower-house castles of the late sixteenth and early seventeenth centuries are usually well provided with musket and pistol loops. They are to be found in the tower-house structure at the entrance door, at various locations in the walls at upper levels, in the battlements, and in the projecting corner structures often positioned half-way up the tower, which have come to be known as bartizans. They also appear in the bawn wall at ground or wall-walk level, in the corner towers or turrets, and at the entrance gateway. The position of many of the loops at doorways and staircases indicates the use of pistols rather than larger firearms. The most usual form of loop is a circular opening about two inches in diameter, with a splayed embrasure on the interior to allow for as wide a field of fire as possible. Other types of loop are horizontal or vertical openings about two inches wide by perhaps eight or twelve inches long, again with an internal splay.

Most attacks on castles in Ireland in the sixteenth century must have been made without artillery, but with an increasing use of firearms by the besiegers and defenders. Without the use of artillery to destroy the walls and make a breech for the assault parties, the capture of the castle had to depend on a surprise attack, treachery in some form, or a long blockade to deprive the garrison of food and supplies. In these circumstances a well-sited castle could put up a good defence and, with a small but determined garrison, was often able to offer greater resistance to attack than a poorly defended walled town. The extensive medieval walls at Athenry did not prevent the capture of the town by the sons of the Earl of Clanricarde in 1574; three years later they again successfully attacked the town. In 1596 Athenry was taken by Red Hugh O'Donnell and sacked, but he failed to take the castle; and he was driven off by cannon fire from the walls when he attacked Galway. In 1570 the walled town of Kilmallock was captured by James FitzMaurice Fitzgerald and the defences of Youghal did not prevent its capture by the Earl of Desmond in 1579.

The walled towns were equipped in varying degrees with artillery; contemporary views of Cork, Youghal and Limerick indicate guns at embrasures in the towers, while at Youghal the *Pacata Hibernia* view of the town depicts artillery on an outwork outside the north gate. The defences of the seaports of Galway, Limerick, Cork and Waterford assumed greater importance as regular sea warfare developed with Spain in the years leading up to the Armada expedition, with the increasing risk of a large-scale Spanish landing in Ireland. Waterford was considered a likely place for an invasion attempt, and in October 1587 commissioners were appointed to muster the able men in the city to be trained under suitable captains; the commissioners were also to construct fortifications in appropriate places.[30]

Work must have started almost immediately on the construction of the fort at Duncannon, which enclosed an earlier castle, sited on a promontory at the eastern side of the estuary. By December work had been in progress for seven or eight weeks; two sconces were completed, with positions for four culverins at the seaward end of the rocky promontory near water level, backed by an emplacement for four more guns at a higher level.[31] On the landward front were a glacis, covered way, dry ditch and ramparts in the form of a *tenaille trace*, while entrance was by means of a drawbridge across the ditch. Work was continuing in 1589, but Lord Deputy Fitzwilliam, writing to the Privy Council, was against plans to complete the fort, 'as it is commanded by a hill lying over it from which the enemy may at his pleasure throw stones into it ...' This criticism of the fort being overlooked by high ground inland was to be repeated on several occasions in the following centuries. In the same year it was reported that demi-cannons and demi-culverins at Limerick were available for the fort, or else some of the guns recovered from the wrecks of the Spanish Armada on the Irish coast.

In January 1590 the order was given for Waterford, Limerick, Cork and Galway to be strengthened with entrenched fortifications or outworks, outside the town walls. In the following month Edmund Yorke arrived at Waterford to supervise the work there;[32] in 1588, the year of the Armada, he had advised on defences of the Norfolk and Suffolk coasts and prepared plans for the strengthening of Yarmouth. Waterford city was to provide 150 labourers a day as long as the construction of the fortifications continued, and Yorke asked for 200 or 300 more men to be levied. Outside the walls of Waterford on the south, earthworks were erected, and a separate work protected the gate at the south-west angle. In May, Yorke was reporting that the works were almost complete at Waterford, the Rock and Duncannon. The Fort of the Rock was sited on high ground north of the River Suir, overlooking the city; it is depicted on a contemporary pictorial map of 1591, which also shows the works outside Waterford, at Passage and Duncannon.[33] The work at the Rock is shown as a low circular tower surrounded by a *tenaille trace* outer work, while the earlier cylindrical tower or blockhouse at Passage is depicted with a similar outer line of

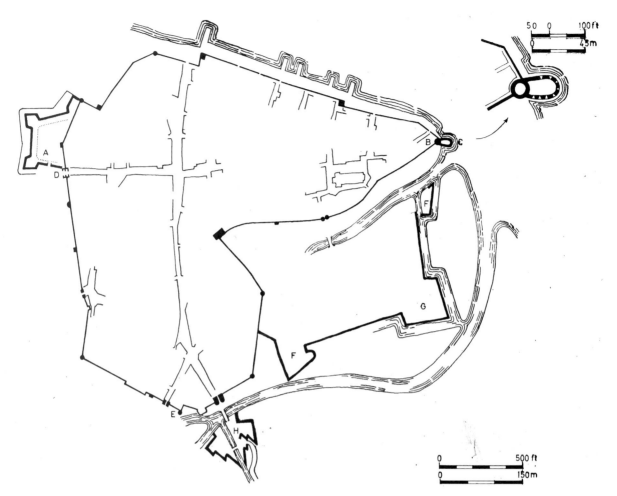

Fig. 22. Plan of the defences of Waterford 1590-1626.
A The Citadel or St Patrick's Fort 1624-26; B Reginald's Tower; C Blockhouse; D St Patrick's Gate; E Watch Tower; F Demi-Bastion; G Bastion; H Outwork to gate and bridge. Parts of the walls and some towers survive. The size and location of the outworks of 1590 are approximate, based on TCD Ms. 4877 (2).

defence, which was built at this time. In 1592 Lord Deputy Fitzwilliam wrote to the mayor of Waterford stating that the blockhouse at Passage was out of repair and useless, to which the mayor replied that the outer wall had been finished some days earlier and only inner works remained to be done to retain the rampart. The Fort of the Rock had been started in 1589.

Carew, writing in 1595, suggested that a force of three thousand Spaniards would be able to capture and hold Waterford—a similar number was to arrive at the walled town of Kinsale six years later and hold it for several months before they surrendered after the defeat of their Irish allies.[34]

A detailed plan of Waterford, originally in the John Hunt Collection, illustrates the works constructed outside the city walls in 1590; a copy is in Trinity College, Dublin.[35] It shows the artillery blockhouse attached to Reginald's Tower, and a similar structure outside the south-west angle of the town walls. The outwork to the south of the town wall has a bastion at the south-east corner and is supported by two demi-bastions, one to the north-east, the other to the west. A short distance from the western demi-bastion is the southern gate of the town, in front of which is an elaborate *tenaille trace* outwork. Just to the west of the gate is the semicircular-ended work at the corner of the town wall, similar to the artillery blockhouse at Reginald's Tower (Fig.22). In October 1590 the earthwork defences were described by Nicholas Lombard, a citizen of Waterford, in a letter to his son; he also noted the work at the Rock and the outer wall built about the blockhouse at Passage.[36]

While work was proceeding at Waterford, defences were also being constructed at Cork and Limerick. Cork was overlooked by high ground to the north and south and was vulnerable to artillery bombardment from these positions. Outside the city walls to the south Sir George Carew constructed a fort some ten years later, but it is not clear what was carried out in 1590; there is a reference to a plan of the fortification at Cork in August that year. Carew felt that because of its situation Cork could not be fortified adequately, but that the river approaches might be fortified at convenient places to obstruct enemy shipping. A pictorial map of c. 1601 shows a small rectangular fort or battery on the corner of a marsh to the east of the city wall, and Carew's new work to the south.[37] Three gun-embrasures appear to be indicated in the parapet of the rectangular fort, facing eastwards, the direction of approach of ships coming upstream to Cork; the early seventeenth-century map of Cork by Speed notes this fort as the 'Entrance Fort,' while Carew's work is the 'New Fort.' It is possible that this fort at the river approach to the city dates from 1590, and it is likely that at certain locations on the river down to Cork Harbour other defences were constructed, possibly in the form of earthwork batteries. Blackrock Castle, three miles downstream, is a good position for a gun emplacement, and it had been provided with artillery by the citizens of Cork in 1585; the present structure dates largely from the early nineteenth century, but incorporates the lower part of the original circular tower, with gun embrasures commanding the

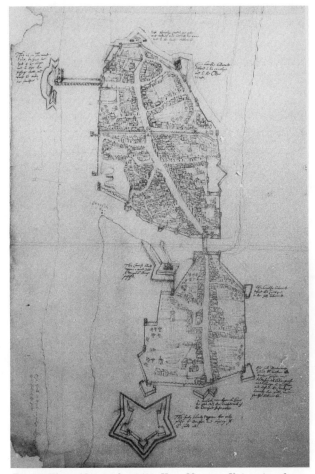

Fig. 23. Plan of Limerick c.1590, Hunt Museum. University of Limerick.A bridgehead defence work protects Thomond Bridge at top left; a ravelin and demi-bastion are on the north and north-east of the English town defences. Bastions and other outworks are added to the walls of Irish Town, where there is a bastioned pentagonal fort at the south-west angle. Not shown is the six-pointed star fort some distance north of English Town. The plan may be by Edmund Yorke.

river,

A plan of Limerick by Sir Richard Grenville—his rough proposals for fortifying the city—depicts proposed artillery works in the form of an Italian-style bastioned trace across Irish Town.[38] This consists of a central bastion flanked by two demi- bastions, each with orillons protecting recessed flanks; three bastions are also shown attached to the south wall of Irish Town. A 'half moon' or semi-circular work is indicated at the west end of the bridge—Thomond Bridge—across the Shannon.

Edmund Yorke had been sent over to Ireland in December 1589 to meet Sir Richard Bingham at Limerick, who was to assist him in the fortifications. In February 1590 four pieces of artillery were to be placed in position at Limerick; in March the castle was to be repaired. A gun-embrasure in the west tower of the gatehouse at second-floor level, with a field of fire to the west across the river below Thomond Bridge, may date from this time.

A much more detailed plan of Limerick than that by Grenville is in the Hunt Museum at the University of Limerick (Fig.23). There are some similarities to the Grenville plan. The artillery outworks at the English Town are: a six-pointed star fort some distance north of the town to protect a ford; a ravelin outside the gate in the north wall; a half-bulwark or demi-bastion on the north-east side; a work covering the gate of the bridge on the Thomond or Clare side of the Shannon; and a work in the form of a *tenaille trace* on the east side of the English Town (this work is not commented on in the plan, unlike the other artillery defences). The Irish Town outworks are a half-bulwark or demi-bastion at the north east corner; a full bulwark or bastion at the south east corner; a *tenaille trace* outwork to cover the gate in the south wall; and a bastion at the south west angle of the Irish Town. In front of this south west bastion is a detached pentagonal fort: the two salient angles flanking the bastion take the form of demi-bastions. The demi-bastions and the three bastions of the fort are shown with straight flanks, unlike the recessed flanks of the larger bastions and demi-bastions attached to the town wall. These works at Limerick depicted on this plan—if they were built (certainly some defence works were undertaken in 1590)—were most probably earthworks, as, except for Speed's map, they do not appear on later plans of the city. The absence of the bastion at the south-east angle of the castle, built by 1611, indicates that the plan is earlier than that

date. There are references to fortifications at Limerick in the first decade of the seventeenth century, but by this time bastions with orillons as depicted on the plan were replaced with bastions with straight flanks, as English engineers were influenced by Dutch practice. The probability is that the Limerick plan depicts works proposed or executed in 1590, as the plan of Waterford illustrating the works carried out there in 1590 appears to be by the same draughtsman, possibly Edmund Yorke. Speed's map of Limerick (1610) contains several of the artillery outworks depicted on the plan in the Hunt Museum. At the English Town are the ravelin at the north gate and the half-bastion at the north east, while the outwork at the bridge is a similar shape. The bastion at the south east corner and the outwork at the south gate of Irish Town are depicted, while the detached fort at the south west angle is also of the same shape.

Fortifications were constructed at Galway at about the time of the Spanish Armada in 1588: the south-west corner of the town at the quay was fortified and equipped with heavy ordnance, and a part of the adjoining wall was built by the corporation. The surviving part of the town wall here, known as the Spanish Arch, is wide enough to mount cannon; seventeenth-century maps and views of Galway indicate guns here.

A report on the situation at Kinsale in 1586 noted that the repairs to the blockhouse—the circular tower projecting from the town wall—started ten years earlier were still not completed.[39] It was suggested that a gun platform should be constructed at Ringcurran Castle on the east side of the estuary, later to be the site of Charles Fort, and that another battery should be built on 'the westerly point', presumably the promontory of Castle Park, where the fort and blockhouse were later to be erected in the early seventeenth century. Much harm had recently been done by pirates, as the harbour was undefended, and it was feared that if an invasion were

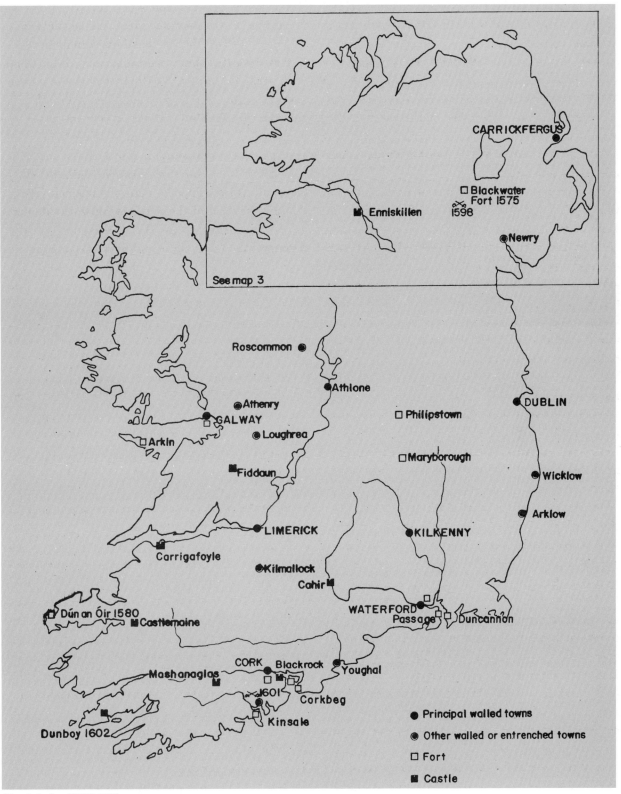

CARRICKFERGUS

☐ Blackwater
Fort 1575
1598

■ Enniskillen

● Newry

See map 3

Roscommon ◉

Athlone

◉ Athenry

GALWAY ☐

● DUBLIN

☐ Philipstown

◉ Loughrea

☐ Arkin

☐ Maryborough

■ Fiddaun

● Wicklow

● LIMERICK

● KILKENNY

● Arklow

■ Carrigafoyle

◉ Kilmallock

Cahir ■

WATERFORD ☐
Passage ☐ ☐ Duncannon

Dún an Óir 1580
■ Castlemaine

CORK ● Blackrock
Mashanaglas ■   ● Youghal
1601 ☐ ☐ Corkbeg
Kinsale ☐

Dunboy 1602 ■

● Principal walled towns

◉ Other walled or entrenched towns

☐ Fort

■ Castle

Map 2. Ireland 1558-1603.

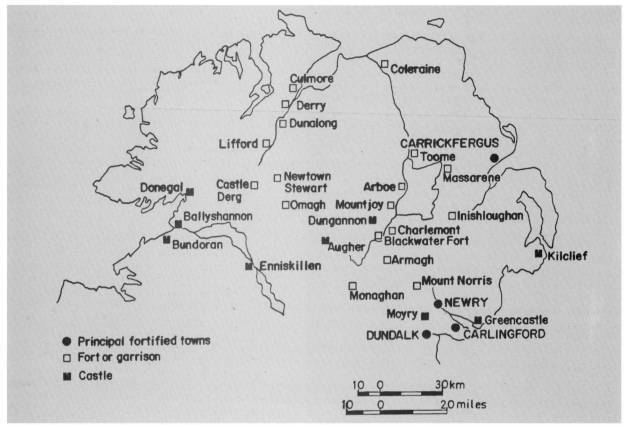

Map 3 Ulster 1594-1603.

attempted it would be at Kinsale, as there was a good harbour and the town would not be able to put up any resistance. Fifteen years later the Spanish expedition arrived at Kinsale and occupied the town and the outposts at Ringcurran and Castle Park, which had not been fortified with artillery works as recommended in 1586. Further west along the Cork coast, Castlehaven and Glandore should each be defended by a 'bulwark' or gun battery at the eastern point of each harbour, and it was recommended that Baltimore be similarly defended. Crookhaven and Berehaven were also mentioned in these proposals for coastal defence in 1586, places that were to be fortified in the following century. The principal concern of the English administration in Ireland with regard to a possible Spanish landing appears to have been to defend the seaports of Waterford, Cork, Limerick and Galway; the sec-

ondary harbours along the south and south west coast were also to be fortified, but little appears to have been done at this time. The armada of 1588 was followed by further expeditions from Spain in 1596 and 1597. The earlier fleet was intended for the invasion of both England and Ireland; on both occasions the ships were dispersed by storms. Military and political events in Ireland in the closing years of the century must be considered with regard to the possibility of Spanish intervention at that time; Sir George Carew, writing in 1595, feared a Spanish landing at Cork or Waterford: he stated that a force of three thousand Spaniards would be sufficient to capture and hold Waterford. It was an expeditionary force somewhat larger than this that landed at Kinsale in 1601 and held the town for more than three months.

The last decade of the sixteenth century was

remarkable for the resistance of Gaelic Ireland to the completion of the Tudor conquest. It was in Ulster that the Gaelic order was to prove most difficult to defeat. After some authority had been established in Connacht and Munster by the English administration in Dublin, attention was turned to the north. The Maguire castle at Enniskillen was taken by the English in 1594, adding a further garrison to those of Carrickfergus, Monaghan, the fort on the Blackwater and Newry (Map 3).

A pictorial plan, possibly of 1568, depicts Newry as consisting of two adjacent rectangular enclosures: the main town with the church and 'new castle' is surrounded by a ditch and rampart; at two diagonally opposite corners are bastions, one an angle bastion with straight flanks, the other rectangular in shape. A contemporary drawing of the castle shows that it was a rectangular tower-house with a spiral staircase in a square projection at the centre of the entrance front, and a square turret of a similar size at one corner of the rear wall. Both the main town and 'base town', which had a simple rectangular enclosure without bastions or other flanking defences, appear to have been defended by earthwork ramparts only.[40] Newry was to remain an important garrison and staging post for English expeditions into Ulster against Hugh O'Neill, Earl of Tyrone.

In February 1595 O'Neill sent his brother Art to attack and destroy the Blackwater Fort and bridge; the war was to continue until early in 1603. O'Neill built a new earthwork on the opposite side of the river, the northern or Tyrone bank; his castle of Dungannon was six miles away to the north-west. In July that year an account of Lord Deputy Russell's expedition into Ulster states that Dungannon had been fortified with 'great ditches with rampiers [ramparts] by the device, as it was said, of a Spaniard he had with him.' Tyrone made use of trenches and field fortifications, and built forts on the western shore of

Lough Neagh later in the war. However, he abandoned Dungannon in 1595, and was to do so again, to conduct a war of movement and ambush: crannógs—timber-palisaded strongholds built on artificial islands in the Ulster lakes—became his places of retreat.

O'Neill's new fort on the Blackwater was captured by Lord Deputy Burgh in July 1597; a contemporary drawing of this attack depicts the work with earthen ramparts forming a rectangular enclosure on the riverbank, with two rounded bastions at the landward corners.[41] Burgh built a new earthwork on or near the site of O'Neill's fort and it was this new English garrison that brought about the Battle of the Yellow Ford in 1598. In an attempt to relieve the garrison, six English regiments marched out of Armagh. This force of some 3,000 men was attacked on the march, and O'Neill and his allies won the greatest victory ever achieved by an Irish army up to that time. For several years the Blackwater river was to be a frontier; attacks were made from Dundalk, Newry, and Armagh, and in the west from Ballyshannon into Donegal. From Carrickfergus an expedition sailed to the Foyle in May 1600, landing at Culmore and Derry, while in the following year English forces sailed across Lough Neagh to the Tyrone or western shore of the lake. A key element in the warfare in Ulster between 1595 and 1603 was the construction of forts, earthworks with timber palisades constructed by the English soldiers to hold captured territory and strategic positions such as river crossings. In places, existing castles were extended by the addition of outworks, and in at least one location, Mount Norris, an Irish ring-fort was incorporated in new defences.

After the Irish victory of the Yellow Ford, O'Neill gained numerous allies in Connacht and Munster, where the plantation was overthrown. English-held territory was reduced to the area around Dublin, the walled towns, and isolated garrisons. In 1599 Robert Devereux, Second

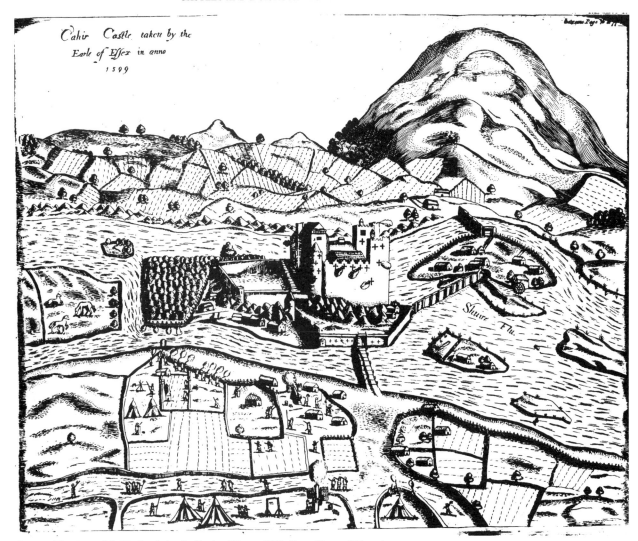

Fig. 24. The siege of Cahir Castle by the Earle of Essex, 1599. From Pacata Hibernia.

Earl of Essex, arrived in Dublin with the title of lord lieutenant; his only success was the capture of Cahir Castle. Instead of attacking O'Neill in Ulster he marched through Leinster and Munster. In his attack on Cahir he had two guns, a cannon and a culverin, which had been sent up river from Waterford to Clonmel. The strength of Cahir Castle consisted mainly in its situation on an island in the River Suir (Fig.24). The attack on the castle with the aid of artillery was in many respects typical of such sieges in Elizabethan Ireland: the cannon and culverin were set up on the east bank of the river in positions that had been prepared under cover of darkness the night before. The cannon's carriage broke at the first shot, and for some time the culverin was out of action, eventually firing some fifty shots. The cannon was sited close to the castle, the culverin farther back. On the third and final day of the siege the shot from the cannon—now repaired—and the culverin destroyed large areas of the walls, and ladders were made ready for the assault parties. During the night the Irish garrison sallied out but about eighty were killed, and the remainder escaped by swimming across the river. The breaches in the walls were repaired and an English garrison placed in the castle.

Queen Elizabeth's scornful letter to Essex

refers to his capture of Cahir:

> *Where upon ensued the taking of Cahir Castle full well do we know that you would long since have scorned to allowed it for any great matter in others to have taken an Irish hold from a rabble of rogues with such force that you had and with the help of the cannon which was always able in Ireland to make his passage where it pleased.*

The following year the castle was recaptured by James Galda Butler, who had defended it at the siege: with sixty men he overpowered the garrison of thirty soldiers. The castle surrendered to the English again some months later. Increasingly the Irish abandoned their castles, particularly if there was the threat of the use of artillery against them: in the Elizabethan wars there was seldom any chance of surrendering on terms that would ensure the lives of the garrison. The forests, hills and bogs were safer strongholds, allowing for a warfare of movement and ambush.

Charles Blount, Lord Mountjoy, arrived early in 1600 as the new lord deputy to replace Essex; he was to maintain a continuous pressure on O'Neill and his allies, secure the establishment of an increasing number of fortified garrisons in Ulster, and use sea power fully to support land operations. In May 1600 Mountjoy sent Sir Henry Docwra to Lough Foyle. His force of 4,000 men sailed from Carrickfergus and landed at Culmore and Derry. The O'Donnells made no effective effort to dislodge the English force that fortified Culmore, Derry, and Dunalong, an O'Neill castle a short distance upstream. Lifford was taken with the aid of renegade O'Donnells and fortified like the other garrisons with earthworks, rapidly constructed by the soldiers. This landing at Lough Foyle was as critical to the outcome of the war as the more well-known events—the siege and battle of Kinsale—some eighteen months later.

In Armagh new forts were under construction as Mountjoy pushed forward to the line of the River Blackwater; Mount Norris was built in November 1600, and in the following year Moyry Castle was constructed. From Carrickfergus English forces moved up to Massarene, close to the site of the later town of Antrim, where a fort was constructed by Sir Arthur Chichester in April 1601. He was later to cross Lough Neagh and raid the Tyrone shore. By July 1601 Mountjoy had crossed the Blackwater and built the third Blackwater Fort on the Tyrone bank of the river, a triangular bastioned earthwork. He was aware of Spanish preparations for an expedition to Ireland, and in September a Spanish force of some 3,500 men landed at Kinsale. By the end of October Mountjoy had assembled almost 7,000 soldiers in Cork.

The Spaniards remained in Kinsale and the outposts of Castle Park and Ringcurran Castle, preventing effective use of the harbour by the English fleet; the inlet further east, Oyster Haven, was used by the English for unloading supplies. Ringcurran surrendered after two days of bombardment by several culverins and a cannon; Castle Park put up a longer resistance, but after the surrender of the small garrison the English placed three culverins here to fire on the town. By the end of November O'Neill decided to march south to Kinsale: the battle outside the town resulted in an English victory, and the Spaniards, under Don Juan del Aguila, surrendered nine days later. There was still fear of a further Spanish expedition, so plans were made for new forts at Kinsale and at Haulbowline Island in Cork Harbour, and a work started outside the walls of Cork was completed. Work also continued on the fort begun in 1600 at Galway, and a work was proposed for Carlingford Lough on one of the small islands at the entrance, possibly the blockhouse described above. Proposals for forts at Berehaven and Baltimore were not carried out.

With the defeat of O'Neill at Kinsale, Mountjoy's attention was again turned to Ulster: Dungannon Castle was taken, and Sir Arthur Chichester built a new fort here; in July 1602 Mountjoy Fort was constructed on the Tyrone shore of Lough Neagh. Like the other campaign forts it was laid out according to the principle of artillery fortification, with earthwork bastions and ramparts. Charlemont Fort, close to the Blackwater in Co. Armagh, had been constructed the previous month.

As pressure mounted on O'Neill in Tyrone, the west Cork outpost of Dunboy Castle was attacked; it had been strengthened with earthworks constructed by the Spanish and Irish garrison. Sir George Carew waited at Bantry for ships that transported his force to Bere Island, avoiding the dangerous overland route. The defence of Dunboy Castle was under the command of Captain Richard MacGeoghegan, presumably one of the followers of O'Neill's midlands leader, Tyrrell, who was defending landing-places nearby. It was at a MacGeoghegan stronghold, Balrath Castle, in Westmeath, that artillery was first used in siegework in Ireland, in 1488.

Two guns were landed north of Dunboy, while the main battery was set up 140 yards to the east; after much of the castle was destroyed by the artillery and an assault made by the attacking force, the survivors of the garrison surrendered, to be hanged the next day. Earthwork defences contructed around the tower-house by the garrison and the remains of the mid-seventeenth century star fort surrounding these works survive on the site today.

In Ulster O'Neill opened negotiations with Mountjoy, resulting in his surrender at Mellifont in March 1603. The war that had started in 1595 now came to an end, with the construction of artillery forts at principal harbours and a network of campaign forts in strategic places across Ulster. These Ulster forts played a significant part in the defeat of O'Neill; many were soon to form the nucleus of plantation settlements.

Contemporary plans and maps survive that provide detailed information on many of the Ulster forts and those at Kinsale, Cork and Galway. At Culmore, Docwra constructed a triangular earthwork fort enclosing an earlier castle in May 1600, situated on a promontory at the mouth of the Foyle. He had the assistance of a Dutch engineer, Jose Everaert, who undertook to complete the work in four months, including a wet moat on the landward side, and a drawbridge.

At Derry the settlement that preceded the walled town of 1614-18 is depicted as an irregular enclosure with three bastions and a demi-bastion; to one side a future extension of the town is shown in a broken line (Fig.25). This extension would have resulted in a seven-sided layout, with angle-bastions at each salient angle. The settlement and proposed extension, which would have resulted in almost doubling the size of the town, was sited further away from the river than the later town with its masonry defences. Between the first settlement and the river a castle is depicted, surrounded by an earthwork defence incorporating two bastions. This settlement at Derry with earthwork defences was overrun in 1608 by Sir Cahir O'Doherty; it was rebuilt to a new layout with masonry ramparts and bastions after 1614.

Upstream from Derry on the opposite bank of the Foyle a garrison was established at Dunalong, a five-sided enclosure with four bastions and a small rectangular work instead of a bastion at the salient angle at the river side. A ruined castle surrounded by a square entrenchment built by Turlough Luineach O'Neill in 1568 and a settlement with a market-place, are depicted in the contemporary plan, while two of the bastions are provided with an artillery piece on a field carriage (Fig.25).

The plan of Lifford shows a triangular enclosure, the river bank forming one side; at the

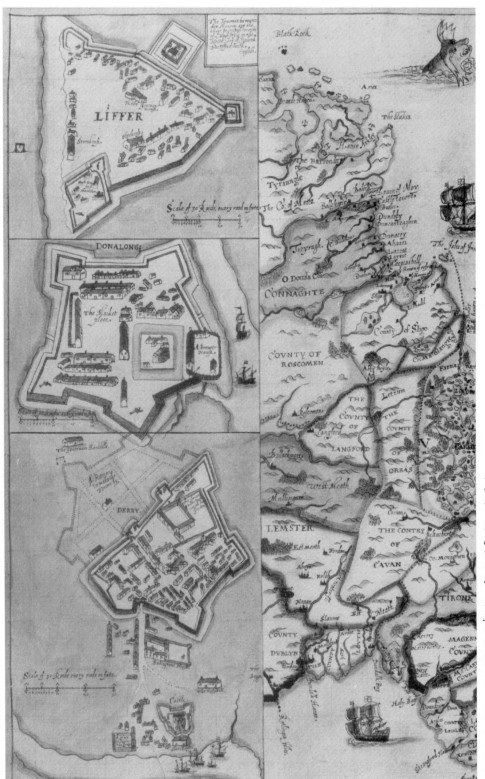

Fig. 25. Lifford, Dunalong and Derry c.1601-02. TCD Ms 1209 (14)

Lifford is depicted as a triangular enclosure, with a fort with two bastions, and two rectangular works which are probably earlier Irish forts.

Dunalong defences include four angle-bastions; the ruined O'Neill castle is surrounded by a square entrenchment constructed by Turlough Luineach O'Neill in 1568.

Derry is depicted surrounded by earthwork defences, with a proposal to enlarge the settlement; these defences were replaced by the more extensive permanent fortifications of 1614-18.

landward salient is a rectangular work in place of a bastion, part of the Irish defences of Lifford before the place was taken by the O'Donnells acting with Docwra. At the other corners of the enclosure by the river are an angle-bastion with a rounded salient, and a fort with two bastions at diagonally opposite corners. Immediately outside the settlement is a building surrounded by a wall or rampart forming a square enclosure with an external ditch, again part of the Irish settlement here before it became an English garrison (Fig.25).

The three settlements, judging by the evidence of these contemporary plans, appear to have been approximately the same size at this time (1600-03), but with a greater concentration of buildings in Derry.[42] Included in *Ulster and other Irish Maps c. 1600*, by G. A. Hayes-McCoy is a map of the Foyle from Culmore to Lifford, which depicts Culmore, Derry, Dunalong and Lifford in pictorial form as they were in December 1600. This book also includes reproductions of a series of contemporary pictorial plans of Ulster forts drawn by Richard Bartlett, a cartographer with Mountjoy: these are Mount Norris, the third Blackwater Fort, Charlemont Fort, Inisloughan Fort, Mountjoy Fort, Monaghan and Augher. Mount Norris was established by Mountjoy in November 1600; it is depicted after it was extended in the following year. An existing Irish ringfort, somewhat modified, formed the original defence work. Two gun platforms, each equipped with a small field-piece, are shown at opposite sides of the rampart, which also has five small houses spaced at intervals around it. A gate and counterbalanced drawbridge lead into an angular outwork, which evidently formed the second stage of the fortification. The third stage is shown as a much larger irregular enclosure with four bastions, to one side of the ring-fort and outwork.

The third Blackwater Fort was constructed by Mountjoy in July 1601, on the north or Tyrone

bank of the river, a triangular fort with three bastions. The first fort on the Blackwater, sited a short distance downstream on the Armagh side of the river, had been constructed by Essex in 1575; it was a large rectangular earthwork enclosure close to a wooden bridge over the river. The fort and bridge were captured and destroyed by O'Neill's forces early in 1595; he then built an earthwork on the opposite bank to guard a ford. This work was attacked and captured by Burgh in 1597, who built a second Blackwater Fort on or near O'Neill's work. Burgh's fort surrendered to the Irish in 1598 after their victory at the Battle of the Yellow Ford close by: this fort was a square earthwork with the four salient angles somewhat extended, and each side slightly convex in plan.

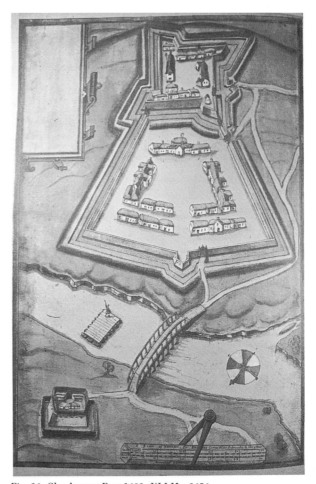

Fig. 26. Charlemont Fort 1602, NLI Ms. 2656.

Charlemont Fort on the Armagh bank of the Blackwater, dating from June 1602, is depicted as a square fort with demi-bastions at the corners and with what appears to be a second stage of construction in the form of an outwork. The outwork is larger in area than the fort, reaching almost to the river bank. A wooden bridge spans the river here; close to the end of the bridge on the Tyrone side is a small square fort or redoubt, an earthwork with a timber palisade forming the parapet. From the scale on the plan it is possible to determine some dimensions: the square demi-bastioned fort is 120 feet across, the outwork 300 feet long by over 400 feet at the widest point. The fort and outwork are surrounded by a ditch, counterscarp, covered way, and short embankment or glacis (Fig.26). The covered way around the fort only is protected by a timber palisade. By 1624 the earthwork fort and outwork had been replaced with a different layout.

Some idea of the size and scale of this demi-bastioned fort may be gained by a comparison with the inner masonry work built a few years later at Castle Park, Kinsale, which still survives in good condition. This structure is a demi-bastioned work, almost square in plan, of similar dimensions to that depicted on Bartlett's plan of Charlemont.

Bartlett's plan of Inisloughan Fort is of particular interest, as it is the only detailed evidence we have of an Irish fortification of this time, apart from the drawing of the attack on O'Neill's earthwork at the Blackwater in 1597, and various illustrations of crannógs, including some by Bartlett. Two lines of palisades and two wet ditches surround a rampart of earthwork and timber, with rounded flankers at two diagonally opposite corners. In one flanker is a tall timber tower; at another corner, where there is no projecting flanker, is a wooden rectangular tower with timber framework visible at the top. The scale on the plan provides information on the size of the fort: the inner work with the rounded

flankers is about 180 feet square, the flankers are 50 feet in diameter and the wet ditches some 25 feet broad (Fig.27). Other Irish forts constructed by O'Neill at this time are shown on maps, perhaps conventionally, as square or rectangular works with angle-bastions at the corners, depicted in much the same way as the English forts. However, there is no reason to suppose that Inisloughan was unusual in layout or construction.

Presumably forts such as Bunvalle, near the mouth of the Bann where it enters Lough Neagh ('Banbrasill' on Bartlett's map of Lough Neagh), Fort Bundorlin, near the mouth of the Blackwater, Toome Fort and other Irish works were similar to Inisloughan.

The Irish built field fortifications to cover the

Fig. 27. Inisloughan Fort 1602, NLI Ms. 2656.

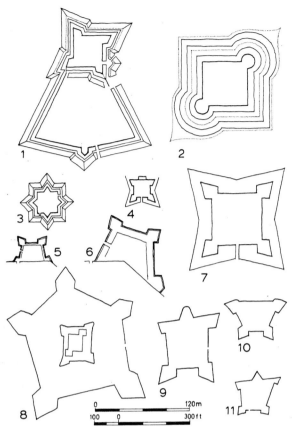

Fig. 28. Comparative outline plans of forts c.1600-1625.

1 Charlemont; 2 Inisloughan; 3 Monaghan; 4 Haulbowline, Cork Harbour; 5 Waterford Citadel proposed by Bodley; 6 Waterford citadel as built; 7 Galway; 8 Castle Park or James Fort, Kinsale; 9 Elizabeth Fort, Cork; 10 fort proposed for the north side of Cork by Bodley; 11 Lifford.

fords of the Blackwater, indicated on a map of the area by Bartlett as trenches on the Tyrone bank of the river. The Moyry Pass, the route between Dundalk and Newry, was fortified by O'Neill in 1600; he constructed trenches and earthwork parapets with barricades across the roadway, and 'plashed' the undergrowth and trees at each side with a barrier of wattles and intertwined branches. Mountjoy failed in his attempt to force his way through these defences in October 1600. The following year Mountjoy built Moyry Castle to protect the route through the pass; this still stands, a small square tower shown on one of Bartlett's maps, with an earthwork bawn similar in shape to the outworks at

Mount Norris and Charlemont, except for two rounded flankers. This earthwork was soon replaced with a rectangular bawn enclosed by a stone wall.

Mountjoy Fort was erected on the western or Tyrone shore of Lough Neagh in 1602, on or near the site of O'Neill's fortification of Clonoe. On the lakeside promontory a triangular work with a redan on its landward front is depicted on Bartlett's plan; inland from this is a symmetrical work with three bastions, each of which mounts a field gun. To the north are two irregular outworks. The scale on the plan provides some dimensions for these defences: the triangular work on the promontory is 240 feet wide; the larger landward enclosure is slightly wider, extending to some 400 feet wide farther inland, the central landward bastion being about 400 feet from the salient of the redan of the triangular work. By 1605 a masonry fort of brick and stone had been built nearby, a small central building with four flankers provided with musket-loops, surrounded by an earthwork rampart, with a ditch and flanking 'bulwarks' or bastions. This work presumably superseded the work depicted by Bartlett described above, although perhaps the houses in the earlier work remained as the nucleus of a settlement here.

Bartlett's plan of Monaghan dates from after May 1602; it depicts the ruined abbey, which had been a garrison in the time of Lord Deputy Fitzwilliam in 1589, as it was again in 1593 and 1595. The soldiers had entrenched the buildings to some extent. However, in 1602 Monaghan was retaken by the English, and the fort drawn by Bartlett was evidently constructed in July of that year; like the other Ulster forts it was an earthwork, soon to be replaced with a fortified settlement and castle. The fort, almost square in plan, approximately 90 feet across, has a triangular projection or redan on each side, and is surrounded by a ditch, a covered way on the counterscarp, and an outer embankment or crude glacis (Fig.28). A short distance from one side of the fort is a square earthwork with rounded corners, provided with embrasures for firearms through the earthen bank or wall; possibly this small work was constructed by the English garrison before construction started on the larger fort.

Augher Castle, Co. Tyrone, was the stronghold of Tyrone's brother Cormac O'Neill, taken by the English in September 1602. The castle was situated on an island in a small lake; on the lakeside nearby the English garrison constructed an outwork or enclosure commanded by the castle. This diamond-shaped work with a bastion at the landward salient was approximately 220 feet wide by 240 feet long from the lake shore to the salient of the bastion. It appears that part of the island was artificial, as it is partly enclosed by a curtain wall of masonry extending from the castle and partly by a palisade of posts and wattle in the manner of a crannóg.

Other forts and castles in Ulster were constructed or occupied as English garrisons in the closing stages of the war: Massarene was built by Chichester in April 1601 on or near the site of the later town of Antrim; a fortified post was established by him at the castle at Toome a year later; and O'Neill's fort, constructed the year before on the opposite bank of the Bann, was taken at about the same time. In Co. Tyrone a garrison was established at Arboe on the western shore of Lough Neagh, possibly at Arboe Point, where traces of a small-scale bastioned front survive at the landward side of the ruined church. The garrison was possibly accommodated in the church. The site is a good position for defence, being somewhat higher than the surrounding countryside. At Dungannon, Chichester built a new fort to replace the O'Neill castle, while at Newtown Stewart and Omagh, English garrisons were established in 1602. At Castlederg a garrison was also set up in the same year; the castle was built some years later by Sir John Davies.

In Co. Donegal, English garrisons were placed at Ballyshannon, Bundoran and Donegal town. Burt Castle was taken by Docwra in 1601 and occupied by an English garrison for some years; a contemporary drawing shows unusual flankers, possibly in the form of casemates to the bawn.[43]

After the battle of Kinsale and the surrender of the Spanish garrison in the town, work began on the construction of Castle Park Fort on the high promontory overlooking the harbour. Construction started in February 1602 on a large pentagonal bastioned fort, which was completed in October 1604 (Fig.28). The engineer was Paul Ive; built as an earthwork, the bastions have straight flanks, the two landward bastions being somewhat larger than the other three. The length of the curtain or rampart between the bastions varies from less than 200 feet to about 230 feet between the larger landward bastions. The dimension from the re-entrant angle of one bastion— where the bastion flank joins the curtain—to the salient angle of the adjacent bastion varies from somewhat under 300 feet to about 350 feet, well within the recommended maximum distance of 200 yards, the effective range of the musket. A plan by Ive depicts the outline of the fort essentially as it is today; the central complex of buildings enclosed by a demi-bastioned work was built later, between 1608 and 1611 (see Fig.32).[44] The size of this central work, almost identical to the demi-bastioned fort at Charlemont, demonstrates how much larger Castle Park Fort is when compared with the Ulster forts built by Mountjoy (Fig.29).

Another fort designed by Paul Ive was that on Haulbowline Island in Cork Harbour, a rectangular bastioned work under construction at the same time as Castle Park (Fig.28). A drawing by Ive of Haulbowline includes a caponnière, noted as a secret casemate in the ditch, but this vaulted structure from the rampart to the counterscarp in the ditch was not constructed.[45]

South of Cork, immediately outside the walls,

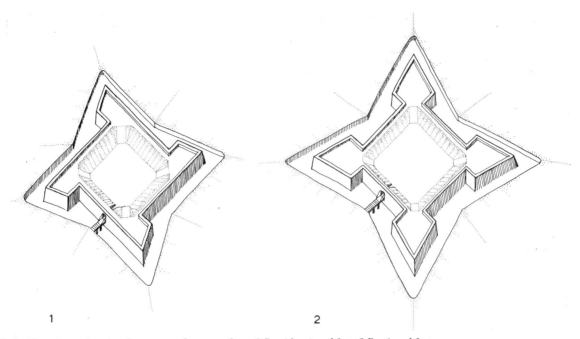

Fig. 29. Typical late sixteenth and early seventeenth century forts: 1 Demi-bastioned fort; 2 Bastioned fort.

Carew constructed a temporary fortification which by August 1602 he had reinforced with a strong rampart. Work had started in 1601 with 200 labourers provided by the city and an equal number paid for by the county, but on the accession of King James I in 1603 the citizens demolished the fort and removed the guns. A plan of Cork of about 1601 shows this irregular work at the south end of the city.[46] Mountjoy regained control of Cork and the fort was rebuilt, but this structure was partly rebuilt by Pynnar between 1624 and 1626. The present fort on the site is essentially the same in outline as this reconstruction by Pynnar (Fig.28).

After his arrival in Ireland in 1600 as lord deputy, Mountjoy put Galway into a state of defence, and a fort was started on the advantageous position of St Augustine's monastery, which commanded the city and harbour. By August 1602 the fort was almost finished. Four demi-cannon and four culverins were to be mounted; in November Mountjoy gave directions for completing the work, and in May 1603 Sir Thomas Rotheram became governor. Several pictorial plans of the fort depict it as a rectangular fort with four bastions.[47] As at Castle Park, Haulbowline Fort and Duncannon, works were carried out at Galway by Sir Josias Bodley between 1608 and 1611, when an outer retaining wall was built onto the fort. Contemporary plans show the fort to have been about 220 feet square, approached by a drawbridge over a ditch; the acute-angled bastions had flanks about 36 feet long and faces approximately 75 feet long (Fig.28). This plan of a rectangular or square fort with bastions at the corners was to be repeated on numerous occasions during the seventeenth century (Fig.29).

Chapter 3
Cannon and Musket: 1603-1691

1
Plantation, new towns, forts, and fortified houses, 1603-1641

WITH THE END OF the war in 1603, many castles continued in use as English garrisons, including Dublin, Leighlinbridge, Wexford, Dungarvan, Castlemaine, Limerick, Athlone, Carrickfergus and Enniskillen. In the north the new forts predominate in contemporary garrison lists, many soon to form the nucleus of plantation settlements. At Boyle the abbey continued as a garrison, an outpost of the Elizabethan settlement in Roscommon in the previous century. A limited amount of artillery was distributed among the garrisons, which included the midlands forts of Philipstown and Maryborough; gunners are listed at some castles and forts. The numbers at most garrisons were reduced at the end of the war, while it is clear that the fortifications were often neglected. Some of the Ulster forts were later rebuilt in masonry; others, such as Dunalong near Derry, do not appear to have been occupied for more than a few years.

Fears of Spanish invasion were again revived with the 'Flight of the Earls' in September 1607, the sudden departure of O'Neill and O'Donnell and their followers. Their departure left the way open for the plantation of large areas of Ulster by English and Scottish settlers, while other plantations followed in the midlands and the south-east of the country (Map 4).

Sir Josias Bodley had been active as a soldier in Ulster and at Kinsale, and was governor of Duncannon Fort from 1604 to 1606. In 1607 he was put in charge of fortifications in Ireland and was to superintend works at Cork, Limerick, Waterford and Kinsale; in 1608 he made a tour of fortifications in Ulster and reported on their condition.[1] By 1611 he was reporting on work he had carried out at Duncannon; Haulbowline Island Fort; St Augustine's Fort, Galway; Castle Park, Kinsale and Limerick Castle.[2] He also prepared plans for a citadel at Waterford, for a fort at Cork and for the layout of the earthwork ramparts and bastions of the new plantation settlement of Coleraine after 1610.

His recommendations on the Ulster fortifications in 1608 included strengthening Moyry Castle with a bawn. He visited Mount Norris and suggested that the ditch around the castle or fort at Mountjoy—a brick and masonry structure—be made wider and deeper, the earthwork parapet increased in thickness and the castle protected with a ditch and drawbridge. The fort at Omagh was little more than half finished and at 'Newtowne' (Newtown Stewart) the place was 'much ruined' and not necessary to hold if the garrisons at Omagh and Lifford were increased; it might be made defensible by repairing the castle.

At Lifford he noted that there was a *sconce* (a detached earthwork fort) 'well ditched and watered' and that the fort of stone beside the river required the expenditure of at least £500 or £600 to be made strong. A plan of this fort, which must have been built between 1603 and 1608—it is not on the earlier plans of Lifford— shows it to have been a bastioned work similar to the fort at Cork and the fort on Haulbowline Island (Fig.28).[3] At Dunalong the 'great entrenchment' was not worth repairing; at Derry he noted the

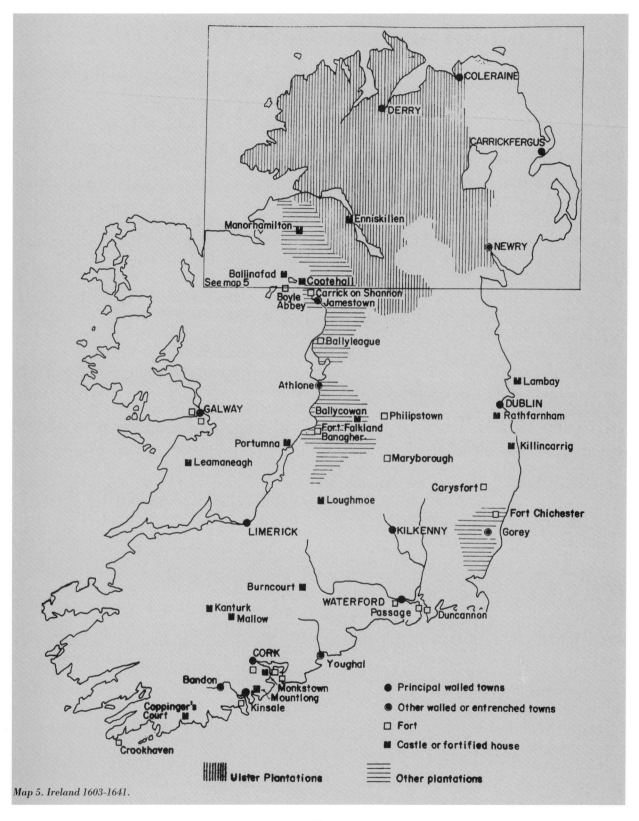

COLERAINE

DERRY

CARRICKFERGUS

Manorhamilton
Enniskillen

NEWRY

Ballinafad
See map 5
Cootehall
Carrick on Shannon
Boyle
Abbey
Jamestown

Ballyleague

Lambay

Athlone
DUBLIN
Rathfarnham

GALWAY
Ballycowan
Philipstown
Fort Falkland
Banagher
Portumna
Killincarrig

Leamaneagh
Maryborough

Carysfort

Loughmoe
Fort Chichester

LIMERICK
KILKENNY
Gorey

Burncourt

Kanturk
WATERFORD
Passage
Duncannon
Mallow

CORK
Youghal

Bandon
Monkstown
Mountlong
Kinsale

Coppinger's
Court

Crookhaven

● Principal walled towns

◉ Other walled or entrenched towns

□ Fort

■ Castle or fortified house

|||| Ulster Plantations   ≡ Other plantations

Map 5. Ireland 1603-1641.

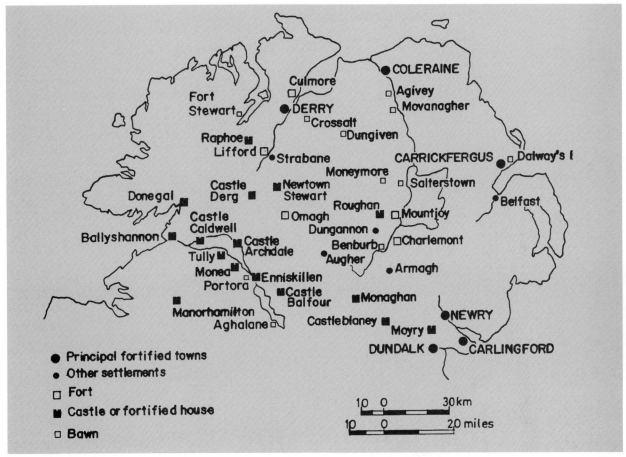

Map 5. Ulster 1603-1641.

'rampier and bulwarkes' (rampart and bastions) as much ruined. This was the settlement surrounded by earthwork defences overrun by Sir Cahir O'Doherty in April 1608; Bodley's report is dated from September of that year. Culmore Fort, also taken by O'Doherty in April, was noted as an earthwork 'much decayed'; Bodley recommended that it should be rebuilt in stone, which, with repairs to the bastions and internal buildings, including apparently the castle in the centre of the fort, would cost some £600 to £700.

At Donegal the old castle and bawn of the O'Donnells was a better place for the garrison than the abbey, which would cost a considerable amount to be fortified; the castle could be strengthened 'with careful contriving' by the expenditure of £300 to £400. At Ballyshannon the bawn and the bulwarks of the bawn on one side should be raised three or four feet higher and a tower or platform was required on the side next to the water. Enniskillen he describes as 'the broken castle of Enniskillen'; he suggested that it be enlarged, at a cost of £500 to £600, to contain larger numbers and yet be defended by a small garrison. He suggests that small sconces be erected at Belleek and Belturbet for the safety of the boats on the Erne waterway. At Killybegs in Co. Donegal there was a good position for a fort to command the road (anchorage?), town and inlet, which would cost £1,200.

In 1611 Bodley reported on works he had carried out at Duncannon, various fortifications in Munster, and at Galway. At Duncannon Fort he increased the thickness and raised the height of

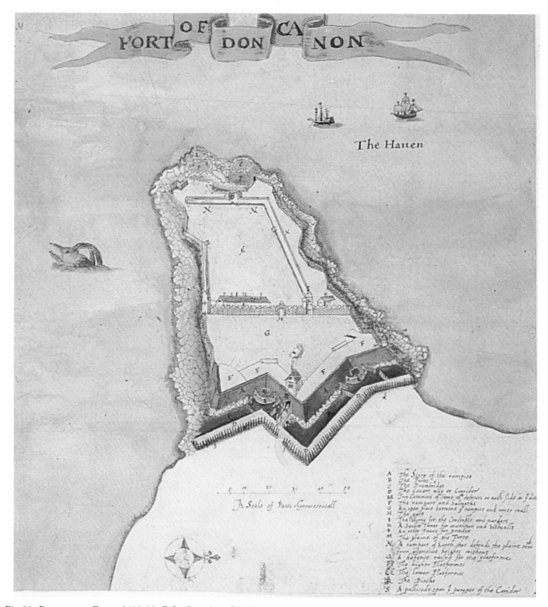

Fig.30. Duncannon Fort c.1608-11, B.L..Cott.Aug. I ii 31.

the landward rampart, in an attempt to improve the strength of the fort here where it was over-looked by high ground. He enlarged the ditch, made a new drawbridge, gate and gatehouse, and placed a palisade on the counterscarp. For the better protection of the garrison Bodley sur-rounded the fort with a stone wall backed by an earth rampart, and on the front overlooking the estuary he raised an earthwork with a mount for defence of the gun platforms. The gun platforms

were enlarged and lodgings for the garrison were repaired (Fig.30).

The Fort on Haulbowline Island in Cork Harbour Bodley found in a ruined condition. He repaired the bastions, ramparts and parapets, completed the gateway with the construction of a gatehouse, and built lodgings for the officers and soldiers and a gun platform for guns to command the shipping. He also constructed a square tower or castle in the centre of the fort, which com-

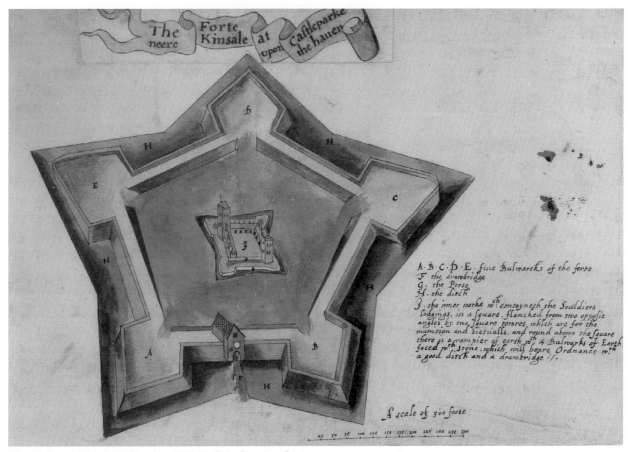

Fig. 31. Castle Park Fort, Kinsale c. 1608-11, B.L..Cott.Aug. I ii 35.

manded the ramparts.

Bodley remarked that the fort at Castle Park, Kinsale was so large that five hundred men or more would be required as an adequate garrison. To reduce the size of the fort would have resulted in a weak, irregular work, so he constructed an inner citadel (Fig.31). This was in the form of a square fort with a demi-bastion at each corner, surrounded by a dry ditch. Bodley noted the perimeter stone wall as being fifteen or sixteen feet high, backed with earth on the inside, the demi-bastions filled with earth to provide gun platforms. Inside this defence work, approached by a drawbridge over the ditch, were two square towers at diagonally opposite corners, which held supplies and munitions. Linking these towers were lodgings for the garrison, built around three sides of an internal court. Bodley also repaired the bastions and ramparts of the main fort and completed the gatehouse and drawbridge (Fig.32). He noted the absence of a lower gun platform to command the harbour fully, an indication that the water-level blockhouse at the north-east end of the promontory was not then in existence. Most of the inner complex of Castle Park survives today; the demi-bastioned work is almost complete, and the two towers and the lodgings around the small central court for the garrison are laid out as described by Bodley.[4]

At Limerick Castle he repaired the foundations of the towers, which had been undermined by the action of the river. The two half-round towers of the gatehouse were repaired, and a bastion was constructed at the south-east corner of the castle capable, according to Bodley, of mounting five or six pieces of ordnance to com-

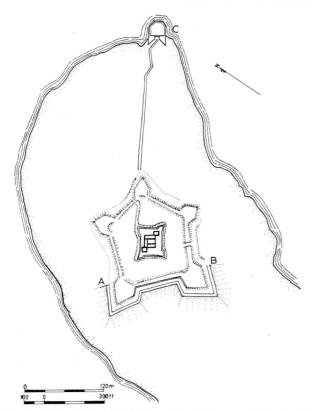

Fig. 32. Plan of Castle Park Fort, Kinsale. Pentagonal bastioned fort 1602-04, with inner demi-bastioned work c.1608-11. A-B - extent of ditch, covered way and glacis on plan by Paul Ive. C Blockhouse.

mand the town. He made or enlarged a ditch around the castle, constructed a new drawbridge at the gatehouse, and laid new planks on the towers and bastion as gun platforms (Fig.33).[5]

The fort at Galway, referred to as 'St Augustine's Fort' by Bodley, was built at first largely as an earthwork: an outer retaining wall built some time earlier some ten to twelve feet high had not solved the problem of the earth tending to slide. Bodley constructed another stone wall, leaving a passageway some four or five feet wide between the walls, the outer wall topped with a five foot parapet of masonry, the inner wall with a new earthwork parapet. This work resulted in a form of *chemin des rondes* or continuous low-level pathway around the fort on the face of the ramparts and bastions. Vaulted passages or tunnels through the inner rampart gave access to this lower outer defence. Bodley

also erected a house for the commander and officers and lodgings for the soldiers, and partitioned the earlier church building to accommodate supplies and munitions (Fig.34).[6] He remarked that the fort had little command over the harbour and suggested the construction of a small blockhouse on an island 'between the mouth of the haven and the fort', at an expense of £200 or £300. This was Mutton Island, where a fort had been proposed some years earlier.

Bodley prepared drawings of a fort or citadel at Waterford, and a plan for a fort for the north side of Cork, probably intended to be sited on the high ground outside the city walls in the vicinity of Shandon Castle (Fig.28). The Waterford proposal is depicted in a drawing dating from 1605 or 1613, a symmetrical, four-sided work with two bastions and two demi-bastions attached to the outside of the city wall, which constituted the fourth side of the citadel.[7] The wall is shown increased in width to form a gun

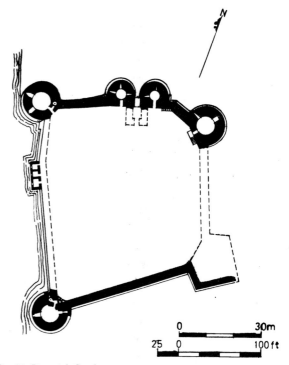

Fig. 33. Limerick Castle.
Angle-bastion constructed c.1608-11; conjectural outline of north flank and east face of bastion shown in broken line.

platform, with four gun-embrasures overlooking the city and four more on the side next to the fort. The title of the drawing is 'The Fort as it is to be made at Waterford', but the gun platform is noted as being in existence: it appears that work did not start on the fort until 1624-26. The dimensions of the fort on Bodley's plan were enlarged on the later drawings of 1624-26 and a demi-bastion omitted at the junction with the city wall at St Patrick's Gate. In the design by Bodley the town gate gives access to the fort; on later plans and in the layout of the fort as it was constructed, the gate remained as a town gate with entry to the city from the country, and the half-bastion here was omitted, with the fort wall linking to the town wall just north of the gateway.

The plan of the fort proposed by Bodley for the north side of Cork depicts a fort of a similar size and shape to that at Waterford but in this instance a detached work, not linked to the city wall.[8] A four-sided work with two bastions and two demi-bastions with a gun platform between them, presumably to command the city below, it was no doubt intended to be sited a short distance north of the town walls. It would have overlooked the city in much the same way as did Elizabeth Fort—the work that replaced Carew's fort in 1603—on the south; it would also have acted as an outwork to the city defences. This northern fort was not constructed (Fig. 29).

By 1611 Bodley had expended some £5,000 on Duncannon, Haulbowline, Castle Park, Galway, the Castle of Limerick and other, smaller works that he had been directed to carry out in 1608. Work on these forts was not yet completed, and for this and for other fortifications, of which Philipstown and Maryborough forts were the most important, a further £2,000 was requested.

A list of ordnance in Ireland of 1611 from the Carew Manuscripts provides information on the distribution of artillery at the more important forts and larger towns. The heavier guns of brass

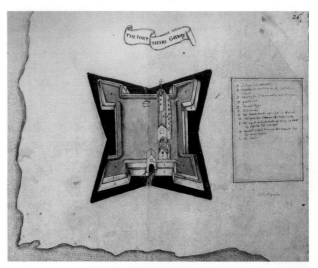

Fig.34. The Fort at Galway, TCD MS 1209 (71)

(bronze) and iron are for the most part at the principal seaports and coastal forts: cannon and demi-cannon of brass are noted at Dublin, Duncannon, Cork, Galway, Limerick, Ballyshannon and Derry; culverins of brass or iron are listed at these forts and towns and at Castle Park and Haulbowline. Smaller guns, such as demi-culverins, sakers, minions, falcons and falconets of brass or iron, are also listed at these places and, inland at Athlone, the midland forts of Philipstown and Maryborough, and the new Ulster forts and settlements.

At Castle Park, Kinsale, the brass ordnance consisted of one culverin, and the iron ordnance of one saker, one falcon and one minion. At Duncannon Fort there were a brass cannon, culverin, demi-culverin, saker and fowler, and iron guns included one demi-culverin and a murdering-piece. The midland forts had only small armaments: a minion at Philipstown, and one falcon and two robinets at Maryborough. In Ulster, forts such as Charlemont, Mountjoy, Mount Norris and Culmore had one or two brass falcons or robinets, or iron sakers or falcons; Dunalong is listed as having one iron saker.

The coastal forts were poorly armed: Duncannon, Castle Park and Haulbowline are listed with one brass culverin each and a few

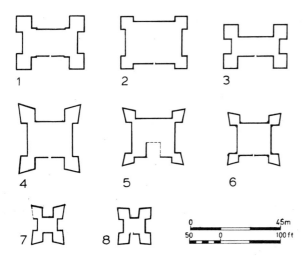

Fig. 35. Comparative outline plans of fortified houses:
1 Kanturk; 2 Portumna; 3 Burncourt; 4 Rathfarnham;
5 Manorhamilton; 6 Raphoe; 7 Lambay; 8 Mountjoy Fort.

smaller pieces. Later in the seventeenth century, batteries of from four to eight 24-pounders or culverins (18-pounders) protected harbours or anchorages, often reinforced by forts mounting far more guns of these sizes. The inland forts, in many instances with one or two small field-pieces as armament, were evidently considered to be strong enough to resist local attack.

Lists of garrisons of early seventeenth-century Ireland, during the period of the plantation of Ulster, give surprisingly small numbers of 'warders' at the various forts and castles. A constable and from ten to thirty men, with in some cases a gunner or boatmen in addition, was a typical garrison. In 1610 the 'ward' of Duncannon consisted of a constable, lieutenant, gunner and thirty warders; at Castle Park, Kinsale, there was a constable, lieutenant, gunner and twenty warders; and there was the same number at Haulbowline Island. At Athlone Castle the ward was a constable and twenty men, while most of the smaller castles and forts had from ten to fifteen warders. In addition to these small regular garrisons there were companies of foot or smaller detachments, or troops of horse, attached to particular castles or forts from time to time.

In certain places small castles had been constructed to provide accommodation for garrisons in the closing stages of the 1595-1603 war, and in the early years of the seventeenth century. Moyry Castle, built by Mountjoy in 1601, is a simple square tower enclosed later by a bawn with a stone wall. Mountjoy Castle or fort, built of brickwork on a stone base, was completed by 1605 and was surrounded by earthwork rampart and bastions, replacing the earlier fort near the lake-shore. The structure consists of a central block somewhat less than forty by thirty feet externally, with flankers about twenty feet square at each corner. Although liberally provided with musket-loops at ground level, the slightly angular corner towers are not adequately flanked by each other; for this they would require their faces to be enlarged and the flanks reduced to about half their length, resulting in a true bastion-shaped plan with salient angles of about 45 degrees (Fig.35).

At the 'Castle of the Curlews' at Ballinafad, Co. Sligo, there is a central block with flankers of a different form; here the main block, some 37 by 24 feet externally, has a cylindrical tower 19 feet in diameter at each corner. One tower contained the staircase, the entrance to the castle being flanked by musket-loops in this tower. The structure was four storeys in height, with timber floors. Descriptions of this castle do not refer to a bawn, but it seems probable that there was some outer line of defence here originally. A reference in 1590 to a new fort in the Curlews may possibly apply to this building: certainly by 1610 the place is listed with other garrisons, having a guard of a constable and ten men. It is perhaps more likely that the date of construction was in the final stages of the war up to 1603, or between that year and 1610. It is remarkably similar in plan to Roughan Castle in Co. Tyrone, a plantation castle of 1618, where the central block is about twenty-three feet square externally, with the corner towers sixteen feet in diameter.[9] Here the entrance is in the staircase tower; the castle was of three storeys and had timber floors.

The period from about 1600 to 1660 marks the transition from the tower-house castle to the undefended country house; after that date only high outer walls enclosing outbuildings and courtyards formed a limited degree of defence for the larger houses. The intermediate stage in this development was the fortified house or 'strong house of stone' and smaller semi-fortified structures of various plan forms. The plantation house of Ulster and other areas such as the mid-lands often formed one side of a bawn or court-yard, which had circular towers or 'flankers' shaped like angle-bastions at the corners. Scots settlers in Ulster brought with them the tradition of castle building, and their tower-houses or for-tified houses often have Scottish characteristics and details.

One type of fortified house of which there are several surviving examples consisted of a rectan-gular or square central block with square or angle-bastion shaped towers at the corners (Fig.35). Musket and pistol-loops provide for defence and are found in the flankers or corner towers and at doors and windows. Bawn or courtyard walls, with flankers and gatehouses, formed an outer line of defence, again provided with loops for firearms, as can be seen at Portumna. At Rathfarnham Castle in south Dublin we have an early example of this plan form (Fig.35). In this fortified house the corner turrets are based on the angle-bastion shape in plan, although it is apparent that here and else-where the builder did not have a clear under-standing of the principle of defence by flanking fire: the faces of the turrets are not at an appro-priate angle and are not covered by fire from the flanks of the adjacent turrets. Rathfarnham, built by Archbishop Loftus, dates from about 1583-1585: a similar but much smaller fortified house from perhaps about the same date, on Lambay Island off the Co. Dublin coast, was altered early this century by Sir Edwin Lutyens (Fig.35). The owners of Lambay Castle were related by marriage to Loftus, which suggests a link in the similarity of the design to Rathfarnham.

Other fortified houses of this general layout are Kanturk, Co. Cork, from before 1609; Portumna, Co. Galway, constructed by 1618; and Burncourt, Co. Tipperary, from 1641—all with square corner towers. At Raphoe, Co. Donegal (1636) and Manorhamilton, Co. Leitrim (1634-38), the central blocks are almost square in plan, while at Manhorhamilton there is a large recess in one side—with corner flankers at both castles of the angle-bastion form in plan at ground level. However, these flankers, like those at Rathfarnham, rendered the buildings some-what inadequate for defence because of their shape (Fig.35). Aghadown House in west Cork, some five miles north of Baltimore, has angle-bastion-shaped flankers, more carefully set out for defence. Two flankers survive of what was probably a rectangular house with a flanker at each corner.

The basic plan of a central block with corner towers is repeated in Monkstown Castle (1636) and Mountlong (1631), both in Co. Cork; but in these instances the corner towers flank a much smaller central block, resulting in a building of taller proportions, with a vertical emphasis, in place of the horizontal emphasis of such build-ings as Kanturk and Burncourt. A variety of early seventeenth-century houses survive, some of U- or L-plan. Others have a staircase housed in a square projection at the centre of the rear wall, with the entrance located in a similar struc-ture on the front facade. These houses are pro-vided with musket and pistol-loops, particularly at the doorways and in the projecting bays, for flank fire along the face of the adjacent walls. Most of the fortified houses have some provision for defence at higher level, in the form of battle-ments or roof parapets, and most have machico-

Fig. 36. *Early classical doorway, Kanturk Castle, Co. Cork.*

lations at this level at corners and over the entrance doorway.

At Mallow Castle, Co. Cork (c. 1600), a rectangular block has two polygonal towers at the corners and one at the centre of the front facade,

while at the back is a bastion-shaped projection housing the staircase.[10] Coppinger's Court in west Cork, built before 1641, is U-shaped in plan with the projecting wings slightly offset, while the rear of the house has a projecting bay for the staircase.[11] These fortified houses share many features and architectural details with the later tower-houses, but generally have larger mullioned windows, particularly on the upper floors, and have a characteristic silhouette of a series of steep gables and tall chimney-stacks (Fig.37). Classical columns and pilasters appear at principal doorways and gateways, as at Kanturk and Portumna (Fig.36).

Another development of the early seventeenth century, part of the transition from tower-house to mansion, was the construction of a multi-storey house at one side of an earlier tower-house. Leamaneagh in Co. Clare is a well-known example, dating from perhaps 1643, the date on the gateway to the bawn, now removed to Dromoland Castle. This three-storey house with attics, L-shaped in plan, is almost as tall as the narrow rectangular tower-house to which it is attached: at one corner, at second-floor level, is a bartizan, providing for a degree of defence by

Fig. 37. *Early Gable, Portumna Castle, Co. Galway.*

firearms of the entrance facade and the end wall of the house. Large mullioned windows contrast with the narrow loops in the tower. Another house constructed as an extension to an earlier tower-house is Loughmoe, Co. Tipperary. On a much larger scale than Leamaneagh, this was of four storeys, with a projecting wing at the end of the entrance front to balance the tower at the other end, an attempt to arrive at a symmetrical arrangement of the facade. These buildings are perhaps a development of the earlier tradition of a single-storey hall structure adjoining the tower-house, in which much of the daily life of the castle went on; many tower-houses show evidence of a hall of this type having been built against them.

Examples of smaller houses are Ballycowan, Co. Offaly, built in 1626, a rectangular block entered by a square staircase tower (Figs. 38, 39); and Killincarrig House, Delgany, Co. Wicklow, from perhaps about the same date or earlier, L-shaped in plan, with the addition of a square staircase turret at the rear.[12] The only

Fig. 38. Ballycowan Castle, Co. Offaly.

defensive features now at Killincarrig are loops for firearms in the stair turret; but as the place was garrisoned in the Confederate and Cromwellian wars, it is likely that there was orig-

Fig. 39. Ballycowan Castle, east face of entrance bay.

Fig. 40. Derryhivenny Castle, Co. Galway.

inally an outer line of defence in the form of a bawn with flankers. The majority of these fortified houses must have had a bawn or courtyard; at Portumna two impressive axially-planned courtyards survive, with gatehouses and circular flanking towers provided with musket-loops. These early seventeenth-century houses reflect a search for more comfort and a move away from the more inconvenient living quarters of the tower-house, a move made possible by the more settled conditions of the time.

Tower-houses continued to be built during the early decades of the seventeenth century, and perhaps one of the latest examples that can be dated is at Derryhivenny, not far from Portumna, Co. Galway (Fig.40). This four-storey tower with two corner machicolations at parapet level has a small bawn with two circular flankers at diagonally opposite corners, and carries a date-stone of 1643. Much larger bawns than this

small enclosure at Derryhivenny were quite a common feature of late sixteenth and early seventeenth-century towerhouses. Several examples of these are in Co. Tipperary: Knockelly; Ballynakill, near Roscrea, perhaps one of the largest bawns in the country (the mid-sixteenth-century fort at Maryborough was of about this size); and the more average-sized rectangular bawn at Moorstown Castle, not far from Cahir, which encloses a circular tower-house (Fig.9). Another more well-known circular tower-house in Tipperary is that at Ballynahow, a five-storeyed structure. At Ballyragget in Co. Kilkenny is another large bawn with circular flankers enclosing a tall rectangular tower-house; this was the castle taken by Essex on his march to Cahir in 1599. The bawn walls, circular flankers and gateways of these tower-houses are provided with a variety of loops for firearms, small circular or rectangular openings with internal splays. No comprehensive study has been published on Irish tower-houses: *The Architecture of Ireland from the Earliest Times to 1880* by Maurice Craig (1982) is the most recent account, which also gives a detailed survey, with plans, of the early seventeenth-century fortified houses.

Following the flight of the northern earls in 1607, plans were made between 1608 and 1610 for the planting of a colony in the six confiscated Ulster counties of Armagh, Cavan, Donegal, Fermanagh, Londonderry and Tyrone. Plantations also continued in Monaghan and were to be established in other areas, such as Leitrim, Longford, Offaly, and in parts of Wexford and Wicklow. In Ulster there were to be three categories of settler: English or Lowland Scots 'undertakers'; 'servitors'—military officers or civilian officials – and Irish 'grantees'. The estates were in three sizes: 1,000, 1,500 and 2,000 acres. The conditions stated that each undertaker should construct a stronghold on his estate and bring in settlers proportionate to the size of his holding. It was intended to be a settlement of villages, each protected by a castle, fortified house, or bawn. Servitors and Irish freeholders had similar obligations but, unlike the undertakers, were not obliged to bring in English or Scottish tenants. Derry and Coleraine were to become the largest towns: by 1630 Derry had the largest population, followed by Coleraine and Strabane; most of the other new settlements were villages rather than towns, or even smaller clusters of houses outside the strong-houses or bawns of the undertakers (see Map 5, p.59).[13]

A survey of each county was carried out in the summer of 1608, under Lord Deputy Chichester, the officials involved including Sir Josias Bodley. Articles of the plantation included a provision that the colonists were to live in settlements each defended by the undertaker's strong-house or bawn. In *A Direction for the Plantation in Ulster,* published in that year, Thomas Blenerhasset, who had received land in Fermanagh, criticised the building of fortified houses and bawns on each estate, as he was convinced that these would be inadequate to protect the colony. He advocated instead a series of larger settlements or corporate towns.

In the Ulster plantation those granted the largest estates were to erect a castle and bawn; those of the middle size a stone or brick house and bawn; while those with smaller estates were to construct a bawn only. In Monaghan after 1618 new English landowners were each to build a strong-house of stone or brick; the Longford plantation in the same year included the condition that those granted a thousand acres or more were to build a castle 30 by 20 feet, 25 feet high, and a bawn of 200 feet perimeter. A typical description of an Ulster house and bawn gives the following dimensions: the bawn 120 by 80 feet, the wall 10 feet high, a stone house occupying one side of the bawn, 18 feet wide, circular corner flankers to the bawn 15 feet high, the fourth flanker, which formed part of the house, being 22 feet high and 14 feet diameter. In the house were

stored arms for about a hundred men, including fifty-two pikes, twelve muskets, ten calivers, pistols, six bows, targets (circular shields), swords, a drum and colours (flags).

The first official survey of the Ulster plantation was carried out in 1611 by Carew and there were to be three further surveys by 1622. A report on the state of the plantation in 1611 gives details of population and building operations at the new settlements. At Dungiven Captain Edward Doddington had been granted £200 by the king towards the cost of his castle and bawn. At Lifford the king had provided £200 towards the cost of the stone fort; at Donegal there was a bawn with flankers and a wall fifteen feet high, and within the bawn was a 'stronghouse of stone' built by Captain Basil Brooke, towards which the king had granted £250. A 'fair and strong wall newly erected of lime and stone', twenty-six feet high, with flankers, parapet and wall walk had been built at Enniskillen Castle by the constable, Captain William Cole, with the help of a grant of £200 from the king.

At Augher a castle was under construction by Sir Thomas Ridgeway. He had ten masons at work on the castle, and the previous year he had brought over twelve carpenters from London and Devonshire. At Omagh materials were being prepared for a stone house or castle; the walls of the castle were 19 by 36 feet, and, at that time, 22 feet high. The Fort of Omagh was noted as a good one, within which 'is built a fair house of timber after the English manner'. A contemporary pictorial plan depicts the fort with two bastions and two demi-bastions, with a small settlement nearby.[14] The Castle of Mountjoy, beside the old fort, is described as 'a fair castle of stone and brick' enclosed by a ditch and ramparts and bulwarks of earth. Moyry Castle is noted as having a constable and ward of twelve men. Both Charlemont and Mount Norris were evidently in good condition, with ditches, ramparts and bastions of earth, and palisades.

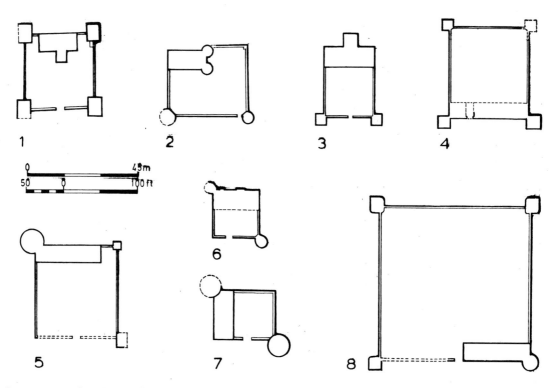

Fig. 41. Comparative outline plans of plantation castles and bawns:
1 Tully; 2 Monea; 3 Castle Archdale; 4 Castlederg; 5 Bellaghy: Vintners' Company; 6 Crossalt, Brackfield: Skinners' Company;
7 Salterstown: Salters' Company; 8 Cootehall.

Plans for the Ulster settlement included the building of twenty-five new towns; these corporate towns or boroughs were to be entitled to send members to the Irish parliament. Those that were incorporated by 1613 included Armagh, Charlemont, Belturbet, Cavan, Ballyshannon, Donegal, Lifford, Enniskillen, Coleraine, Limavady, Derry (re-named Londonderry) and Strabane. Other places, such as Mountnorris, Raphoe, Dungiven, Mountjoy and Omagh were proposed but not incorporated. Other towns that were incorporated but were outside the area of the official plantation were Belfast (1613), Killyleagh, Bangor, Newry, and Newtownards. Carrickfergus had an earlier medieval charter. Most of the settlements remained quite small, only a few places such as Derry and Coleraine developing into urban centres, while reports indicate that many undertakers failed to meet the requirements regarding for-

tified houses and bawns, some of which were abandoned in an unfinished state after a few years.

The houses and bawns at Salterstown and Crossalt (Brackfield), Co. Derry, may be considered as typical, with a house occupying one side of the enclosure. The Salters' Company bawn at Salterstown is a rectangle about 95 by 70 feet, with two circular flankers 30 feet in diameter at diagonally opposite corners. The house occupied one end of the bawn, and the walls and flankers are provided with musket-loops. Much of the structure survives, but the original house has been replaced with a later building. The Skinners' Company bawn at Crossalt has a similar layout, but the bawn and flankers are smaller, the bawn being just over 60 feet square, and the flankers, not quite circular in shape, about 15 feet across (Fig.41).[15]

The largest surviving plantation castle of

Scottish character is at Monea, Co. Fermanagh. It was built by Malcolm Hamilton by 1618, the bawn being under construction in 1622. The castle or tower-house is about 55 feet long by a little less than 30 feet wide, with two circular towers at one end (Fig.41). These change to a square shape at a higher level, supported on corbelling, terminating in crow-step gables; other Scottish features are the small turrets at the other end of the castle (Fig.42). The bawn is approximately 110 by 95 feet, with two circular flankers. Other Scottish-style castles are at Lisnakea and Tully, also in Co. Fermanagh. The bawn at Tully was 100 feet square with four flankers; one of the square flankers remains, as do the walls of the castle, which are somewhat smaller than Monea. The entrance and staircase at Tully are in a square projection, resulting in a T-plan for the house (Fig.41). There is a stair turret above the entrance wing corbelled out at high level, while there was another turret on one corner of the house, which was of two storeys with an attic. At Castle Balfour, Lisnakea, there are corbelled turrets to a tall T-plan building that was under construction in 1618.[16]

The Scottish architectural features of these castles and fortified houses included crow-stepped gables, conical-roofed turrets, often supported on moulded corbel courses, and rounded stair-turrets containing spiral stairs often corbelled out from the face of the building at high level. The western lowlands of Scotland have numerous examples of late sixteenth and early seventeenth-century castles with these characteristic details, and it was from this area that many of the new Scottish settlers came to Ulster.

The watergate at Enniskillen Castle, at one time thought to be part of the original Maguire stronghold, is also of Scottish style, with corbelled conical-roofed turrets. It is now considered to be from the plantation period; it is not on a view of the castle under attack by the English in 1594, and no structure of this type is depicted on a plan of 1611 that shows the Maguire tower-house enclosed by a curtain wall with two angular and two circular flankers.[17] The watergate does not appear to have been a gatehouse, as there is no structural evidence for a gateway.

Another T-plan fortified house in Co. Fermanagh is Castle Archdale, built by an English settler, John Archdale, in 1615 (Fig.41).[18] The house occupied the full width of the bawn at one side and, unlike Tully, the staircase projection, square in plan, is on the exterior wall of the house. Loops for firearms in the stair wing allow for flank fire along the exterior of the house; there were evidently two flankers at the opposite side of the bawn and these provided for defence of the other three walls of the enclosure.

At Castlederg in Co. Tyrone Sir John Davies constructed a house and bawn with four square flankers at the corners.[19] The house occupied one side of the bawn through which, near one end, was the entrance passage. The bawn, about a hundred feet square, extended to the bank of the River Derg, where the two flankers are smaller than those adjoining the house at the opposite side of the enclosure. The house was a gabled structure of two storeys, only fifteen feet wide (Fig.41). Davies also built a more elaborate house at Castle Curlews, of which part survives.

Pictorial plans made by Thomas Raven for Sir Thomas Phillips's survey of 1622 depict a variety of bawns and houses. The 'strong house and bawn' belonging to the London Drapers' Company at Moneymore is shown at the end of a settlement consisting of two streets crossing at right angles, with timber-framed and stone houses. Occupying one side of the bawn is a large three-bay house of three storeys with attic rooms above. A flanker adjoins the house at one end, and at the diagonally opposite corner of the bawn is another flanker of square or angular shape. The gatehouse to the bawn, on the axis of one of the streets of the settlement, is a half-timbered pitched roof building—unsuitable materials for a

Fig. 42. Monea Castle, Co. Fermanagh.

gateway to a defensive enclosure. The house was noted as nearly completed but without floors or partitions, the timber rotting and the walls decaying with the weather, and having been in this condition for six years. In 1619 Sir Thomas Roper had become the tenant, but was an absentee: he reappeared to establish a fort and settlement at Crookhaven on the coast of west Cork some years later.

Other bawns illustrated by Raven were the Mercers' at Movanagher, the Ironmongers' at Agivey, the Goldsmiths' at Clondermot, the Vintners' at Bellaghy, and those of the Salters at Salterstown and the Skinners' Company at Crossalt, described above (Fig.41). These vary in layout and in the position of the house. At Movanagher three round flankers have conical roofs, while similar roofs crown taller round turrets at the corners of the house, one end of which adjoins the centre of one of the walls of the bawn. The bawn at Agivey has one side that appears to be formed of a timber palisade, there are no flankers, and the house, with four corner turrets, is free-standing within the bawn. At Clondermot three round towers serve as flankers to the bawn, one of which has a conical roof; the other corner is occupied by a house of U-shaped plan. The bawn at Bellaghy is depicted as having two circular towers at opposite corners and a

smaller square tower at another corner, while a gabled house adjoins one of the circular towers, occupying most of one side of the enclosure. Surviving structures confirm some of these features of the layout: a bawn of 120 by 110 feet, and the tower adjoining the house 30 feet in diameter.[20]

A gun platform at Bellaghy inside one wall may be a later addition. The bawn is of brick on stone footings; other materials used in the construction of bawns were masonry, earthworks, or timber palisades. Some ring-forts were adapted and settlers' houses built within them: it is recorded that in the Elizabethan settlement of Roscommon a number of Irish forts were modified for occupation in this way.

Dalway's Bawn, at Bellahill, near Carrickfergus, is probably the best-preserved bawn in Ulster. The rectangular enclosure with three round flankers was built about 1609; similar structures were built elsewhere in Ireland. In the midlands, at Tinny Cross near Tullamore, are the remains of a bawn with four circular towers at the corners. The bawn at Cootehall was possibly the residence of Sir Charles Coote when he was building Jamestown, seven miles to the south-east. The enclosure is somewhat less than two hundred feet square. Much of the bawn wall and corner flankers survive: one flanker forms part of the present house, which may incorporate the original structure. One of the largest bawns is that built by Sir Richard Wingfield at Benburb, Co. Tyrone, about 1611, on high ground above the Blackwater on the site of an O'Neill castle.

The principal fortified towns in Ulster in the early decades of the seventeenth century were Carrickfergus, Newry, Derry and Coleraine (Fig.43). The earthwork defences at Carrickfergus were gradually replaced with stone walls and bastions at the end of the Elizabethan period and during the first two decades of the seventeenth century. As early as the 1565-66 scheme for a plantation in Antrim it was proposed that Carrickfergus be walled in stone and the castle repaired; at the same time the friary was garrisoned and entrenched, and in 1568 Sidney was to consider how this entrenching might be achieved. Essex asked for someone skilled in fortification to be sent to Carrickfergus to lay out the defences in 1573.

A plan that may date from shortly afterwards depicts a rampart with two rounded bastions at two corners of the town—an old-fashioned approach at a time when the Italian angle-bastion was well established. The Blackwater Fort also had similar bastions, established by Essex in 1575, while the settlement at Roscommon built by Malby in 1581 had a semicircular and a round corner bastion linked by what must have been earthwork ramparts; Malby had been in Ulster with Essex, and was granted the castle and lands at Roscommon in 1577.

The town defences at Carrickfergus were evidently still largely earthworks in 1596, when a corner flanker—presumably an angle-bastion—was built in stone. By 1610 more permanent works were under construction, and in the following year soldiers were working on the town walls. The defences were still unfinished in 1624. A number of plans survive of Carrickfergus during the Elizabethan period, depicting a variety of defences around the landward side; the later drawings show stone walls and towers on the waterside. One plan shows two angle-bastions on the landward front, and notes the town ditch, town wall and the rampart; this may be an early seventeenth-century copy of a plan by Lythe. It appears that by 1624 the bastions and ramparts around the town, of masonry backed by earth, were largely complete and the most accurate plan that we have of these is that of 1685 by Thomas Phillips.[21] There are three broad obtuse-angled bastions, an angle-bastion at the north corner and demi-bastions where the landward defences join the wall on the waterside. The bastion at the northern corner, extensive lengths of wall, one of

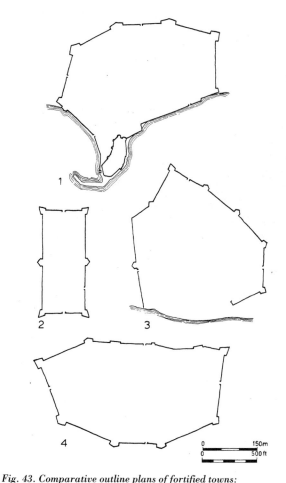

Fig. 43. Comparative outline plans of fortified towns: 1 Carrickfergus; 2 Jamestown; 3 Coleraine; 4 Derry.

the obtuse-angled bastions and parts of the other two survive at Carrickfergus today.

The northern bastion has faces some 80 feet long and flanks of about 25 feet; the dimensions of the flanks of the other surviving bastion are similar, the faces slightly shorter. The length of the curtain between these two bastions, somewhat over 300 feet, was repeated for the lengths of town wall between the three obtuse bastions, providing for an even spacing of the landward defences. When the layout and dimensions are compared with the fortifications of Derry, the bastions of the latter are seen to be more widely spaced, some 350 to 450 feet apart. The acute-angled bastion at the western salient of the city walls is similar in dimensions to the corner bastion at Carrickfergus, while one of the four obtuse-angled bastions—King James's Bulwark—is about the same size as the similar one at Carrickfergus, the other three being slightly smaller in the dimensions of their faces. The walled towns of Carrickfergus and Derry were of approximately the same area, and the similarity of the bastions might suggest that the same designer was responsible for both fortifications.

In May 1600 Sir Henry Docwra arrived at Lough Foyle and landed with over 4,000 men at Culmore, where he entrenched a fort around the old castle. Leaving a garrison of 600 soldiers there, he pushed on to Derry, which was protected on one side by the Foyle, on the other by a bog. Here there were the ruins of an abbey, some other buildings, and a castle near the river. Docwra constructed earthwork defences, the upper or great fort on the hill, and a much smaller work around the castle, with two bastions. The church buildings were converted into barracks for the troops. He held out against the Irish and moved inland, placing garrisons upstream at Dunalong, at Lifford, taken for him by renegade O'Donnells, and at Omagh. O'Cahan deserted O'Neill in 1602, and then served against him on the English side, to be followed by the MacDonnells, thus enabling an English garrison to be established at Coleraine.

The settlement declined at Derry when the war ended in 1603 and the garrison was reduced; however, it was incorporated as a city in 1604. After the place was burnt by Sir Cahir O'Doherty in 1608 the earthwork defences around the settlement and the castle were repaired, although these temporary works had been criticised before 1608 as inadequate. A plan of 1611 shows the layout of the proposed new town, with a grid plan of streets, much larger than the original settlement;[22] there were then over 500 workmen at Derry, and Captain Vaughan and Captain Hart were to advise on the new fortifications. The plan of 1611 is different in some details from later plans, although in general a similar area was enclosed by the fortifications. On this early plan the castle is at one corner of the walls, on later plans it is shown enclosed by the town defences. There are no fortifications on the river frontage, which was later fortified, and the outline of the walls and the number of bastions are not the same as when it was finally constructed.

In 1614 Bodley reported on the progress at Derry: work was proceeding on the walls, stone being prepared and earthworks under construction, but no masonry work started on site. In the following year a planned revolt among the Irish in Ulster revived fears of Spanish invasion. In 1616, when Thomas Raven was in charge of setting out and measuring the fortifications, the wall at Derry was half completed. It was intended to be 16 feet high, but this was considered to be too low; a dry ditch extended from the western salient of the defences at Prince's Bulwark along the south side of the town 30 feet wide and 8 feet deep. There were two drawbridges to be completed here.

Captain Nicholas Pynnar's survey of works in Ulster, from December 1618 to the following March, reported that Derry was now enclosed by a strong wall 24 feet high, 6 feet thick and over 5,000 feet in perimeter. There were nine bastions and four gatehouses—two with portcullis and two with drawbridges at the dry ditch—but there were no gates in position. Inside the wall was an earth rampart 12 feet thick. The fortifications were all well built, but lacked guard-houses and platforms for artillery; the walls had been completed in May 1618. A plan of the town made at the time of Pynnar's survey depicts the settlement completely enclosed, including the river frontage; the old castle is shown at one corner, two main streets crossing at a central square and other streets forming a grid plan similar to the 1611 proposals. There are seven full bastions on

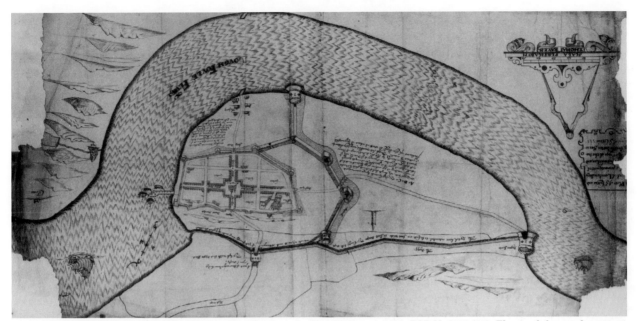

Fig. 44. The River of Lough Foyle with the city of Londonderry by Thomas Raven, 1625, TCD Ms 1209 (22). The city defences of ramparts and bastions are depicted with reasonable accuracy: proposed outer defences are also shown.

the town walls and three other projections or gun platforms on one side, two of which must have been included in Pynnar's nine-bastion total.

Captain Pynnar had arrived in Ireland with Docwra at Lough Foyle in 1600; after some time abroad he was granted a thousand acres in Co. Cavan and, on the death of Sir Josias Bodley, he and Sir Thomas Rotheram became 'directors general and overseers of the fortifications and buildings' early in 1618.

With regard to the progress of the Ulster Plantation in general, Pynnar concluded that some 107 castles with bawns (fortified houses would be included here), 19 castles without bawns, 43 bawns and nearly 2,000 houses had been constructed. Both Derry and Coleraine needed more inhabitants and houses.

A new survey from August to October 1622 was carried out by Sir Thomas Phillips, covering the areas of Co. Donegal and Co. Londonderry (formerly the county of Coleraine). Maps and pictorial plans by Thomas Raven include Derry, Culmore and Coleraine, and form part of the Phillips report. The description of Derry by Phillips is similar to Pynnar's report, but by now

the gates were in position, the number of bastions was noted as eight, and the town hall was under construction. In the central square a proposed fortified structure is shown on Raven's plan. The old castle, which had been in the centre of Docwra's small riverside fort, is shown as a store—noted as a magazine in the report. The principal streets are named, as are the bastions: King James's Bulwark, Prince Charles's, the Lord Deputy's, London Bulwark, Lord Docwra's, Lord Chichester's, the Governor of the Plantations' Bulwark, and the Mayor of Londonderry's Bulwark. In the central square or market-place the proposed 'citadel' or fortified town hall is depicted as a classical structure with guns emerging from embrasures at low level, the upper level supported on an arcade of columns and more artillery on the flat roof. Rising up through this upper level from the raised ground floor is a square battlemented structure. This strange fortified market-house—of very doubtful value as a fortification—was not constructed: a later plan of Derry by Raven depicts a more conventional market-house in the central open space (Fig.44). In 1622 Derry was garrisoned by a company of foot under the command of Captain John Vaughan, and what was evidently an additional 110 well-armed men were available from among the townspeople. Proposals by King James I to the city of London in 1609 concerning plantations involved the area later known as Co. Londonderry, including Derry and Coleraine. In 1613 both towns were incorporated by charter, Derry became the city of Londonderry, and the London companies became responsible for the plantation settlements in the county. There was again fear of a Spanish invasion after October 1623, with the possible consequence of those Irish in Spanish service returning to Ulster; and in 1624 further improvements were ordered in the defences at Derry. Oak platforms for the artillery and sentry boxes were to be made, and twenty pieces of ordnance were to be provided. War broke out with Spain late in 1625 and lasted for five years; and from 1627 to 1629 England was also at war with France, leading to concern about the state of the fortifications in Ireland. Forts were rebuilt and some new works constructed.

Pynnar's survey of 1618-19 had noted the fort at Culmore, downstream from Derry, as in good condition; the 1622 survey by Phillips describes the triangular fort, giving dimensions, the landward side being over 100 feet in length, the other sides somewhat shorter. The three bastions (the two flanking the land front each composed of what might be termed two demi-bastions, the salient at the waterfront ending in a semicircular projection) were each capable of mounting four pieces of artillery. The wall was 14 feet high and 4 feet thick, and the two waterside walls were provided with gun embrasures. The landward wall had a gate, gatehouse and drawbridge. The old castle was 21 feet square, to which was attached a stone house of two storeys for the commander of the fort and his family.

While work was under way at Derry in the early years of the century, a town was developing at Coleraine under Sir Thomas Phillips, which was defended with temporary fortifications. Under articles of agreement of 1610, which stipulated that 200 houses were to be built at Derry with room for more, Coleraine was to have 100 houses with room for a further 200. Coleraine is depicted on a map of 1611 as an irregular hexagon, the River Bann forming the western side, the other five sides being earthen ramparts with an external ditch, having seven bastions, and gates at two locations. A grid plan of streets with a central square or market-place is similar to that proposed for Derry at this time. The rampart, 12 to 14 feet thick, was only about half the intended height of 12 feet. The ditch was from 36 to 40 feet wide, and 3 feet deep. One bastion had been completed, another was almost finished and the rest were under construction. By November 1612 most of the works at Coleraine were completed, apart from the gates and drawbridges. Bodley's report of 1614 noted the completion of the walls; he had evidently approved the original plan, but it is not clear to what extent he was the designer. The original scheme had not been followed, and the ramparts were too small, the ditch needed to be made deeper, and the gatehouses should have been of stone, not of half-timbered construction. By 1616 it was reported that the fortifications at Coleraine were too extensive and too costly; the earthwork ramparts gradually decayed, and two drawbridges had been built.

The survey by Pynnar of 1618-19 noted the decaying earthworks, the ramparts too narrow and the bastions too small for artillery. The gatehouses were still of half-timbered construction. The town was too thinly populated, with not enough men to defend one-sixth of the wall. Phillips's survey of 1622 notes the circuit of the defences as something over 2,000 feet, less than half the perimeter of Derry. The rampart was 12 feet high and 10 feet thick—certainly very narrow for an earthwork structure. Six small bastions and two half-bastions, a ditch full of water

CANNON AND MUSKET: 1603 – 1691

Fig. 45. Aerial view of Derry (Cambridge University Collection of Air Photographs APE 82). Since this photograph was taken the terrace houses close to the outside of the city walls in the foreground have been demolished.

and two small gates with drawbridges completed the defences. Again the walls were reported as decaying and the timber-frame gatehouses were inadequate. It was recommended that stone gatehouses be built and the riverside boundary of the town fortified. A facing of mortared stonework was required for the wall, in the market-place a fortified building should be constructed as a citadel and town hall, while a bridge should be built across the river. In 1624 it was again proposed that the earthwork defences at Coleraine be faced with stone, the town provided with sufficient artillery and munitions, and the riverside enclosed by a stone wall. In reply it was stated that Coleraine had been built under the direction of Bodley (it is not clear if this was so) and that the place was adequately defended by the wet ditch. In the following year the town was again to have stone gatehouses, and a keep or citadel was required.[23]

The outstanding new fortification in Ulster was Derry. The ramparts and bastions survive, with some later alterations: by far the most impressive seventeenth-century town defences in Ireland (Fig.45).[24] At Newry, early Elizabethan earthwork defences do not appear to have been replaced with stone walls. Elsewhere in Ireland other new settlements were under construction in the first decades of the seventeenth century, including the fortified towns of Bandon, Co. Cork, and Jamestown, Co. Leitrim.

A settlement had been founded as part of the Munster plantation at Bandon in 1588, evidently surviving the warfare of the last years of Elizabeth; by 1608 houses were being built on the north side of the river and a bridge was erected. In 1613 Richard Boyle, First Earl of Cork, acquired an interest in part of the town; in 1619 he obtained more of the property and by 1625 owned the town on both sides of the river Bandon. In 1613 the place became the borough of Bandon Bridge. The construction of the town walls by Boyle began in 1620, although there is a reference to town walls in 1616; they were completed about 1625. Several plans of Bandon show proposals for the layout of the town and walls, and one depicts the scheme by Christopher Jefford of 1613 for the settlement on the north side of the river.[25] This was a grid plan of streets, four gateways, two large angular bastions at the northern corners, and a smaller bastion on the eastern wall. Of particular interest are two forts, one evidently in existence when this proposal was drawn up, noted as 'Carew's Old Fort'. Depicted as square in plan with two bastions at the corners of the west wall, the rear wall is formed by the east wall of the proposed defences, the fort being situated inside the town. Carew's fort presumably dated from the end of the Elizabethan wars;

it is shown as about 150 feet square. The smaller fort outside the walls for the 'Lord President of Munster' appears to have been a proposal; sited a short distance outside the walls to the west, it is shown as 90 feet square with two bastions at diagonally opposite corners. The circuit of the town walls in this proposal for Bandon is only slightly shorter than that of Derry, and just over twice that of Coleraine.

The other two plans of Bandon show the town before it was finished—as drawn up for Carew—and 'as it is now built'.[26] The plans vary in the details of the defences and street layout; in the later plan the round or semicircular towers (it is possible that these were solid bastions or gun platforms rather than towers) are almost twice the diameter compared with those on the plan for Carew. The circuit of the walls is shown as almost a mile in length. Boyle boasted that the walls of Bandon were stronger, thicker and higher than those of Derry: they are said to have been nine feet thick and from thirty to fifty feet in height, and about a mile in length. North of the river, a street that runs diagonally from the end of the bridge is North Main Street; this is also on Jefford's plan, suggesting that it was part of the early settlement, as was South Main Street, before the grid plan of streets was set out on these proposals. South of the river another enclosed area is depicted on these plans, with round towers or flankers at the corners and tall gatehouses at the east and west like those of the northern town. An interesting detail of the plan of Bandon 'as built' is that the walls between each tower or gatehouse are angled forward in plan into a slight obtuse salient, each part of the wall parallel to the line of flanking fire from one tower to the front of the next. It seems unlikely that this unusual refinement in the layout was constructed. Plans of the Bandon gatehouses show a twin-towered arrangement, two half-round towers flanking a gateway similar to those of Norman castles such as Limerick. While

Boyle's claims for Bandon in relation to Derry might be partly true, the arrangement of curtain walls, towers and gatehouses would not have resisted an attack by artillery, and lacked the broad earth rampart inside the wall at Derry. The position of the walls as known by tradition in the late nineteenth century, and as depicted on the Ordnance Survey for certain parts of the perimeter, do not follow the rectangular layout on the plan of Bandon 'as built'. The line of the walls south of the river approximate to the layout on the plan, but the walls to the north of the river were more irregular. Just north of Christ Church, built in 1610, they ran from east to west for about 150 yards, then northwards 100 yards to the north-east corner of the town.

In October 1621 Sir Charles Coote agreed to build a walled corporate town in Co. Leitrim, beside the Shannon. There were to be two gates and a watergate, the walls 14 feet high and 6 feet thick, with a parapet or battlement of 6 feet, the wall to be 'compassed on the outside 160 perches, 18 feet to the perch', a length of 2,800 feet. The dimensions of Jamestown from the first edition of the Ordnance Survey indicate the area enclosed by the walls as a rectangle approximately 900 by 380 feet, while according to Coote's agreement the circuit of the walls was comparable to that of Coleraine (see Fig.43).

The work was under way in 1622, and it was also intended to build another settlement on the opposite bank of the river. From eighteenth-century maps the layout may be seen to have been a long rectangular enclosure, a central main street on the long axis with a gate at each end and another street crossing at right angles leading to a gate in the wall near the riverside.[27] There was an angle-bastion at each corner, and one at the centre of each of the long sides. The bastions were most probably solid, to act as gun plat-forms, but it is possible that they were open structures loopholed at ground level for firearms, as were many of the flankers of the Ulster plantation bawns. It seems unlikely that the town walls were backed by an earth rampart, as it would have considerably reduced the space inside the walls; no rampart is indicated on the eighteenth-century maps. In 1973 the arch of the surviving gate at Jamestown was removed, to facilitate road traffic.

Another settlement that was to grow into a larger town than Jamestown was Monaghan. By 1611 the earlier earthwork fort of 1602 had been replaced with a fortified house constructed by Sir Edward Blayney surrounded by a large bawn and a fortified town, depicted on a contemporary plan.[28] The new castle or house and the town for-tifications were noted in 1614; the castle was at the centre of the town, surrounded by a square bawn with angled flankers at diagonally opposite corners. A large formal garden with fishponds extended from the bawn to the town wall, some-what larger in area than the bawn. The town was enclosed by a wall with three angled corner bas-tions, two angle-bastions at mid-point on two of the walls, and four gateways. Situated between two lakes, the town defences were surrounded by a wet ditch. The castle consisted of a small cen-tral block with four square towers, similar in plan to such castles as Monkstown and Mountlong in Co. Cork. The bawn and the town are some 200 feet square and 700 feet square, respectively.

Sir Edward Blayney was also involved in building a house and bawn at 'Baile Loergan', the Castleblaney of today. A plan of this (with the plan of Monaghan) depicts a bawn just over two hundred feet square, with two circular and two angular flankers at diagonally opposite corners. The house is shown as of H-plan, with short pro-jecting wings, situated near one side of the bawn; a report of 1611 notes this bawn with a stone wall eighteen feet high, a gatehouse and the house under construction (Fig.46).

In west Cork Sir Thomas Roper, involved in the Ulster plantation at Moneymore in 1619, had

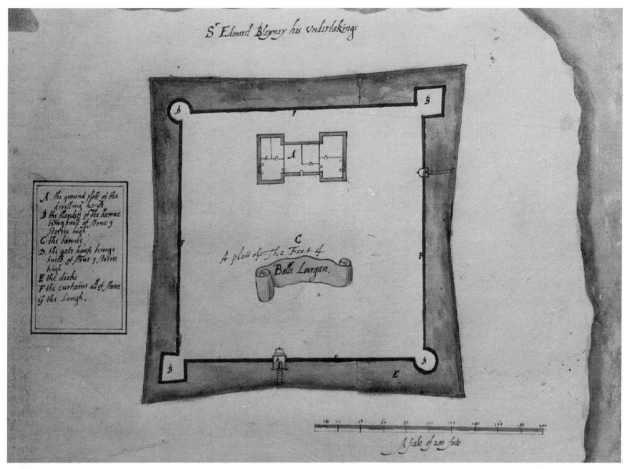

Fig. 46. Sir Edward Blayney's house and bawn at Castleblaney, TCD Ms 1209 (32).

established a fort and settlement at Crookhaven by 1622; the fort is listed with other coastal forts later in the seventeenth century. Roper is noted as constable of Castlemaine in 1610, one of the five wards in Munster in that year (the others being Dungarvan Castle, Limerick Castle, Castle Park and Haulbowline). Coastal defence was brought into prominence with the outbreak of war with Spain in 1625 and with France in 1627, but piracy was a constant problem, and it was remarked that the forts of Castle Park and Haulbowline were so badly maintained and garrisoned that they could easily be taken by pirates. In 1631 Baltimore was raided by Algerians, who carried off some two hundred of the inhabitants. The English navy of the time of James I and the early years of Charles I was

neglected compared with the days of Elizabeth, but it was realised that the ships were essential to protect the coast: five years after the Baltimore raid there were plans to establish an admiralty in Ireland at Kinsale, to use the place as a winter harbour for warships and to construct a dock, wharf and warehouses.[29]

Captain Nicholas Pynnar reported on the state of the forts in Ireland in 1624, with maps of Waterford Harbour, Cork Harbour, and Carlingford Lough.[30] The map of Waterford Harbour depicts Duncannon, Passage and Waterford, with the battery at Reginald's Tower. The plan of Duncannon Fort is similar to that by Bodley, which shows works carried out by him between 1608 and 1611; Pynnar noted Duncannon as 'much out of repair', the platforms rotten and the ordnance lying on the ground. A drawing of the fort at Waterford, the citadel by St Patrick's Gate proposed by Bodley some years earlier, is included, with the remarks that it was unfinished and that within the fort was a timber-framed house a hundred feet long to accommodate a hundred men, but not roofed and in a poor condition.[31] The fort on Haulbowline Island in Cork Harbour was also noted as in poor condition and is depicted with the central tower or castle built by Bodley. Pynnar notes the fort at Cork as 'of lime and stone' but not finished or defensible. Kinsale Fort or Castle Park was decayed, with ordnance on the ground; the pictorial plan shows the inner works completed by Bodley in 1611 surrounded by the 1602-04 pentagonal work by Paul Ive.

Pynnar noted the castle of Limerick as in a reasonable state and having three good pieces of brass ordnance mounted. The forts at Culmore and Galway are described; the fort of Galway is similar in Pynnar's pictorial plan to the drawing by Bodley of 1611, but it was in a poor condition in 1624, 'much decayed' and with no parapet and no lodgings for the soldiers but with a house for the captain and officers. The recently completed fort at Banagher or Fort Falkland was 'built of lime and stone' and in good repair. Charlemont Fort is depicted as a regular rectangular bastioned fort with a 'strong-house or castle within' noted as 'lately built', which had replaced the campaign fort of 1602.

Pynnar's map of Lough Neagh, evidently largely copied from earlier maps, shows the Mountjoy Fort built by 1605, enclosed by a rectangular bastioned work, with the earlier campaign fort of 1602 indicated nearby on the lakeside. The map of Carlingford Lough depicts Narrow Water Castle and the town of Newry, with no defences indicated; the walled town of Carlingford is shown, but nothing is in evidence on the two islands at the entrance to the lough, which again raises the question of the island

blockhouse here. The blockhouse is listed as a Cromwellian garrison; the character of the structure is sixteenth-century. Pynnar in 1624 and Bartlett in 1602-03 in his map that included Carlingford Lough do not show this coastal fortification.

The fort at Banagher included in Pynnar's report was proposed in 1621, the land being taken from Sir John McCoughlan, the local chieftain. By October 1624 the fort was completed, but two years later Sir Arthur Blundell was still to be paid for the construction. The pictorial plan of the fort shows a rectangular masonry enclosure with a twin-towered gatehouse similar to those at Bandon. At one corner near the Shannon is a circular tower, while at the diagonally opposite corner close to the gatehouse is a small turret or bartizan. A long narrow building in the fort is most probably a barrack for the garrison. Fort Falkland, as the Banagher fort was named, is also shown on a map of Banagher of 1629, at the end of the small settlement; it is depicted as a rectangular shape with a round flanker at each corner and a gatehouse centrally placed in one wall on the axis of the street of the town.[32]

Both Haulbowline and Cork forts are shown by Pynnar as square forts with two bastions, two demi-bastions and a projecting gun platform on one side; at Haulbowline the platform is rectangular, at Cork it is in the form of a redan or triangular work with a rounded salient (Fig.47). The Cork fort remains largely intact today; the line of the bastions and ramparts is complete except on the east and south sides, where later structures and alterations have obscured the line of the curtain. The fort is an irregular quadrilateral with demi-bastions at the northern corners and the redan in the centre of the north side, overlooking the city below. At the corners at the south side of the fort are the two bastions. It was intended that the guns on the two demi-bastions and the redan should command the city, and the

Fig. 47. The New Fort at Cork erected by Nicholas Pynnar 1626, TCD Ms 1209 (50).

drawing of December 1626 by Pynnar depicts five pieces of artillery here, one on each demi-bastion and three on the redan.[33] The fort at Lifford attributed to Sir Richard Hansard is remarkably similar in plan to the fort at Cork, but somewhat smaller.

Captain Pynnar's plan of the fort at Waterford of December 1626 notes the gatehouse completed, the stone walls of the fort six feet thick backed by earth ramparts twenty-five broad, the house to lodge 120 men, and the gatehouse of St Patrick's Gate and two wall towers of the town forming part of the fort.[34] The fort is larger in scale than that proposed by Bodley some years earlier, enclosing a greater area extending farther north from St Patrick's Gate; the length of the curtains between the bastion flanks is depicted as from 120 to 130 feet, compared with a distance of 50 feet on the plan by Bodley. The bastions are also

correspondingly larger on Pynnar's plan.

Fear of a Spanish landing at Galway brought about the construction of a new fort there in 1625; situated at the west end of the bridge over the Corrib to protect the city from attack from the west, it is shown on a contemporary plan of Galway as a rectangular bastioned fort.[35]

At Youghal in 1627 there was a proposal by an Ensign Steward for a new battery at the old blockhouse, the circular tower on the quay. The mayor of Youghal stated that the town was prepared to construct and maintain the new work; it was agreed that for the protection of the harbour the most convenient place was at the old block-house. A battery fifty feet square, a parapet six feet thick and a curtain wall of the same thick-ness at the quay wall were proposed. Six pieces of artillery were requested for the new battery in addition to the two brass guns already at the blockhouse. In the following year St Leger, lord president of Munster, and the Earl of Cork were considering the plan for the new fortification, but it appears that nothing was undertaken, as these proposals were referred to in 1643, when it was remarked that there was no place to mount ordnance to defend the harbour. In 1616 the blockhouse at Youghal had been leased as a storehouse, and the ordnance was useless for want of carriages and munitions and the absence of an officer in charge. The corporation of Youghal was to resume control of the blockhouse and equip the ordnance with carriages and munitions, and an officer was to be appointed. In 1622 it was stressed that the blockhouse was to be in the charge of the mayor of Youghal, and powder and at least a hundred shot were to be available for the ordnance. Four years later it was ordered that Balthazar Porthingall was to have the keeping of the key tower or blockhouse and the charge of the two pieces of ordnance there.[36]

It is clear from numerous references and reports that the coastal forts were neglected and the artillery in a poor condition during the early decades of the seventeenth century. From time to time attempts were made to remedy these defects when there was fear of invasion, as there was after the flight of the northern earls in 1607, and at the outbreak of war with Spain late in 1625. In November 1625 it was reported that the harbour and fort at Kinsale were without defence: there were only six dismounted cannon in the fort where there should have been twenty guns. Sir Thomas Button, governor of the fort, had carried out repairs and paid the garrison at his own expense; it was remarked that the central works at Castle Park would resist the Irish, but not a foreign enemy.

Lord Deputy Falkland was requesting means to proceed with works at Castle Park and with 'King John's Fort'—the fort of Corkbeg at the entrance to Cork Harbour—in January 1626. A plan of Castle Park indicates a proposed blockhouse at the north-east end of the promontory, where one was later built; the first suggestion for this appears to have been in 1621, when it was noted that a blockhouse was required closer to the channel. The plan of January 1626 and the particulars given in the state papers that describe it include an enclosure on the east side of the promontory below the fort, another proposed blockhouse: this, with the blockhouse to the north, might be built with platforms for the ordnance and a house for the guard and gunners for £300. It was also proposed that the narrow neck of land to the south of the fort be entrenched to prevent the approach of an enemy from that direction; a dry ditch and earth rampart with a half-bulwark and a drawbridge, might be constructed here for £200.[37]

It seems most likely that the blockhouse at water level at the end of the promontory below the fort was built as a result of these proposals in 1626. The blockhouse is a semi-octagonal fronted battery with double-splayed embrasures for seven guns, approximately seventy feet in length and width; the three short walls forming the seaward end of the structure each have one gun-embrasure, the two side walls each two embrasures. The wall is about six feet thick and stands today six to seven feet in height above the level of the embrasure cills; the guns here commanded the estuary to the south and the channel some 400 yards wide to the north-east. The artillery at the embrasures in the north and north-west walls of the blockhouse had a field of fire northwards and towards the small settlement at Scilly outside the town of Kinsale, some 700 yards to the north-west. The landward front of the structure is defended by two demi-bastions, with the entrance to the blockhouse placed centrally between them; a small square room in each demi-bastion flanks the entrance passage. The blockhouse was vulnerable to attack from the landward side, being overlooked by high ground and out of sight from the fort just over 200 yards away because of the intervening hill.

By 1632 it was realised by those in authority that ships were essential to protect the Irish coast. In 1634 it was suggested that naval vessels should winter in Kinsale under the guns of the fort, as it was the best harbour. In July 1636 King Charles I ordered that his ships on the Irish coast should be stationed at Kinsale, as it was the best anchorage, and stores and equipment were to be provided. Captain Pynnar reported on the condition of the fort and the expense of repairing it, and it was proposed to construct a storehouse, a wharf, a crane and officers' quarters. The fort was noted as being 'in ruins'. The following year Captain Thomas Kettleby was visiting Kinsale to advise on building a dock and storehouses;[38] the dock was subsequently constructed to the southwest of the fort. Kinsale was to be an important port during the warfare of the next decade and the wars of the second half of the century, an importance reflected in the construction of additional artillery fortifications by Prince Rupert and by Lord Orrery.

Inland, the line of the Shannon with the fortified towns of Jamestown and Athlone and Fort Falkland at Banagher also had defended crossing-points at Ballyleague (Lanesborough) and Carrick Drumrusk (Carrick-on-Shannon), where there was a fort and wooden bridge by 1623. These places were to be important strategic posts in the warfare after 1641. In the south-east, Fort Chichester in Wexford had been built by 1610; in Wicklow the 'Fort of Cariesfort' (Carysfort) was under construction in 1628. Sir Henry Cary, Viscount Falkland, lord deputy of Ireland between 1622 and 1629, planned to set up a plantation on the lands of the O'Byrnes in south Wicklow; the establishment of Carysfort as a new corporate town was part of this scheme. Both Fort Chichester and Carysfort were taken by the Irish in 1641. Lord Deputy Wentworth obtained permission to construct a rectangular fort at Cosha, Co. Wicklow, in 1638; this was to have corner bastions, a hornwork and a ravelin.[39] Two years earlier it appears that construction had started on Wentworth's large mansion at Jigginstown, near Naas, the largest unfortified house of the time; the brick-vaulted basement and part of the upper level survive today. It was only partly completed when Wentworth, by this time Earl of Strafford, was called to London in 1640; his trial and his execution in May 1641 were followed by the outbreak of rebellion in Ireland in October. Less than a year later, civil war broke out in England between the forces of Charles I and the parliament in August 1642 and for the next ten years Ireland was to become a battlefield for various factions fighting for control of the country. In this warfare the defence of the fortified towns, forts and castles was to play a prominent part.

2

The Confederate wars and Cromwellian conquest, 1641-1660

The rising in Ulster broke out in October 1641. A plan to seize Dublin Castle failed, but in the following month Drogheda was under siege by the insurgent forces. By the end of the year an alliance had been formed between the Gaelic Irish and the Old English, and by June 1642 the Confederate Catholics were established with the city of Kilkenny as their headquarters.

In July, Owen Roe O'Neill, nephew of Hugh O'Neill, Earl of Tyrone, landed at Doe Castle, Co. Donegal, bringing with him Irish officers from the Spanish forces in Flanders. From June to August 1640 with Ulster troops of the Spanish army he had defended the town of Arras against the French. O'Neill was to take charge of the Ulster forces and create the most effective army of the Confederacy. In August 1642 the Civil War started in England when King Charles I raised his standard at Nottingham. In the following month Colonel Thomas Preston landed at Wexford; another Irish soldier in the service of Spain, he was to become the principle rival to O'Neill among the generals of the Confederacy. By the end of the year the General Assembly of the Confederates was meeting at Kilkenny, controlling most of Ireland other than parts of Ulster, areas around Dublin and Cork, and some isolated garrisons (Map 6). The following year they had negotiated a truce with the royalist James Butler, Earl of Ormond, soon to be appointed lord lieutenant of Ireland by Charles I.

The English forces in Ireland were divided between king and parliament; in Ulster the Scottish settlers sided at first with the parliament, reinforced by a Scottish army under Robert Munro, who, like O'Neill and Preston,

was a veteran of the Thirty Years' War. These soldiers brought with them from Europe the current ideas on artillery fortification and siegecraft, but in Ireland the resources were generally lacking for constructing the permanent, large-scale fortifications and outworks of the Continent, and the equally elaborate and costly siegeworks. Medieval town walls and castles were strengthened with earthworks, and fieldworks were constructed at strategic river-crossings and at 'passes' through hills, bog or forest. Contemporary accounts indicate that the numerous garrisons in castles and fortified houses added to their defences with outlying earthworks. The shortage of heavy artillery in Ireland, and the difficulties of transporting the available artillery in a countryside with few adequate roads, gave isolated garrisons in castles a considerable importance on frontier territory under dispute between the various sides in the confused warfare between 1641 and 1652. The several armies of the Confederacy and the English and Scottish forces fought a series of limited campaigns based on fortified towns and castles as depots for their supplies and munitions. Rivers such as the Barrow were used to transport artillery and gunpowder to garrisons and to provide an easier means of transporting guns and equipment of the field forces.

In Ulster, O'Neill strengthened the rectangular bastioned fort of Charlemont by constructing outworks, and successfully resisted attack from the Scottish army under Alexander Leslie, which had arrived in the spring of 1642. Later that year Leslie returned to Scotland, and the Scottish forces came under the command of Munro. Also in 1642 Belfast was enclosed by a rampart, presumably the rampart and bastions depicted on Phillips' plan of 1685. The town walls of Kilkenny are said to have been strengthened by Dutch engineers in the same year. At Dublin Castle, master gunner Thomas Stutevile was paid £100 for the making of outworks there in

Map 6. Ireland 1641 – 1660.

December 1641.[1] St Augustine's Fort at Galway, held by an English garrison that eventually sided with the parliamentary forces, was strengthened with outworks in 1642; in the following year Roger Boyle—one of the sons of the Earl of Cork—was involved in constructing entrenchments around the town of Tallow, and in 1644 he was concerned with the repair of the town walls of Youghal.[2] In 1690 there were remains of earthwork defences near the south gate here, which had been constructed when the town had been besieged by Castlehaven in 1645.

Nicholas Lalloe, a French military engineer, was based at Kilkenny as 'engineer-general' to the Confederates; in 1645 he supervised the siege operations when Duncannon Fort was attacked by Preston. Artillery was placed in position—both cannon and mortars—and a zigzag approach of trenches excavated by the besieging force. Batteries were constructed to drive off English ships anchored off the fort. A contemporary plan depicts the fort with the trenches and batteries of the Irish forces protected by *gabions*, wickerwork baskets filled with earth.[3] The siege, which had started in January, ended two months later when the garrison surrendered. It was the opinion of Castlehaven that the siege of Duncannon was the only 'regular' siege in Ireland during this decade of warfare: the only place where trenches and batteries were laid out systematically by the attackers. In many instances there were blockades rather than sieges, and Cromwell in his attacks on Drogheda and Wexford stormed those walled towns rather than setting about the slower process of excavating trenches and setting up batteries.

In 1646 another English garrison, at Bunratty Castle on the Shannon estuary, surrendered; the place had been surrounded by earthwork defences, including a fort, which helped the parliamentary forces to prolong the defence.[4] Like Duncannon, Bunratty was of strategic importance, controlling an important estuary; at both places artillery was able to command the navigable channel, and the garrison was supported by warships of the English parliament. Bunratty was the seat of Barnaby O'Brien, Sixth Earl of Thomond, who has been described as being royalist, roundhead and Irish rebel at one and the same time: many of those who survived with their estates at the Restoration in 1660 had the ability to change sides at the appropriate time. Another O'Brien, Lord Inchiquin, changed his allegiance from king to parliament in 1644, and four years later changed back again. Lord Broghill, at first a royalist, assisted Cromwell in his campaign in Ireland and was prominent during the Commonwealth and Protectorate. He helped influence the acceptance of the Restoration of Charles II in Ireland and was rewarded by being created Earl of Orrery.

Contemporary accounts, such as *An Aphorismical Discovery of Treasonable Faction*, note the frequent construction of fieldworks. After Preston suffered a defeat at Clonard it is recorded that he retired to the border of Co. Westmeath, 'where Captain Bernaby Geoghegan kept his post ... and made his half moons and redoubts'—evidently an important position between King's County and Westmeath. Not far away, at the castle of Richard Geoghegan at Laragh, a large triangular outwork was built to the south of the tower-house; it is shown on the first edition of the Ordnance Survey, and the line of the western side may be seen today in a slight change of level in the ground. It seems most probable that this outwork was constructed during the warfare of the 1640s.

A fortified house at Dollardstown, Co. Kildare, is noted in the *Aphorismical Discovery* as defended by sconces (detached earthwork forts) with ditches when it was captured by a Captain Gerald Fitzgerald under Castlehaven in 1643. Some nine miles away to the north the Fitzgerald castle at Ballyshannon was surrounded by more elaborate fortifications.

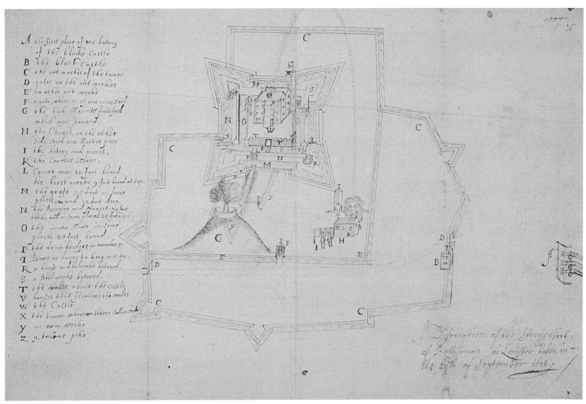

Fig. 48. Ballyshannon, Co. Kildare, 1650. B.L. Add. Ms 21427..

Ballyshannon was an important stronghold on the route from Dublin to Kilkenny, a Confederate garrison apparently too strong to be attacked by Ormond in 1643. The place held out for the Confederates after their defeat in 1647 at Dungan's Hill by Colonel Michael Jones, commanding the forces of the English parliament, when many of their castles and garrisons in north Leinster surrendered. However, in September 1648 the Ballyshannon garrison surrendered to Jones; he had been before the place in February of that year but was unable to take it then. When the Confederates, now in alliance with Ormond, advanced on Dublin in 1649, Ballyshannon was blockaded by a small detachment of their forces commanded by Pierce Fitzgerald, the owner of the castle; the only other place still holding out in Leinster for the parliament was Dublin.

Following the defeat of the combined Confederate and Royalist army at Rathmines in August 1649 by the parliamentary forces under Jones, Ballyshannon was induced to surrender after the garrison was persuaded that Jones had been defeated. Part of the army commanded by Cromwell that landed later that month at Dublin advanced into Kildare under Colonel John Hewson at the end of the year; in February 1650 Hewson marched from Naas to 'Ballisonan'. His report describes the place as a strong garrison with double works and wet moats and a mount with a fort upon it. He had with him one culverin, a demi-culverin and a mortar.[5]

The town, outlined on the contemporary plan with a wet moat and bastioned defences—presumably earthworks—was abandoned by the garrison, but a detachment held the fort on the mount, evidently the motte of an Anglo-Norman earthwork castle, which still survives. A short distance to the west a later Church of Ireland church stands on the site of the earlier one depicted on the plan. Part of what appear to be the inner works surrounding the castle remain to the south in the form of a ditch or trench some 150 feet long, approximately 20 or 25 feet wide and 6 feet deep, running from north to south. Joined to this at the south end at right angles to it is an embankment some 210 feet in length, ending in what may be the remains of part of the south-west bastion of the defences. The embankment changes direction here, angled out for a distance of some 45 feet. The first edition of the Ordnance Survey depicts an embankment forming three sides of a square, of which the surviving ditch and embankment form the east and south sides. The plan depicts a tower-house castle or fortified house surrounded by a bawn, a circular flanker at the north-east with rectangular flankers at the south-east and northwest corners (Fig.48). The bawn appears to have been about 150 feet square, judging by the dimensions given for parts of the defences; surrounding the bawn was the wet inner moat, noted as being in places 40 feet broad. Enclosing this inner moat is a square bastioned work, the rampart and parapet noted as 30 feet thick and in places 25 feet high. This earthwork defence must have effectively masked the masonry of the bawn wall from artillery fire. According to the dimensions of these elements of the fortification, and assuming the plan to be drawn with reasonable accuracy, the bastions at the four corners had flanks of some 20 to 25 feet and faces 80 to 90 feet long. The length of the curtains between the flanks of the bastions appears to have been some 170 to 200 feet. The outer wet moat is noted in the list of details with the plan as being 25 feet wide in places and 12 feet deep. The covered way on the counterscarp was 12 feet wide, protected by a breastwork 9 feet broad, presumably inclined on the exterior to form a rough glacis or embankment down to the original ground level. Five drawbridges are noted and dams to retain the water in the moats. A 'new work' is shown on the plan in broken line, a form of outwork or hornwork protecting the entrance to the castle and apparently extend-

ing to the foot of the mount, which is depicted with a circular wall or breastwork enclosing the summit. The plan has the remark that Ballyshannon was taken (by the parliament) on 24 September 1648: presumably the new work was constructed by the Confederate forces that replaced the parliamentary garrison after August 1649.

Hewson constructed a battery and opened fire on the fort on the mount and to some extent on the castle and outworks. The guns are depicted close to the church, the mortar being placed to the south of it, shown firing a shell into the castle. Before any breach was made, the garrison surrendered, being allowed to march out with the honours of war. The bastioned earthworks surrounding the castle and town of Ballyshannon were typical of the additional defences constructed at many garrisons in Ireland during the warfare from 1641 to 1652. At Dunsoghley Castle, north of Dublin, an outpost of the English garrison of the capital, earthwork defences in the form of parapets and bastions were constructed. At Castlelyons, Co. Cork, the Down Survey map depicts an extensive work with six bastions surrounding the castle or fortified house; the place was taken by Castlehaven in 1644. It is evident that in some instances the representation of defence works on the Down Survey maps is conventional, but at other places, such as Bunratty and Portumna castles, the buildings are depicted with reasonable accuracy.

At Trim Castle, another outpost of Dublin for much of the 1640s, an earth embankment or gun platform was constructed behind the curtain wall on the south-west side, probably in 1647. Three of the semicircular-fronted towers here were filled in at this period, presumably to convert them into solid bastions to mount artillery. It is possible that the medieval town walls at Trim and at other walled towns such as Ardee, Drogheda and Dundalk were strengthened to some extent by similar earthen ramparts inside the curtain

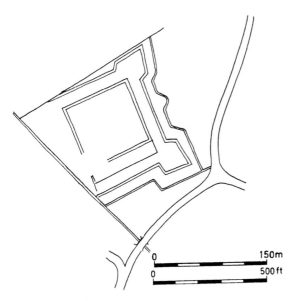

Fig. 49. Plan of Tircroghan, Co. Meath.

walls. At Wexford the town defences were strengthened by an external entrenchment, and buildings along the inside of the walls were removed to improve the communications of the defenders.[6] This work was carried out late in 1641 by the insurgent forces, and Wexford, an important port and naval base for the Confederates, remained under Irish control until taken by Cromwell in October 1649.

In Ulster the walled town of Carrickfergus, with defences of early seventeenth-century artillery bastions and ramparts, was the most important base for the Scottish forces in that province. Behind the similar defences of Derry an English garrison held out for the parliament. The smaller-scale artillery defences of Jamestown in Co. Leitrim made the place an important garrison on the Shannon. Other important posts on the river were Carrick-on-Shannon, where a strong fort was held for Clanricarde when attacked by the forces of Owen Roe O'Neill in 1648; Ballyleague (later Lanesborough), one of the last Irish garrisons to surrender in 1653, where a fort on the Longford side of the river controlled the crossing-point here; and Athlone, where a wall had been constructed around the town on the east bank of the river. This had been erected by Viscount Wilmot during the seventeen years before 1635, the two gatehouses having been built during the Elizabethan period. Athlone was a key post on the route from Dublin to Galway and the town and castle were held by various factions during the warfare of 1641-52.

An important stronghold on the road from Dublin to Athlone was Ticroghan or Queen Mary's Castle, less than two miles south of Clonard, Co. Meath. It was one of Owen Roe O'Neill's midland garrisons, and his son Henry married Elena, daughter of Sir Luke Fitzgerald, owner of Ticroghan. Ormond was at Ticroghan when Cromwell was attacking Drogheda in September 1649; the parliamentary forces under Hewson and Reynolds attacked and captured the place in 1650.

The central castle buildings, depicted in an eighteenth-century view, no longer survive, but extensive outworks of ramparts and bastions remain on the site. The first edition of the Ordnance Survey shows two bastions linked by a rampart, and two other ramparts evidently originally forming a square enclosure, suggesting that the fortification was a regular work with a bastion at each of the four corners (Fig.49). These earthworks may date from the period of Confederate occupation, or from the Cromwellian or Restoration period. The scale of the works is considerably larger than the outworks surrounding the castle at Ballyshannon, and larger than the Cromwellian forts in Ireland such as Bantry, Bellahy and Sligo, possibly indicating that the defences were built or remodelled during the reign of Charles II, when Ticroghan was a garrison. The bastion flanks are depicted on the Ordnance Survey first edition at an obtuse angle to the curtain, which also suggests a later date than the middle of the century.

Some twenty-seven miles to the north-west there was an important 'pass' from Leinster into Ulster at Finnea. Remains survive of a quadrangular bastioned fort on the south bank of the river joining Lough Kinale and Lough Sheelin, to the west of the bridge. In 1644 the post was taken by Munro and his Scots but abandoned on the advance of O'Neill and Castlehaven. A castle and fort at Finnea were captured by parliamentary forces in March 1651 under Colonel Hewson and Theophilus Jones. Also in Westmeath, midway between Mullingar and Athlone, was a fortification at Ballymore: a house and fortification were recorded in 1642, and later there was an English garrison here. Remains of earthwork bastions and ramparts and a ditch originally filled with water from the nearby lake survive on the site. As at Ballyshannon, there is a Norman motte at Ballymore, north of the earthwork defences. The place was held by Jacobite forces in 1690. Sir Henry Piers, in A *Chorographical Description of the County of Westmeath* (1682), describes Ballymore:

> *Here was formerly a strong garrison of the English forces, towards the latter end of the war; this garrison seated on the skirts of the lake, was divided from the mainland by a graff [moat] deep and large with ramparts of earth and bulwarks; the ditch was so low carried, as to receive three or four foot of . . . water of the lake, over which was by a drawbridge the entry to the fort .*

Before the arrival of Cromwell in 1649 the Confederate and royalist forces had been involved in harbour defence works at Dublin, Wexford and Kinsale. Sir Bernard de Gomme's maps of 1673 depict a small fort at the end of the peninsula of Ringsend, commanding Dublin Harbour and the approach of ships to Dublin. The fort is also shown on a later map by Phillips and a chart of Dublin Bay by Captain Greenvile Collins. It is shown as a square bastioned fort, and on one map by Phillips of 1685, evidently copied to some extent from earlier maps of 1673,

it has a more irregular outline, some 250 by 200 feet. The fort probably originated with the proposal in 1644 for a blockhouse for Dublin Harbour, an additional defence of the capital for the royalist garrison under Ormond. In 1646 earthwork defences were also built to protect the eastern suburbs of Dublin. In 1655 it is recorded that the Ringsend fort was no longer to be maintained as a fortification, and early in the following year Colonel Oliver Fitzwilliam, the owner of the estate of Merrion and Thorncastle on which the fort stood, was given permission to demolish the four bulwarks (bastions) of the fort. It is possible that the more irregular outline of the fort on Phillips' map of 1685 represents the place in a partly demolished condition.

When Cromwell attacked Wexford in October 1649 his forces first captured a rectangular bastioned fort on Rosslare Point, commanding the harbour entrance. Constructed by the Confederates about 1642, it was at first armed with five pieces of artillery, including a brass field-gun from Ferns Castle; when taken by Cromwell the armament consisted of seven guns.[7] It is depicted on the Down Survey map 'Barony of Forth' as 'Roselare Forte', a square-bastioned work. In March 1654 the fort and Wexford Castle just outside the town walls were to be maintained as garrisons under the Cromwellian Protectorate. The fort was still in existence in 1798, when it was occupied by the insurgent forces, but the site is largely submerged today.

Prince Rupert was at Kinsale with a squadron of royalist ships in 1649. He constructed outworks south of Castle Park Fort to strengthen the defences on the landward side, and works overlooking the estuary farther south for harbour defence. A map of Kinsale that must date from about this time depicts these works and others near the town, presumably also built by Prince Rupert.[8] Two square redoubts or earthen forts are shown south of Castle Park Fort, linked by an entrenchment or parapet between them. A

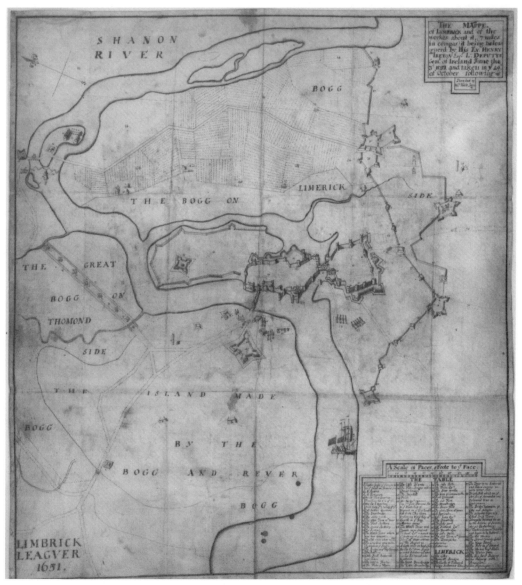

Fig. 50. Siege of Limerick 1651 by William Webb, Worcester College Oxford Ms. YC 20, ccvi.

redoubt and platform are depicted on a headland at the west side of the harbour entrance, with a gun platform on the opposite headland on the east. Guns here at each side of the entrance to Kinsale Harbour covered the approach of shipping, the batteries being half a mile apart. Linked to the western side of the walled town of Kinsale, a demi-bastion and a line of fortification with two bastions run southwest to an inlet of the River Bandon, noted as 'the new line'. The blockhouse north-east of Castle Park proposed

in 1626 is also depicted on the map (see Map 8).

Like many other places in Munster, Kinsale was at various times under royalist or parliamentary garrisons. In 1645 Captain William Brocket commanded Castle Park Fort for the parliament, having superseded the royalist Captain Kettleby. In 1649 Prince Rupert spent most of the year at Kinsale, his squadron using the harbour as a base for attacks on shipping of the parliament. Late in 1649 Kinsale declared for Cromwell and Broghill sent troops to attack the fort and occupy the town; the fort surrendered to Broghill and a few days later Bandon and Youghal also surrendered to the forces of the parliament.

By the winter of 1649-50 Cromwell was in control of the eastern seaboard of Ireland, extending from the walled city of Derry in the north to west of Kinsale in the south. Early in 1650 he marched from Youghal to attack Kilkenny, linking up with a force under Hewson that had marched from Dublin. Kilkenny surrendered after some resistance, and in April, Cromwell was before Clonmel, which was defended by Hugh Dubh O'Neill and a force of Ulster troops. Hugh O'Neill had been taken prisoner at the Irish defeat at Clones in 1643, but was exchanged after the victory of his uncle Owen Roe O'Neill at Benburb. At the time of the death of Owen Roe in November 1649 the Ulster army was moving south to join with Ormond in resisting Cromwell. Hugh O'Neill's defence of the medieval walls of Clonmel with a garrison of some 1,200 men included the technique of building internal barricades some distance behind the breach made by Cromwell's cannon in the north wall. The attacking force, allowed into the breach, found themselves in a trap and under fire from musket and cannon: Cromwell lost over a thousand men at Clonmel, the greatest loss the parliamentary forces suffered in Ireland. O'Neill and the survivors of his garrison escaped from the town across the bridge over the Suir, while the townspeople negotiated surrender terms.

O'Neill later defended Limerick against Ireton, who commanded the English forces after Cromwell returned to England shortly after the fall of Clonmel in May, 1650. That summer Carlow, Waterford and Duncannon Fort surrendered to the parliament; in the north, Charlemont Fort, the last Irish stronghold of importance in Ulster, also surrendered. By the end of the year the Irish forces were driven back to the line of the Shannon, holding Athlone and Limerick as key positions. Ireton made prepara-

tions for the siege of Limerick in the summer of 1651 (Fig.50). He constructed two forts about half a mile east and south-east of the walls of Irish Town, while a battery near the west end of Thomond Bridge bombarded the castle. The parliamentary forces captured an Irish fort on the west side of St Thomas's Island, in the Shannon one-and-a-half miles north of English Town, which enabled them to construct a floating bridge across the river. An attack on Thomond Bridge resulted in the capture of the gatehouse near the Clare side of the river, but the garrison destroyed some arches of the bridge, preventing any advance of the besiegers by this route. After an unsuccessful attack by boats on King's Island outside the city walls on the north side—it was defended by breastworks or earthwork parapets along the river bank—Ireton decided to starve the town out. O'Neill's garrison made large-scale attacks on the besieging forces from time to time and held out until the end of October, when a peace party among the defenders seized the castle gatehouse and trained the castle guns on the city. At the same time Ireton's artillery made a breach in the walls of Irish Town, where there was no backing in the form of an earth rampart, apparently the east wall, which was later rebuilt before the sieges of 1690-91. The party in the castle admitted 200 English soldiers while the garrison of the city, now reduced from about 2,000 to 1,200 men, negotiated terms of surrender. O'Neill's gallant defence of the medieval walls of Clonmel and Limerick was outstanding at a time when so many towns, forts and castles surrendered after only a token resistance to the forces of the English parliament. The only fortified town of any consequence now remaining in Irish hands was Galway. Athlone had capitulated in June 1651, when the Cromwellian forces threatened the place from both sides of the Shannon; the town was soon fortified by Colonel John Reynolds, with the engineer Major Myles Symner in charge of the works. By August 1651

Reynolds and Sir Charles Coote were blockading Galway, which was defended by a combined garrison of Irish and royalists under Preston. With other leaders Preston left by sea, leaving Clanricarde in command, determined to hold out as long as possible. The surrender of Galway was agreed in April 1652 without his consent.

At the outbreak of the rising in 1641 the town and fort of Galway had been put into a state of defence by Clanricarde, but a dispute developed between the townspeople and the garrison of the fort, resulting in the construction of a battery by the citizens. Clanricarde attempted to send provisions into the fort by sea, and heavy guns in the fort fired into the town. The fort's garrison eventually went over to the parliament, and in 1643 it was besieged by forces under the command of Colonel John Burke, who had been appointed lieutenant-general of Connacht by the Confederation of Kilkenny. Troops were posted at Athenry and Claregalway to prevent any attempts by Clanricarde to relieve the fort. Two bulwarks and batteries were erected by the Confederates, one on a headland to the west, the other at Rinmore on the opposite side; the fort surrendered in June 1643 when Castlecoote, Loughrea and Portumna were still holding out for Clanricarde.

Between 1643 and 1650 improvements were made to the walls of Galway, which were strengthened by the addition of artillery bastions and ramparts on the east, the side open to attack from the land. By the end of 1643 the east and south-east ramparts were completed: the ramparts were constructed in advance of the curtain wall, with a large bastion in front of the east gate, a demi-bastion at the northern corner of the defences, and a bastion at the south-east corner, close to St Augustine's Fort. The demi-bastion at the northern salient was completed in 1645, being in front of the Lyons Tower, the corner tower of the town walls. Other works were completed in 1647 and armed with twelve pieces of

artillery, including four iron 18-pounders. The gates were repaired and the bastion outside the east gate constructed by 1649; other works completed the fortifications in 1650.[9]

A detailed pictorial map shows Galway with these artillery fortifications and the siege lines and forts of the parliamentary forces in 1651.[10] St Augustine's Fort is depicted—which was dismantled to some extent by the townspeople after it was taken in 1643—and a triangular bridgehead defence at the western end of the bridge over the Corrib. In front of the bridgehead work is the square bastioned fort that had been constructed in 1625 to defend Galway from attack from the west. The fort on Mutton Island a mile to the south of Galway was included in the surrender terms drawn up by Coote in April 1652. The artillery defence works of ramparts and bastions, added to the medieval defences of Galway, were the most ambitious permanent town fortifications undertaken in Ireland between 1641 and 1652, and from Phillips' survey of the town of 1685 it is possible to determine their dimensions.[11] The demi-bastion in advance of the Lyons Tower had a face of 110 feet and a flank of 45 feet; the central bastion in front of the east gate had flanks of some 25 to 30 feet and faces of 40 to 50 feet, while the bastion at the south-east corner had flanks of 90 feet with faces of 110 feet. The rampart linking these works was from 100 to 150 feet in advance of the curtain wall forming the eastern boundary of the city.

Galway was considered to be of special strategic importance because of its links with the Continent. It was thought to be the most likely landing-point for a foreign force: for some time the defenders of Galway had been negotiating with the Duke of Lorraine for assistance. After October 1651 there was the possibility of war with the Dutch, which broke out in the following year. There was the fear of Dutch ships transporting foreign troops to Ireland, and in 1655 Spanish invasion was thought likely, resulting in concern for the defence of Galway.

An important outpost of Galway was the garrison of Arkin at Killeany, Inishmore, the largest of the Aran Islands. An English garrison had been established at Arkin in 1588, but it is not clear what form the castle or fort had at this time. Clanricarde hoped that Arkin might be a convenient base for the promised aid from the Duke of Lorraine, and he sent a garrison of 200 men and three pieces of ordnance there in April 1651. The post was included in the surrender of Galway a year later, and the fort was undergoing reconstruction when the English garrison was overcome by an Irish force from Inishbofin at the end of 1652. In January 1653 the place was recaptured by the parliamentary forces, who garrisoned Arkin; in 1659 the recommended garrison was a hundred men.

A wall remains facing the harbour, with a blocked-up doorway at low level. At the eastern end is a projecting square tower with machicolations supported on corbels similar to those on some tower-house castles. Parts of other walls survive further inland. A detailed survey is required to establish the original form of the fort. A sketch plan forming part of a military report of the defence of Galway Bay of 1796-98 depicts two square towers, one at each end of the sea-front wall, from where walls run inland to two circular towers. The enclosure, of irregular outline, approximately rectangular, contains three buildings of rectangular plan. A round tower is noted in 1821 and 1839, while a more recent description gives the dimensions of the seaward wall as some 4 feet thick and 200 feet long, the wall extending inland from the square tower about 120 feet in length. The form of the original layout appears to have been comparable to a bawn, with two square flankers on the sea front and two circular towers on the landward side, linked by an irregular layout of walls.

Another island outpost off the west coast was on Inishbofin. There was an Irish garrison here, presumably on the site of what is depicted on the first edition of the Ordnance Survey as 'Cromwell's Barrack'.[12] Tradition associates the place with Bosco, a Spanish or Danish pirate, who is said to have had a castle here and placed a cannon on Gun Rock nearby to protect the harbour. Sited on a rocky headland with the harbour to the north and west, there is an enclosure of approximately 120 by 80 feet, from which project bastions, those on the eastern or landward front being linked by a wall 45 feet long and 6 feet thick, in which there is a centrally placed doorway. The north, west and south sides are protected by rocky cliffs, with a demi-bastion and a square projection forming the northwest and south west corners of the fort. In addition a semicircular turret projects from the south wall. A list of expenditure on fortifications of 1664 gives the cost of building the fort of Inishbofin as £1,000, the same amount being recorded for the fort of Arkin. Although it was suggested that the Inishbofin garrison be withdrawn and the fort dismantled, this advice was not taken, and works were continued in 1656. In 1659 the recommended garrison here was a hundred men, with the same number at Arkin.[13] Inishbofin had been one of the last Irish outposts to surrender in 1653.

The Commonwealth and Protectorate were times of considerable activity in the construction of fortifications in Ireland. Town walls were repaired, citadels constructed and forts built for coastal defence. Inland forts and castles were erected at strategic positions such as 'passes' and river-crossings. After the regular Irish forces surrendered the Cromwellian garrisons had considerable trouble with bands of 'tories', and military escorts had to be provided for convoys travelling from one strong-point to another.

At Athlone a sum of £2,000 was to be levied for fortifications, £500 to be raised in each province, and the commissioners of the parliament instructed Reynolds to proceed with the works in December 1651.[14] The fortification of Athlone appears to have continued from 1652 to 1654.On the Leinster side the earlier wall was strengthened by an earth rampart on the interior, an external ditch and the addition of angle-bastions. Earthwork ramparts and bastions protected the part of the town west of the Shannon, with the castle forming a strong-point or citadel here overlooking the west end of the bridge. Phillips' plan of 1685 shows the layout of the defences, and the line of the walls and bastions on the Leinster side may be traced by the surviving walls, a bastion and parts of two other bastions. The circuit of the defences formed a rough semi-circle, starting with a demi-bastion at the north by the river. The wall ran some 450 feet to the north-east to an angle-bastion of irregular outline, the eastern face and flank of which still survive. From this bastion a surviving length of wall runs eastwards, and changes direction slightly at a small semicircular turret, which may be part of the defences built by Wilmot before 1635. The next bastion is complete, the flanks some forty feet long, the faces about sixty feet. The flanks and faces are *battered* or inclined inwards some two to three feet in the present height of about twelve feet. The curtain wall is vertical, in contrast to the bastions, perhaps further confirmation that this is the wall constructed by Wilmot, to which the bastions were added in 1652-54. The wall continues south-eastwards for about a 100 feet, the next 200 feet to the remains of the next bastion having been demolished. Some 200 feet farther south, at Dublin Gate Street, is the site of the east gate of the town, which was defended by a bastion-shaped outwork, parts of which remain, forming external or party walls of existing buildings. From here the wall ran southwards to the river, where it ended in a demi-bastion. The earthwork ramparts and bastions of the Connacht town enclosed a somewhat smaller area, with a circumference of some 700 yards (see Fig.62).

Other fortifications on the line of the Shannon included a new castle at Termonbarry, a castle at Banagher, a fort at Meelick, and the city defences of Limerick, where a citadel was constructed. A castle was also built on the west bank near Clonmacnois, to protect a ford a short distance downstream. Also on the Shannon there were garrisons at Carrick-on-Shannon, Jamestown, Ballyleague, Banagher and the Black Castle at Portumna, a short distance from the fortified house known as Portumna Castle.[15] The garrisons varied from eighteen men at Portumna to forty at Jamestown and Killaloe; at Banagher and Meelick there was a combined force of sixty men. At Athlone the recommended garrison in 1659 was 100, with 100 at Limerick.

At Termonbarry, an important crossing-place on the upper Shannon, work started after 1655 and was still in progress in the following year; what must have been a relatively small structure cost £390. For a recommended garrison of twenty men in 1659, the castle was sited on an island here. There is no evidence for it on the first edition of the Ordnance Survey.

A small castle much altered during the construction of the Shannon defence works during the Napoleonic period after 1803 stands at the west end of the bridge at Banagher. It is known as Cromwell's Castle, an irregularly shaped tower with the upper part rebuilt as part of the early nineteenth-century defences of Banagher. This structure appears to be the castle recommended to be built at Banagher, where it was noted there was a small fort, evidently the fort constructed in 1624, which had seen action in the warfare of the 1640s. A short distance downstream there was another Cromwellian garrison at Meelick on Cromwell's Island: a fort here was the scene of fighting between the Irish and parliamentary forces in 1651. It was captured by the Irish under Colonel Richard Grace, who also took the parliamentary post at Rachra (now Shannonbridge) in the same year. The fort at Meelick was taken at the third attempt by Sir

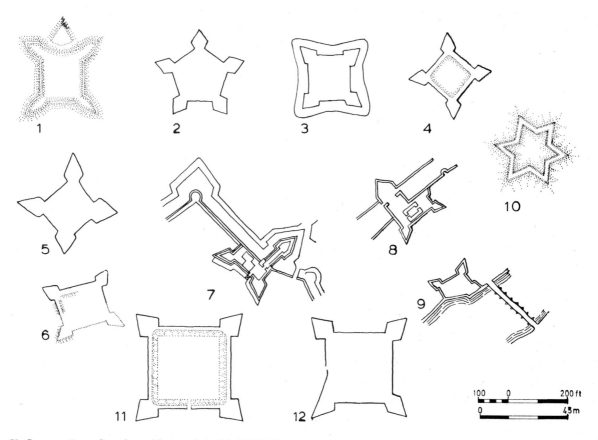

Fig. 51. Comparative outline plans of forts and citadels 1641-1660:
1 Duagh; 2 Coolyhune; 3 Fort Cromwell, Bellaghy; 4 Green Fort, Sligo; 5 Bantry; 6 Finnea; 7 Limerick Citadel; 8 Upper Citadel,
Galway; 9 Lower Citadel, Galway; 10 Massy's Hill, Tarbert; 11 Hillsborough; 12 Ross Carbery.

Charles Coote and continued as a garrison from then onwards.[16] The Down Survey map 'Barony of Garriecastle' depicts a square bastioned fort: the island was later the site of a battery of the Napoleonic period, possibly constructed on the remains of the earlier fort. Both fort and battery were built to protect a ford across the river here. Grace continued a guerrilla war against the parliamentary forces for almost a year, ranging over much of Leinster as far as Ticroghan and Kildare. By August 1652 he was holding out in an island named by the Cromwellian Colonel Sankey as 'Inchicore', which has been identified as Inchicoura, an island in Lake Coura, Co. Offaly. It was described by Sankey as a fort surrounded by a stockade in the water, with a well-flanked breastwork or rampart twelve feet high and with a castle within the fort. The remains of a circular

tower-house survive here. Grace was able to surrender on terms at Birr, and was to defend Athlone in 1690 for King James II.

Cromwellian garrisons in Connacht, where many existing castles and some new castles and bawns were used as local strong-points, included two new forts at Bellahy and Bellamoe. At Bellahy in Co. Sligo, on the border with Co. Mayo, 'Fort Cromwell at Bellaghey Pass' was under construction in 1656 (Fig.51).[17] It was of masonry backed by earthwork, the rampart was sixteen feet broad and there were timber-framed houses within the fort. The first edition of the Ordnance Survey depicts a typical mid-seventeenth-century square bastioned fort, about 150 feet square, the distance from salient to salient of the bastions some 200 feet, the bastions having flanks of 25 feet and faces of 50 feet linked by

curtains of about 100 feet. The fort was surrounded by a ditch or moat. On the later maps of
the late nineteenth century the fort is shown in
outline only, the site has later buildings and is
noted as the fair green.

At Ballymoe Bridge on the Galway border with
Co. Roscommon another fort was under construction in 1656, which was so far advanced as
likely to be completed in that year.[18] It was
known as Fort Fleetwood, named after Charles
Fleetwood, the lord deputy of Ireland from 1654
to 1657, when he was replaced by Henry
Cromwell. The first edition of the Ordnance
Survey does not indicate the remains of this
work; a report of 1662 notes a masonry fort of
four bastions, no doubt similar to Bellahy, which
cost £2,200—the fort at Ballymoe cost £2,050,
suggesting that it was of about the same size.

At Sligo an earthwork fort known as the Green
Fort survives on high ground north of the town
(Fig.51). It seems probable that this defence
work originated in the wars of the 1640s, as the
Cromwellians constructed what was known as the
'new fort' at Sligo at the south end of the bridge,
listed with a recommended garrison of sixty men
in 1659.[19] The Green Fort is of similar dimensions
to Bellahy, 140 by 150 feet, from salient to salient
of the bastions 200 feet, the faces of the bastions
some 50 feet, the curtains about 100 feet. The
fort is shown on the Down Survey map 'Barony
of Carbury' as a rectangular bastioned work; the
new fort is depicted on a map of Sligo of 1689 as
similar in size and shape to the earlier fort. It
was still unfinished in 1666, a sum of £1,620 having been noted for the cost of construction in a
list of the fortifications of 1664. It was a masonry
work, noted as the 'Stone Fort' on the map of
1689, which illustrates the fortifications of Sligo
constructed by the forces of King James II.

At Finnea the remains survive of what was
originally a rectangular bastioned fort: 160 by
140 feet, the bastion faces from 35 to 45 feet long,
the flanks about 20 to 25 feet, to judge by the

surviving evidence on the site (Fig.51). This fort,
at an important 'pass' between Westmeath and
Cavan, was garrisoned under the Cromwellian
regime and during the Restoration.

In Ulster a square fort with corner bastions
was constructed at Hillsborough some years
before 1660 by Colonel Arthur Hill; it is almost
300 feet square, the bastions having faces about
65 feet and flanks 25 feet long linked by curtains
some 215 feet in length. The masonry walls are
backed by an earthen rampart and, like the
other mid-seventeenth-century forts, the bastion
flanks are at right angles to the curtain (Fig.51).
The gatehouse was remodelled in the middle of
the eighteenth century with corner towers and
battlements by the Hill family. The fort is now in
State Care as an historic monument.[20]

Coastal defence, particularly in the west and
south-west of the country, was reflected in the
number of garrisons at castles and at new forts.
In addition to the forts at Inishbofin and Arkin
there were outposts at Broadhaven, and possibly
at Inver, where a small castle was garrisoned in
the early years of Charles II, while at
Lettermullan, on Gorumna Island, there was
another small castle, which maintained communication with the garrison at Arkin. On the
Shannon estuary the castles of Carrigaholt and
Carrigafoyle were garrisoned and provided some
protection for the coast here. New forts were
constructed on Valentia Island, at Nedeen at the
head of Kenmare Bay, at Bantry and at Dunboy,
around the earlier castle overlooking the western
entrance to Berehaven.

Two forts were built on Valentia Island, one at
the north of the island where a bastioned defence
cuts off the northern promontory and the other
at the south; both are noted as 'Cromwell's Fort'
on the Ordnance Survey first edition, which
depicts the southern fort as an almost square
enclosure. Only the southern work is shown on
the Down Survey map 'Barony of Iveragh',
noted as 'Fort'. Valentia is listed in 1659 with

Dingle as having a total garrison of sixty men. These forts protected the approaches to the anchorage between the island and the mainland.

Another 'Cromwell's Fort' is noted on the Ordnance Survey first edition, at Nedeen, at the head of Kenmare Bay: it appears on the Down Survey map 'Barony of Glanerought' as Needeene Fort. The site is at the north end of the present bridge, on the west side of a promontory projecting from the north side of the estuary. The fort was an earthwork and was only used for a short time; a description of about 1685 notes it as ruined, having been built in Cromwellian times.

At the head of Bantry Bay, Lord Broghill built a square bastioned fort at the time of the first Dutch War, 1652-54.[21] Sited at Newtown, about a mile north of the present town of Bantry, the fort protected a small settlement nearby and provided some degree of protection to the anchorage sheltered by Whiddy Island. It was similar in dimensions to the other Cromwellian forts: 150 feet square, the bastion faces about 75 feet, flanks 25 to 30 feet, and the curtains about 75 feet in length (Fig.51). A perspective view of the fort by Phillips in 1685 depicts it with two large buildings in the central space,[22] while a plan of some five years later by Goubet indicates three buildings here. The recommended garrison in 1659 was 100 men, although a report of 1677 indicates accommodation for 200 in the fort, which at that time was in bad repair, as were the drawbridge and gates. The earthworks of the fort survive, much overgrown.

At Dunboy Castle, overlooking the western entrance to Berehaven, Broghill constructed a 'star fort' or tenaille trace work around the castle, which had been one of the last Irish outposts to hold out in the south-west after the Battle of Kinsale.[23] Broghill may have constructed this work during the warfare of the 1640s, as he implies that it was demolished during the Cromwellian period. The work is depicted as a rectangular bastioned fort on the Down Survey map 'Barony of Beare and Bantry', with the inscription 'The towne and forte of Bearhaven'. Parts of Broghill's tenaille trace survive on the site, around the ruin of the castle.

At Crookhaven in west Cork the fort built by Sir Thomas Roper in 1622 was another coastal garrison, with a recommended strength of thirty men in 1659. Although not included in the list of 1659 of garrisons 'thought fit to be constantly kept if any invasion should be made into Ireland,' Sherkin Island or 'Innesherkin' is included in such lists in the early 1660s and later, so it is probable that there was a Cromwellian post here. A fort at Castletownshend erected about 1648 or 1650 is somewhat unusual in combining the functions of fortification and private dwelling. Constructed by Colonel Richard Townshend, who arrived in Ireland in 1647, the fort has a number of embrasures for small cannon and loopholes for firearms, and is just under thirty feet square internally with a bastion at each corner.[24]

Captain Robert Gookin erected a fort at Ross Carbery at his own expense to accommodate a garrison of 100 horse and foot; in 1654 300 people were settled 'within musket shot of it'. Gookin petitioned for expenses in fortifying the place, and in 1655 it was stated that the buildings he was constructing required a further £400 for completion. An eighteenth-century estate map depicts the plan of the fort, situated to the south of the main street.[25] A rectangular enclosure some 250 by 230 feet with bastions at the corners, by 1788 one of these was in the form of a demi-bastion: most probably a partial reconstruction of an earlier bastion (Fig.51). The fort is of similar size to that at Hillsborough, Co. Down, and typical of the square or rectangular bastioned forts of the middle of the seventeenth century.

Orders were given in August 1652 for the 'new blockhouse' at Kinsale to be fitted out with guns

Fig.52. A Prospect of the New Fort at Kinsale by Thomas Phillips, 1685, NLI Ms. 3137 (22). Charles Fort, recently completed is in the foreground, Castle Park or James Fort is in the background. To the right of Castle Park is the Cromwellian period tower and below this to the right is the water-level blockhouse.

and equipment to secure the anchorage, referred to as 'the only harbour in these parts' where the warships of the parliament could take on supplies and refit. The implication may be that the blockhouse was recently constructed, perhaps during the 1640s: Kinsale was considered to be of more importance than Cork Harbour or Youghal. A tower was built between the blockhouse and Castle Park Fort, prominent in the perspective view by Phillips of 1685 (Fig. 52). Major Hodder, governor of Kinsale, built this tower, similar to a tower-house, between 1654 and 1656. The upper levels of the tower would have provided a better view of the harbour to the north than was possible from the fort.

At Cork Harbour the entrance fort of Corkbeg and that on Haulbowline Island were recommended to have a total garrison of forty men in 1659. Coastal defence was carried out by naval patrols of the Commonwealth, reaching a high degree of efficiency, which was allowed to lapse to some extent after the restoration of King Charles II. Duncannon Fort and Passage defended the estuary of Waterford Harbour; at

Wexford the fort on Rosslare Point commanded the harbour entrance, while at Wicklow the Black Castle was repaired. At Carlingford a garrison of sixty men was recommended in 1659, to be distributed between the town (presumably at the castle) and at the blockhouse on the island at the lough entrance. The first reference to the Carlingford Lough blockhouse, apart from the proposal for building such a structure by Mountjoy in 1602, appears to be in 1649, when the forces of the parliament marched north after taking Drogheda, finding Carlingford and the blockhouse held by their opponents.

Another feature of the fortifications of the Commonwealth in Ireland was the construction of citadels. These were erected at Limerick, Galway, Clonmel, Derry and Coleraine, while the forts overlooking Cork and Waterford were repaired. At Limerick the citadel consisted of a small rectangular enclosure with two bastions built against the inside of the south wall of Irish Town (Fig.51). A bastion-shaped work projected outside the wall, forming part of the citadel, flanking the adjacent St John's Gate. Phillips' plan of Limerick of 1685 depicts the citadel, part of which still survives: it was approximately 140 by 80 feet, the bastion faces 60 to 70 feet and the flanks some 25 feet. The bastion-shaped ravelin forming part of the citadel outside the city wall had faces some 70 feet in length and flanks of 50 feet. Entrance to the citadel from within Irish Town was by means of a drawbridge across a ditch. Part of the wall of the western bastion, some seven feet in thickness, remains on the site. A ravelin outside the western gate of Irish Town on Phillips' plan dates from the 1640's. When Limerick was defended by Hugh Dubh O'Neill in 1651 there were outworks outside the walls of Irishtown including three bastions as shown on a contemporary plan of the siege (Fig.50).

Two citadels were built at Galway similar to that at Limerick: the upper citadel was sited inside the walls on the east side at the east gate, the lower citadel on the west side of the town close to the bridge across the Corrib. The construction of the upper citadel effectively blocked the passageway of the east gate; with direct access from the citadel to the new bastion outside the gate, the arrangement was similar to that at Limerick. Galway upper citadel was approximately the same size as Limerick citadel, but with bastions somewhat smaller; the lower citadel at Galway was smaller in area but similar in plan, with two bastions overlooking the town (Fig.51). Both citadels at Galway are depicted on Phillips' plan of 1685. Work was continuing on the citadels at Galway in October 1657 when the engineer William Webb was writing from there to Henry Cromwell in Dublin, pointing out the absence of a gatehouse and iron portcullis and the need for a sally port. The recommended garrison for Galway in 1659 was 200 men, possibly 100 at each citadel.

At Clonmel a citadel was constructed during the Cromwellian period and the recommended garrison there in 1659 was sixty men. The Down Survey map 'Barony of Glaneyhyry' (Co.

Waterford) shows the medieval curtain walls and towers surrounding the town, with an inner wall built diagonally across the south east corner; the resulting triangular space may represent the citadel, which was started in 1652 and demolished in 1673.

In Ulster, citadels were constructed at Derry and Coleraine. At Derry the citadel was built inside the walls backing onto Church or King James's Bastion and enclosing the cathedral. The plan of the citadel was similar to the layout at Limerick and Galway. Work was under way at Derry in 1653, but by 1685 only the outline of the citadel was depicted on Phillips' plan of the city, with the note 'The church formerly a citadel'. At Coleraine a stone fort or citadel was begun during the 1650s, and it was recorded in 1662 that it was ten to twelve feet in height on the river side but that the walls were not finished or backed by ramparts; it was evidently not completed. The fort of Coleraine is listed with other fortifications in 1664 constructed or repaired in the previous decade.

In addition to the new forts and citadels, repairs were carried out at existing forts, castles and town walls. At Wexford the castle was repaired and an outwork constructed; the forts at Duncannon, Passage and Waterford were also repaired. Elizabeth Fort at Cork, Castle Park at Kinsale, Banagher Fort and the fort at Ballyleague on the Shannon and the fortifications of Kilkenny were also renovated. Works were carried out at Maryborough Fort in 1651-52; in Ulster, Doe Castle, Carrickfergus Castle and Charlemont Fort were repaired. The castle or fortified house at Raphoe cost £25 for repairs.

Early in 1652 the Commonwealth forces had over 350 garrisons in Ireland and a further 100 were required in Wicklow, the midlands, Connacht and Ulster; the army should not be less than 30,000 men. It was remarked at this time of the use of the bogs and woods by the Irish forces that 'these fastnesses are of better use to them than walled towns'. The surrender terms granted to commanders such as Colonel Richard Grace reflect the difficulties the parliamentary forces had in overcoming the resistance of the Irish detachments holding out in the countryside, who were fighting a guerrilla war, making skilful use of the terrain.

The surrender of the Irish forces and the shipping of many of the soldiers overseas made possible the reduction of the Cromwellian army in Ireland, many of the disbanded officers and men being granted land made available by the transplanting of Catholic landowners to Connacht. Due to the policy of transplanting, garrisons in Clare and Connacht were of particular importance: outposts on the islands and along the coast were intended to act against intervention from abroad; garrisons along the Shannon effectively formed a barrier against the rest of the country, and throughout the western counties there was a network of strong-points in existing castles or new forts. In August 1656 there were over thirty garrisons in Co. Clare and Connacht, including those for coastal defence and those at crossing-places of the Shannon.[26].

The recommended garrisons in Ireland in 1659 to be retained in case of invasion totalled more than sixty, those in Clare and Connacht being one-third of these, with a similar number in Munster and the remainder divided between Leinster and Ulster. The number of soldiers required for these garrisons was over 3,000, with 200 men at Limerick and Galway, 100 men each at Dublin Castle, Kinsale, Bantry Fort, Arkin, Inishbofin, Bellahy or 'Fort Cromwell', Athlone, Derry, Enniskillen and Charlemont Fort. At Philipstown, Maryborough, Kilkenny Castle, Cork Fort, the new fort at Sligo, Ballymoe or 'Fort Fleetwood', Carrickfergus and other garrisons, detachments of 60 men were advocated. Smaller castles and forts such as Ballyleague and Termonbarry on the Shannon, Wicklow Castle, Crookhaven Fort in west Cork and some of the

smaller Connacht garrisons had between 20 and 40 soldiers.

A list of walled towns in Ireland of 1657 includes the more well-known examples and some surprising additions and omissions.[27] Naas and Kildare are included in Leinster; in Munster, Cahir is listed but Bandon is omitted; in Ulster, Armagh and Strabane are listed as walled towns but Derry is not included. In Connacht, in addition to Athlone, Galway, Athenry and Jamestown, five other towns are noted as walled— possibly enclosed by earthwork defences: Loughrea, Roscommon, Sligo, Elphin and Leitrim. Over forty walled towns are listed, all evidently of some military significance to the government of Ireland during the Cromwellian Protectorate.

The Cromwellian settlement, in which the establishment of garrisons at walled towns, citadels, forts and castles played an important part, transferred wealth and power from Catholics to Protestants. A new Protestant land-owning and mercantile class was created, which for political and economic reasons became assimilated with the earlier Protestant settlers of the Elizabethan period and early seventeenth-century Ireland.

Fortifications that may originate from the 1641-1660 period include forts at Tarbert, Co. Kerry; Boyle, Co. Roscommon; Coolyhune, Co. Carlow; Mylers Park, Co. Wexford; and Duagh, south of Waterford city. The fort at Tarbert was similar in outline but somewhat larger than the *tenaille trace* work at Dunboy Castle constructed by Broghill at this time. It is shown on the first edition of the Ordnance Survey as a small star fort situated on the mainland just south of the west end of Tarbert Island. It was some 250 feet across with a distance of 125 to 150 feet between the salient angles, a small six-pointed star fort. Later editions of the Ordnance Survey show the outline less clearly; the plan form may suggest a date from the beginning to the middle of the seventeenth century, and the similarity to the work at Dunboy may indicate a Confederate or Cromwellian origin.

At Boyle the remains survive of a regular pentagonal fort on high ground approximately 400 yards north-west of the town centre. The much-eroded outline may be seen on the site today; the first edition of the Ordnance Survey depicts the fort clearly, the later edition indicates less of the outline. The dimension from salient to salient of the bastions was about 200 feet.

Some two miles east of Graiguenamanagh, at Coolyhune, is a regular pentagonal fort sited on the top of a small conical hill. The dimensions are similar to those at Boyle, the distance between the salient angles of the bastions being some 200 feet (Fig.51). A masonry wall four to five feet thick and in places six feet high forms the curtains and bastions, the wall battered on the exterior to a slope of approximately 1:5. The curtains are some 80 feet in length, the faces and flanks of the bastions approximately 50 and 25 feet, respectively. There is no indication of an earth rampart on the interior and no evidence survives of gun-embrasures or loops for firearms. It is possible that references to a fort at St Mullin's in 1581, and the 'new fort' of St Mullin's in 1582, may be connected with this structure.[28] However, the fort in 1582 was built to command the River Barrow, and this fort at Coolyhune is over a mile from the river at the nearest point to the south-west and over three miles north of the religious settlement of St Mullin's. A more likely period for the construction of the fort at Coolyhune may be between 1642 and 1649, perhaps as a Confederate outpost overlooking the route between Enniscorthy and Graiguenamanagh and the road from New Ross northwards via Pollmounty and Borris to Leighlinbridge. In March 1643 Ormond abandoned his siege of New Ross and on his return to Dublin was attacked in the glen of Pollmounty by the Leinster army of the Confederates command-

ed by Preston, five miles south of the fort at Coolyhune.

Some four miles south-east of New Ross, at Mylers Park, are the remains of an earthwork fort approximately 200 feet square; the first edition of the Ordnance Survey indicates projections at the corners, which may have originally been bastions. The form suggests the typical bastioned fort of the seventeenth century except that the bastions are somewhat smaller than usual. The Down Survey map 'Barony of Bantrie' shows 'Millers parke', but no fort is indicated. A more recent survey indicates virtually no projections at the corners, and the work has been interpreted as a medieval moated site.

Three miles south of Waterford, at Duagh, just to the west of the Waterford to Tramore road, a rectangular bastioned fort is depicted on the first edition of the Ordnance Survey, much less clearly indicated on later editions. The fort was 150 by 160 feet, the distance between the salients of the bastions some 240 to 250 feet, the curtains 100 to 115 feet in length (Fig.51). On the north side, masking the curtain between what may have been two demi-bastions, a ravelin is indicated, with faces that may originally have been some 70 feet long. The site is connected with Cromwell's camp in December 1649 during his siege of Waterford. While the fort was protected to some extent by marshy ground to the north and west, to the southeast it was overlooked by higher ground.

The contemporary accounts of the Confederate and Cromwellian wars suggest that many more fieldwork fortifications in Ireland remain to be identified. The elements of fortification remained essentially the same throughout the seventeenth century, and as many permanent and temporary works were reoccupied and modified later in the warfare of 1688-91, the closer dating of these sites will depend on further documentary evidence or archaeological excavation.

3
The Restoration and the Jacobite War, 1660-1691

In May 1660, Charles II was proclaimed king in Dublin. Ormond returned to Ireland and from 1662 was to be lord lieutenant for most of Charles's reign. The Irish Catholics, many having served the king in Ireland and abroad, looked forward to the recovery of their lands; but the Protestant army officers of the Commonwealth, who had agreed to the return of the king, were determined to keep the Irish estates they had acquired. No satisfactory solution was found to these incompatible claims, and the garrisons established by the Cromwellian government in Ireland were for the most part retained under Charles II, to ensure that the country was under Protestant control and that the land settlement, apart from some minor changes, remained basically unaltered.

In February 1661 Captain John Paine was appointed director-general and overseer of the king's fortifications in Ireland. In August the following year he submitted a detailed estimate for repairs to the fortifications of Dublin. Apart from work on seven drawbridges, four new gates and 'courts of guard'—presumably guard-rooms—the major part of the defences to be repaired were earthworks, most probably constructed during the years of Ormond's control of Dublin in the 1640s and the subsequent period of Jones' parliamentary garrison and the Commonwealth. The line of defences noted at over 7,000 yards was more than five times the length of the city walls, excluding those on the riverside, and it is clear that the defence line must have included extensive suburbs outside the walls, possibly extending north of the river to enclose the settlement there. More than 5,000 yards of trench needed to be cleaned out, the trench being 18 feet wide at the top, 10 feet wide at the bottom and 8 feet deep, at a cost of some £500. The remaining part of the trench—some 1,800 yards—having been filled in, was required to be 'new sunk' or excavated; and over 2,400 yards of it, being of loose earth, were to be sodded from the bottom to the top of the rampart, at a cost of nearly £900. The rest of the rampart and parapet was to be repaired. The seven drawbridges were to cost in total over £200, the four new gates £8 each. Other expenses involved palisades, turnpikes and watercourses, giving an overall total of £2,680. The dimensions of the trench or ditch—the excavated material from which the rampart and parapet were formed—suggest that the rampart may have been of similar width and perhaps some eight feet in height.[1]

It is not known if any repair works were carried out arising from these estimates. It appears that the fortifications were allowed to fall into disuse or were removed to make way for new roads and buildings, as in June 1667 there was some alarm at the defenceless state of Dublin following the Dutch attack on Chatham and their blockade of the Thames Estuary. There were proposals to 'cast up a trench which shall surround the whole city and suburbs'. However, in the following month fears of invasion diminished, as did 'the impatience of the citizens ... to have it fortified.' A map of 1673 does not indicate defences other than those of the city walls, Dublin Castle and the extensive citadel proposed at this time.

Also in August 1662 a list of the ordnance, arms and ammunition in the king's stores in Ireland was drawn up, and from this some indication is available of the armament at the garrisons and forts.[2] The artillery ranges from one brass 'cannon of 8' at Limerick and four brass 'cannon of 7'—one each at Dublin, Kinsale, Limerick and Athlone—down to the smaller calibre ordnance such as sakers and minions. There were thirteen demi-cannon (32-pounders) dis-

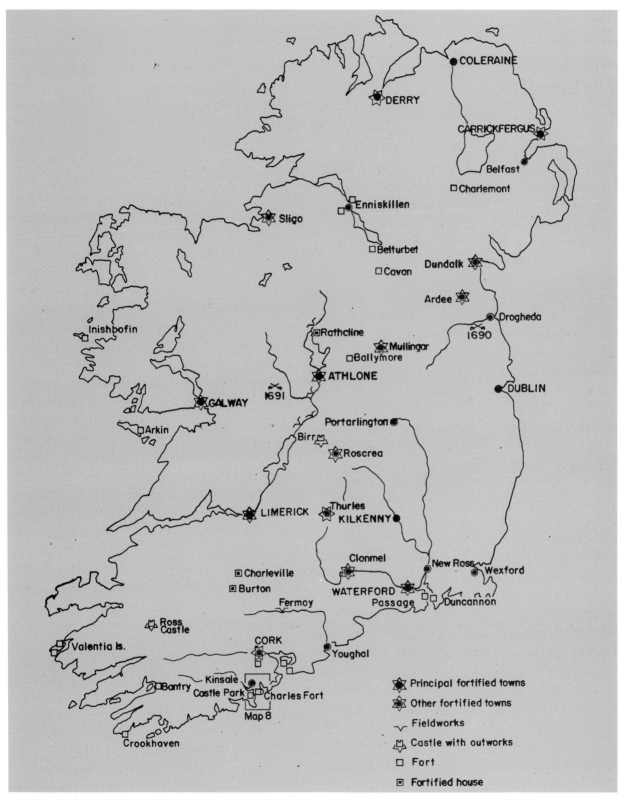

COLERAINE

DERRY

CARRICKFERGUS

Belfast

☐ Charlemont

☐ Enniskillen

Sligo

☐ Belturbet

☐ Cavan

Dundalk

Ardee

Drogheda
1690

Inishbofin

☐ Rathcline

Mullingar

☐ Ballymore

ATHLONE

DUBLIN

1691

GALWAY

Portarlington

☐ Arkin

Birr

Roscrea

Thurles

LIMERICK

KILKENNY

Clonmel

New Ross

☐ Wexford

Charleville

Burton

WATERFORD

Passage

☐ Duncannon

Fermoy

Ross
Castle

☐ Valentia Is.

CORK

Youghal

Kinsale
Castle Park

☐ Bantry

Charles Fort

Map 8

Crookhaven

	Principal fortified towns
	Other fortified towns
⌄	Fieldworks
	Castle with outworks
☐	Fort
⊡	Fortified house

Map 7. Ireland 1660 – 1691.

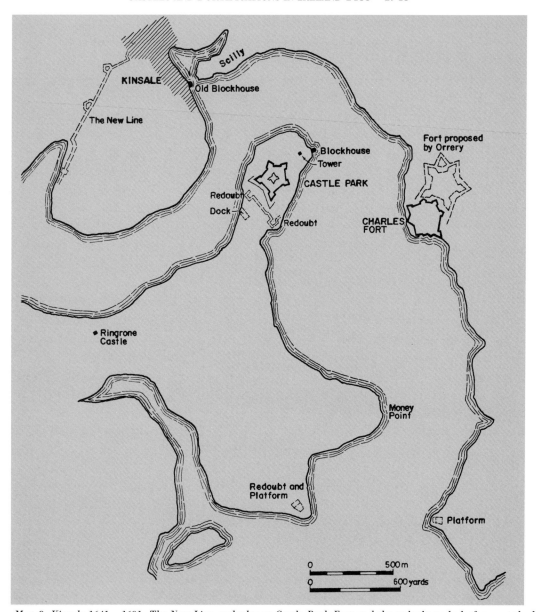

Map 8. Kinsale 1641 – 1691. The New Line, redoubts at Castle Park Fort and the redoubt and platforms at the harbour entrance are based on a map in the National Maritime Museum, Greenwich, Dartmouth Collection of Irish Maps No.1 (16). These works were evidently constructed by Prince Rupert in 1649.

tributed between Dublin and other towns; one unmounted 24-pounder at Limerick, and thirty-two culverins at Dublin and other garrisons, including some of the smaller forts. Eleven 12-pounders, 72 demi-culverins, 126 sakers and 124 minions were also listed, with a number of smaller pieces such as falcons, falconets and robinets.

At Kinsale, presumably at Castle Park Fort and the blockhouse, there were one brass cannon

of 7, one brass and one iron culverin, seven iron demi-culverins, ten iron sakers, seven iron minions and two iron falconets. Among the smaller garrisons such as Crookhaven, Sherkin Island, Bantry, Arkin and Inishbofin the smaller pieces of ordnance predominate: at Bantry there were one demi-culverin, three sakers, three minions and one falcon; at Inishbofin there were one 12-pounder, two demi-culverins unmounted, one saker, twelve minions—of which only three were mounted—and two falcons. At most places a certain proportion of the guns were unmounted, indicating gun carriages in need of repair or replacement. At Arkin in the Aran Islands the culverin, two demi-culverins and four sakers that comprised the armament, all iron pieces, were unmounted; the two iron sakers that formed the armament at Crookhaven were also unmounted. Apart from Athlone, Enniskillen, Charlemont, Clonmel and Kilkenny, the garrisons listed were all on the coast or were seaports on navigable rivers, such as Limerick, Cork and Derry (Map 7).

A list of master-gunners and quarter-gunners of 1666 shows that they were stationed at Dublin, Duncannon, Athlone, Galway, Sligo, Arkin, Inishbofin, Waterford, Limerick, Cork, Haulbowline, Youghal, Kinsale, Crookhaven, Sherkin Island, Valentia, Derry, Culmore and Carrickfergus. From an account of the ordnance in Ireland in March 1668 it is clear that there was little change in the number of guns when compared with the list of 1662 except for an increase in the number of some of the smaller calibre pieces such as sakers and minions. Garrisons of 1662 included 73 officers and men at Castle Park, Kinsale, with a sergeant, a corporal and twelve men at the blockhouse; 98 officers and men at Bantry Fort; 32 men at Ballymoe Fort; 78 officers and men at Bellaghy; and at Arkin and Inishbofin there were 45 soldiers and some officers at each garrison.

Some of the citadels and forts under construction during the Cromwellian period were not completed or were demolished during the Restoration. In 1664 the citadel at Coleraine was reported to be unfinished and it appears that it was not completed; the citadel at Clonmel was demolished in 1673. Captain William Webb was paid for his work at Sligo and Ballymoe between August 1660 and March the following year, but in June 1666 there was a proposal to demolish these

new forts at Sligo and Ballymoe Bridge. Lord Kingston, writing to Ormond, stated that he would not undertake their demolition until obtaining Ormond's agreement, and stressed that they had cost at least £4,000 to construct. A report some three months later described the unfinished fort at Sligo with four small bastions; £2,500 had been spent on its construction, and more funds were required to complete it and the accommodation for the garrison. The fort was still in existence in 1688 when Sligo was held by the forces of King James II. Ballymoe continued as a military post after 1666, being listed as a garrison in 1668, 1678 and 1680, although it is recorded that Ballymoe Fort, 'a ruinous place and not worth repairing—and if replaced would be useless as it is an inland place and on no pass' was to be granted to a Colonel Dillon in 1669.

Other inland fortifications included repairs at Charlemont Fort after 1663, a new fort at Belturbet and works surrounding the new settlement of Portarlington. At Belturbet the townspeople on the instructions of Ormond erected a fort in 1666 at their own expense, at a cost of £300, 'in resistance to Costello, Dillon, Nangle and divers other rebels, which then infested the whole country....'[3] Sited on high ground surrounding the church and graveyard, the earthwork bastions and ramparts of a rectangular fort still survive around much of the perimeter. Belturbet was garrisoned by Cromwellian forces under Venables in 1651, and it seems probable that he would have occupied this strategic site; the size of the work is comparable to the Green Fort at Sligo and other mid-seventeenth-century forts. It is recorded that during 1689 Colonel Wolseley fortified this site, and it is possible that he modified or repaired the earlier structure of 1666 here. The new town of Portarlington was set out in 1667: a plan of 1678 shows bastioned defences around the place, which is further protected by a loop of the River Barrow serving as an outer line of defence on three sides.[4]

The principal concern of those responsible for fortifications in Ireland during the Restoration was coastal defence. In 1666 Orrery reported that the western forts of Valentia, Bantry, Sherkin Island and Crookhaven were in a poor condition; he noted that the fort at Dunboy, which he had built, had been demolished, and that Kinsale was in as bad a condition as the other Munster forts.[5] The Second Dutch War, 1665- 67, in which the Dutch were joined by the French after January 1666, emphasised the lack of adequate coast defences in Ireland. The Dutch attack on the Medway at Chatham in June 1667 stressed the urgency of defences at Kinsale, and Orrery was active in the following two months strengthening Castle Park Fort and constructing earthworks to defend the harbour (Map 8).[6]

He strengthened the earthworks of Castle Park, where there were twenty-five pieces of ordnance: culverins, demi-culverins, and some sakers. One brass cannon of 7, three culverins and three iron demi-culverins were placed in the blockhouse, and a new work was constructed at Ringcurran Castle on the east side of the harbour. At Ringcurran on the lower platform there were six demi-cannon, eight culverins and six demi-culverins; an inner work here in the form of a *tenaille trace* mounted ten pieces of ordnance. It appears that the lower platform was the courtyard of the old castle, which Orrery repaired and backed with an earth rampart on two sides to resist gunfire from enemy ships. There were two foot companies and seventy gunners and matrosses (gunners' mates) in garrison at Ringcurran, with ten troops of horse drawn up in reserve nearby. Orrery reported that this site commanded all ships entering the harbour of Kinsale by means of the guns mounted on the southern platforms, and vessels sailing past the fort came within musket shot and under the guns facing westwards.

To fire on ships that might anchor to open fire on Ringcurran a battery was constructed on the opposite side of the estuary below Castle Park Fort, mounting ten pieces of ordnance. From the blockhouse at water level north-east of Castle Park a nineteen-inch cable was run across the harbour, six feet below the water; some distance within the cable was a boom, at the east end of which Orrery constructed a 150-foot long breastwork. At the west end of the boom a twelve-gun battery was erected, which mounted twelve demi-culverins. A nine-gun battery was constructed at Scilly, to the west of which was 'Queen Elizabeth's Old Tower'—the tower repaired by Sidney in 1576—where Orrery placed ordnance.

Two outworks or redoubts built by Prince Rupert in 1649 were repaired—these were on the narrow neck of land south-west of the fort—while within Castle Park there were five companies of foot, forty gunners and matrosses, and two hundred seamen. Should an enemy take the fort, Orrery concluded that all shipping in the harbour would be lost.

In addition to the new work at Ringcurran and the new batteries there were fireships, warships within the boom, and three ships south-west of the fort to provide flank fire on an enemy landing party. But these elaborate defensive preparations at Kinsale were not put to the test, as peace was signed at Breda in August 1667 with France, Denmark and the United Provinces of the Netherlands.

In November that year Orrery was in communication with Ormond stressing the need to retain Ringcurran as a garrison. He noted the old castle courtyard, where the wall was strengthened on two sides with an earth rampart to resist gunfire from ships, a new work within this, and 'without Ringcurran a bastion and a half hornwork, and I think more good cannon than any fort in Ireland.' In July, during the preparations for defence of the harbour, Orrery had requested permission to use timber from a ship in Kinsale for gun platforms, with the ribs for sleepers and the planks for platforms. He remarked that all the guns were on ships' carriages and they required timber platforms, as platforms made up of small stones were unsuitable for demi-cannon or culverins mounted on carriages with trucks or small wooden wheels. In 1672 the engineer Paulus Storff was in charge of alterations to Ringcurran Fort, for which he received payments from Orrery, but it was not until six years later that the decision was made to construct a permanent fort on the site.

William Robinson, engineer and surveyor-general of Ireland, was involved in works at Charlemont Fort in 1673. Repairs were carried out to the walls and bastions, and work was under way on the ditch fronting the ravelin and a new drawbridge. It is not clear if the ravelin was constructed by Owen Roe O'Neill, who strengthened the defences in 1642, or if it was a work built by Robinson. An account of 1689 implies that Robinson constructed a demi-lune or half-moon there, which must refer to the ravelin. Also in 1673 the lord lieutenant, the Earl of Essex, suggested that a citadel was required at Dublin, and Sir Bernard de Gomme, who was chief engineer to Charles II, visited Dublin and drew up proposals for a large citadel between the city and Ringsend, at an estimated cost of over £131,000.[7] One proposal depicts a pentagonal bastioned fort with ravelins covering each curtain and counterguards in front of each bastion, sited approximately in the area later occupied by Merrion Square. The length of each curtain was some 400 feet, with bastion faces of 350 feet and the flanks approximately 150 feet. The overall diameter including the outworks was some 2,800 feet. Another scheme has a similar fort but with less extensive outworks—there are only two ravelins—sited across the narrow peninsula of Ringsend; the small earlier fort of Ringsend is also depicted. At both sites extensive piling and land reclamation would have been necessary, adding considerably to the expense and difficulties of construction. In 1685 Thomas Phillips was

to propose a citadel sited on the higher ground of St Stephen's Green, overlooking the city, without the construction problems of the site nearer to the river and at Ringsend. [8]

In October 1677 Bantry Fort was described as 'built of lime and stone', with four bastions; the buildings within the fort to accommodate 200 men were in poor condition, the 'gates and drawbridge decayed'. The dry ditch surrounding the fort was also to be cleaned out, all at a cost of £400. Eight guns on standing carriages were required, at £56, eight more carriages were to cost £16, and repairs to the magazine £80. Twenty miles to the south-west, at Crookhaven, the fort was described as built of 'stone and clay, on a rock by the harbour side, having only two small bastions to the landward.' Some £500 was required to repair the fort; to mount the five guns and make platforms an additional £55 was needed.[9]

The fort at Kinsale was also in need of repair in 1677. The inner work or citadel required repairs to the masonry walls and buildings, while the outer line of ramparts and bastions of earthwork, and the blockhouse, were also defective. Repairs were estimated at £2,000, with a further £600 required for a 'large double platform' to the south-east of the fort overlooking the estuary on or near the site of a redoubt or battery constructed in 1667. Gun platforms in the fort and gun carriages for forty guns were also required, costing £360.[10]

Construction started in March 1678 at the opposite side of the harbour on a new permanent work at Ringcurran.[11] Robinson was in charge of the project, assisted by Captain James Archer. In accordance with instructions issued on 7 February at Dublin Castle, Archer was to remain on the site and take directions from Orrery, including advice on the hiring of masons and other workmen.[12] Work was to start on the seaward defences to secure the harbour from attack, followed by the defences on the landward side to the east and north. Castle Park Fort was to be inspected, repaired and improved. The instructions of February included details of materials and rates of pay: for each day's work the labourers were to receive sixpence, starting at five in the morning 'at beat of drum', with three breaks until seven in the evening, 'making in all twelve hours labour at all of which periods of time the drum shall beat to give notice throughout the works....' Five officers or overseers are listed: Captain John Martin, Captain William Crispin, James Bulgier, John Deoran and George Harvey. Martin, as general overseer, was paid three shillings a day; Crispin was 'clerk of the cheque'; and Harvey, as gunner's assistant, was 'to keep account of all tools and instruments'. Articles of agreement were signed on 12 March between Robinson and Archer 'on behalf of his Sacred Maj. Charles the Second', and Thomas Smith and William Armstead of Charleville 'to make contract ... with artificers and others building the work....' The contract was concluded with the approval of Orrery; Smith and Armstead agreed to build as directed by Robinson and Archer 'in and about where the old fort now standeth'. The contractors were to provide all materials and workmen, including 'masons, labourers, quarrymen, boatmen, carmen, instruments, tools, boats, ladders....'

The angles or quoins of the ramparts and bastions were to be built of hewn stone or ashlar, the gun-embrasures and sally ports to be similarly finished. The contractors were to be allowed to use material on the site forming the earlier fortification and the stones of the old castle of Ringcurran. The first stage of the contract appears to have been the lower batteries next to the sea, with the understanding that the contractors were to be retained to complete the rest of the fortifications.

Articles of agreement were also drawn up with Thomas Chudleigh of Kinsale, shipwright, on 7 April 1678, to make gun carriages to be delivered to Castle Park Fort when completed. Twenty-seven carriages were required, varying in cost from £3 6s for a saker or minion, culverins at £3 15s, and £4 4s for a demi-cannon. Chudleigh was also offered the option of making gun carriages for the new fort at Ringcurran at the same rates, where thirty-one guns were required. The carriages are described as platform or standing carriages, to be similar to those of the seven guns at the blockhouse below Castle Park.

An early plan of Ringcurran depicts a proposal for a regular pentagonal bastioned fort with a small ravelin protecting the entrance on the landward side, probably drawn by Robinson.[13] A section through the fort shows casemated gun positions at two levels on the sides overlooking the estuary; the lower level of gun-embrasures is masked by the wall of an external battery, a mistake unlikely to have been made by an experienced military engineer such as Archer, which perhaps reinforces the probability that the drawing is by Robinson. The bastions of this proposed fort have faces 77 feet long, the flanks 40 feet, similar in dimensions to those built eventually at Ringcurran; the flanks of the bastions are at right angles to the curtain, the system common in the first half of the seventeenth century. By the 1670s an obtuse angle here was accepted as better practice, making the flank at right angles to the 'line of defence' to the salient of the adjacent bastion. Ringcurran, later to be named Charles Fort, was to be built with the bastions in this improved form. The fort as built was a considerable modification and enlargement of this early proposal of a regular pentagonal fort; no bastion was constructed at the south-west angle, and the defences along the waterfront consisted of two levels of batteries only. An estimate that appears to be related to the early proposal for a pentagonal fort on the site of the present work, 'The Fort of Ringcorran calculated with the outworks', gives a total cost of over £10,000.

Another plan of the fort indicates it at an

intermediate stage of construction, and significantly the title of this plan is 'The Crown Work of Charles Fort'. [14] A crownwork was an extensive outwork to a fortress, and it appears that Orrery had proposed a regular pentagonal fort immediately to the north-east, in such a position that the siting and shape of the work that later became Charles Fort suggests that it was originally intended as an outwork. The plan depicts the works on the seaward side completed but parts of the landward defences unfinished; the three landward bastions made up of unmortared stonework 'for the present closing the crownwork' were to be removed with the outworks— the covered way and glacis—when the fortification was completed by the construction of the large pentagonal work inland. With the omission of these three landward bastions and outworks the layout takes the form of a crownwork to an adjacent fort on the higher ground to the northeast. The angle between the faces of the enclosure at each side of the central temporary bastion of unmortared stone is such that it would fit exactly between and in front of two bastions of a regular pentagonal fort. As further evidence there is the redoubt or citadel of the fort—an unusual arrangement in a relatively small fort designed for all-round defence; but a triangular work of this form with its own ditch, at the rear of a crownwork, was a further obstacle to an attacking force and provided additional protection to the curtain or length of rampart between the two flanking bastions of the principal work.

It seems that lack of finance to build Orrery's proposed pentagonal fort on the high ground inland led to the crownwork—its outwork to the south-west—becoming a fort that had the basic defect of being commanded by the higher ground to the rear. The plan of the fort depicting the landward bastions of unmortared stone must date from after August 1681, when Ringcurran was renamed Charles Fort following a visit by Ormond. In its half-finished state, with only the

seaward defences completed, the work could not have been defended against a properly conducted siege on the landward side. The fort was essentially a gun platform for artillery to defend the harbour until it was fully completed.

Ormond remarked during his visit in August 1681 on the difficulty and expense of making the work defensible on the landward side. In the following month, writing to the Earl of Longford, Ormond discussed the problem of completing and manning the fort: he said that he

should be as well pleased His Majesty would cause Fort Charles to be perfected to the full extent of the largest design if there could be any reasonable expectation of finding money to finish it, or if out of this little army it were not impossible to man it when finished…. Yet I am sure four frigates as they may be employed would be more for the service of the king and both kingdoms than a fort that will not probably be erected in seven years, nor then sufficiently manned considering that the sea batteries already finished do, or may when furnished with guns, secure the harbour to seaward… [15]

In February 1683 it was estimated that £1,500 was required to complete Charles Fort (by this time the proposed pentagonal fort on the high ground must have been abandoned): presumably the completion of the landward bastions and counterscarp in mortared stone, and the provision of barrack accommodation. At the same time over £7,000 had been expended on repairs to fortifications in Ireland. [16]

Charles Fort today is basically unchanged from its seventeenth-century layout. Minor changes have taken place in the ramparts and bastions, such as the blocking up or widening of some gun-embrasures; the interior of the fort has several later barrack blocks and ancillary buildings; but the external appearance of the fort is

Fig.53. Charles Fort Kinsale - the sea batteries from the north, before conservation work.

Fig. 54. Charles Fort Kinsale - the southern sea batteries and Charles Bastion, after conservation work.

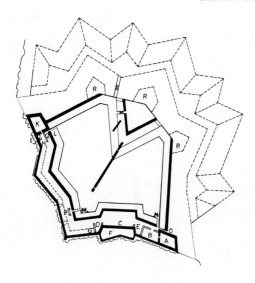 

Fig. 55. Plans of Charles Fort. Kinsale c.1681-1695:
Left: A plan of the crownwork of Charles Fort (after Staffordshire County Library Ms D 1778/v/3).
A Lighthouse Battery; B Princess Battery; C Ormonde Battery; D West Flank; E East Flank; F Orrery's Battery; G-H Royal Battery; I Storehouse; K Kinsale Battery; L-M Clarendon's Battery; M-N Queen's Battery; O Caves Port; P Ringcurran Port; Q Kinsale Port; R Bastions made up of un-mortared stone.
Right: The fort after plans by Phillips 1685, NLI Ms 3137 (31) and by Goubet, c. 1690, NLI Ms 2742. Traverses, place d'armes, and pow-der magazine as on plan by Corneille 1694-5, NLI 15 B 14 (11) are shown in broken line.

much as it was when drawn by Phillips in 1685. On the seaward fronts, on the south and west, two levels of gun batteries command the approach to Kinsale Harbour; at the south-east and north-west ends of the batteries or ramparts are demi-bastions with casemated gun emplace-ments at low level and gun platforms at high level (Figs.53, 54). Ramparts following the slope of the hillside link the demi-bastions with the landward bastions on the higher ground inland. The three landward bastions are solid gun platforms. The flanks of the demi-bastions and bastions are at an obtuse angle to the curtains, approximately at right angles to the 'line of defence' from the re-entrant angle to the salient of the adjacent bas-tion (Fig.55). Backing on to the central landward bastion is the triangular redoubt of the intended crownwork, originally protected by a ditch to the south and west. Entry was by means of a draw-bridge over the ditch and through the existing arched gateway. From the salient angle of the ditch of the redoubt a high traverse or wall ran towards the southwest angle of the sea batteries,

dividing the fort in half. This traverse provided some protection to the east side of the fort from low-trajectory fire from ships on the estuary to the west, and the west side of the interior from fire from the high ground inland to the south-east. Most of this traverse survives today, the part to the north nearer to the redoubt having been demolished in the middle of the eighteenth century to allow for the construction of the west-ern wing of the barracks built at that time.

The earliest barrack accommodation in the fort was a continuous line of buildings following the zigzag line of the inner side of the upper ram-part of the sea batteries on the west and south; this position gave them the maximum protection from cannon fire from enemy ships. One of these buildings was the governor's house, situated close to the southern end of the traverse. The ruined structure on this site may be the original build-ing, and it has a fine classical doorway, indicat-ing a late seventeenth or early eighteenth-century date. The terrace of barrack accommodation below the western sea batteries, now a ruined

Fig. 56. Charles Fort from the south-east, 1980 (Photo courtesy Dr. Daphne Pochin Mould).

shell, may incorporate part of the original build-ings, built here before 1685. The lower floor and cross walls are of masonry; the first-floor walls are brickwork, indicating perhaps extensive rebuilding. By the middle of the eighteenth cen-tury this terrace had been reduced in length to its present extent by the removal of several bays to the north, while the 'lodgements' or barracks behind the rampart of the southern batteries, east of the governor's house, had been removed, new accommodation being provided by the new square of barracks in the eastern half of the fort (Figs.56 and 57).

In 1685 Captain Thomas Phillips visited Ireland to carry out an inspection of the chief harbours, forts and fortifications; he was also to prepare plans and estimates for improvements. Phillips held the rank of third engineer and acted under the instructions of the master-general of the ordnance, Lord Dartmouth. Following an order in council by King Charles II in August

1684, Dartmouth instructed Phillips to go to Ireland and in conjunction with Robinson to sur-vey all the ordnance, arms and ammunition in the country. In addition Phillips was to view the 'several forts, castles and garrisons' and prepare plans of them, with proposals for improvements and estimates of costs. His report included Dublin, Duncannon and Passage, Cork, Waterford, Kinsale, Limerick and Scattery Island, Galway, Athlone, Derry Woragh on Lough Neagh, Culmore, Belfast and Carrickfergus.[17]

Of these places Phillips suggested that only Dublin, Passage, Kinsale, Limerick, Derry Woragh (replacing Charlemont Fort) and Culmore were capable of being fortified to resist a large army. His detailed survey and proposals were submitted to James II in March 1686. Phillips noted that many inland towns formerly considered strong, 'being encompassed with bogs and rivers', were no longer so because of improvements in the draining of bogs and the construction of new roads and bridges. As a result, inland places formerly of strategic importance were now of little consequence.

Dublin, as the capital of the country, was 'to be secured against all attempts....' The castle was in a poor condition following a recent fire and was unsuitable both as a residence for the lord deputy and as a store for arms, ammunition and powder. The Royal Hospital at Kilmainham, recently completed, was 'fit to receive the powder and the train of artillery' but was too far from the sea to be considered as a strong garrison (Fig.58). As both castle and hospital were unsuitable to be made into magazines or fortifications of any strength, Phillips revived the earlier project of a citadel for Dublin.

Phillips' scheme for a pentagonal citadel at St Stephen's Green was on a similar scale and layout to that proposed by de Gomme in 1673. The curtains were 380 feet in length, bastion faces 270 feet and the flanks some 125 feet. The overall diameter of the citadel from the salient angle of the counterscarp at a ravelin to the corresponding salient fronting a counterguard at the opposite side was some 2,500 feet. Counterguards or outworks in front of the bastions had faces 400 feet long (Fig.59). An armament of 250 iron guns for the work was estimated at £8,725, while the total cost of the citadel was over £126,000, compared with some £131,000 for the 1673 proposal by de Gomme. Phillip's proposal for a citadel at Dublin was on a much larger scale than any fort or citadel built in Britain or Ireland at that time, and may be compared with Tilbury Fort and Plymouth Citadel, both designed by de Gomme and then recently completed. Work started at Tilbury in 1670, continuing until 1683; it had been estimated to cost £47,000, an amount greatly exceeded in the construction. The overall dimension across the work from the counterscarp of the outer moat is some 1,800 feet, while the bastions are considerably smaller than those of

Fig. 57. Charles Fort- Guérite or sentry box on the south west salient of the sea batteries, before conservation work.

Fig. 58. The Royal Hospital Kilmainham, Dublin. Construction started in 1680. The architect, William Robinson, was also involved - with the engineer James Archer, on Charles Fort, on which work started in 1678.

Fig. 59. A Draught of the Citadel to be built over Dublin by Thomas Phillips, 1685, NLI Ms 3137 (2).

the proposed Dublin citadel. At Plymouth Citadel, which was under construction between 1666 and 1671, the bastions are of similiar size to those at Tilbury, while the overall dimensions including the out-works were some 1,200 by 900 feet. The Dublin proposal, containing extensive outworks of ravelins and counterguards, with bastion flanks having two levels of gun-embrasures, was much more ambitious and elaborate than Tilbury or Plymouth: Phillip's design reflects the developments in fortifications taking place on the Continent under military engineers such as Vauban and Coehoorn. In June 1684 Phillips had met Vauban at Luxembourg and visited the siege works there. He also studied the defences of the fortress towns of northern France, and was well qualified to comment on the state of the Irish fortifications in the following year.

Phillips' report continues with a discussion of

Duncannon Fort, which he considered incapable of being strengthened, being overlooked by high ground. He stressed the importance of Waterford Harbour, leading to three navigable rivers, but dismissed any idea of fortifying the city of Waterford and stated that it was too far from the sea to be relieved. His plan of Waterford depicts the medieval defences of curtain walls and towers, the layout of the streets, the blockhouse below Reginald's Tower and St Patrick's Fort or Citadel. For the defence of Waterford Harbour Phillips recommended Passage as a suitable place for a new fortification, on the hill to the west overlooking the village and the earlier blockhouse, at an estimated cost of some £44,000 including a chain and boom for the river. His plan of the proposed new work shows a rectangular fortification with two demi-bastions on the west front surrounded by a dry moat, noted as some eighty feet wide and twelve feet deep. On

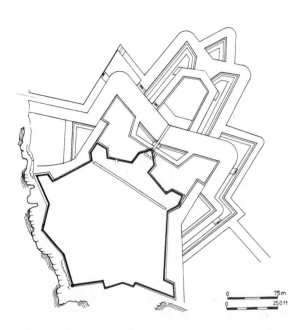

Fig. 60. Charles Fort: proposed outworks by Thomas Phillips, 1685, after NLI Ms 3137 (21).

the axis of the west front a ravelin masked by a counterguard protected the curtain. Two traverse walls linked the work to the waterside north and south of the blockhouse, each ending in a square redoubt. Phillips' perspective view of Passage includes the sixteenth century circular blockhouse surrounded by the *tenaille trace* outer work; in the distance is Duncannon Fort.

Cork Harbour was regarded as 'one of the most convenient places for an enemy to invade this kingdom.' Phillips proposed a blockhouse and boom at Haulbowline Island and redoubts or blockhouses to 'secure the passes' from Great Island. To secure the harbour would cost some £42,000. Phillips regarded Cork city as 'incapable of being made strong', as it was overlooked by hills to the north and south. A redoubt was proposed for the high ground north of the city at Shandon. To the south another redoubt was advocated on the 'Catt', the high ground commanding Elizabeth Fort; no work was constructed here, and the position was easily taken by the Williamite forces in their siege of Cork in 1690.

Phillips remarked on the advantage of Kinsale Harbour with its ready access to the sea, the town providing supplies for merchant ships, but there were other harbours of larger extent and greater depth of water. He noted the boom to provide security for shipping as 'quite rotten and destroyed'. Charles Fort was well built, but 'as to the strength to landward, or its terror to sea, I can say nothing, for it being so ill situated under the command of hills, that it is a very hard matter to cover the inhabitants thereof, on any occasion that they shall have to stand by the guns, or the sea batteries, the hills being so very near....' Phillips proposed an extensive outwork on the high ground north-east of the fort, the three landward bastions being replaced with this work, which was in the form of a large hornwork with a ravelin (Fig.60). His estimate for this was some £23,000, with an additional £300 to alter the barracks and storehouses in the fort. These were

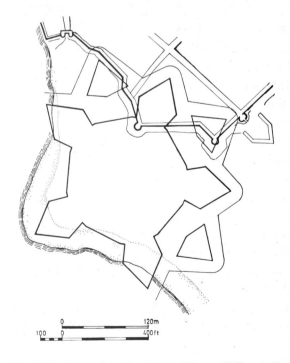

Fig. 61. Proposed citadel at Limerick by Thomas Phillips, 1685: a pentagonal citadel with three ravelins, overlapping the western wall of Irish Town. It was of similar size to Charles Fort, but with bastions twice the size. After NLI Ms 3137 (26).

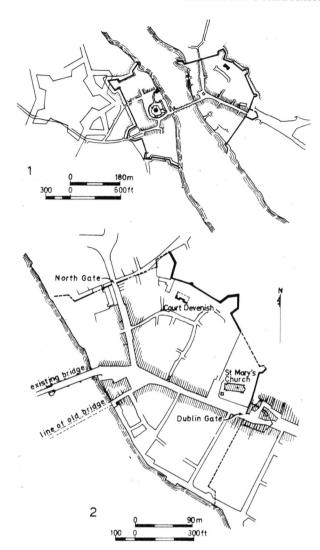

works at Castle Park, and facing the exterior of the rampart and interior of the parapet with brick or stone. The ditch was to be deepened, the platforms below the fort and the storehouse of the blockhouse were to be repaired, and two rows of barracks were to be built within the fort. With the building of a redoubt to the south-west and the construction of a boom, these works came to an estimated total of almost £6,000. With Waterford, Cork and Kinsale secured, Phillips was of the opinion that other harbours on the south coast were of no use to an enemy, while the harbours on the west coast, which had such a wild hinterland, were unsuitable for the landing of an invasion force.

Limerick had been reported to be the strongest place in Ireland, but Phillips found the walls in a poor condition, with Irish Town commanded by higher ground. He advocated the construction of a citadel to the west of Irish Town, occupying the ground between the north-western wall and the Shannon (Fig.61). This pentagonal bastioned work with three ravelins is depicted on his plan of Limerick, which shows the town walls, the castle and the Cromwellian citadel, as well as the layout of the streets and suburbs. Also shown on the plan (in broken line) is a proposal to enclose Irish Town with a large-scale bastioned trace on the south-east and east. It was also proposed that Scattery Island in the Shannon Estuary be fortified. The total cost of the Limerick works, including some £14,000 for enclosing Irish Town with bastioned defences and £8,000 for a work on Scattery Island, came to an estimated £78,000. The proposed citadel was somewhat larger than Tilbury Fort if the outworks at Tilbury are excluded, and smaller than that proposed for Dublin.

Phillips' plan of Galway depicts the town walls, the bastions and outer rampart built by the Confederates, and the two Cromwellian citadels. He proposed replacing the upper citadel with a much larger work, occupying the eastern

defective in being joined to the rampart, presumably leading to dampness damaging the timber work. Included in the estimate were platforms and carriages for seventy guns. Several guns were needed to complete the batteries in the fort, while repairs were needed at Castle Park Fort and a new boom was required to secure the harbour.

Phillips recommended repairing the earth-

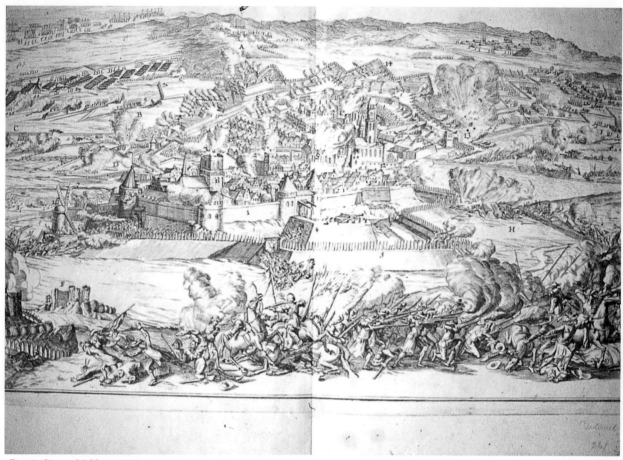

Fig.63. Siege of Athlone, 1691.

front of the town (it is shown in broken line on the plan, superimposed over the east wall and the outer rampart and bastions). A central bastion is flanked by demi-bastions to the north and south, while inside the town wall two more demi-bastions are indicated, of somewhat larger dimensions. This proposal for a new citadel at Galway was estimated at over £24,000. Phillips also suggested a redoubt on Mutton Island, of the same design as those proposed for Cork Harbour, and another on Fort Hill on the site of the early seventeenth-century fort dismantled by the Confederates; the Mutton Island redoubt was to be built first.

At Athlone the castle was noted as in good repair, but unsuitable for lodging a train of artillery. The plan depicts the masonry defences of wall and bastions enclosing the part of the town on the Leinster side of the Shannon, while on the western bank of the river the settlement around the castle was enclosed by earthwork bastions and ramparts of the Cromwellian period. Phillips proposed that a pentagonal bastioned fortification be sited on the high ground immediately west of Athlone; it was of the same layout and dimensions as his proposed citadel for Limerick (Fig.62).

In Ulster, Phillips described Charlemont Fort as surrounded on three sides by bog, but commanded by several hills. He advocated the construction of a new work some seven miles away to the north-east at 'Derry Woragh', a high peninsula projecting into Lough Neagh. As well as the natural strength of the position, the advantage of the lake as a means of communication was stressed, being some four hours' journey across Lough Neagh by boat, compared with the alternative of at least two days' march around the lake. The fortification proposed consisted of a form of hornwork on the landward front with two demi-bastions and a ravelin, the end of the promontory to be occupied by a pentagonal bastioned work. The estimated cost of the fortification was some £45,000, compared with £43,000 for the proposed pentagonal work at Athlone.

Derry was overlooked by hills and regarded by Phillips as 'incapable of being fortified' adequately . He advocated instead a fortification at Culmore, at a cost of some £18,000, including a boom across the river, which would secure the city and the estuary of the Foyle. His plan for Culmore depicts the small early seventeenth-century triangular fort at the end of the promontory backed by a much larger proposal of a complex fortress to mount 100 guns. Carrickfergus, 'an old strong castle', might be repaired and garrisoned, and the plan depicts a proposal for a front of two demi-bastions and a bastion as outworks between the castle and the town.

At Belfast he proposed a pentagonal bastioned citadel that incorporated a small harbour, the size of the fortification being somewhat larger than the works proposed for Limerick and Athlone. The Belfast citadel, estimated at just over £42,000, was to mount 250 guns, the same number as the citadel intended for Limerick. Phillips' plan of Belfast also shows his proposal for a bastioned trace enclosing the town, on a very much larger scale than the existing ramparts and bastions depicted, which are probably those constructed in 1642.

The fortifications in Phillips' report total over £554,000 in estimated cost. He concluded by suggesting that only six places be fortified as strongly as possible: Dublin with the proposed citadel, Passage, Kinsale, Limerick, Derry Woragh and Culmore, at a total of some £331,000, to which he added the works at Cork Harbour at £14,000.

Also included in the report is an abstract of ordnance in Ireland. Charles Fort, Kinsale, with seventy-five pieces of artillery and one mortar, was the strongest fortification with regard to the number and calibre of guns, including six demi-cannon or 32-pounders, three 24-pounders, twenty-one culverins, and a variety of smaller pieces. Phillips was critical of the armament here: 'There are several guns wanting to complete the batteries, those which are already there, being of different natures, and much less than they ought to be....' At Duncannon Fort there were only one 24-pounder and two culverins, the other ordnance of smaller calibre amounting to a further thirty-nine pieces; better batteries and larger guns were proposed for the defence of the channel here. The distribution of ordnance in Ireland recorded by Phillips in 1685 generally follows the pattern of some twenty years earlier: a few large-calibre pieces are noted at Dublin, Limerick, Galway, Cork, Athlone and other locations, while the smaller forts such as Bantry and Crookhaven are listed with demiculverins, 6-pounders, sakers and minions. Forts in earlier lists that are omitted from the 1685 abstract of ordnance include Inishbofin, Arkin and Valentia Island, while a variety of small calibre guns are listed at Wexford, New Ross, Kilkenny, Youghal, Carrickfergus, Drogheda, Carlingford and other towns.

Phillips' ambitious proposals for fortifications included a considerable increase in the ordnance in Ireland. The Dublin, Limerick and Belfast citadels were each to be armed with 250 guns, Derry Woragh with 125, and Athlone and Culmore each to be equipped with 100. The proposed outwork to Charles Fort was to mount 70 guns, almost doubling the armament there. In contrast, the abstract of ordnance lists only some 555 pieces of artillery and some mortars for all the fortifications in the country, the majority being medium to small calibre guns.

Captain Phillips' designs for new works were not carried out, but his plans and maps provide a valuable record of the principal towns, forts and harbours of Ireland as they were in 1685. Accurate plans of Carrickfergus and Derry depict the street layout and fortifications of these early seventeenth-century fortified towns. Similar plans of Dublin, Galway, Limerick, Waterford and Cork are of equal importance, and the surveys of Belfast and Athlone provide the earliest plans of those towns. His plans of Duncannon, Charles Fort and Charlemont and his perspective views of towns, harbours and forts are the earliest detailed and accurate drawings of these places (Fig.52).

Late seventeenth-century views by Francis Place include a drawing of Waterford in 1699 from the north (Fig.64).[18] The sixteenth-century blockhouse at Reginald's Tower, the riverside walls and the citadel appear to be accurately depicted when compared with Phillips' plan of the city. Thomas Dineley's sketches of the 1680s are more crudely drawn but include views of Limerick and Youghal and some country houses. The principal defensive element of these houses was a high wall enclosing the house, out-buildings and courtyards. Charleville, Co. Cork, designed by Orrery in 1661, was evidently enclosed by a walled courtyard and was unusual in being capable of defence by sixteen guns. A plan of 1671 of Burton House, also in Co. Cork, shows the house surrounded by a symmetrical layout of courtyards enclosed by a wall with square flankers at the corners. The flankers in this proposal for Burton are shown with walls battered at the base to form a slight salient angle, resulting in a plan form at ground level similar to an angle-bastion. Another house surrounded by walled enclosures with corner flankers was Rathcline, near Lanesborough, Co. Longford. Within the enclosures were the outbuildings and garden; the one containing the house and outbuildings—a less formal layout than that proposed for Burton—

was some 65 by 75 yards, the walled garden attached to this enclosure being of similar dimensions. There were square flankers at the corners of the house enclosure and at the outer two corners of the walled garden. A contemporary plan depicts a canal supplied with water from Lough Ree, ending in a formal layout with a large artificial island, noted as a redoubt. The ruins of the house, perimeter walls and gateways survive at Rathcline today.[19] Within the house enclosure is part of an early seventeenth-century house with remains of buildings of the 1660s and later structures.

The accession of the Catholic James II in 1685 appeared to threaten the power of the Protestant minority in Ireland. However, in 1688 William of Orange landed in England, and James fled to France. In March 1689 James landed at Kinsale in an attempt to recover his throne. The war between the supporters of James II and William of Orange from 1689 to 1691, brought into prominence several inland towns that had not been surveyed by Phillips in 1685, as his concern was principally with the seaports and harbours liable to attack from overseas. In Ulster the Protestant colonists at Derry and Enniskillen held out against the Jacobite forces.

The defenders of Derry held out for some four months until the siege was raised at the end of July 1689. The early seventeenth-century ramparts and bastions were strengthened with a ravelin outside Bishop's Gate, and Windmill Hill was held by the besieged with redoubts and trenches. The attacking force had few heavy guns and mortars, and the attack on Derry became essentially a blockade, as the walls could not be breached by gunfire. Downstream a boom was constructed across the Foyle under the supervision of the French naval officer Pointis, and redoubts were built at each end of the boom on the river bank, to mount guns to fire on ships attempting to break the boom and sail upstream to relieve the city.

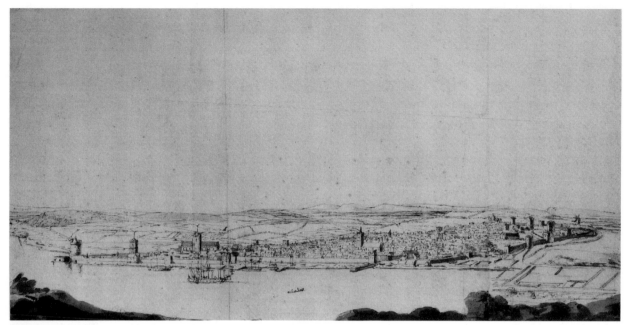

Fig. 64. A view of Waterford by Francis Place, 1699. On the left below the Reginald's Tower is the blockhouse, on the right is the citadel or St.Patrick's Fort. Courtesy of National Gallery of Ireland No.7533.

In September 1689 it is recorded that the soldiers of the Irish army were busy fortifying Dublin, 'trenching streets', setting up gates and palisades, and establishing a garrison in Trinity College. It seems likely that earthwork defences and trenches may have been constructed in the suburbs, outside the walled city; however, Dublin does not appear to have been fortified as much as other centres such as Sligo, Dundalk, Athlone, Limerick and Galway. After the Battle of the Boyne in July 1690 no attempt was made by the Jacobite forces to hold Dublin, which suggests that little effort had been made to strengthen the city with additional fortifications.

At Sligo, extensive fortifications were constructed surrounding the town, with the Green Fort forming a salient strong-point. The town changed hands several times during the Jacobite War and was of strategic importance on the route from Ulster into Connacht. Williamite supporters held Sligo early in 1689 but left in March, intending to join the Derry garrison, leaving the town to be occupied by their opponents, who used it as a base for attacking Enniskillen. Later that year

the Jacobite forces under Sarsfield abandoned Sligo, and the Williamites again garrisoned the place. A force from Sligo advanced on Boyle, where an engagement took place resulting in a Jacobite withdrawal; it is possible that the pentagonal fort just north of Boyle may have been constructed by the Irish, or by the Sligo forces who held Boyle for a short time. When Sarsfield again advanced on Sligo the Cromwellian fort near the river was held by a force commanded by a French Huguenot captain, St Sauveur, while the Green Fort was garrisoned by an Enniskillen detachment. After a gallant resistance, Sligo surrendered to the Jacobites, and a contemporary plan depicts the fortifications around the town and additional works at the Green Fort constructed by them at the end of 1689. The fort of the Cromwellian period close to the bridge is noted as the 'Stone Fort', while the earlier Green Fort on the high ground to the north-east is named the 'Earth Fort'. To the north-west a detached redoubt was sited a short distance outside the fortifications.[20]

In the summer of 1690 Charlemont Fort surrendered to the Williamites, and the commander of the garrison there, Sir Teague O'Reagan, was placed in charge of Sligo. He brought the guns from the Stone Fort up to the Green Fort, which he considered the key point of the defences. Sligo held out until September 1691, the Green Fort having at that time a Jacobite garrison of 600 men and sixteen guns; it was regarded by their opponents as a strong fortification. The earthwork ramparts and bastions survive on the site today, but the outworks constructed in 1689 have disappeared.

A contemporary plan of Dundalk by the Williamite engineer Goubet indicates extensive fortifications outside the medieval walls, including a ravelin to the west, a ravelin outside the south gate, which is flanked by a bastion and demi-bastion, and works to the north of the town extending to the river bank and bridge.[21] These fieldworks were either constructed by Schomberg, the Williamite commander who advanced from Ulster as far as Dundalk late in 1689, or by the Irish army, which took over Dundalk when Schomberg retreated north to Lisburn. The town was held by the Jacobites until June 1690.

After the Boyne an attack was made on Athlone, where the Irish forces held the town on both sides of the river under Colonel Richard Grace. The garrison evacuated the Leinster town on the approach of the Williamite force and successfully defended the bridge. Works had already started at Athlone under the French engineer, Loziers d'Astier, late in 1689 and additional defences were being considered in November 1690. Early in 1691 work started on these fortifications, delayed by bad weather and shortage of labour. Proposals included two ravelins, a counterguard, a covered way, and other improvements to the works on the west side of the town. Robert, the French engineer stationed at Athlone, advocated defending the town on both sides of the river and proposed strengthening the

masonry wall of the Leinster town with earthen banks, presumably in the form of a rampart behind the wall. However, Noblesse, the chief engineer, ordered the works on the Connacht side to be carried out, evidently stopping the works intended by Robert on the eastern side of the river, so that little was done to strengthen the town here. The defences of the town were essentially as they were in the Cromwellian period, a masonry wall with bastions surrounding the Leinster town, with earthwork ramparts and bastions enclosing the Connacht settlement around the castle. The two parts of the town were linked by the masonry bridge built in 1566-67.[22]

A plan of Athlone is included in an account of the war by George Story, who was with the Williamite army.[23] A ravelin is depicted outside the rampart of the Connacht town, which must have been built by the French engineers; otherwise the plan generally agrees with an earlier French plan that shows a covered way with places d 'armes and traverses on the counterscarp of the ditch on the Leinster side—evidently a proposal that Robert was unable to carry out. When the Williamite forces attacked Athlone for the second time, in June 1691, they besieged and captured Ballymore in Westmeath, which lay in their line of march from Mullingar. This earthwork fortification was not a strong position and was taken after bombardment. The Jacobite garrison held what was essentially the mid-seventeenth-century fieldwork here, with perhaps some minor improvements and rebuilding, but the place was overlooked by high ground and exposed to cannon and mortar fire.[24] The Leinster side of Athlone was taken by the Williamites despite some strong resistance by the Irish garrison, who withdrew across the bridge; the western side of the town and the castle were then bombarded, and eventually assaulted at the end of June (Fig.63). Disagreement between the French engineers had resulted in little work being carried out on the Leinster town defences, while the works carried out on the Connacht town made it much more difficult for any attempt to be mounted to drive the Williamites out of Athlone.

The Jacobite defeat at Aughrim in the following month cleared the route to Galway, where French engineers had also been active in strengthening the fortifications. Galway was most open to attack from high ground on the east, and it was the eastern wall of the town that had been reinforced with an outer line of ramparts and bastions by the Confederates in the years before the Cromwellian forces besieged it. The eastern side of the fortifications was also the site of Captain Phillips' proposal for a large-scale citadel in 1685, and it was here that the French engineers attempted to improve the defences. *A Continuation of the Impartial History of the Wars of Ireland* by Story has a plan of Galway. A ravelin and covered way in advance of the east front of the earlier fortifications, a counterguard masking the south-east bastion, and some distance in advance of this a detached triangular work or redoubt flanked by two *lunettes* or ravelins, appear to have been constructed under the supervision of the French engineer officers. The redoubt, not quite completed, was attacked and the defenders were driven out. Two gun batteries are depicted on Story's plan on or near the site of the early seventeenth-century fort or citadel and close to the captured redoubt, overlooking the town; the Williamite guns and mortars here at these batteries induced the beginning of negotiations for a surrender. Phillips in his report had proposed the construction of a redoubt here on the site of the earlier fort. In fact Galway surrendered before the besieging force had brought up their heavy artillery, and with a more determined garrison might have held out for some time.

There were two sieges of Limerick during the Jacobite War. After the Boyne the city became the main strong-point of the Irish army, and in July and the first week of August 1690 efforts were made to improve the defences. A ditch was excavated outside the walls—probably the cleaning out or enlarging of an existing dry ditch or moat—and a covered way constructed on the counterscarps protected by a palisade. Some detached works or redoubts were built outside the walls of Irish Town and houses in the suburbs destroyed to provide a clear field of fire for the defenders. As in the siege of 1651, Irish Town was the place most open to attack, particularly from the south and east, where the two Cromwellian siege forts still survived on the high ground. The forces under William of Orange established themselves in this area about half a mile from the walls of Irish Town, but the destruction of their siege train of heavy guns by Sarsfield a week later was a considerable loss and delayed preparations for the siege. The raid on the convoy of guns and ammunition wagons resulted in the loss of ammunition, gunpowder and two of the siege guns—24-pounders—and was to contribute to the ending of the siege at the end of August.

The eastern wall of Irish Town to the north of the south-east corner tower was breached by batteries set up some eighty yards away: the breach is recorded by Story as having been twelve yards wide but was considerably wider according to Boisselau, the French governor in command of the garrison. New Road crosses the line of the wall today on the site of the breach. Boisselau made a retrenchment behind it on which he mounted artillery, and the Williamite assault was repulsed with some particularly hard fighting, during which the attackers reached the Black Battery, a platform on the rampart adjacent to the corner tower of Irish Town. Guns on the eastern bastion of the Cromwellian citadel contributed to the defence of the breach.

Phillips' survey of Limerick provides an accurate plan of this part of the city as it was five years earlier.[25] Irish resistance, bad weather and shortage of ammunition as a result of Sarsfield's attack on the siege train all contributed to the withdrawal of the Williamite forces from their positions outside Limerick, and the Irish army held the line of the Shannon for another year.

In September 1690, after the siege of Limerick had been abandoned, an expedition under Marlborough arrived off Cork Harbour with the intention of taking Cork and Kinsale. The ships were fired on from the eastern side of the harbour entrance, either from Prince Rupert's Tower or from Corkbeg Fort. The plan of Cork Harbour by the Williamite engineer Goubet shows a battery here with six embrasures in advance of a work incorrectly noted as Corkbeg Fort, which is in fact Rupert's Tower. Phillips' plan of the harbour shows this work with Corkbeg Fort and its detached battery overlooking the harbour entrance a short distance to the north; on the opposite headland on the west side of the harbour entrance a battery is indicated. Goubet depicts a square bastioned fort here with two lines of gun-embrasures overlooking the harbour entrance just to the east of the fort.[26] It seems probable that these works on the site of the later Ford Camden were erected by the Jacobites. A more determined defence of the narrow harbour entrance here might have prevented or delayed the attack on Cork and Kinsale.

After landing at Passage West, Marlborough's troops marched to Cork and established a position at the Cat Hill overlooking Elizabeth Fort and the southern part of Cork, guns being set up here to fire on the city, and Danish troops advanced on the city from the north to attack outworks at Shandon Castle. Cork was vulnerable to attack from the high ground to the north and south, and both the outpost on the Cat Hill and the works at Shandon, which included a redoubt and a ravelin, were abandoned by the Irish troops. The Williamites now had possession of these heights, bombarded Elizabeth Fort, and fired on the city from the north, from batteries near Shandon. A breach was made in the south-

ern part of the eastern wall, and a combined assault was launched by English and Danish troops; negotiations were opened to discuss terms of surrender, and the Williamite forces occupied Elizabeth Fort, entering Cork on the following day.

The forces of the Prince of Orange moved on to Kinsale, where the Jacobites had abandoned the walled town and were holding out in the two forts, Castle Park or the Old Fort and the new Charles Fort on the eastern side of the estuary. A French account of Kinsale some six months earlier, in April 1690, describes work in progress at Castle Park, and it seems probable that the masonry facing to the south-west curtain and the two flanking bastions here on the landward front dates from this time. One of the bastions of Charles Fort was undergoing repairs, and the covered way was evidently not in existence, being only marked out at the time of the French report, which also noted that the place was commanded by the high ground inland.[27]

Castle Park was attacked and taken by storm on 3 October 1690, and on the same day trenches were begun before Charles Fort. Six 24-pounders and two mortars opened fire on the fort on 12 October, and two more 24-pounders arrived the next day. On the 15th a breach was made by the Danish gunners, and the counterscarp was in the possession of the attacking force; terms of surrender were agreed, and the next day the garrison marched out, being allowed to go to Limerick. The attack had been concentrated on the central landward bastion, and the adjacent curtain was breached. Goubet's plan of Kinsale shows the two forts and the two siege batteries inland of Charles Fort. The *chemin couvert* or covered way of the fort is depicted on his larger-scale plan of the fort, and from this it is evident that the covered way must have been completed to some degree since the French report the previous April. A Danish account notes the absence of traverses on the covered way—confirmed by their absence on Goubet's plan—as contributing to the garrison abandoning this part of the fortification; the troops here were exposed to enfilade fire, and traverses flanking the *places d'armes* would have provided them with some protection. Traverses were added to the covered way some years later, when it was rebuilt to some extent when repairs were carried out to other parts of the fort. According to Würtemburg, who shared the command of the Williamite forces with Marlborough, there were 94 guns in Charles Fort, including 34 of brass.

Fortifications constructed during the Jacobite War included forts at Enniskillen and works at Belturbet constructed by the Williamite forces, defences at Ardee erected by the Irish army, and works to cover bridges and fords on the Shannon, also built by the Jacobite forces, who held the line of the river after their defeat at the Boyne in July 1690. Outworks were built at Clonmel by the Danish troops of William of Orange; there were also fortifications constructed by his forces at Mullingar, Roscrea, Thurles and Birr Castle, while Ross Castle in Co. Kerry was one of the principal Jacobite strongholds in the south-west, strengthened with outworks. Williamite forces captured two forts in Kerry in their attempt to take Ross Castle late in 1690. Fortifications are recorded at the Danish garrison at Fermoy Bridge in December 1690. It is clear that fieldworks were constructed at most of the towns occupied by the soldiers of each side where there was a possibility of attack from their opponents. Encampments and strategic positions were also fortified. Many works erected during the warfare of 1641 to 1652 must have been occupied and rebuilt to some extent; at Youghal earthen outworks at the south wall and gate constructed when the town was besieged by Castlehaven in 1645 were to be repaired by the Williamite forces in September 1690.

At Enniskillen two square bastioned forts were built as outworks to the town; on Fort Hill to the east of the town one of these survives today with later modifications.[28] Constructed in 1689 when Enniskillen was held by Ulster forces fighting for the Prince of Orange, it is 100 feet square, the bastions having faces some 40 feet in length and flanks of about 20 feet. The fort on the west side of the town was evidently smaller than the east fort, according to a map of Enniskillen depicting the place at the time of the Jacobite War. The site of the west fort is now occupied by a late eighteenth-century redoubt. On Trannish Island on Upper Lough Erne is a square earthwork fort with demi-bastions at the corners: it is possible that this also dates from 1689-90, but equally possible that it originates from the Confederate or Cromwellian wars or from the Elizabethan period, when this form of fort was quite common.[29] At Belturbet, Williamite forces under Colonel Wolseley are recorded as having fortified the churchyard, presumably occupying and improving the earlier fort here. At the eastern side of the town he constructed another work, apparently at the place known as the Deanery Banks, where there seems to have been a square fort or redoubt. These fortifications were constructed in 1689, and early in the following year Wolseley was preparing to attack a Jacobite fort at Cavan.

During the winter of 1690-91 Sarsfield commanded detachments holding the line of the Shannon, with headquarters at Athlone. There were fortifications and entrenchments at all the important bridges and fords, including Portumna, Meelick, Banagher, Raghra (later Shannonbridge), Lanesborough and Jamestown. At Lanesborough there was an earthen fort close to the bridge early in 1691 when Williamite forces made an ineffective attempt to cross the Shannon here.[30] Sarsfield also had garrisons in Westmeath and other areas east of the Shannon at this time, but he made the mistake of considering Ballymore to be a strong position, the place being easily taken by the Williamites in 1691.

A plan of Birr in 1691 by the engineer Michael Richards, who served under Ginkel, depicts the town and castle with fortifications erected by the Williamite garrison. An irregular line of defences enclosed the church and linked onto the castle, while the plan is also of interest in showing a more extensive line of defence or entrenchment dating from the Cromwellian period enclosing the town.[31]

Goubet's plan of the walled town of Clonmel shows the layout of the town and medieval walls with the addition of works outside the gates and corner towers: these were erected by Brigadier Elnberger of the Danish contingent with the Williamite army. A report of October 1690 notes that he constructed six ravelins with a counterscarp. Goubet's plans of Irish fortifications include Derry, Culmore, Carrickfergus, Belfast, Charlemont, Athlone, Galway, Bantry Fort, Charles Fort and Kinsale, Cork, Cork Harbour, Waterford and Duncannon, as well as those of Dundalk, Limerick, Kinsale and Clonmel described above.[32] While not as detailed and perhaps not as accurate as the plans and maps in the report by Captain Phillips of 1685, they are of value in depicting the additional fortifications built during the war and the siegeworks at several places such as Derry, Athlone, Limerick and Kinsale.

At the end of August 1691 Limerick was again under siege, by forces under the command of Ginkel, who had taken Athlone and Galway in the previous months. A plan of Limerick by Goubet shows a line of outworks consisting of earthwork bastions and ramparts outside the wall of Irish Town on the east, south and west. The counterscarp of the moat is shown with a covered way having *places d'armes* at intervals. The north and west of English Town were protected by a moat and glacis, more regular and extensive than the ditch depicted on the plan by Phillips of six years earlier. To the north of English Town a square bastioned fort with ditch,

covered way and glacis was constructed by the Limerick garrison and is shown on Goubet's plan. It is indicated in a much simplified outline on the first edition of the Ordnance Survey, and was evidently about 150 feet square, comparable in size to such mid-seventeenth century forts as the Green Fort at Sligo and Bantry Fort. Correspondence from Noblesse, the chief engineer of the French forces in Ireland, mentions the construction of a fort at Limerick to be completed by the end of May 1691, most likely a reference to this work. Also in that month the bastions and ramparts surrounding Irish Town were to be completed in a few weeks, with the covered way on the counterscarp finished and fitted with palisades. There are references to other works at English Town, and a plan that accompanied the correspondence of Noblesse depicts six bastions linked by ramparts outside the walls of Irish Town; one of these encloses an earlier ravelin outside the south-west gate, which is shown on Phillips' plan of 1685.

These earthworks planned by the French engineers and constructed after the first siege of Limerick appear to have been the most extensive fortifications built by the forces of King James II. As a result of these new works Irish Town in particular must have been much stronger at the time of the second siege, by which time the breach in the east wall must have been repaired. Siege batteries were established to the east of English Town and south-west of Irish Town. Ginkel's troops crossed the Shannon and occupied the west bank, cutting off communications between the garrison and Co. Clare. By the end of September a cease-fire had been agreed, and this was followed by negotiations for surrender. Limerick was still a place of strength, with adequate provisions and ammunition, the garrison expecting aid from a French fleet due to arrive with money and supplies at any time.

The 'Articles of Limerick' included the agreement that those Irish soldiers who wished to go to

France were to be transported there by shipping provided by Ginkel, and those officers who decided to stay in Ireland were to retain their estates. Sarsfield and some 14,000 men left Ireland, to form the basis of the Irish regiments in the French service and other European countries.

The Jacobite War brought to Ireland many foreign military engineers: with the forces of James II were French engineers responsible for works at Ardee, Athlone, Galway, Limerick and other places; with inadequate tools and equipment they also supervised the siege works at Derry and redoubts to protect the boom across the River Foyle. Many of the engineers serving William of Orange were Huguenots, such as Rudolph Corneille, who was later to work on repairs to Charles Fort and barracks at Kinsale and elsewhere. The principal involvement of those engineers who were to stay in Ireland after the end of the war was to be the repair of fortifications and the design and construction of the many new barracks that were to form an important part of the Williamite settlement of Ireland. For the following century the Royal Navy was to provide the principal means of defence against external attack, and few new fortifications were constructed until the threat of invasion combined with insurrection compelled the British government to embark on the most ambitious scheme of defence works ever undertaken in Ireland.

Chapter 4
A Century of Neglect, 1691-1793

THE HUNDRED YEARS THAT followed the Treaty of Limerick in 1691 passed without regular military conflict within Ireland, in contrast to the preceding century, which witnessed three periods of intense warfare in which both inland fortifications and the walled seaport towns played an important part.

In order to secure the Williamite settlement, an ambitious scheme of barrack building was undertaken in the closing years of the seventeenth century and the opening decade of the next. As well as accommodation for horse and foot in barracks situated at most of the important towns throughout the country, a number of smaller defensible barracks or redoubts were constructed in areas where there was considerable activity on the part of tories or rapparees and at strategic locations such as 'passes' in isolated or difficult terrain. The redoubts were surrounded by a wall or rampart and in some instances were situated within an earlier fort, such as those at Finnea and Bellaghy. The more numerous cavalry and infantry barracks were enclosed by a high perimeter wall, usually with no particular consideration given to defence.

In the years immediately following the Jacobite War and in the first two decades of the eighteenth century a certain amount of activity is recorded in the repair of fortifications, including works at Charles Fort, Kinsale, and at the defences of Athlone, Galway, and Limerick. Mutton Island Fort at Galway was rebuilt, and there were proposals for a new redoubt near the Cromwellian fort at Bantry. A plan was also drawn up for a fort on the site of Dunboy Castle at the western entrance to Berehaven.

There appears to have been less activity in repairs to fortifications after about 1720— both town defences and coastal forts were neglected— and by the middle of the eighteenth century the walls of such places as Galway and Limerick were in a ruinous condition. An ambitious proposal to build an arsenal in the form of a star fort in the Phoenix Park, Dublin, in 1710 was not completed, and some twenty-five years later the Magazine Fort was erected nearby. Soon afterwards the fort at Cove (Cobh) overlooking Cork Harbour was constructed. Repairs are recorded at Charles Fort, Duncannon, and Charlemont, works carried out from time to time and in response to the threat of war or invasion. Britain relied on the sea power of the Royal Navy to retain colonies overseas and for home defence, a reliance that was an important factor in the neglect of coastal fortifications.

Thurot's raid on Carrickfergus in 1760, resulting in the capture of the castle there, demonstrated that naval power alone was not enough to ensure protection against enemy attack. John Paul Jones captured the small fort at the English seaport of Whitehaven in 1778, which resulted in the construction of several new batteries to protect the harbour. For a time during the American War of Independence the French navy challenged that of Britain, and for some weeks the combined French and Spanish fleets controlled the English Channel. In Ireland the Volunteers were organised to resist invasion, and new fortifications were constructed at Cork Harbour and in the Shannon Estuary. After the war these works were abandoned but had to be occupied again some ten years later, in 1793, when war with the French Republic renewed the need for coastal defence.

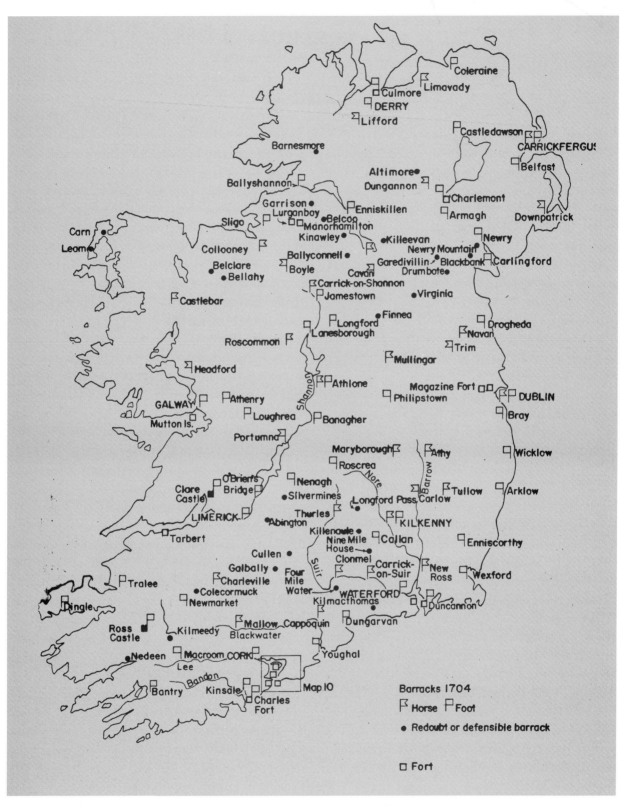

Map 9. Ireland 1691-1793.

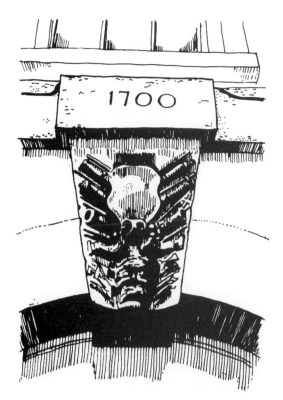

Fig. 65. The keystone of Ballyshannon Barracks, Co. Donegal, 1700.

Apart from Fort George near Inverness, built after the Jacobite rising of 1745-46, the principal fortifications constructed in Britain during the eighteenth century were works to defend the naval bases of Plymouth, Portsmouth and Chatham. The fortifications at Cork emphasised the growing importance of the harbour as a naval anchorage and as an assembly point for convoys of merchant vessels sailing to and from North America or the West Indies.

By 1704 there were over ninety new barracks in Ireland, of which about one-third were cavalry barracks, located principally in the midlands and at inland towns.[1] Of the infantry barracks some twenty-five were classed as redoubts, each noted as accommodating a company of foot in 1704 but in 1727 listed as housing a half-company. At most of the cavalry garrisons there was a troop of horse, and at the infantry barracks one or two companies of foot. At larger towns such as Kilkenny, Cork, Waterford, Galway, Athlone and Carrickfergus, the barracks housed much greater numbers, while the largest barrack complex was in Dublin (Map 9).

Among the earliest barracks constructed were those at Athlone in 1697 and at Cork in 1698. At Ballyshannon Barracks there is a date-stone of 1700; the building may have been designed by Thomas Burgh, who succeeded Robinson as engineer and surveyor-general at that time (Fig. 65). Another barrack that survives is at Bray, Co. Wicklow, now converted into private houses; it was constructed by 1700 and must have been one of the first new garrisons close to Dublin.

Records indicate that barracks at Navan and Drogheda were constructed by 1702, and at the same time the Dublin Barracks (now Collins Barracks) were under construction. The engineer Rudolph Corneille was involved in the construction of the barrack at Cork in 1698, and may have been responsible for the erection of that at Waterford on the site of the citadel, for which a contract was drawn up in the same year. His plan of the barrack at Kinsale is dated 1701.

In Connacht there were redoubts at Carn and Leam, near Mullet (Belmullet), which probably housed the two companies of foot listed for Mullet (Table 1).

The redoubts were concentrated in the southern part of Ulster, from Fermanagh across Cavan

Fig.66. The north-east bastion, at Manorhamilton, Co. Leitrim.

Leinster

Horse:		Foot:		
Athy		Arklow	*Finnea	
Carrick-on-Suir		Bray	Enniscorthy	
Carlow		Callan	Kilkenny	
Dublin		Carlingford	Philipstown	
Kilkenny		Dublin	Wicklow	
Longford		Duncannon	Wexford	
Maryborough		Drogheda		
Navan				
New Ross				
Tullow				
Trim				

Munster

Horse:		Foot:		
Cappoquin		*Abington	Limerick	
Clonmel		Bantry	*Longford Pass	
Charleville		Cork	Macroom	
Mallow		*Colecormuck	*Nedeen	
Thurles		*Cullen	Newmarket	
		Dungarvan	Nenagh	
		Dingle	*Nine Mile House	
		*Four Mile		
		Water	Ross Castle	
		*Galbally	Roscrea	
		*Kilmacthomas	Tralee	
		Kinsale	Waterford	
		*Kilmeedy	Youghal	
		*Killenaule	*Silvermines	

Connacht

Horse:		Foot:		
Athlone		Athenry	Carrick-on-Shannon	
O'Brien's Bridge		Athlone	Galway	
Boyle		Banagher	Jamestown	
Castlebar		*Bellaghy	Lanesborough	
Collooney		*Belcare	*Mullet	
Headford		Clare Castle	Sligo	
Loughrea				
Portumna				
Roscommon				

Ulster

Horse:		Foot:		
Belturbet		Armagh	Charlemont	
Cavan		*Altmore	*Drumbote	
Carrickfergus		*Ballyconnell	Enniskillen	
Downpatrick		*Belcoo	*Garrison	
Dungannon		Ballyshannon	*Garedivillin	
Lifford		Belfast	*Killeevan	
Limavady		*Blackbank	Derry	
		*Kinawley	Newry	
		Culmore	*Newry Mountain	
		Coleraine	*Virginia	
		Carrickfergus		

*redoubt

Table I. Barracks in use in Ireland in 1704.

and Monaghan to south Armagh; in the west there were two in Mayo and two in Sligo; in Munster they were located in Tipperary, Waterford, east Limerick, and north-west Cork, with one at Nedeen in Co. Kerry, at the site of the Cromwellian fort. The only redoubt in Leinster appears to have been the fort at Finnea in Co. Westmeath, which was a garrison during the reign of Charles II.

The regimental records of the Royal Scots Regiment note that several detachments occupied redoubts in Ireland in the early decades of the eighteenth century. In 1716 half-companies of the Ist Battalion were stationed at six of the redoubts in Munster, while the 2nd Battalion was quartered at Charlemont Fort, the redoubts at Altmore, Drumbote and Garedivillin, and at other barracks. The regiment had half-companies at various redoubts in 1718 and again in 1727-28 and 1730. Later records show detachments of the Royal Scots at redoubts in Ulster and Munster between 1733 and 1740. Evidently, by 1727, a number of these outposts were not occupied, and many were not continuously garrisoned. It appears that by the middle of the century most were no longer in use, the troops being quartered in the barracks in the towns and cities.

At Longford Pass redoubt in Co. Tipperary, south of Urlingford, earthen ramparts enclose the ruins of a two-storey masonry building.[2] It is possible that this post was first established during the Jacobite War to control the river crossing here: the Williamite engineer Romer was engaged on fortifications at Cork, Thurles, and Longford —presumably Longford Pass—late in 1690. At Barnesmore in Co. Donegal remains survive of the redoubt: a stone building with musket-loops in the southern wall commanding the Pass or Gap of Barnesmore. A number of the redoubts are shown on the first edition of the Ordnance Survey maps, variously noted as 'Old barrack' or 'Barrack (in ruins)', but the exact location of many of them awaits more detailed investigation.

The redoubts may be compared to the fortified barracks built in Scotland between 1717 and 1723 following the Jacobite rising of 1715: these were rectangular enclosures with bastion-shaped projections at two diagonally opposite corners; within this perimeter defence were barrack buildings three storeys in height.[3] These four Highland garrisons held larger detachments than the half-companies in the Irish redoubts, and were more extensive as a result. The smaller fortified posts in Ireland appear to have been much less ambitious architecturally than the defensible barracks in Scotland, which may more readily be compared to the fortified barracks along the Wicklow Military Road that were constructed in the opening years of the nineteenth century.

During the eighteenth century new barracks for cavalry and infantry were built from time to time, in some instances replacing those constructed between 1697 and 1704. At Galway, barracks were constructed adjacent to the Cromwellian upper citadel, inside the south-eastern angle of the town wall, in 1734; in 1749 a barrack was built on the site of the lower citadel beside the bridge; and in the same year Lombard Street barrack was erected. In Cork, in addition to the barrack constructed in 1698 (unusual in having bastion-shaped projections at the corners of the perimeter wall) new accommodation was built for troops in Elizabeth Fort nearby in 1719, noted on Rocque's map of Cork of 1759 as the 'New Barracks'.

In Co. Leitrim two barracks evidently constructed before 1722—in 1727 they each housed a company of foot—were Lurganboy and Manorhamilton. At Lurganboy traces of earthen ramparts and angular bastions survive on the site. On the first edition of the Ordnance Survey a rectangular enclosure is depicted with acute-angled bastions at each corner, the enclosure being some 200 by 220 feet, the curtains about 175 feet, the bastion flanks being some 40 to 50 feet and the faces 60 to 70 feet in length. One of the remaining bastions, now much eroded, has today somewhat smaller dimensions. No trace of barrack buildings survives, and none are indicated on the Ordnance Survey first edition, which notes the place as 'Old Barrack Yard', the townland being Barrack Park.

Some two miles to the east, at Manorhamilton, a rectangular bastioned enclosure of similar dimensions to that at Lurganboy is sited in a strong defensive position on high ground. A battered masonry wall forms the curtains and the bastions, the flanks and faces of which vary from some 30 to 35 feet and 55 to 60 feet, respectively (Fig. 66). The centre of the enclosure is occupied today by the Church of Ireland church, and there appears to be no trace of military buildings; the church was completed in 1783. There is no reference to Manorhamilton in a list of regiments in Ireland—*Quarters of the Army in Ireland, 1769*—from which the barracks in use at that time may be identified. It appears that Lurganboy and Manorhamilton were in use only during the first half of the eighteenth century; like some of the redoubts, the places may have originally been the sites of fortifications built during the warfare of the seventeenth century, possibly from the period of the Jacobite War.

The police function of the military establishment in Ireland during the first half of the eighteenth century is demonstrated by a memorial addressed to the lords justice from the townspeople of New Ross in 1730.[4] They state that the barrack erected some years previously was in need of repairs and that the removal of the troop of horse quartered there would leave them 'utterly defenceless'. The 'security of the Protestant interest' and the use of the soldiers to counteract the activities of smugglers required the retention of the garrison at New Ross for the protection of 'His Majesty's Protestant subjects'. The barrack here was situated within the walled town and was noted as being in 'good repair' in 1729, in a report on the barracks of the regiments of horse

and dragoons in Ireland. A map of the town of about 1700 depicts the barrack as a two-storey building with a steep pitched roof and short projecting bays at each end; a late nineteenth-century plan shows a building of the same layout with troop stables at ground level and officers' and soldiers' quarters at first-floor level, presumably the barrack building of the early eighteenth century.

The layout and dimensions of the New Ross barrack are typical of the smaller and most numerous type of barrack in Ireland: a main block some 130 feet long, between 25 and 30 feet wide, with projecting bays at each end some 20 feet square. The building was free-standing in a walled enclosure approximately square in plan, with some smaller ancillary structures built against the perimeter wall.

Town defences and forts were repaired in the years following the end of the war in 1691. Works were carried out at Galway, Athlone and Limerick, to reconstruct the fortifications damaged during the sieges of 1690-91; repairs and improvements were undertaken at Charles Fort, Ross Castle, Charlemont Fort, Carrickfergus Castle and Derry. There were also proposals for new coastal forts at Bantry and Berehaven and an elaborate scheme for extending the defences of Derry.

Rudolph Corneille, appointed second engineer in Ireland in 1692, was involved from 1694 onwards in repairs to the Limerick fortifications, and also prepared a plan and estimate for a citadel here. At Galway the Jacobite outwork at the south-east corner of the town walls was repaired, and fortifications—presumably earthworks— erected outside the East Gate and also at the west end of the bridge over the Corrib. A fort was built or reconstructed on Mutton Island: a plan by Goubet, presumably drawn in 1691, depicts a work here at that time. The fortification was armed with ten guns and the castle was repaired. The fortifying of Mutton Island is noted in 1702 as providing protection for shipping; a company of soldiers was stationed on the island, at Arkin in the Aran Islands and at Inishbofin. In 1719 the engineer John Corneille and Major-General Wynne were paid for works at Galway, which evidently resulted from a fear of Spanish invasion the year before.

Also in 1719, Major Jacques Wybault and Brigadier Borr received payment for fortifications at Athlone, presumably repairs to the existing works; in 1701 Wybault had dedicated a manuscript book of fortification plans to the Second Duke of Ormond (now in the Irish Architectural Archive). Alterations were in progress at the fortifications of Limerick in 1718-19, where the engineer was de Pagez, who had earlier been in charge of the works at Galway.[5]

A plan of Charles Fort by Rudolph Corneille of 1694 details repairs and improvements to be carried out in 1694-95, including the upper and lower sea batteries, the counterscarps, covered way, and glacis.[6] The plan depicts a covered way different in layout from that on Goubet's plan of 1691, having an additional *place d'armes* on the north-west, flanked by traverses to provide protection from enfilade fire. Other traverses are depicted on the covered way, evidently an attempt to strengthen this outer line of defence. During the siege of 1690 there were no traverses here, and as a result the garrison abandoned this part of the fort after some days. Plans of the sea batteries of Charles Fort drawn in 1691 by Corneille detail proposals to improve them by adding *banquettes* or firing steps between each embrasure and replacing wide, single-splayed gun-embrasures with narrower embrasures, double-splayed in plan. Between 1702 and 1709 the surveyor-general, Thomas Burgh, supervised works at Charles Fort, including the existing gateway, probably replacing the original gatehouse, which seems to be depicted on Phillips' perspective view of 1685 with a pyramidal roof. Some £2,000 was expended in 1712, and there

was an estimate for further repairs in 1719.

Three new fortifications were constructed in Ireland during the first half of the eighteenth century: the Star Fort and the Magazine Fort, both in the Phoenix Park, Dublin, and the battery or fort at Cove overlooking Cork Harbour. The star fort or 'Lord Wharton's Fortification' in the Phoenix Park was evidently designed by Thomas Burgh, 'Engineer and Surveyor General of Her Majesty's Fortifications and Buildings', acting on the orders of the lord lieutenant, Lord Wharton, in June 1710. The cost of the works was not to exceed £15,000 in the first year. It was intended to serve as an arsenal, but by October Burgh was addressing a memorial to the lords justice, complaining of abuses and corruption during the construction, some £2,900 having been expended up to the previous month.[7] The work was never completed, but from later maps and plans it is possible to determine the design and dimensions. A square earthwork with a redan projecting from each side resulted in a 'star fort' plan surrounded by a ditch, covered way, and glacis. Internally the work was some

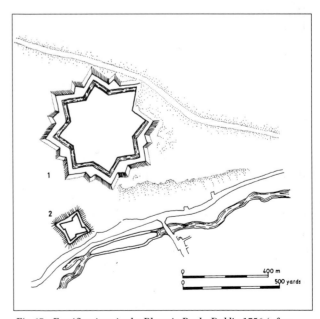

Fig.67. Fortifications in the Phoenix Park, Dublin 1756 (after Rocque's Map Of Dublin, 1756): 1 The Fortification or Star Fort. 2 Magazine Fort.

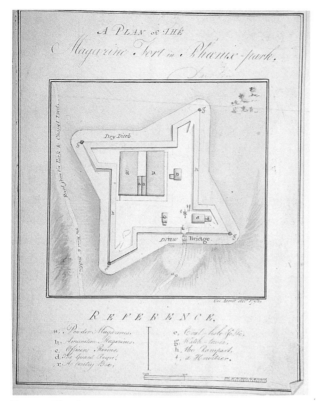

Fig. 68. The Magazine Fort Phoenix Park, Dublin, 1793, NLI 16 G 17 (42).

300 yards square, the overall dimension from the extremity of the glacis at the salients opposite the redans some 600 yards. It appears that there was a wet moat, indicated on contemporary maps, of which the Citadel Pond seems to be the only part remaining today, having originally formed one side. A map of the Phoenix Park of 1789 shows the work as almost complete except for one corner: it is depicted on Rocque's map of Dublin of 1756 as somewhat less regular in outline (Fig.67).

Also depicted on Rocque's map is the Magazine Fort, sited to the south-west of the Star Fort, on high ground with the only easy approach from the west. The date-stone that survives from the demolished gateway is inscribed 1736; it is recorded that the first powder and shot for the fort was supplied in 1738. It is a square work with a demi-bastion at each corner, surrounded by a ditch with sloping bank forming the counterscarp—there is no ravelin depicted on the entrance front on early maps and plans, includ-

ing those of 1789 and 1793, which do, however, indicate a slight embankment or breastwork in advance of the drawbridge.[8] The fort is just over 200 feet square, the demi-bastions having faces some 75 feet and flanks 35 to 40 feet in length. Two large magazines occupy a large part of the interior on the west side (Fig.68).

Jonathan Swift's comment on the building of the fort questioned the need for such a structure—which in fact arose from the danger of a magazine being situated, as formerly, in Dublin Castle:

> *Behold a proof of Irish sense;*
> *Here Irish wit is seen:*
> *When nothing's left that's worth defence,*
> *We build a magazine.*

The battery overlooking Cork Harbour, known as Cove Fort, was built by 1743, evidently superseding several temporary batteries then in existence at various locations around the harbour. A demi-bastioned front close to the water level mounted a battery commanding the main shipping channel from the harbour entrance, at the point where vessels turned to the west to sail north of Spike and Haulbowline Islands upstream to Passage and Cork (Figs 69 and 70). Reports later in the eighteenth century were to be critical of this work, in particular the fact that it was overlooked by high ground at the rear and

Fig.69. Plan of Cove Fort Cork Harbour, 1778, from Vallencey's Military Survey

Fig.70. Elevation of Cove Fort, 1778, from Vallencey's Military Survey.

that proposed landward defences in the form of two bastions were not built. An early nineteenth-century report indicates batteries here at three levels; the demi-bastioned lower battery and an archway at an upper level survive on the site today, with some flanking walls for musketry defence on the steeply sloping hillside.

Apart from these new works, improvements and repairs were carried out at Duncannon and Charles Fort from time to time, while at Limerick and Galway the ruined state of the town fortifications gave rise to suggestions for new defence works to protect these important ports. Reports on the condition of the walls of Galway indicate that most of the ordnance was dismounted and the defences seriously neglected. In 1747 there were numerous breaches in the parapets and walls, and embrasures were filled up and overgrown: it was recommended that certain bastions and gun batteries should be repaired and that the battery on Mutton Island and the small barrack there be rebuilt. It seems that no action was taken to carry out these proposals.[9]

Some of the smaller coastal forts of the seventeenth century are included in a list of 1706 with the larger forts and walled towns, in which the ammunition, small arms and ordnance are detailed. Passage, Inishbofin and Sherkin Island are each listed with ten serviceable pieces of ordnance; Mutton Island and Valentia Island are not included. It seems that many of the smaller posts, such as those at Dunboy and Crookhaven, were no longer in use by the early years of the eighteenth century, although a plan of a square-bastioned fort proposed for Dunboy dates from this time.[10]

At Youghal in 1736 the mayor was to be allowed the cost of the 'four new great guns' and to have liberty to sell as many of the old guns in the fort as were no longer of use. The fort was the blockhouse or circular tower at the end of the quay, evidently constructed in the sixteenth century. A new gunner was to be appointed in 1762; however, by February the following year it was decided that the fort was to be used as a fish market, and the gunner was to be paid until June 1763 and no longer.[11] It appears that from this time onwards there was no artillery at Youghal Harbour. In 1779 two light 6-pounder field-guns and a detachment of the Royal Irish Artillery were ordered to Youghal; and similar arrangements were made at Carrickfergus, Galway, Waterford and Limerick at the same time to provide some degree of defence.

At Charlemont Fort in 1746 there were proposals for a new barrack and other buildings and repairs at a cost of £1,000. A report of September 1748 by Arthur Jones-Nevill, engineer and surveyor-general, on barracks to be built, rebuilt or repaired includes a barrack of forty-eight rooms for Charles Fort.[12] This new accommodation was evidently built by April 1751, and is noted in January the following year as 'New barracks lately built .. . three sides of a square three stories high'. This is the barrack complex in the eastern part of Charles Fort, which survives today with later additions and alterations.

In November 1763 the ordnance at the forts was listed as:

Duncannon Fort:	ten	24-pounders
	fifteen	18-pounders
Cove Fort:	eight	24-pounders
Charles Fort:	eleven	24-pounders

These were all iron guns. Fifty-one mortars were listed at Dublin, mostly of small calibre. In March 1769 the armament listed at the forts was the same, with a hundred rounds of shot for each piece. The gun carriages at Cove and Charles Fort were unserviceable, and new carriages were to be made to replace them. In the same year, eight 6-pounder guns were required for Charlemont Fort, although the place was not considered defensible, as houses were built near-by and there were no gun platforms. The rela-tively limited armament at Duncannon, Cove and Charles Fort reflects their use as harbour defence batteries rather than fortifications capa-ble of effective resistance to attack from both land and sea.

In August 1765 Lieutenant-Colonel Thomas Eyre, chief engineer of Ireland, had submitted a memorial to the lord lieutenant on the ordnance establishment in Ireland. He was critical of the forts and the defences of the walled towns: they were of little importance in strength and situa-tion, and were inadequately equipped with artillery. It seems probable that this report resulted in the detailed inspection carried out in the following year by Colonel William Roy. In 1766 Colonel Roy, appointed the previous year surveyor-general of coasts and engineer for mili-tary surveys in Great Britain, made a short tour of that part of Ireland south of a line from Dublin to Galway.[13] His report gives a general description of the countryside from a military viewpoint, including the rivers and their cross-ing-places at bridges and fords; he considered the roads to be very good, better than in any other country. Under the heading 'Concerning the Principal Towns, Harbours and Forts in the South Part of Ireland', Roy discusses the defences of Dublin, Duncannon Fort, Waterford, Cork, Cork harbour, Kinsale, Limerick, Galway and Athlone.

Dublin was 'entirely open without either castle or fort....' The Magazine Fort in the Phoenix Park with its demi-bastion flankers had 'scarcely any appearance of a ditch around it'. Nearby were the remains of the ditch and glacis of the incomplete Star Fort, about which Roy had diffi-culty in obtaining information. He remarked that it had been built too far from the city to com-mand it and was too far away from the sea. The place for a citadel was Ringsend: this would secure the harbour entrance, to some extent command the bay, might always be supplied by sea and was not overlooked by nearby higher ground. The use of the River Dodder would add to the defences. Roy gives no indication that he was aware of the proposal by de Gomme for a citadel at Ringsend in 1673. The establishment of the Pigeon House Fort on the South Wall of Dublin Harbour in 1798 derived from the same strategic considerations: a strong-point for the garrison commanding the harbour entrance.

At Duncannon Fort defending Waterford Harbour 'a few rotten planks are at present made use of instead of a drawbridge'. The fort had barracks for four companies of foot and one of artillery and there were ten 24-pounders and fifteen 18-pounders mounted on the sea batter-ies. However, the place was commanded on the landward side by high ground two hundred yards away, and although the deep-water channel lay close to the fort, with a favourable wind and a flood tide he felt that ships would be able to sail quickly past with the aid of the strong current and soon be out of range of the guns. The bar-racks at Waterford were situated 'in what was formerly a kind of citadel', of which only some parts remained—a reference to St Patrick's Fort.

Cork was not tenable, and any attempt to defend the place by means of forts, redoubts or lines on the high ground north and south of the city would require a very large garrison. Roy remarked on the poor situation of Elizabeth Fort and the Old Barracks nearby, overlooked by high ground to the south and now surrounded by suburbs. This faulty siting applied to almost all the barracks in Ireland: many of the smaller barracks 'might have been so placed as to have become afterwards good posts, when times and circumstances made it necessary to enclose them as redoubts, or works of any other kind.' A citadel might have been built on the high ground south of Cork before the growth of the suburbs there; but defences would also be required on the north side, and no works could completely defend Cork from a superior force. Roy's reference to redoubts and lines to defend Cork reflects new approaches to the design of fortifications emerging in the second half of the eighteenth century, a move away from continuous bastioned defences towards detached works.

At Cork Harbour Roy did not refer to any works existing at the harbour entrance, the sites of the later Forts Carlisle and Camden. He described the fort at Cove as being a battery, as it had no landward defences. The battery of eighteen guns at the water level with a barrack for four companies was overlooked by high ground inland to the north; it was intended that landward defences be built in the form of side walls and a rear wall, with a bastion at each landward angle, but Roy dismissed this proposal as ineffective, as the place would still be commanded by the hillside on each flank and in the rear. He suggested a site some three hundred yards to the west nearer to Cove as a better position for a battery, with a fort inland on the high ground behind it.

Roy was convinced that batteries without good landward defences were of very limited use, liable to capture by enemy landing parties; he has surprisingly little to say about fortifying the headlands at the harbour entrance, but regarded Spike Island as an excellent site for a fortress to command the harbour. The east end of the island, noted as the highest part, with cliffs some fifty to sixty feet high, was later to be the site of the fort built by Vallancey during the American war.

At Kinsale, Compass Hill overlooking the town and the disused fort of Castle Park were each considered by Roy as a good site for a fortress. Charles Fort was armed with only eight iron 24-pounders on the lower sea battery and contained barracks for a regiment of foot, a small powder magazine and casemates sufficient for part of the garrison. Roy noted that a considerable amount had 'been expended at the commencement of the late war, in the repairs of this fort, particularly in making a new covered way.' The covered way is remarkably similar in details, such as the traverses, to that at Fort George, Inverness, where this element of the defences was under construction in 1749; work continuing for a number of years after the fort received its main armament in 1760.

Roy remarked that Charles Fort was commanded by high ground inland, particularly that

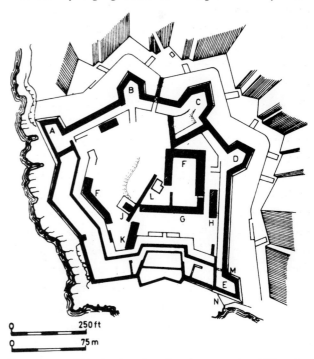

Fig.71. Plan of Charles Fort, Kinsale, after 1751; after NLI 15 B 14 (39). A Kinsale Bastion; B West Bastion; C Prince of Wales Bastion; D East Bastion; E Charles Bastion; F Barracks; G Officers' Barrack; H Sutlery; J Magazine; K Governor's House; L Storehouse; M Sally port; N Quay.

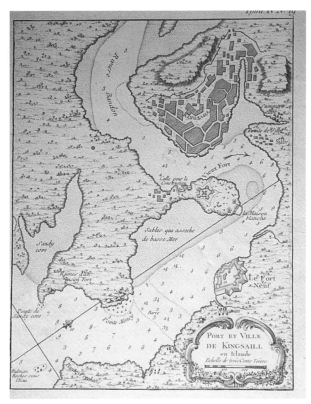

Fig. 72. French Chart of Kinsale, mid-eighteenth century.

some 150 yards to the southwards—here he must have been referring to the hillside to the southeast, where the land is about 100 feet above sea level. He thought Castle Park a better position than Charles Fort: the barracks in Kinsale were in such a poor condition that they should be rebuilt—perhaps new barracks might be constructed instead at Castle Park and the fortifications there repaired (Fig. 71). The small dockyard for the ships of the Royal Navy was also noted by Roy; but from about this time onwards Cork Harbour began to supersede Kinsale as the principal south-coast anchorage both for naval and merchant vessels (Fig. 72).

Limerick had previously been thought of as the place of greatest strength in Ireland, and Roy suggested that the best site for a citadel here was on the Clare side of the river, close to Thomond Bridge. An alternative site was some three hundred yards from the Mungret Gate in the western

wall of Irish Town, but Roy pointed out that this would require the demolition of the suburb here; Phillips' proposed citadel in 1685 was to have been sited just to the north of this location.

The town wall of Galway was described as most ruined on the river side, and Roy advocated that the high ground to the east be fortified by 'repairing the present redoubts [possibly a reference to the Cromwellian-period siege forts] and adding some new works.' He remarked that 'it is said that the walls of Galway and Limerick are to be pulled down. This may be right as it is better to have no works at all, than to have bad ones.' He gave two possible alternatives for a citadel at Galway: on the west side of the Corrib, commanding the anchorage, or on high ground near the East Gate. In either case demolition of parts of the suburbs would be necessary.

At Athlone the castle contained a barrack for one company, the rest of the barracks being situated in 'a kind of entrenchment, being the only part that now remains of the old fortification of the place.' This refers to the Cromwellian earthwork defences, which had been modified by the French engineers with the Jacobite forces in 1690-91. This western part of the town—noted as 'Irish Town' by Roy—was 'commanded by Gallows Hill beyond the new canal'. To include the high ground here and that on the east of the town, works would be too extensive, 'yet by occupying these heights by redoubts, depending upon the principal works—the place might sometimes be maintained.' It was on Gallows Hill that temporary works were to be erected in 1798, and more extensive fortifications were under construction here in 1804 as part of the scheme of defence on the Shannon.

Cork or Galway was considered to be the most likely invasion point, while Roy thought Limerick an unlikely target, because of the difficulty of navigating the Shannon. The Fergus was navigable as far as Ennis, and at Clare Castle the military post was of considerable importance where the Limerick-to-Ennis road crosses the river. He noted the extent of the navigable rivers such as the Nore, the Suir, navigable as far as Clonmel, and the Blackwater, navigable as far as Cappoquin and tidal to Lismore. The possibility of invasion of the south of Ireland required an assembly point for the defending army: Roy noted that 'during the late wars the army usually assembled and encamped at Thurles', evidently to be in a central position if a landing were effected at Galway, Limerick, Cork, or Waterford. He considered the place too far from Cork, and advocated instead the Ardfinnan-to-Clonmel area as the best location for the army, to be able to advance on an enemy landing at Cork or Waterford, and which would also serve in case of invasion at Galway or Limerick. An alternative position was near Mitchelstown. These plans for troop movements influenced defence proposals when French invasion was feared during the American War of Independence, and again during the war with the French Republic, when the Bantry Bay expedition exposed the difficulties of concentrating scattered detachments and garrisons to oppose a large invasion force.

In October 1770 the viceroy, Lord Townshend, reported on the military state of Ireland, considering the possibility of war with France and Spain following the seizure of the Falkland Islands.[14] Townshend remarked that Ireland had not 'one good and permanent fortress in the whole kingdom.' The security of the country with the 'wretched and oppressed' Catholics outnumbering the Protestants in three out of the four provinces depended on the 'constant protection of the British fleet and the submission of the wealthy Catholics to His Majesty's Government.'

He noted that £8,000 had been spent on Duncannon after 1753, and an application was under consideration for the expenditure of a further £1,000 here. Townshend described Duncannon as 'a weak, ill-shaped, contemptible fort... full of defects, both in situation, construc-

tion and ... scarcely capable of withstanding a frigate.' He noted Cove Fort as a 'miserable battery' and recommended Dognose and Ram Head, the entrance headlands of Cork Harbour, as much better positions for fortification. Spike Island and Haulbowline Island should also be fortified.

Concerning Kinsale, Townshend stated that Charles Fort was 'if possible more faulty than Duncannon'; Oyster Haven, between Cork Harbour and Kinsale, was a good landing place. He noted that £10,000 had been spent on Charles Fort against the opinion of the engineer in 1753, that Cork Harbour was preferred as an anchorage for naval vessels because of the bar at the entrance to Kinsale, and that it was surprising that the Old Fort (Castle Park) or Compass Hill, which overlooks it, were not used as military posts.

In the Shannon Estuary, Clare Castle was noted as an important post and possible enemy landing place, easier than sailing up to Limerick, for which two tides were necessary. Townshend was concerned about the distribution of the barracks in Ireland, 'built where they answered no military purpose'. He was critical of their situation in the middle of towns: if they had 'been more judiciously placed, they might have, with a little additional ground or buildings been turned into very good depots in time of public danger, by being places near passes, bridges, or fords they might with occasional works have become very good posts....' Of importance in this regard he noted the River Bandon, the Lee, Blackwater, Suir, Nore, Barrow, and 'particularly the passes of the Shannon'. He suggested that more barracks were required to protect depots and to command particular situations, with the potential to become strong-points for a defending army; barracks in the north would possibly contribute to the suppression of smuggling there.

New barracks were proposed for areas of Cork and Kerry, and Townshend suggested that barracks situated on promontories or at junctions of rivers where they were not overlooked by high ground might be 'of very great use in times of emergency, particularly in the absence of the army. The gentlemen of the country and their Protestant tenants who are generally well armed, might occupy these posts.' He advocated building a large fortification to the south of Cork, accessible by sea. 'It should be purely military to contain such a garrison that an enemy could not venture to leave behind. If inland it should be on some great river, or the confluence of two rivers, where the tide reaches, for the cheap conveyance of all stores.' Somewhat in contradiction to his suggested site south of Cork he proposed Mount Elliott, at the confluence of the Nore and Barrow, as a good place for a fortress to hold magazines and stores. It would be difficult to defend the interior of the country against an enemy that had established itself in Munster. The importance of the tidal reaches and the crossing points of the Suir, Blackwater, Nore and Barrow were emphasised as possible lines of defence.

Townshend was in favour of the Ardfinnan area as an assembly point for the army in Ireland: two days' march to Cork, three days' march to Limerick, five days' march to Banagher on the Shannon, and two days' march to Waterford. He considered Cork the most likely place for invasion, or the harbours of Kerry; an army corps should have headquarters at Bandon with detachments at Ross (presumably Ross Carbery, where the barrack was in the earlier fort), Dunmanway, Macroom, and Millstreet.

The connections with France and Spain, the shipping of recruits from west Cork and Kerry to the Irish regiments of those countries and the 'uncivilised and dangerous state' of the countryside here led Townshend to suggest the formation of special detachments of infantry, light artillery, and dragoons, and a chain of barracks. He considered that the ruined state of the walls of Galway left it open to the enemy, and that the

line of the Shannon had to be considered as a frontier, although troops retreating from Loughrea 'might take up a defensive position on the Suck'—presumably at Ballinasloe—to delay the enemy before it reached the Shannon. Banagher was suggested as a good position for a depot, communicating by the projected canal with Dublin which would be useful for transporting artillery and stores. The situation of the barrack at Athlone was criticised, the military authorities having neglected to occupy the heights there—presumably those to the west, where the batteries were constructed some thirty-five years later during the Napoleonic wars.

The reports by Townshend and by Roy some four years earlier on the defence of the south of Ireland emphasised strategic considerations that were to reappear again during the invasion scares of the American war and the wars against the French Republic and Empire. Townshend regarded the Shannon and the Suir as critical lines of defence in the event of an enemy landing in the west or in Munster. A fortress 'to secure the records, valuable effects and the arsenal' was essential at Dublin. The site advocated was 'a neck of land containing a dirty fish town called Ringsend just at the harbour's mouth.... This place has a very narrow front towards the country, by the outfall of a very small mountain river called the Dodder.' Townshend suggested the creation of an inundation between Ringsend and Dublin by means of a defended sluice, protecting the place from attack from the direction of the city. A 'fine citadel' might be constructed here. In this proposal Townshend was repeating what had already been suggested by Colonel Roy four years earlier, and much of his report follows Roy's ideas: his report concludes with praise for 'Mr Roy's abilities and his valuable observations'.

Also in October 1770 Townshend outlined proposals for barracks in Ireland.[15] Some £46,000 had been expended on the repair and completion of barracks since 1766. 'All the important passes of the Shannon remain unoccupied and one barrack at Limerick in ruins....' The barracks at Cork, Kinsale, and Waterford, 'all situations of consequence', were in the same state. There were no barracks on the Blackwater or Suir that commanded passes over those rivers. He emphasised four main points with regard to the barracks: the defence of the country and support of the magistrates; suppression of smuggling in Co. Kerry and Co. Down and the activities of lawless gangs in Kerry in particular; the convenience of subsistence and assembly of the army; and the setting up of a chain of barracks for regiments sent to Ireland from the north, and their regular movement southwards.

In 1771 Townshend's proposals were approved, but it seems that little was done to put the principal suggestions into effect. New barracks were recommended at Limerick, Cork, and Waterford and at Nedeen on the Kenmare River, where the Catholics were connected with France and Spain and 'are very ungovernable'. A barrack for two troops of light horse should be erected at Rush, Co. Dublin, 'where there is a nest of outlawed smugglers'. With his proposals Townshend enclosed a plan for an 'enclosed barrack' to be built 'upon advantageous spots', perhaps a form of defensible barrack similar to those built in Scotland early in the century or those later built on the Military Road in Co. Wicklow.

In March 1778, just before the outbreak of war with France, a report was prepared concerning the possible invasion of Ireland, and appropriate defence measures.[16] It was expected that the ports of Brittany or the Bay of Biscay were the most likely places from which invasion might be launched. An attack on Dublin or the east coast was thought unlikely: Carlingford, Dundalk and Dublin Bay were regarded as the only practicable landing places. Waterford was regarded as a likely invasion target, with several

navigable rivers flowing into Waterford Harbour and several routes to Dublin available. The defects of Duncannon Fort were again noted; Dungarvan was not well placed for an invasion attempt, and the bay there was not safe for a large fleet; at Youghal there was a 'spacious and landlocked' harbour, but the bar at the entrance prevented the entry of large vessels. The city of Cork was regarded as 'the next most important object of attack after Dublin'. The fort at Cove was described as 'a miserable battery too far up the bay to prevent ships coming in'.

At Kinsale, Charles Fort was 'more defective if possible than Duncannon, commanded even by musketry' and not tenable for twenty-four hours. The bar at Kinsale prevented large ships of war entering the harbour and made Cork the principal anchorage; the French might attack Cork or Kinsale if the Royal Navy was in the English Channel a sufficient distance from Brittany or the Biscay ports. Further to the west, Clonakilty, Ross Carbery and Baltimore were regarded as inferior harbours, while Bantry seemed 'too far removed from Cork'. Kenmare, Dingle and Tralee were too far to the west, the Shannon Estuary was easily navigated as far as Tarbert and there were good roads to Limerick. The remains of the old works might be repaired at Galway, but it was not considered likely that an invasion would be attempted on the coast northwards from Galway to the north of Ireland.

The probable objectives of a French fleet would be first Cork, next Limerick, then Waterford or Galway. The situation in the north, where there was widespread support for the American cause, made it necessary to leave a considerable force there. Possible steps required to put Ireland into a state of defence included strengthening Duncannon Fort, Charles Fort and Carrickfergus Castle, the artillery mounted in them to be adequate to resist attack from shipping, and each to have provisions for ten or twelve days. At Cork Harbour a temporary work and battery of heavy guns should be placed on Spike Island and a work near Crosshaven to defend the Carrigaline River; at Kinsale a battery was required in advance of Charles Fort to protect more effectively the harbour entrance or to obstruct a landing at Oyster Haven.

Sites for works to cover the bridges and crossing-places of the Shannon should be surveyed, and also locations for works and batteries in the estuary. Scattery Island, Carrick Island, Tarbert and Kilkerin Point or Foynes Island are noted. All these were to be sites for batteries—Tarbert within a year or two, the other locations during the Napoleonic period. As in the earlier military reports, the principal routes to Dublin and the crossing-places of the important rivers are discussed, together with points of assembly for troops to act against an invading force. Of the proposed establishment of some 12,000 men, 3,000 infantry were to be in the Cork area, including Kinsale and Youghal, to oppose a landing at Kinsale or Cork Harbour. However, a memorandum of July 1779 noted that 'the mouth of Cork Harbour is at present in no degree defended, and an enemy may immediately enter from the Ocean....' The battery at Cove was too far away to be effective: batteries should be erected on the two headlands at the harbour entrance, and also a battery at the entrance to Carrigaline River, presumably opposite or east of Crosshaven. These might at least delay an enemy attempting to enter the harbour or to land troops.

The importance of the line of the River Blackwater was again stressed: the principal part of the army must defend the area from Mallow to Fermoy, and entrenching tools should be stored at Kilkenny, Clonmel, and Kilworth. The absence of walled towns and military posts that might be easily fortified exposed depots and magazines to attack.

In 1777-78, Lieutenant-Colonel Charles Vallencey, later to become director of engineers in Ireland, began a military survey of the southern half of the country, the same area toured by Roy eleven years earlier. He noted in particular the details of the harbours and coastline, the roads leading towards Dublin, and the rivers that formed obstacles to a possible enemy advance from the south or west. With regard to the defence of Waterford Harbour, Vallencey, like Roy before him, noted that 'Duncannon Fort affords a very trifling defence to this harbour. One thirty-gun frigate would silence it in a few hours, at least would keep up its attention, while the enemy's flat bottom boats may pass, between the frigate and the western shore, one mile distant from the fort.' Six 12-pounders placed on the commanding ground—the hillside inland of the fort—would force the immediate surrender of the garrison; the banks and ditches around the fort provided ready-made entrenchments for an attacking force.[17]

A battery of five guns had formerly existed at Passage, of which the walls still remained. It was a good position, as the guns would rake every ship or boat that had passed Duncannon. Vallencey recommended the reconstruction of this battery and the construction of another battery at Faithleg Point farther upstream. Each should be equipped with six 24-pounders and with mortars. These works would delay the landing of an enemy force and obstruct a fleet of transports or boats. Waterford should be defended by detached redoubts equipped with cannon and mortars, these works to be sited on heights overlooking the city; in particular a redoubt should be placed on the high ground north of the river, with a garrison of two hundred regular soldiers.

Vallencey repeated the earlier critical comments on the barracks in Ireland: that they were built without consideration for the defence of the country in the event of invasion or insurrection. Should the garrison of Dublin move out to oppose an invading force, the arsenal, magazines and treasury would be exposed. A strong fort was required in or near Dublin to contain these stores and records, and the perimeter walls of barracks should be built to allow for defence by country gentlemen and others 'well affected', while the regular troops were in action elsewhere. The proposal by Townshend of a line of fortified barracks from Cork to Limerick is repeated by Vallancey, only in this instance it is taken to be from Clonmel to Limerick, 'each barrack a defensible post'.

Cork Harbour is noted as 'very defenceless in its present state'. Batteries were formerly sited at the harbour entrance, on Haulbowline Island and on Battery Point on Great Island west of Cove. These were now abandoned and ruined, and only the battery at Cove, with twelve guns, was now in use. This battery was quite inadequate when the extent of the harbour was considered. It appears from Vallencey's survey that the construction of the battery at Cove resulted in the other batteries being abandoned. He was very critical of the battery, noted that it had been intended to complete the landward defence with two bastions, and that the hillside at the rear completely commanded the batteries over the roof of the barracks. Batteries should be built at Ram Head and at Dognose, and at Roche's Tower on the opposite side of the harbour entrance, 'rebuilt in more proper places than the old ones were in,' and also a battery on Spike Island and on Battery Point, each to be mounted with six 24-pounder cannon and with mortars (Map 10).

Another battery was required at Crosshaven, where there was a good landing place for baggage and artillery. Vallencey noted that in 1756 Lieutenant-General Skinner, chief engineer of Great Britain, had surveyed Cork Harbour and reported on the importance of Crosshaven and recommended that the earlier batteries should be rebuilt, a new one added at Spike Island, and a fort constructed at Battery Point, which was esti-mated to cost £50,000. These proposals had not been acted upon, and no defence works had been constructed. Vallencey considered a battery was sufficient at Battery Point and that half the amount of Skinner's estimate might be used instead on the defence of the city of Cork. Two redoubts should be built on the high ground north of Cork, on Windmill Hill and Fair Hill, or alternatively one work on Windmill Hill flanked by temporary batteries on the other hill. These works would, in Vallencey's opinion, delay an enemy for several days until it had landed and brought up its artillery. A powder magazine was noted some distance from the barrack on the south side of the city: this magazine is depicted as a fort on a map of Cork of 1801. Vallencey advocated that all military buildings be sited on high ground on the north side; and in the early years of the following century a large new barrack was to be erected here.

Oyster Haven, between Cork Harbour and Kinsale, was a possible landing place, a suitable anchorage for transports: here a battery of six 24-pounders and some mortars should be erected to command the entrance. Kinsale Harbour, a safe anchorage and more easily defended than Cork, had begun to be superseded by Cork Harbour. At Charles Fort there were eleven 24-pounders on the lower battery, commanding the channel but not effectively commanding the harbour; a battery of six 24-pounders should be constructed at the old fort opposite and four 12-pounders mounted at the blockhouse below it, and mortars should also be added to the armament of the old fort. Skinner in 1756 had advocated that no money be spent on Charles Fort because of the commanding ground overlooking the place inland, and that instead the old fort should be reconstructed for half the amount required for improvements to Charles Fort. This advice was not followed, and some £14,000 was expended on the repairs, including presumably the construction of the new covered way noted by

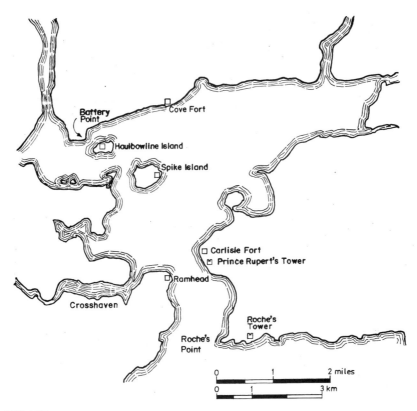

Map 10. Cork Harbour 1775-1783.

Roy. Vallencey remarked that the lower batteries of the fort were commanded by the maintops (the fighting platforms on the masts manned by marines and equipped with small swivel guns) of a frigate lying alongside. The parapets here were too thin to resist cannon, and the embrasures too narrow. The upper batteries commanded ships' tops but they were not equipped with artillery: as at Duncannon, Vallencey thought that Charles Fort must surrender to even a thirty-gun frigate.

His survey of the area from Youghal to Bantry included a detailed examination of the harbours and possible landing places, and the roads leading from them towards Cork. The best anchorage at Bantry Bay was to the east of Whiddy Island, and while there were good landing places at Berehaven and Glengariff there were no adequate roads from these places suitable for artillery. Some other harbours, such as Crookhaven, Baltimore, and Castlehaven, were

suitable for transports: Vallencey notes a barrack at Inchigeelagh for a company of foot, surrounded with a wall forming a square with four bastions—a rare example at this time of a fortified barrack. Ross Carbery barrack was also similarly described; in this instance the square bastioned fortification was the mid-seventeenth-century fort. Other barracks are noted, one for two troops of cavalry at Bandon and one for two companies of foot at Clonakilty, while Vallencey repeats the proposal for a chain of redoubts between Limerick and Clonmel to accommodate new barracks. A general line of defence was to run from Kinsale by the River Bandon to Bandon and Macroom, an advanced line from Clonakilty to Dunmanway, in the event of an enemy landing in the south west.

France entered the war on the side of the American colonies in June 1778 and was joined by Spain a year later, leaving Ireland open to the

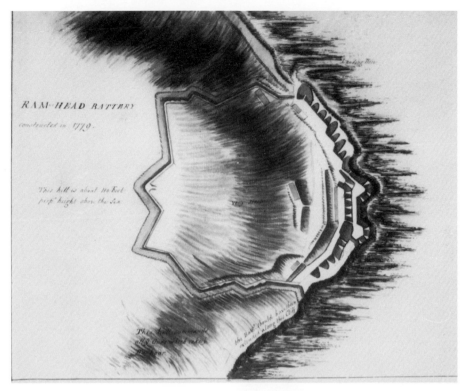

Fig. 73. Ram-Head Battery, Cork Harbour, 1779, PRO MPF 159 (3).

possibility of invasion,which was thought likely in 1779 and again in 1781.

Most of the batteries advocated by Vallencey for Cork Harbour were constructed between 1779 and 1781; works were not erected at Crosshaven or at Battery Point on Great Island west of Cove. At Ram Head, later the site of Fort Camden, on the west side of the harbour, a fortification was erected in 1779 with batteries at two levels overlooking the harbour entrance. The landward defences consisted of a ditch and rampart in the form of a *tenaille trace* (Fig. 73).[18] In 1781 the armament was eight 24-pounders and one 8-inch and four $5\frac{1}{2}$-inch howitzers; by 1783 this had been increased by the addition of five 18-pounders and six 12-pounders. The Royal Irish Artillery detachment stationed here consisted of one subaltern, two non-commissioned officers, and thirty-six men; there was a barrack for the artillerymen.[19]

On the opposite headland over two hundred feet above sea level, on the site of the earlier Corkbeg Fort, another fortification was constructed, linked by an entrenchment on the landward side to Rupert's Tower some distance to the south. It was known as Carlisle Fort, after the Earl of Carlisle, who was appointed lord lieutenant in December 1780 (Fig 74).[20] The armament in 1783 consisted of twenty 24-pounders, ten 12-pounders, thirty 6-pounders, and two 8-inch and twelve $5\frac{1}{2}$-inch mortars. One-and-a-half miles to the south of Carlisle Fort at Roche's Point was a battery on two levels,armed with twelve 24-pounders in 1783.[21] The three works at Ram Head, Carlisle and Roche's Point commanded the harbour entrance with a cross-fire from their guns.

At the eastern end of Spike Island a battery was constructed, mounting in 1783 eighteen 24-pounders and one 8-inch mortar. The guns here commanded the centre of the harbour and the main shipping channel to the south and east,

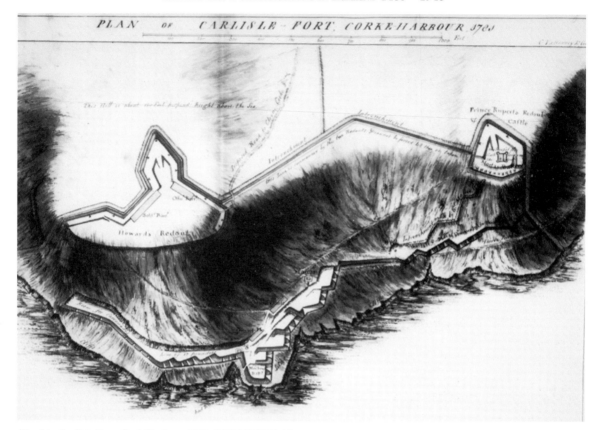

Fig. 74. Carlisle Fort, Cork Harbour, 1781, PRO MPF 159 (4).

overlapping in their field of fire with guns at Ram Head and Carlisle capable of firing northwards over the harbour. A contemporary plan of Spike Island depicts the battery here, the principal emplacement facing south-east over the harbour, an irregular landward defence with four salients completing the enclosure.[22] One landward salient was formed by a square blockhouse, the platform of which, thirty feet high, mounted five 6-pounders and six swivel guns. At each of the other salient angles was a 6-pounder. The wall enclosing the work was intended to be from seventeen to twenty feet high, evidently for musketry defence, apart from the 6-pounder guns and swivels. The surrounding ditch was ten feet deep, a depth arrived at by excavating six feet into the rock and raising the counterscarp four feet. Two barracks, a magazine and three shot furnaces behind the main sea battery are also shown on the plan. The parapet of the block-

house and part of the perimeter wall on the north side were to be increased in height. Although well provided with ammunition, the garrison was not sufficient to man half the guns on the battery. Two 12-pounders were located in a flank of the battery to command the low-water landing place. The plan is signed by Vallencey, with the rank of major-general and director of engineers, which dates it to 1793 or later, as he obtained these ranks in October and November that year (Fig. 75). It seems probable that the layout depicts the battery as it was at the end of the American war some ten years earlier: a storehouse and guardhouse are shown in broken outline, with the note that they were yet to be built, the materials being on the site.

At the battery at Cove in 1783 there were no guns, only a small detachment of the Royal Irish Artillery lodged in the infantry barrack there. At Charles Fort, Kinsale, eleven 24-pounders were mounted in 1783, the same armament as existed some twenty years earlier; no extra guns were mounted at the old fort opposite or at the water-level blockhouse, and no battery was erected at Oyster Haven, as advocated by Vallencey. By 1783 there was a battery of eight 24-pounders at Tarbert Island in the Shannon Estuary.[23] In September 1779 ten 12-pounders and two $5\frac{1}{2}$-inch howitzers were to be sent to Limerick to be mounted on temporary batteries to protect East India Company ships then lying in the river; in 1781 the Limerick merchants had petitioned the Lord Lieutenant, Carlisle, to erect a battery on Tarbert Island. A late eighteenth-century view of the river and Tarbert Island indicates a gun battery at water level on the north side of the island to command the deep-water channel.

Duncannon Fort in 1783 was equipped with ten 24-pounders and ten 18-pounders, while across the estuary at Passage the battery had been brought back into action with an armament of five 24-pounders and three 12-pounders, with a barrack to accommodate the artillery detachment.[24] Vallencey's proposal for a battery upstream at Faithleg Point was not carried out, and his suggestion that Waterford and Cork be defended by redoubts on nearby high ground was not acted upon by the military authorities.

The batteries constructed between 1779 and 1783 at Cork Harbour, Tarbert and Passage were abandoned or disused for the next ten years, repeating the eighteenth-century pattern of the neglect of fortifications alternating with repairs and reconstruction in times of war or fear of invasion. On the outbreak of war with the French Republic in 1793, these works were again occupied or reconstructed, and other temporary works were to be erected in response to the threat of invasion. The renewal of the war in 1803 was to result in the most extensive scheme of fortification ever undertaken in Ireland.

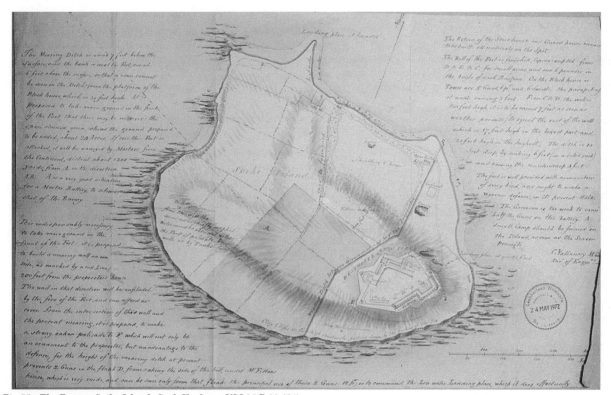

Fig.75. *The Fort on Spike Island, Cork Harbour, NLI 15 B 22 (54).*

Chapter 5

The French are on the Sea, 1793–1815

1

Historical background

IN FEBRUARY 1793 THE French Republic found itself at war with Britain and with those Continental countries that aimed to restore the monarchy in France. In Ireland the Society of United Irishmen, founded in November 1791 at Belfast and inspired by the ideals of American independence and the French Revolution, attempted to achieve an independent Ireland governed by a truly representative parliament. Forced by government pressure and arrests to become a secret society, the leaders turned increasingly to the idea of French military intervention to help them establish an Irish republic by force of arms.

The military authorities reviewed the defences of the country and considered the probable landing places of an invading force. Military reports at this time repeat many of the salient points of the surveys by Roy, Townshend and Vallencey earlier in the century: the probability of a landing in Munster or on the west coast, the importance of Waterford Harbour, Cork Harbour and the Shannon Estuary, and the assumption that the east coast was an unlikely target for a French fleet to land troops. One of these reports, 'Thoughts on the Defence of Ireland' of August 1796, discussed the possibility of invasion of Ireland following the recent successes of the French on the Rhine and in Italy.[1] Ireland was thought a more likely target than England, the invaders having the expectation of being joined by 'a large body of the disaffected inhabitants' and having a greater chance of avoiding the British fleet. The east coast was considered well protected by naval patrols based on Cork, Liverpool and Glasgow. Waterford Harbour was

of great importance but inadequately protected by Duncannon Fort. Depots for stores and artillery should be established at Clonmel, Cork, Limerick and Galway, with others at Athlone, Banagher and Portumna on the Shannon. There was little reason to expect a landing on the coast between Galway and Lough Swilly. Provisions for three weeks should be provided at the batteries at Cork Harbour, Tarbert, Duncannon Fort, Charles Fort, Charlemont Fort and Carrickfergus Castle.

In June 1793 Colonel Charles Tarrant of the Royal Irish Engineers reported on the condition of Athlone Castle and recommended that it be repaired and put in a state of defence. He also surveyed Carrickfergus Castle in the same year and inspected Cork and Waterford harbours; his report on Waterford in 1796 included the proposal to reconstruct the now derelict battery at Passage to provide a cross-fire with the guns of Duncannon Fort.

Between 1796 and 1798 there were several proposals for invasions of Ireland, with French naval and military forces to be combined in some of these plans with those of Spain or Holland to assist the United Irishmen. The first of these expeditions arose from Wolfe Tone's efforts to persuade the French government to send a large force to Ireland: in this he had the enthusiastic support of General Lazare Hoche, who was given command of the enterprise. After many delays the French sailed from Brest on 16 December 1796, the fleet of more than forty ships carrying a force of some 14,000 soldiers. The British Channel Fleet was too far from the French coast, so the French ships of war and transports were able to sail to Ireland without opposition—at first it was thought that the French had Portugal as their objective.

Eight ships of the line and seven other vessels arrived at Bantry Bay on 21 December, with twenty other ships offshore, tacking against a strong easterly headwind. The wind increased to gale force, and on 24 December there were sixteen ships at anchor in the bay south of Bere Island: at this time some 6,000 men and artillery might have been landed under the command of Generals Grouchy and Humbert. Plans for disembarkation arranged for the following day were not carried out, as the weather deteriorated further and the ships were driven out to sea. Over the next ten days other ships reached Bantry Bay and anchored close to Whiddy Island. During the first week of January 1797 there was the possibility of landing a force of 4,000 men; but with no reinforcements arriving over the next few days these vessels returned to France. The absence of the military and naval commanders-in-chief—General Hoche and Admiral Morard de Galles, who were on board a frigate that failed to reach the Irish coast—combined with the gale force winds and the indecision of the senior officers to prevent a landing.[2]

The French expedition had avoided contact with the Channel Fleet of the Royal Navy both on the voyage to Ireland and on the return journey to France, emphasising the risk involved in relying on naval protection to defend Ireland. It was estimated that had the French landed they could have marched to Cork from Bantry in four days, capturing the city and the important naval base of Cork Harbour. There was no adequate military force in west Cork to oppose the French during the time they were at anchor in Bantry Bay. An attempt was made to concentrate troops between Bantry and Cork, but contemporary military opinion was that the regular, fencible and militia regiments in Ireland would have been no match for the veteran troops of the French expeditionary force.

French and Spanish ships at Toulon in 1796 were ordered to join the French fleet at Brest to take part in the Bantry expedition, but the French squadron arrived at Brest too late to join the fleet for Ireland, and the Spanish fleet was intercepted off Cape St Vincent in February 1797 by a British fleet and defeated. During the summer of 1797 some 15,000 troops were on board Dutch ships at the Texel awaiting a favourable wind for Ireland. For several weeks the Royal Navy had been paralysed by the mutinies at Spithead and the Nore, and there was nothing to prevent the Dutch and French fleets putting to sea—but nothing was ready. The expedition was abandoned or postponed in September; General Hoche died later that month, and with him died much of Tone's hope for a large-scale invasion of Ireland. The Dutch fleet was defeated the following month at Camperdown.

General Bonaparte's departure from Toulon with his large fleet of warships and transports in May 1798 was at first thought by Nelson to be intended for Ireland. Later that month the 1798 Rising broke out. Nelson discovered the French fleet at Aboukir Bay in Egypt, and at the battle there destroyed most of the French ships of the line. Meanwhile several smaller expeditions to Ireland were being planned in France, now too late to assist the rising, which had been suppressed by the end of June.

The first of these expeditions, under the command of General Humbert, left from Rochefort on 6 August aboard three frigates, with just over 1,000 men, including Tone's brother Matthew, Bartholomew Teeling, and other Irish officers on Humbert's staff. They arrived at Killala on 22 August 1798. This small force, with Irish insurgents, defeated a superior British force at Castlebar, but finally surrendered at Ballinamuck, Co. Longford, having marched over a hundred miles in seven days. Another contingent left Brest on 16 September, Commodore Bompard commanding a squadron consisting of the ship of the line *Hoche*, eight frigates and a schooner. Aboard the *Hoche* on the staff of General Hardy was Wolfe Tone; the ships carried some 3,000 soldiers. Off the coast of Donegal the squadron was intercepted on 11 October by a superior British force under Commodore Warren; after a hard-fought action the *Hoche* surrendered, followed by three of the frigates.

Three more of the frigates were captured over the next few days and the *Hoche* was taken into Lough Swilly, where some of her guns were mounted at temporary batteries.

Commodore Savary, who had transported Humbert to Killala, set out again with the same three frigates and a corvette from Rochefort on 12 October with 1,090 soldiers on board. Arriving off Killala on 27 October and hearing confirmation of Humbert's defeat, he returned to France. A smaller expedition to Ireland was the voyage of James Napper Tandy in the corvette *Anacreon:* she sailed from Dunkirk on 4 September carrying a small force of soldiers and artillerymen, three guns and 1,000 muskets as a reinforcement to Humbert's army. Arriving off the Donegal coast on 16 September and landing on Rutland Island, Tandy re-embarked his small force after receiving confirmation of Humbert's defeat at Ballinamuck. In October 1798 two Dutch frigates were captured in the North Sea en route for Ireland; they had on board three hundred French troops intended as reinforcements for Humbert, and carried six thousand stand of arms and military stores. Had Humbert been successful, General Kilmaine at Brest was preparing an expedition of 5,500 men to sail under Admiral Martin to Ireland.

The response to these invasions and expeditions was the construction of temporary batteries at Bantry Bay and Lough Swilly, while work continued on strengthening the Cork Harbour forts. The blockade of Brest was reorganised with a strong offshore squadron in touch with the Channel Fleet farther west. The location of the Channel Fleet was the key to England's defence, positioned to block another attempt on Ireland or to move up the English Channel in the event of a French attempt to invade the south coast of England. In Ireland troops were concentrated in the south-west and midlands to resist a French landing on the south or west coasts.

The renewal of war in 1803, after the short period of the Peace of Amiens (Bonaparte, now first consul of France, had hoped for a longer period of peace in which to train and exercise the French fleet) highlighted the lack of coastal defence works in Ireland. Robert Emmet's rising in July 1803 must have renewed fears of another French invasion: a few days after the rising, orders were issued concerning the defence of the Shannon south of Athlone and for equipment to be ready to demolish the bridge at Banagher. During the next few months estimates were prepared for defence works on the Shannon here, and these temporary fortifications were completed by April 1804. In the same year Martello towers were under construction along the coast near Dublin, at Bantry Bay, and at Rosslare Point and Baginbun in Co. Wexford, while work continued on the forts at Cork Harbour and Lough Swilly.

French plans for an invasion of England between 1803 and 1805 included sending a large force to Ireland: in addition to 130,000 men assembled between Boulogne and Ostend there was an army corps under Marmont in Holland of 20,000 men, and some 15,000 troops under Augereau at Brest, which were both intended for Ireland. In January 1804 the troops in Brest were to be ready for a descent upon Ireland with the twenty ships of the line there, while the Toulon fleet combined with a squadron from Rochefort was to cover the crossing of the English Channel of the army assembled for that purpose.

A new plan was drawn up in September 1804. Eighteen thousand men under Marshal Augereau were to sail with Admiral Ganteaume in twenty ships of the line far out into the Atlantic from Brest, then head for the north of Ireland from the west. Thirty-six hours were to be allowed for landing troops, then the fleet was to return to the Straits of Dover to cover the crossing of the Grand Army to England, or to convoy Marmont's army corps in Holland to Ireland. The Toulon and Rochefort fleets were to create a diversion to the West Indies, departing in October and November 1804; the Irish expedition was to await the departure of the other fleets, and it was hoped that it would depart before the end of November. Forming part of the army corps at Brest was the Irish Legion, including in its ranks many of those who had taken part in the 1798 and 1803 risings in Ireland.

In December 1804 Spain came into the war on the side of France and new plans were drawn up. The Toulon fleet was again intended to play a leading role and Spain was to provide twenty-five ships of the line. The Rochefort squadron sailed to the West Indies in January 1805. The fleet at Brest was to join with the Spanish, sail to the West Indies and return with the Rochefort squadron as a combined fleet to escort the French army across the English Channel to the south coast of England—by now the Irish element of the plan had been abandoned. However, when the French fleet came out of Toulon, Admiral Nelson again assumed Ireland was the objective and at first was intending to take up a position between the Channel Fleet and Ireland, off the Scilly Islands; but he eventually followed the French to the West Indies. There was alarm in Dublin at this time as to the objective of the French, and in July 1805 the Admiralty assumed that the French ships returning from the West Indies would sail north of Scotland to join up with Marmont's army corps in Holland for a descent on Ireland.

The threat of invasion of Ireland between 1803 and 1805 stimulated work on the programme of coastal defence and on defences on the middle reaches of the Shannon as a barrier to a French advance on Dublin following a landing on the west coast. The defeat of the French and Spanish fleets at Trafalgar in October 1805 removed some of the urgency concerning these defences, but work on the Martello towers, batteries and signal towers continued into the following year. By the time of Trafalgar, Napoleon had already abandoned his invasion plans, and his army corps were on the march from the French coast to the campaign that ended with his victory at the battle of Austerlitz.

Early in 1808, following French successes in Spain and Portugal, there was again fear of invasion of Ireland among the officials at Dublin Castle. Junot's army in Portugal was expected to land some 25,000 French and Spanish troops in the south-west of Ireland, embarking them on Portuguese and Russian ships of the line. In January 1808 General Dumouriez, formerly in command of the French army in 1793 but who later went over to the forces fighting against the French Republic, submitted a memoir on Irish defence to the British authorities. He assumed the possibility of attack from Spain or Portugal, and put forward proposals to organise the army in Ireland in five divisions, with three of them as advance guards at Cork, Limerick and Enniskillen, a reserve division at Athlone, and a rearguard at Dublin; the Athlone division was to move to support the three advanced guards as required, and to have a detached brigade at Galway. These suggestions assumed a landing on the west coast, or possibly in Munster or in the north-west. Dumouriez also suggested a number of locations around the coast for gun batteries, including a number of sites in the Shannon Estuary at which they were later constructed.

The warships of the French and their allies, although for the most part in port and inadequately equipped and manned, formed a constant threat and forced the Royal Navy to undertake continuous blockades and patrols of enemy naval bases. There was always the possibility of a combination of wind and tide with a faulty disposition of the blockading squadron that would allow a fleet to escape from port. The French had additional ships of the line under construction at Brest, Toulon, Rochefort, Genoa, Naples, Antwerp and Venice.

In January 1809, following Moore's retreat and death at Corruna, it was again feared that an invasion of Ireland might be launched from Spain or Portugal and that a large-scale landing of enemy troops would be the signal for a considerable rising of insurgents in Ireland. In this regard it may be noted that most of the barracks under construction in Ireland during the Napoleonic wars were provided with defensible perimeter walls with musket-loops and with particular attention paid to defence of the gateways.

In September 1810, Napoleon was considering

sending to Ireland or Scotland four divisions: 32,000 infantry, 4,000 artillerymen, 6,000 cavalry, 3,000 artillery horses, and 120 field-guns. In July 1811 he was planning an expedition to Ireland of 36,000 men, and Lieutenant Luke Lawless of the Irish Legion was sent to obtain information on the state of the country.[3] Lawless reported after his return to France in November that most of the regular troops in Ireland were in the west and south; there was little to be said with regard to fortifications, and the 'Fort of Athlone' was the only one that might give any trouble—a reference to the Athlone batteries. He noted the construction of the Martello towers on the coast, but it seems that these were not regarded as being of any importance.

Information late in 1811 on the possibility of French attempts on Ireland led to concern at the distribution of the troops, a large proportion of which were detached in small contingents away from their barracks. Until the French attack on Russia in 1812 there remained the possibility of an expedition to Ireland, and it appears that whenever a fleet of French ships evaded a British blockading squadron and got to sea, preparations to meet a French invasion of Ireland were renewed.

There was a second phase of building activity at this time, after 1811: defences were under construction at Lough Swilly and along the Shannon south of Athlone, in most places rebuilding as permanent works the temporary earthwork batteries and redoubts. Martello towers were under construction, of a different design from those built in 1804-06, at Duncannon Fort, Cork Harbour, Galway Bay, Lough Swilly and Lough Foyle—some in conjunction with batteries—and inland on the Shannon at Meelick and Banagher. The extensive bridgehead defence was under construction at Shannonbridge farther upstream, replacing the earlier earthwork defences constructed in 1804. It seems that the military authorities were aware of the French proposals of 1810-11 to send a large-scale expedition to Ireland; the war with the United States from 1812 to 1814 must also have influenced the deci-

sion to continue building coastal towers and batteries. Enterprising American naval officers and privateer captains were capturing merchant vessels off the Irish coast and even in the Shannon Estuary.

How effective would the coastal defence works have been in obstructing, delaying or containing a large French expeditionary force landing in Ireland? A large-scale landing, the landing parties in ships' boats covered by gunfire from warships within range of the beaches or harbours, would have been delayed by fortifications, and the invading troops would have suffered considerable casualties. Fortifications without the assistance of large numbers of regular troops forming a line of defence would not prevent a landing; but any delay to the invasion force was of value in enabling the defending troops to take up positions to resist the enemy moving inland. The bridgehead defences at Shannonbridge, Athlone and elsewhere on the Shannon, and similar works on the Erne at Enniskillen, Belleek and Ballyshannon, might also delay an invasion force for some days, providing time for reinforcements to arrive to strengthen these river crossing-points. The new barracks, with their defensible perimeter walls and gateways, provided local strong-points that might be considered adequate to resist insurgent forces not equipped with artillery.

The permanent fortifications and the large barracks constructed in Ireland during the Napoleonic wars constituted the greatest expenditure on defence works and military buildings ever undertaken in the country. Some £425,000 was the estimate of July 1804 for coastal defence in the Dublin area, the Pigeon House Fort, defence works on the Shannon, Bere Island and the Northern District, the signal stations around the coast, Dublin Castle and the Barrack Department. In December 1805 the towers and batteries on the coast near Dublin were estimated at £67,000, not including many extra items such as the traversing carriages, equipment and site works. Defences at Athlone and at the crossing-points of the Shannon to the south were to cost

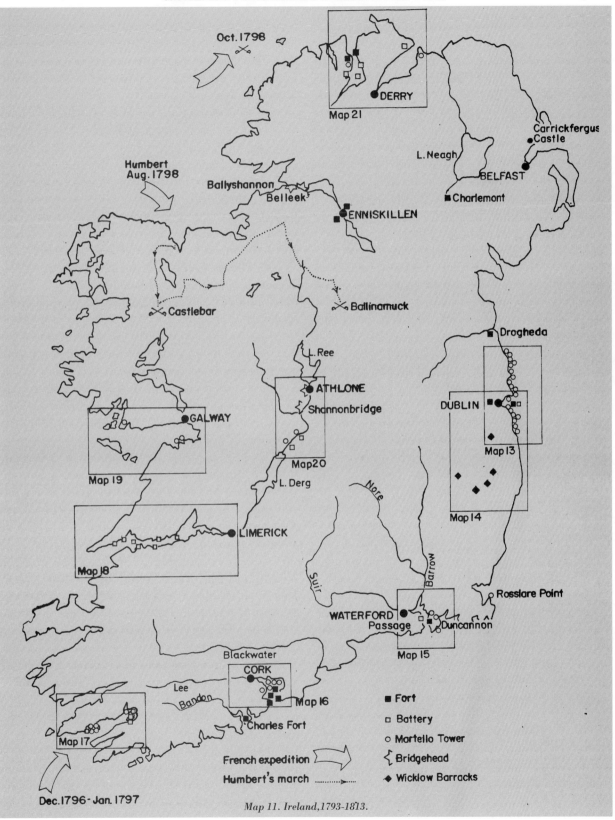

Oct. 1798

Map 21

DERRY

Carrickfergus Castle

L. Neagh

BELFAST

Humbert Aug. 1798

Ballyshannon
Belleek

Charlemont

ENNISKILLEN

Castlebar

Ballinamuck

Drogheda

L. Ree

ATHLONE

Shannonbridge

GALWAY

DUBLIN

Map 13

Map 19

Map 20

L. Derg

Nore

Map 14

LIMERICK

Map 18

Suir

Barrow

WATERFORD
Passage

Rosslare Point

Duncannon

Map 15

Blackwater

CORK

Map 16

Lee
Bandon

Charles Fort

Map 17

■ Fort

□ Battery

○ Martello Tower

〈 Bridgehead

◆ Wicklow Barracks

French expedition

Humbert's march ....▸

Dec.1796 - Jan. 1797

Map 11. Ireland, 1793-1813.

£42,000, and the Bere Island works £22,000.
When the Shannon defences between Meelick
and Shannonbridge were rebuilt as permanent
works after 1811, there was an additional expenditure of over £52,000. An inquiry into the fortifications on Bere Island in 1809 revealed that
over £45,000 had been required and that a further sum of £7,500 was necessary for repairs.
There was also the large expenditure on the three
Cork Harbour forts, in particular the new Fort
Westmoreland on Spike Island, the defences of
Lough Swilly and Lough Foyle, other works such
as the circular redoubts on Whiddy Island, and
the Galway Bay Martello towers. Large new barracks in Dublin, Newbridge, Fermoy, Cork and
elsewhere increased the military estimates, as did
the construction of the smaller fortified barracks
and the Military Road in the Wicklow
Mountains.

This massive programme of fortification and
barrack construction resulted from the threat of
invasion combined with the fear of a simultane-
ous insurrection on a large scale. After the small-
scale works and repairs undertaken from time to
time during the beginning and middle of the eighteenth century, dismissed as inadequate in the
surveys of Roy, Townshend and Vallencey, the
military authorities were now able to embark on
a comprehensive scheme of defence (Map 11).

2
The signal towers

The T-telegraph of Claude Chappe in France
dates from the period of the French Revolution;
the system of a pivoted arm at each end of a T-
shaped frame may have originated in the practice
of signalling by arranging windmill sails in certain positions. By 1794 a line was in operation
between Paris and Lille; the line from Paris to
Brest, with fifty-five stations, opened in August
1798. The system was in operation in Belgium
and Denmark by 1802.

The term 'semaphore' appears to have been
first applied to the French coastal telegraphs,

which were in operation by 1803. A vertical staff
with three movable arms, it was more versatile
than the Chappe telegraph and capable of a larger variety of signals. In England a telegraph
known as Murray's system was set up by the end
of 1796; it consisted of six large shutters or pan-
els, fixed in pairs in a large frame. The shutters
were operated by ropes from a building at the
base of the frame, and various arrangements of
closed and open shutters related to coded messages, letters and numbers. There was a line of
these shutter telegraphs between Portsmouth and
London, and another line between the Kent coast
and London, with a branch line to Chatham.

The Admiralty also set up a coastal signalling
system at this time, established in 1794 along the
south and east coasts of England between Land's
End and Yarmouth. By 1795 there were seventy-
four stations, intended to communicate with
ships of war by a system of balls and flags, and
not necessarily to communicate with each other.
At each station there were a lieutenant, a midshipman and two signalmen. A rectangular flag,
a blue pendant (narrow triangular flag) and four
black balls made of hoops covered with canvas
were hoisted in various arrangements to convey
certain signals. The signal post consisted of an
old topmast of fifty feet with a cap, cross-trees
and fid (conical wooden pin) to secure the thirty-
foot flagstaff, and a thirty-foot gaff or spar set at
an angle from the mast, to which the canvas-cov-
ered balls were hoisted.

This ball-and-flag system was the one introduced on the Irish coast in 1804. In 1810 the
Admiralty began to replace this system on parts
of the English coast with an arrangement similar
to that in France.[1]

The signal stations around the coast of Ireland
were established between 1804 and 1806. At most
of them a 'defensible guard house' or signal
tower was erected, except for a few locations
where the signal crew and military guard were
accommodated in a fort, Martello tower, or lighthouse. The first proposal appears to date from
August 1803, when the lord lieutenant, the Earl
of Hardwicke, confirmed in correspondence to

London that signal stations and flagstaffs were to be erected in west Cork; orders had been issued to the officers of the ordnance to carry this into effect. In the following month the commander of the forces in Ireland ordered Colonel Fisher of the Royal Engineers to send an experienced officer to Co. Cork to investigate the proposed locations of the signal posts to convey intelligence by signals from Berehaven to Cork. He pointed out that the signal houses used in England would not be suitable in Ireland, where a defensible stone building to lodge six men would be required, and suggested the possibility of a two-storey round tower some twenty feet high. This was to have a flat roof, the entrance at high level to be approached by ladder and the door to be covered in iron sheeting against attack by fire. The tower outlined had elements both of the Martello towers and signal towers that were soon to be under construction on the Irish coast.[2]

In January 1804, Hardwicke was again in communication with London, having been advised to investigate the possibility of building 'Corsican towers' or Martello towers at the signal stations, a suggestion that had come from the Admiralty. The plan for 'defensible guard houses' or signal towers at the signal posts was under way at this time, and Hardwicke thought it best to proceed with these less expensive structures while further consideration might be given to the placing of Corsican towers on the coast in situations where they might be necessary for defence.[3]

The reference in this correspondence to the signal stations of the southern coast implies that the west Cork area was still a priority. In March the question of the issue of bedding, fuel and candles for the Cork stations was raised, the supplies to be issued as soon as the military guards were in occupation. Signal lieutenants were appointed to several of the Cork signal stations in 1804, while by the following year all of them had a military detachment in residence.

By June 1804, Rear-Admiral Whitshed was advising on coastal defence measures, including the siting of the signal stations, Martello towers, and batteries. Some of the stations were established on the southern coasts and a plan had been decided on for signal posts from Dublin southwards around the coast to Malin Head. The locations had been fixed, and work started on some of the towers and defensible guardhouses. Whitshed had selected the sites, and the works were to be carried out under the direction of the commanding officer of the military district in which they were located. Military expenses for July 1804 included the sum of £40,000 for the signal stations with defensible guardhouses then under construction on the coast.[4] Later lists of the stations show that the costs of the signal towers varied from about £600 to £900 each, possibly including the signal mast and other equipment; to meet the overall estimate of £40,000 the cost of each signal post—tower and equipment—should not have exceeded an average of about £540.

Hardwicke was again in communication with London in September 1804, stressing that the construction of the signal posts was well advanced; they were evidently intended as a line of communication from Dublin to Bantry Bay and from Bantry around the west coast to Malin Head. The remote locations of many of the signal stations had resulted in their cost being larger than estimated.[5] In August 1805 the commander of the forces, Lord Cathcart, in communication with Hardwicke, expressed his concern that the signal stations visited by the lord lieutenant had defects in their construction, but stated that in the absence of an overseer and with only occasional visits of an architect, in some instances it was inevitable that there would be defects in this form of contract work.[6]

The towers were generally of two storeys, square in plan or with the rear wall opposite the entrance door increased slightly in thickness at the centre to form a slight salient angle, perhaps to accommodate the fireplace and chimney on this side. The tower at the Old Head of Kinsale is some fourteen feet square internally, the walls being about two feet thick. The entrance was at first-floor level, approached by a step ladder. Directly over this axially placed doorway is a

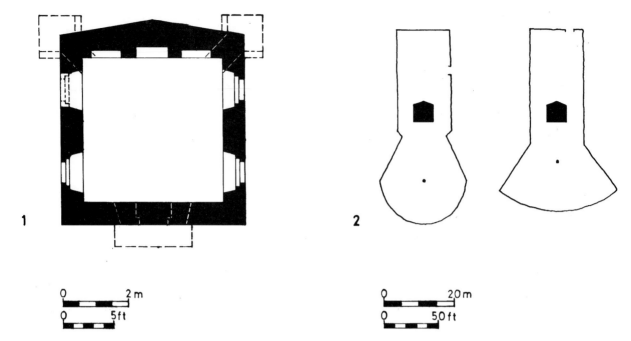

Fig. 76. Plan of Old Head of Kinsale signal tower and plans of typical Cork signal tower enclosures.

machicolation, with two more at the landward corners of the tower. There was a flat roof—two rows of sockets for timber joists here suggest a particularly strong structure—protected by a parapet incorporating the three machicolations. The ground-floor windows are relatively small square openings, the first-floor windows of the same width but of taller proportions, typical of Georgian domestic architecture. With the entrance door at first-floor level on the seaward elevation, the two flank walls contain the windows at ground and first floor, while the splayed rear wall is blank, with fireplaces and chimney. The tower was originally clad in weather slating, a feature it shares with several of the other Cork towers. The height from ground level to parapet is some thirty feet (Fig. 76).

The signal towers farther west at Kedge Point and Toe Head are slightly larger in plan than that at the Old Head of Kinsale, being fifteen feet square internally, nineteen feet externally. The tower at Carrowmably on the Sligo coast is of similar dimensions, with a splayed rear wall to accommodate the fireplace and chimney as at the tower at the Old Head of Kinsale. It is evident

that there was a standard design for the signal towers, perhaps drawn up by the Royal Engineers. Contemporary sketches of the Donegal towers at Fanad Head and Malin Head depict the same type of tower as elsewhere on the coast.

A series of site plans of the Cork coast signal stations in 1806 depicts most of them within a rectangular enclosure with a semicircular or fan-shaped extension on the seaward end, where the signal mast was situated (Fig. 76).[7] From this position there was a view out to sea and along the coast in each direction to the next signal station. The enclosure was formed by a stone wall or turf bank, having in some instances a glacis on the exterior, providing a limited defensive perimeter for the military guard. When this survey was carried out between September and November 1806 the towers and enclosures were completed but the roads leading to some of them were unfinished. The plans were drawn by John Hampton, who some years later was to survey the ground at Gallows Hill, Athlone, in connection with the acquisition of land for the batteries there.

The signal tower at Dalkey Hill, the first sta-

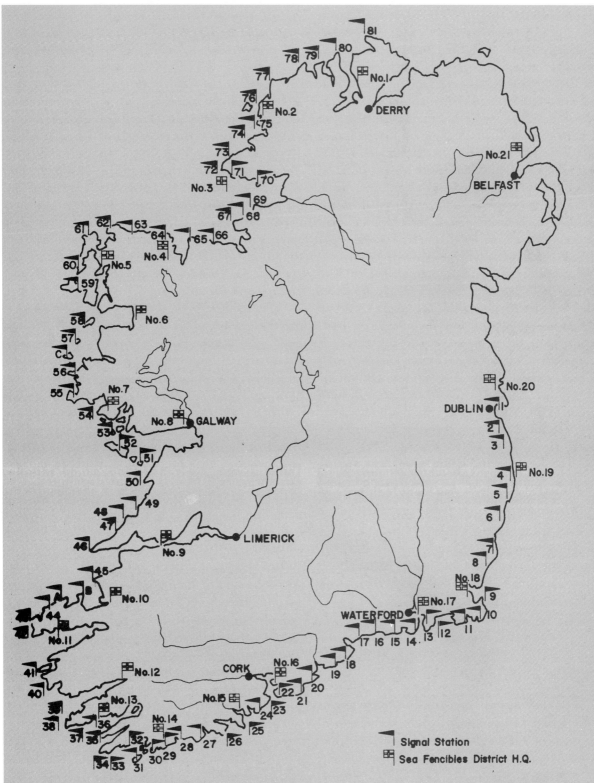

Map 12. Ireland; Signal Stations, 1804–1806. Signal towers not included in the 1804-06 lists: A near Brandon Head; B Kilshannig Point; C Inishbofin.

tion south of the Dublin terminal at the Pigeon House Fort, is nineteen feet square externally, with an additional structure built onto the seaward side. Some distance in advance of this extension—some twenty-six feet from the seaward side of the signal tower—is a shallow depression in the rocky ground surface twelve inches in diameter, in the centre of which is a deeper depression three inches in diameter; this recess appears to have been the socket or mast step for the base of the signal mast. The tower was altered later in the nineteenth century, but the outline of the original entrance doorway may be seen at first-floor level, partly blocked up, above the ground-level doorway inserted later.

Two 'signal defensible guardhouses' at the mouth of the Shannon, at Kerry Head and Loop Head, were ready for occupation in October 1804.[8] However, at Kerry Head the naval lieutenant and signal crew—one midshipman and two signalmen of the sea fencible district with headquarters at Tarbert—were not appointed until October 1805. A sergeant or corporal with six men of the Clanmaurice Yeoman Infantry under Captain Ponsonby served periods of two weeks as the military guard to protect the signal crew.[9] The Kerry Head signal tower was visited in August 1806 by Arthur Wellesley, later the Duke of Wellington, on a tour of the defences of the south and west coasts.[10] He noted the great distance between this tower and that at Ballydavid, and thought that as the Blasket Island station light was visible from Ballydavid, the intermediate station on Sybil Head was unnecessary, indicating perhaps the use of a system of light signals at night. Edward Wakefield, in *An Account of Ireland, Statistical and Political* (1812), volume 2, describes Kerry Head signal station, which he visited in 1808:

The signal station consists of a square tower thirty-four feet in height, each side of which is thirteen feet wide. It is committed to the care of a lieutenant and a guard. The door is in the upper storey, the only access to it by means of a small ladder, which can be hauled

up in a moment. It is built of stone, and might be defended by half a dozen men against any number, unless provided with cannon.

He noted the building contract price as £630. The first floor was divided by a partition to provide a room for the lieutenant, the remaining space at this level being a passageway with access—presumably by ladders—to the ground floor, where the military guard was accommodated, and to the flat roof above. The annual expense of each signal station was about £600 though they were much neglected, particularly in the supply of ropes; Wakefield noted that the next station, on Brandon Height (Ballydavid Head), had never been used.

In December 1805, Captain Lecky, commanding the sea fencibles on the coast of Mayo and Sligo, is mentioned in correspondence concerning furniture, firing and candles for 'defensible guard houses'—the signal towers in No. 4 Sea Fencible District, with headquarters at Killala.[11] These were the towers from Creevagh to Killcologue Point or Mullaghmore, a total of six signal stations. The signal lieutenants had been appointed at Creevagh and at Rathlee in July that year. On the Cork coast in 1805 there were military guards at all signal stations, most of them local yeomanry: at Robert's Head were the Robert's Cove Infantry; the Oyster Haven Infantry had five men at Barry's Head; the Clare Militia provided a detachment of seven men at the Old Head of Kinsale. District No. 14 of the sea fencibles, with responsibility for the seven signal stations from Glandore to Mizen Head, had five men of the Carbury Infantry at each station. Apart from two signal stations in Wexford and the two most northerly towers, at Fanad Head and Malin Head, there were no military guards at the other signal posts in September 1805. In July 1805 twenty-five of the signal stations that were reported as completed required officers to command them; by April 1806, forty-five signal officers were still required for the signal stations—mainly those on the west, south-east and east coasts, as the nineteen stations on the Cork coast were only short of one officer. In July the following year there were detachments of the 32nd Foot at the signal stations at Seven Heads and Galley Head.[12]

In Co. Donegal the contract for building the four signal towers or defensible guardhouses at St John's Point, Carrigan Head, Malin Beg and Glen Head, under the supervision of Major-General Sir Charles Ross, was for a total of £2,404. A list of signal towers of 1804 details the cost of most of the towers and notes that at St John's Point at £438 and the most expensive of the four, at Carrigan Head, at £696. It is evident from the 1804 list that in Cork, Kerry and elsewhere towers were built in groups by one contractor, such as the four towers from Bolus Head to Sybil Head at £720 1s 4d each. The four towers from Bere Island to Hog Island were estimated at £910 10s each, while the twelve towers from Inisheer to Glensky were to cost £650 each.

Major-General Hart was responsible for the construction of five of the Donegal towers, which he reported to Lieutenant-General Campbell at Armagh as completed in October 1806. Richard Taylor of Derry was the architect for three of the Donegal towers: those at Melmore, where work started in August 1804, Horn Head and Bloody Foreland.[13] The remote locations of most of the signal towers must have added considerably to the cost and to the delay in completion of many of them. Although the establishment of the signal stations was considered to be urgent in 1804, only a small number were finished or nearing completion then; others were completed in 1805, and some were still not finished in 1806. At some of the stations on the Cork coast and at the signal posts at Fanad Head and Malin Head, the signal lieutenant and crew were accommodated in wooden huts while the signal towers were under construction.

Sketches of the signal posts at Fanad and Malin by Sir William Smith, who was the engineer responsible, depict small huts near the signal masts.[14] These drawings, made between 1804 and 1812, include the signal mast and hut at Malin Head in 1804 before the tower was constructed, and a sketch of 1808 of the signal tower with the ladder leading to the first-floor entrance door, the wooden hut, and the signal mast with the flagstaff lowered (see Fig. 80). The signal mast was supported by three struts instead of rigging. There are similar sketches of the hut and signal mast at Fanad in 1804 and later sketches here that include the signal tower, drawn in 1812. A complete list of the signal stations in 1804-06 can be consulted in the appendix (p.xx); the numbers are keyed to the accompanying map (Map 12).[16]

The first signal post in the chain around the coast was at the Pigeon House Fort on the south wall of Dublin Harbour, which had become a military establishment in 1798. Six miles to the south-east was the second station, on Dalkey Hill, where the signal tower is a prominent landmark. The next signal station was at Ballygannon, seven miles south of Bray and eleven miles from the Dalkey tower. Ten miles south of Ballygannon, the next signal post was at Wicklow Head. The lighthouse here provided accommodation for the signal crew; this interesting structure still survives inland of the later lighthouses on Wicklow Head. Further south along the east coast were the signal towers at Mizen Head, Kilmichael Point, Cahore Point and Blackwater, from nine to twelve miles apart. From Blackwater there was communication with the signal post at the Martello tower on Fort Point, which commanded the entrance to Wexford Harbour. Some seven miles to the south-west was the next station, no. 10, at Hill Castle some miles inland. Nine miles farther to the south-west was signal station no. 11 at Crossfarnoge or Forlorn Point; ten miles to the west was the next signal post, at the Martello tower on Baginbun Head, which commanded the anchorage here. Unlike the Martello at Fort Point, the tower at Baginbun still survives.

From Baginbun the line of communication continued to Hook Tower five miles to the south-west, still in use as a lighthouse. Signal towers at Brownstone Head, Islandikane (west of

Tramore), Bunmahon, Ballyvoyle Head and Ballynamona (probably Mine Head) continued the chain of signal posts to Ardmore, some five to eight miles apart. The first of the nineteen signal posts in Co. Cork was at Knockadoon Head, signal station no. 20 from the Pigeon House Fort. From Knockadoon the line continued to Ballynacotta (presumably this tower was situated in the townland of Ballymacotter, between Ballycotton and Roche's Point). The next signal post was at Carlisle Fort at the entrance to Cork Harbour, the signal crew being accommodated in the fort; just over eight miles to the south was the next signal tower, at Roberts Head. Four miles south-west was the next signal post, at Barry's Head, in sight of the signal tower some eight miles to the south-west on the Old Head of Kinsale.

From the Old Head the line of signal posts continued westwards: Seven Heads, Galley Head, Glandore Head, Toe Head, Kedge Point (or Ballylinchy) signal tower, to Cape Clear, where the signal tower was on the east side of Clear Island. These stations vary from five to ten miles apart. Some seven miles north-west of Clear Island was station no. 32 at Leamcon, just over two miles west of Schull. South-west from Leamcon about eight miles was the signal tower on Brow Head; from here it was only a little over two miles to the signal tower at Mizen Head, which communicated with that on Sheep's Head, some six miles to the north. The signal station on Sheep's Head watched over the southern approaches to Bantry Bay, in sight of the signal tower on high ground at the western end of Bere Island six miles distant.

The Bere Island tower communicated with that on Black Ball Head (Fig. 77) some six miles to the west, which linked with signal station no. 38 on Dursey Island. Lists of 1804-06 include a signal station on Hog Island (or Scariff Island, as it is known today): however, by 1806 no construction had been undertaken here, and it seems that no signal tower was built. Some seven miles to the north-west the next station is recorded at Bolus Head: foundations survive of a tower at Bolus

Fig. 77. Black Ball Head signal tower, Co. Cork.

Point a short distance to the north-west, which seem to be the remains of the signal tower.[17] The enclosure with four flankers at the corners near Bolus Head and noted as 'Bolus Signal Tower' on the first edition of the Ordnance Survey must be a later structure. A similar enclosure is also depicted on the Ordnance Survey, sited near Hog's Head, some six miles to the east across Ballinskelligs Bay.

Some seven miles north-west is the signal tower on Bray Head, Valentia Island, which was followed by that on Great Blasket Island fifteen miles distant. The next station was at Sybil Head seven miles to the north, followed by Ballydavid signal tower five miles to the north-east. Wellington during his visit to Kerry Head signal tower in 1806 remarked that the next station was at Ballydavid (incorrectly called Brandon Head). However, it appears that at some time after 1806 two additional signal towers were constructed between Ballydavid and Kerry Head, as the first edition of the Ordnance Survey maps indicate signal towers about a mile to the south of Brandon Head and at Kilshannig Point. That at Kilshannig is depicted as the same type of rectangular enclosure with corner flankers as that at Bolus Head and at Hog's Head; there is a reference to Kilshannig in state papers of 1812 con-

Fig. 78 Carrowmably signal tower, Co. Sligo.

cerning signal and Martello towers.

Kerry Head signal tower, no. 45 in the 1806 list, is twenty-two miles from Ballydavid: it is noted on the first edition of the Ordnance Survey as 'Barrack and Signal Tower (in ruins)'. Ten miles to the north was the signal station known as Loop Head; the signal tower was over a mile to the north-east of Loop Head, noted as 'Telegraph (in ruins)' on the first edition of the Ordnance Survey, situated in a large ring-fort.

The line of signal posts continued northwards along the Clare coast: Knocknagarhoon, Baltard Hill in Ballard townland, Mutton Island (which is not in the 1804 list of stations but is included in 1805), and Hag's Head tower, some 400 feet above sea level. The towers along the Clare coast were from six to nine miles apart; the tower on Hag's Head communicated with the next signal station, on Inisheer, some four miles distant, where the tower survives in good condition. The next station was on Inishmore, where the tower still stands next to a later lighthouse structure.[16] From here the chain of signal posts continued across to Golam Head, Lettermullan Island, and north-west eight miles to the hill north-east of Ard Castle. From here it was ten miles to the tower near Slyne Head (no. 55 in the signal sta-

tion list of 1806). The next signal post was at Cleggan Hill ten miles to the north of Slyne Head; the first edition of the Ordnance Survey depicts a signal tower on an island at the entrance to the harbour on Inishbofin close to the structure known as Cromwell's Barrack (Inishbofin is five miles from Cleggan). The Inishbofin signal tower is not included in the 1806 list of signal stations and is possibly a later addition to the chain. The Cleggan tower communicated with that on Inishturk nine miles distant; the next station was on the western end of Clare Island, which linked to the signal tower on Achill Island thirteen miles to the north.

From Achill the line of communication continued to Termon Hill some seven miles to the north ('Glash Signal Tower' on the first edition of the Ordnance Survey), then to Slievemore or Tower Hill north of Belmullet. Some seven miles northwest from Slievemore was the signal tower near Benwee Head: this station was not in the 1804 list and first appears in the signal station list of 1805 as 'Benmore', perhaps an addition to the original line. The next station was at Glinsk some eight miles to the east; under the parish of Kilcommon this place is noted in the *Parliamentary Gazetteer of Ireland* (1844) as Signal Tower Mountain. The next signal post was at Creevagh fourteen miles farther east; Creevagh is three miles north-west of Kilcummin, where the French under the command of Humbert landed in 1798. On the east side of Killala Bay nine miles farther east was the next signal tower, at Rathlee (no. 65 in the 1806 list).

The tower at Carrowmably some four miles east of Easky was the next station; the well-built tower survives in good condition here within a large ring-fort (Fig.78). From here the line continued to Knocklane Hill ten miles to the northeast across Sligo Bay: the first edition of the Ordnance Survey notes 'Ruins of Telegraph' just to the east of Roskeeragh Point here. The chain of signal posts continued north-east to a station noted as Stridagh or Streedagh, and to that at Killcologue Point or Mullaghmore, followed by that at St John's Point on the north side of

Donegal Bay, the first station in Co. Donegal.

Ten miles west from St John's Point was the next signal tower, at Carrigan Head, followed by that at Malin Beg, which survives on a bleak headland on the western extremity of Co. Donegal (Fig. 79). Some four miles north is the tower at Glen Head, the next at Dawros Head ten miles to the north-east, which linked to the station at Crohy Head seven miles north. The line continued to Mullaghderg near Kincasslagh, to Bloody Foreland nine miles farther north, and to Horn Head thirteen miles to the north-east. Eight miles farther east the tower at Melmore Head communicated with the station at Fanad Head; twelve miles north-east from Fanad was the last signal tower, at Malin Head, no. 81 in the 1806 list of signal stations (Fig. 80).

Most of the signal towers may be located on the first edition of the 6-inch Ordnance Survey maps published some thirty to forty years after they

Fig. 79. Malin Beg signal tower, Co. Donegal.

Fig. 80. Malin Head Naval Signal Post and Signal Tower 1808 by Sir William Smith. The flagstaff is lowered; the signal tower is described as "Defensible Guard House and Barrack". TCD Ms 942/1/24.

were constructed, variously recorded as 'Telegraph', 'Signal Tower', 'Watch Tower', or 'Signal Tower (in ruins)'. A considerable number of them were disused or in ruins, although some were incorporated with coastguard stations, such as those on the east coast at Kilmichael, Cahore and Blackwater. Many of the signal towers survive, including a number of those on the coasts of Cork and Kerry; the tower on Hag's Head in Co. Clare; the two towers on the Aran Islands; at Golam Head on the north side of Galway Bay; on the coast of Sligo; and many of those on the Donegal coast.

Another telegraph system was set up in Ireland for communication between Dublin and Galway by Richard Lovell Edgeworth (father of Maria Edgeworth) and his brother-in-law Captain Francis Beaufort RN (who was later to devise the Beaufort wind scale and become hydrographer to the Admiralty).[17] It was a signalling system using triangular pointers, each pointing like the hands of a clock in different directions. It was possible with the use of a telescope to see the signals at a distance of twenty miles—an interesting point in relation to the spacing of the coastal signal stations, which were generally nearer to each other than this. Edgeworth had worked on his telegraph in 1794, and in 1796 he had demonstrated it to the government. In October 1803 he submitted a plan for a telegraphic system radiating from Dublin, with lines to such places as Malin Head, Erris Head, Slyne Head, Dingle and Bantry. He was asked to establish a line from Dublin to Galway via Athlone, in which he was assisted by Captain Beaufort; work started late in 1803, and the line was completed and ready for operation by June 1804. Messages are said to have taken only eight minutes to go from Dublin to Galway. There were huts at the signal stations for the signal crew, and by July 1804 the Edgeworthstown Yeomanry were on duty at the stations between the Royal Hospital (Kilmainham) and Galway as a Yeomanry Telegraphic Corps.

The construction of the Shannon defence works in 1804 appears to have reduced the importance of the telegraph stations west of Athlone; it is not clear how long the telegraphic system was maintained after the years 1804-05, when there was constant expectation of a French invasion. The Dublin-to-Galway line formed only a part of Edgeworth's proposals; it was realised that the huts at telegraph stations were vulnerable to attack, and the plan was for defensible guardhouses to be built at each of the stations.

By June 1808, there were difficulties in keeping the signal stations on the west coast in repair, and it was proposed to build signal towers on lines radiating across the country from Dublin, which may have derived from Edgeworth's proposals. These lines were to link up with a number of the coastal stations, which were to be retained, while many of the other signal posts, particularly on the west and north-west coasts, were to be closed down. These proposals were not carried out. In 1808 also, the possibility of converting the signal stations between Cork and Dublin into telegraphs had been considered by setting up a mast and yard within each signal tower—perhaps an arrangement based on the French semaphore system.

In September 1809, Admiral Whitshed was informed that the government had decided to abandon all the signal stations between Malpas Hill (Dalkey) and Carlisle Fort, and from the tower on Inishmore to Horn Head, retaining those leading into Lough Swilly—presumably those at Melmore, Fanad and Malin Head.[18] Whitshed had suggested converting the towers on the east coast into telegraph stations, but they were closed down. During the American war of 1812-14 it appears that some of the signal stations that had been abandoned were brought back into operation; American naval vessels and privateers were active in Irish waters at this time and captured a large number of merchant vessels.

The signal stations set up in 1804 came under the command of Whitshed, who was also in charge of the sea fencibles and gunboat establishment. They were intended to play a part in coastal defence in conjunction with the Martello towers and batteries then under construction.

The sea fencibles were organised in twenty districts in 1804, an additional district covering the coast from Howth to Balbriggan being added by 1806. In nineteen of these districts the sea fencibles manned the signal stations, the number in each district varying from two to eight. The force was made up of local fishermen and merchant seamen commanded by naval officers, including the signal lieutenants at the signal posts. In addition to a large number of small boats in each district, in June 1804 there were gun vessels at Lough Swilly, the Shannon Estuary, Galway Bay, Killala and Dublin.[19]

The sea fencible districts in April 1806 were as follows:

District	Headquarters	Signal Stations
1. Malin Head to Horn Head	Buncrana	4
2. Horn Head to Teeling Head	Rutland	4
3. Teeling Head to Donegal	Killybegs	4
4. Ballyshannon to Killala	Killala	6
5. Killala to Blacksod Bay	Broadhaven	4
6. Blacksod to Killary Harbour	Westport	3
7. Killary to Greatmans Bay	?	4
8. Greatmans Bay to Black Head	Galway	2
9. Loop Head to Kerry Head	Tarbert	6
10. Kerry Head to Blasket Island	Tralee	2
11. Blasket Island to Valentia	Dingle	2
12. Valentia to Dursey Island	Kenmare	2
13. Dursey Island to Mizen Head	Berehaven	4
14. Mizen Head to Galley Head	Castletownshend	7
15. Galley Head to Cork Head	Kinsale	5
16. Cork to Youghal	Cove	3
17. Youghal to Waterford	Passage	6
18. Waterford (Hook Tower) to Arklow	Wexford	8
19. Arklow to Killiney	Wicklow	5
20. Howth to Balbriggan	Malahide	–
21. Donaghadee to Larne	Carrickfergus	–

A list of sea fencible districts in 1804 gives only twenty districts, with Donaghadee-to-Larne as no. 20, and no Howth-to-Balbriggan district. In this list the headquarters of no. 7 District is Birtebui or Bertraghboy Bay.[20]

3
Dublin and Wicklow

Dublin and the adjacent coast was not felt to be as open to invasion as the south and west coasts; however, contemporary military reports indicate that there was some fear of a landing north or south of the city. This would leave the capital vulnerable to insurgent forces as garrison troops opposed a landing on the beaches. Dublin would be the ultimate objective of a landing by enemy forces anywhere else in Ireland, as it was the administrative and military centre of the country; and the United Irishmen also realised that the capture of Dublin was the key to a successful rising.

A report in March 1795 by the Earl of Carhampton, commander of the forces in Ireland the following year, emphasised how exposed the country was to attack by the French.[1] A force of 3,000 men with a few field guns assembled at Brest, L'Orient or Rochefort might land in the vicinity of Dublin, the best place for a disembarkation being Killiney Bay, where frigates might anchor within a thousand yards of the firm, sandy beach. The enemy would be well established ashore before the soldiers of the garrison at Dublin had marched even half way towards them. There was the possibility of a landing at Dalkey, Bullock or Dunleary (Dún Laoghaire), or to the north of Dublin at Balscadden Bay near Howth, at Skerries or Balbriggan. The garrison of some 2,000 men was hardly adequate to hold the capital in case of insurrection, and many of the city's population of 130,000 might be prepared to join the enemy.

The castle, the ordnance stores, the banks and the prisons all had to be defended. Carhampton even felt that the enemy commanders would be better informed on the details of the approaches to the city than those commanding the garrison. The landing and advance on Dublin might be carried out within a few hours. Assuming an army in Ireland of some 41,000 men, he felt this might be sufficient as a garrison to hold the country against an uprising, but quite inadequate to repel invasion. A force of some 11,000 to 12,000 men, comprising infantry, cavalry and artillery, should be stationed near Dublin. To defend Killiney Bay and Dublin Bay some 5,000 were required south of Dublin, with 3,000 north of Dublin, the rest to remain in the city as a reserve and to move north or south as required.

The jail just completed might serve as a fortress to hold 800 men—evidently a reference to Kilmainham Jail. Carhampton advocated associations for the defence of the city: artificers, the law, the merchants and shopkeepers, to be provided with arms and uniforms by the government—an early suggestion for such units, some time before the yeomanry corps was established. These part-time forces would hold the city against insurrection, with the assistance of a few regular troops and some artillery. Temporary or permanent batteries would be required at places along some forty miles of coastline; Balscadden Bay, Sutton Creek, Malahide and Rush should be defended. Any encampment for defending troops should be at least two miles from the coast, out of range from 24-pounders aboard gunboats or shell-fire from bomb ketches.

The author of another military report, 'Thoughts on the Defence of Ireland' of August 1796, considered invasion of Ireland likely following French successes on the Continent, but the east coast was thought an unlikely target as the Irish Sea was protected by naval patrols.[2] A landing between Bray and Drogheda was considered impracticable, as within twenty-four hours 5,000 men might be on the coast to oppose them: a very different assessment from that of Carhampton the previous year. The report advocated plans to oppose an enemy landing on the south or west coasts, particularly at Waterford Harbour, Cork, the Shannon Estuary, or Galway.

Following the attempted invasion by the French at Bantry Bay in late December 1796, a report from General Dalrymple in February 1797 discussed possible landing places in the south-west; he thought the east coast unlikely as a French objective, particularly for the large French ships of war that were used in the Bantry expedition.[3]

In June 1795 a camp was established at Loughlinstown, about a mile inland from Killiney Bay, another camp was set up at the Naul in north County Dublin, and each camp was to take about 4,000 men. Other camps were at Ardfinnan, near Clonmel, and Blaris, near Belfast. Loughlinstown camp, occupied largely by militia and fencible regiments and detachments of the Royal Irish Artillery, was in operation until 1799, and the camp here and at the Naul evidently reflected to some degree the concern expressed by Carhampton in 1795 for the defence of the coast near Dublin. Major le Comte de la Chaussée, a Frenchman serving with the British army in Ireland, prepared a report in February 1797 on Killiney Bay and in the following month he submitted a survey of the roads and terrain between Cork and Bantry.

His study of Killiney Bay as far south as Bray identified the absence of cliffs in certain places, the formation of the landscape, the possible deployment of forces, the position of batteries on the coast and defensive works inland. After the Peace of Amiens in 1802 and the outbreak of war in May 1803 the military authorities were soon engaged on an ambitious programme of defence works, including those on the Shannon at Athlone and south to Meelick, towers at Wexford and Baginbun, towers and batteries on Bere Island, and by far the largest expenditure—estimated at over £67,000 —on the towers and batteries on the east coast from Bray to Balbriggan.

Work was under way on the Martello towers and batteries in the vicinity of Dublin in 1804, a year earlier than the construction of those on the Sussex and Kent coasts in England. The circular gun tower was not a new type of coastal fortification but is a form of defensive work that may be traced back to the early sixteenth century. The origin of the name and to a much lesser degree the form of the Martello tower may be traced to a tower at Cap Mortella in Corsica. The French

Fig. 81. Machicolations of Dublin area Martello towers: 1 Sandymount; 2 Seapoint; 3 Sandycove; 4 Bray, tower no.2.

garrison of the tower, which was equipped according to some accounts with two 18-pounders and one 6-pounder gun, repulsed a British naval attack, forcing the 74-gun ship of the line *Fortitude* and the 32-gun frigate *Juno* to withdraw with considerable damage and many casualties. Shortly after this engagement, in February 1794, the tower was captured by a landing party. The strong defence of this tower caused great interest among the naval and military authorities, and similar towers were built in 1796 in South Africa and later in Halifax, Nova Scotia. The best-known examples of what were later to be known as Martello towers were those built along the south and east coasts of England and around the Irish coast between 1804 and 1815.

In November 1798 a British expeditionary force landed at Adaya on the north-east coast of Minorca, and soon occupied the island. During the occupation, from 1798 to 1802, a number of coastal defence towers were constructed, including one at Adaya. The design of these towers may well have been based on Spanish examples in Minorca or elsewhere, while similar towers are to be found in the Canary Islands from earlier in the eighteenth century. The tower at Adaya is remarkably similar in design to all the Dublin towers, with the exception of those at Dalkey Island and Williamstown (near Blackrock). [4] The most likely connection with the Minorcan towers seems to be that the engineer officer Captain Birch was sent to Ireland, having served with the Egyptian expedition that had set off from Minorca. Another engineer officer, Dyson, left Minorca for Ireland in July 1802. Birch was in Ireland from July 1803 to April 1805, including some months at Bantry Bay in 1804, concerned with Martello towers there. In December 1804 Captain Birch was noted as an advocate of Martello towers, in an account of a tour of inspection of Irish defence works and possible enemy landing places carried out by General Cathcart, commander of the forces in Ireland. [5]

The Dublin area Martello towers were under construction between 1804 and 1805. Colonel Benjamin Fisher of the Royal Engineers was instructed to start work on them in June 1804, and by December 1805 the towers were all armed and complete except for some minor details and approach roads. [6] At this stage several of the towers and batteries had been garrisoned for some time.

Fig. 82. Gun platform and parapet of Bullock Martello tower, Co. Dublin.

The towers are circular in plan, almost 40 feet in diameter at ground level; the external wall surface is battered or sloping inwards, resulting in a diameter smaller by some 4 feet at parapet level, about 25 feet above the ground (see Fig.85). The entrance is at first-floor level on the landward side, originally reached by a step ladder. The door was heavily constructed of two thicknesses of timber planking, covered with iron sheeting on the exterior. Above the doorway is a *machicolation* or projecting loop-holed structure supported on corbels at parapet level, to provide for close defence of the approach and doorway (Fig.81). The small chamber behind the machicolation formed within the thickness of the parapet was provided with a 'murder hole' (a square opening in the floor above the entrance passageway), a feature to be found in most of the medieval tower houses in Ireland. This opening is also likely to have been used for hoisting ammunition or equipment up to the gun platform.

The first floor provided living accommodation for the small garrison, while the vaulted ceiling of this area supports the gun platform above, which

forms a flat roof to the tower. Access to the gun platform and to the stores and powder magazine on the lower floor is by means of a narrow spiral staircase in the wall thickness. At roof level a massive parapet surrounds the circular gun platform; the perimeter iron track and the smaller central track and iron pivot carried the revolving traversing platform on which the gun carriage was mounted (Fig.82). Built into the thickness of the parapet is a shot furnace: the iron 18-pounder or 24-pounder shot when heated red-hot was capable of setting fire to the wooden sailing ships of the period (Fig.83). The parapet, some 7 to 8 feet thick, slopes down at an angle of about 30 degrees. In proportions, layout, size and external appearance the Dublin area towers closely resemble the Minorcan tower at Adaya, illustrated in *Journal of the Late Campaign in Egypt* (1803) by Captain Thomas Walsh, and it seems clear that the Minorcan towers were the model for those on the Dublin coastline.

The towers vary in small details of design and layout. Those to the south of Dublin are built of regular courses of granite ashlar blocks, while those to the north are built more often in rubble masonry finished externally in rendering. The towers at Williamstown and Dalkey Island are of a different design: the tower on Dalkey Island has no machicolation and is larger than the other towers, having a gun platform some 34 feet in diameter, compared to the average of 20 to 21

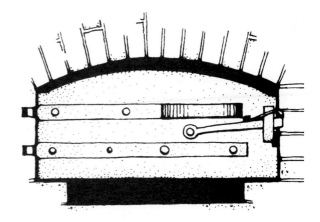

Fig. 83. Iron door of shot furnace, Sandycove Martello tower, Co. Dublin.

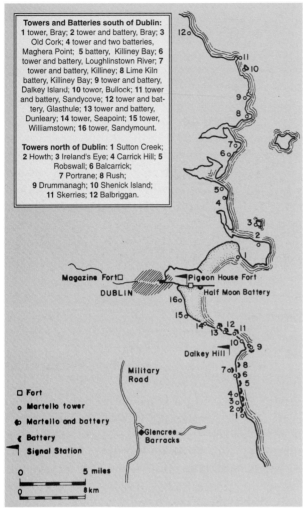

Towers and Batteries south of Dublin:
1 tower, Bray; 2 tower and battery, Bray; 3 Old Cork; 4 tower and two batteries, Maghera Point; 5 battery, Killiney Bay; 6 tower and battery, Loughlinstown River; 7 tower and battery, Killiney; 8 Lime Kiln battery, Killiney Bay; 9 tower and battery, Dalkey Island; 10 tower, Bullock; 11 tower and battery, Sandycove; 12 tower and battery, Glasthule; 13 tower and battery, Dunleary; 14 tower, Seapoint; 15 tower, Williamstown; 16 tower, Sandymount.

Towers north of Dublin: 1 Sutton Creek; 2 Howth; 3 Ireland's Eye; 4 Carrick Hill; 5 Robswall; 6 Balcarrick; 7 Portrane; 8 Rush; 9 Drummanagh; 10 Shenick Island; 11 Skerries; 12 Balbriggan.

Map 13. The Dublin Area 1793-1815.

feet, the increase in size being due perhaps to the extra space required for two guns: it is listed as a 'double tower'. Williamstown tower is unusual in having a parapet supported by two continuous corbel courses; there is no machicolation projecting out over the doorway, although a similar defensive arrangement is arrived at by two openings in the corbelling, one at each side above the door. Like the Dalkey Island tower, Williamstown was listed as a 'double tower', and is somewhat larger in diameter than the average. The third tower on the south side of Dublin that mounted two guns, that at Sandymount, also appears to be larger than the standard pattern.

Contemporary lists give details of the towers and batteries and provide some information on armament and garrisons. The towers and batteries south of Dublin are numbered from 1 to 16, but there were only fourteen towers, as at two locations there were batteries only, while several of the towers were close to adjacent batteries. North of Dublin a list of February 1805 notes ten towers, while later lists have twelve; from these it appears that two towers were added to the original line, those at Carrick Hill and Balcarrick. The names of the locations vary in some instances, but the sites of the towers and batteries can all be identified. Several of the towers and batteries south of Dublin no longer exist, but most of these can be located on the first edition of

	Location	24-pounder	18-pounder	10-in mortar
1. Tower	Near Bray Hd	-	1	-
2. Tower and battery	Bray Point	4	1	-
3. Tower	Old Cork	-	1	-
4. Tower and two batteries	Maghera Point	4	1	-
5. Battery	Killiney Bay	4	-	-
6. Tower and battery	By Laughlinstown River	4	1	-
7. Tower and battery	Tarrow Hill, Killiney	3	1	-
8. Battery	Lime Kiln or Sherwoods Field	4	-	-
9. Tower and battery	Dalkey Island	5	-	-
10. Tower	Bullock	-	1	-
11. Tower and battery	Sandycove	5	1	2
12. Tower and battery	Glastoole (Glasthule)	3	1	-
13. Tower and battery	Dun Laoghaire	4	1	2
14. Tower	Seapoint	-	1	-
15. Tower	Seafort Parade, Williamstown	-	2	-
16. Tower	Sandymount	-	2	-

Table 2, towers and batteries south of Dublin.

Fig. 84. Dalkey Island Martello and battery.

the Ordnance Survey. All the towers north of Dublin survive (Map 13). A complete list of the towers and batteries south of Dublin can be found are listed in Table 2.[7]

The first tower was situated on the waterfront at Bray, and survived until the closing decades of the nineteenth century. About half a mile to the north from the site of this tower is no. 2, which survives with the four-gun battery on the seaward side. Of the four guns in the battery mounted on their traversing platforms, three were arranged to fire northwards and eastwards across Killiney Bay, while the fourth gun was sited to enable it to fire southwards along the beach towards tower no. 1 and to the east over the sea.

Tower and battery no. 2 protected the estuary of the Dargle River—there was no harbour here in the early nineteenth century. Half a mile north was tower no. 3, sited on a low cliff overlooking the beach; this no longer survives, but a mid-nineteenth-century plan indicates it surrounded by a glacis a short distance from the tower. A mile and a quarter north was tower no. 4, flanked by two batteries. Another mid-nineteenth-century plan depicts this tower with semi-circular glacis to the east and west, with a battery some 500 feet to the south and a similar bat-

tery 500 feet to the north.[8] The tower and batteries stood on the cliff some sixty feet above the beach; the coastline has suffered from erosion here and the tower was dismantled in the early years of this century. Large pieces of masonry on the beach here may be from the Martello, but there seems to be no trace of the two batteries, each of which presumably mounted two guns—four 24-pounders and one 18-pounder were listed for no. 4 in December 1805.

Approximately three-quarters of a mile farther north is battery no. 5 at Killiney. Sited on a sandy cliff some fifty feet above sea level, the rear wall of this four-gun battery still survives with the remains of what may have been a magazine and two other buildings within a triangular salient. The wall is loopholed for musketry and protected on the outside by the remains of what is today a shallow ditch. No trace is visible on the seaward side of gun emplacements or parapet: by 1815 the battery had been abandoned, noted as dismantled on a map of the Eastern Military District of that year.[9] Coastal erosion here may have been the reason for abandoning the battery at a time when all the other towers and batteries were garrisoned.

Tower and battery no. 6 are half a mile north of no. 5. The armament here was the same as no. 2: four 24-pounders in the battery and one 18-

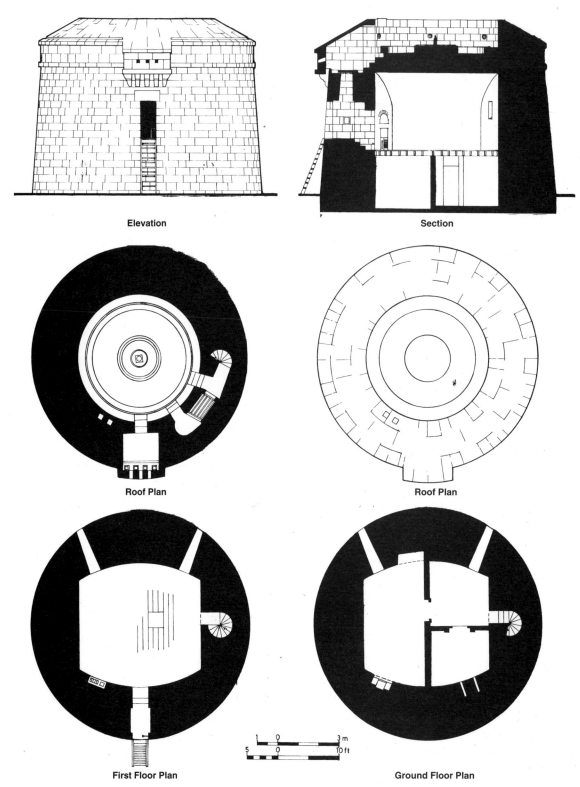

Elevation

Section

Roof Plan

Roof Plan

First Floor Plan

Ground Floor Plan

Fig.85. Bullock Martello tower. (Surveyed by Paul Kerrigan and R.W. Stapleton).

Fig. 86. Doorway and machicolation, Bullock Martello.

pounder on the Martello. The tower, converted into a residence with an additional structure built on top of it, survives behind the semicircular battery on the seaward side, sited a few feet above the level of the beach.

Half a mile to the north-west from no. 6 and just under a quarter of a mile inland are tower and battery no. 7, some 250 feet above sea level. Here the tower and battery survive, the three-gun battery (of 24-pounders) linked to the tower on the south-east side. Built against the tower and at the rear of the battery is a single-storey structure, covered until recently by a lean-to slate roof. There was access from this building to the first-floor level of the tower by means of a vertical recess within the wall thickness of the tower.

About half a mile to the north, situated on a low cliff some fifty feet above sea level and overlooking the beach, was battery no. 8. It was evidently demolished by the railway company in 1868 and was the site for the first Killiney station (a few hundred yards north of the present station) where the coast road turns inland. Almost one-and-a-half miles to the north-east is Dalkey Island, where tower and battery no. 9 are situated. The three-gun battery at the southern end of

the island with its iron rails and pivots for the traversing platforms is still largely intact, backed by a ruined guardhouse. Just under 200 yards to the north-west—that is, within musketry range—is the Martello tower: larger than the other towers, and with no machicolation, there were two 24-pounders mounted on the circular gun platform (Fig. 84). Mid-nineteenth-century plans depict the original entrance in the parapet of the tower, approached by a step ladder; there was one floor level within, serving as gunner's room and magazine. The present doorway is a later insertion, located like those in the other towers some distance above ground level. The field of fire of the battery guns was generally southwards over Killiney Bay, overlapping with the gunfire from battery no. 8 and to a lesser extent with the guns at tower and battery no. 6. The towers and batteries along the shore as far as tower no 1 at Bray all overlapped in their field of fire, and the solid iron shot of the 24-pounders had a range of somewhat over a mile; loaded with canister or grapeshot the guns of the towers and batteries could cover the full extent of the beach at low tide. The concern expressed by Carhampton in 1795 about Killiney Bay as a convenient landing place for an enemy force was now answered ten years later by the construction of these coastal defences.

North-west of Dalkey Island at a distance of just over a mile is tower no. 10, overlooking the approach to Bullock Harbour, in sight of the Dalkey Island tower and the next tower further to the north-west at Sandycove. Sandycove tower, no. 11, similar in basic design to those at Bullock (see Figs. 85 and 86) and Seapoint, is now the James Joyce Museum (Fig. 87), the tower is the setting for the opening chapter of *Ulysses*. The battery here is a short distance from the Martello, on a promontory forming the eastern end of Scotsman's Bay; there were five 24-pounders here mounted on traversing platforms and two 10-inch mortars.

Tower and battery no. 12 were sited just over half a mile to the west of Sandycove, and are depicted on early nineteenth-century maps of the

Fig. 87. Sandycove Martello- the James Joyce tower.

district; the tower was located in the area now occupied by the People's Park. The three-gun battery was some 200 yards to the north, overlooking the rocky shoreline just to the east of the present swimming pool. A plan of 1842 depicts the three traversing platform rails behind a broad parapet, linked by two flank walls to a building at the rear (Fig.88). Tower no. 12 is shown in the cartouche of Duncan's map of Co. Dublin of 1821 with the battery in the background; tower and battery are each provided with a flagstaff flying a large Union flag.

Three-quarters of a mile north-west was tower no. 13, with the battery about 200 yards away on the shoreline to the north-east. The tower was demolished when the railway was constructed in 1834; the battery is depicted on early nineteenth-century maps on or near the site of the present Irish Lights depot. The tower and battery protected the original Dunleary Harbour, the small inner harbour that still survives as part of the very much larger harbour, on which construction started a few years after the end of the Napoleonic wars. Early plans of this new harbour of 'Kingstown' depict towers and batteries

nos. 12 and 13.

Three-quarters of a mile to the west is Seapoint tower, no. 14, a standard tower for one 18-pounder gun. A little over one-and-a-quarter miles farther west is the unusual tower no. 15 at Williamstown, the parapet supported on two courses of quadrant-shaped corbels. The tower is larger than usual, having a diameter of about 44 feet. One-and-a-half miles to the north-west is the last tower south of Dublin, tower no. 16, at Sandymount. The two guns mounted here would have overlapped in their field of fire with the two-gun tower at Williamstown and with the guns mounted at the Pigeon House Fort just over a mile to the north across Sandymount Strand.

Twelve towers were constructed north of Dublin: each tower mounted one 24-pounder, apart from the tower on Ireland's Eye with two 24-pounders. No batteries were constructed with these towers. The towers north of Dublin were:

1. Sutton Creek
2. Howth
3. Ireland's Eye
4. Carrick Hill (Portmarnock)
5. Robswall (Malahide)
6. Balcarrick
7. Portraine (Portrane)
8. Rush
9. Drummanagh
10. Shenick's Island
11. Skerries
12. Balbriggan

Tower no. 1, on the south-west side of the Howth promontory, protected Sutton Creek in the mudflats of the north side of Dublin Bay. The tower survives in poor condition, empty and derelict, having previously been converted into a residence. Tower no. 2 is on high ground overlooking Howth Harbour and Balscadden Bay and in sight of tower no. 3, on the western side of Ireland's Eye, one-and-a-half miles to the north. Tower no. 4 at Portmarnock, 'Carrick Hill' in contemporary lists, is three miles north-west of the tower on Ireland's Eye. The tower at

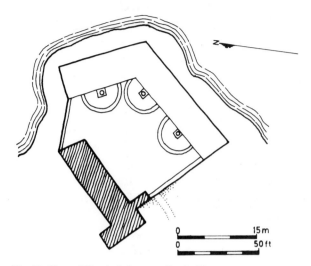

Fig. 88. Plan of Glasthule battery, Co. Dublin.

Portmarnock has also suffered from conversion, including the addition of a crenellated parapet. Northwards along the coast about one mile is Robswall tower, no. 5, overlooking the entrance to Malahide Harbour: it has been converted into a house with a conical roof, one of the few conversions of a Martello tower carried out with some care and sympathy for the original structure.

Somewhat over two miles to the north is tower no. 6, 'Balcarrick' in contemporary lists,which survives in a derelict condition. A mile farther north is tower no. 7, at Portrane, converted into a residence. Some two-and-a-half miles to the north is the next tower, no. 8, at Rush, on the promontory to the east of the town and south of the harbour. Just under one-and-a-half miles north is tower no. 9 at Drummanagh, a promontory south of Loughshinny. Tower no. 10 is on Shenick's Island some two miles to the north and just over half a mile from the coast; it is possible to walk out to the island at low water.

One mile to the north-west is Martello tower no. 11 on Red Island, originally linked to Skerries by a narrow causeway; this tower has also been converted into a residence but is now in a derelict condition. The 24-pounder on this tower provided some protection for the harbour at Skerries, and with the gun on the Shenick's Island Martello provided some defence for the

extensive beach to the south. The last tower north of Dublin is no. 12, a short distance north of the harbour at Balbriggan, the most ruined of the north Dublin towers.

The absence of the additional fire-power of batteries in support of the northern towers indicates that the north Dublin coastline was not considered as vulnerable to attack as the southern section from Bray to Sandymount. The provision of thirteen 24-pounders in twelve towers to the north of Dublin, with gaps of three miles between Ireland's Eye and Carrick Hill towers and four miles between the Martellos at Skerries and Balbriggan, may be compared with an armament of fifty-five guns and four mortars mounted on the southern towers and batteries. The largest distances between the southern towers or batteries is one-and-a-half miles; the length of coastline between towers 1 and 16 is some twelve miles, compared with the twelve towers north of Dublin that were to protect some twenty-four miles of coast.

The sites for the northern towers had been marked out for the contractor, a Mr Ross, by the end of August 1804. By February 1805 most of the towers and batteries south of Dublin were ready to receive barrack furniture and stores.[10] The garrison for a one-gun tower was to be a sergeant and twelve men, for a two-gun tower two sergeants and twenty-four men. Batteries 5 and 8 were each to have a garrison of one officer, one drummer, one sergeant and eighteen men. Dalkey Island tower and battery were to have an officer and forty men, while battery no. 11 had one officer and thirty men.[11]

By the end of October 1805 the towers at Ireland's Eye, Malahide (presumably Robswall) and Portrane were reported as completed; tower no. 16 at Sandymount was finished by the following month, when there was a request that it should be furnished.[12] A detailed report of December 1805 by Colonel Fisher of the Engineer Office, Dublin, describes the works under construction on the Shannon, Bantry Bay and elsewhere, including the Dublin area Martello towers and batteries.[13] The Dublin towers and batteries were all complete except for fixing the flagstaffs and some other details and several were garrisoned by this time and in need of small repairs.

The estimated cost of construction of the towers and batteries had been some £64,000, but this had not included the traversing platforms, the copper-work to the magazines, the bedsteads for the troops, levelling the ground around the towers and other items, including the purchase of boats required for the garrisons on Ireland's Eye and Dalkey Island. The towers and batteries south of Dublin were estimated to cost somewhat over £43,000, those to the north some £20,000, while the towers at Robswall and Balcarrick were estimated at £3,600 or about £1,800 each. In May 1806 towers 6 and 7 and battery no. 8 south of Dublin were to be fitted out with barrack furniture, each to receive a detachment of the North Cork Militia. Militia or other infantry detachments must have assisted a relatively small number of artillerymen at each tower or battery in manning the guns.

A map of the Eastern Military District of 1815 notes battery no. 5 south of Dublin as dismantled, but apart from this and a slight difference in the totals of guns at the southern towers and batteries, the details are essentially as they appear in earlier lists. John Carr in his account of a tour of Ireland, *The Stranger in Ireland* (1806), describes the Martellos as he saw them near Dublin in 1805:

Upon the sides of this coast is a long chain of equidistant Martello towers, which, if they have been constructed to embellish the exquisite scenery ... the object of building them has been successful; and the liberality of the late administration cannot be too much commended for having raised so many decorations of picturesque beauty at the cost of several thousand pounds ....I believe it would require the inflamed imagination of the hero of Cervantes to discover one possible military advantage which they possess, placed as they are at such a distance, on *account of the shallowness of the bay, from the possibility of annoying a hostile vessel.*

Carr repeats in some degree the criticism then being made of the Martellos under construction in England, but seems to have been unaware of their defensive role in repelling a landing from ships' boats, when gunfire from the towers would have been particularly effective at ranges of a few hundred yards. Grapeshot or canister would have had a devastating effect on enemy infantry coming ashore. Military opinion at the time was divided about the effectiveness of the gun tower for coastal defence: it was remarked that the only advantage it had over a battery was its greater security against an infantry attack by escalade. It was also pointed out how vulnerable the gun and gun crew on a Martello were to shell-fire from howitzer or mortar, which might dismount the gun and kill or disable the crew. Those who advocated the use of towers stressed that batteries were also open to attack by shell-fire. At half the locations south of Dublin a tower provided a strong-point to an adjacent battery, while three of the towers were 'double towers', with two guns each. The construction of the numerous batteries south of Dublin considerably strengthened the line of towers here.

Two other elements in the line of coastal defence in Dublin Bay were the Pigeon House Fort and the nearby Half Moon or Five Gun battery. The Pigeon House, a small harbour and hotel on the South Wall of Dublin Harbour, was established as a military post shortly before the outbreak of the 1798 Rising. It was intended to serve as a citadel for Dublin and as a refuge, with its own harbour for the Dublin administration and garrison. Military reports earlier in the eighteenth century had stressed the need for a citadel, with Ringsend as a suggested site: the establishment of the Pigeon House Fort followed on the same principle of an isolated strong-point with its own harbour. Some distance east of the Pigeon House on the South Wall was the Half Moon Battery, evidently constructed in the mid-1790s, providing some defence of the port of

Fig. 89. Gun embrasure Pigeon House Fort, Dublin. This part of the south wall has since been demolished.

Dublin and Sandymount Strand to the south. An addition was made to the battery in 1795. Part of the structure survives, but not enough to establish how the guns were arranged.

At a distance of one-and-a-half miles from Ringsend, the South Wall curved northwards some 400 feet and then continued eastwards to the Poolbeg lighthouse. On the north side, within the space of this quadrant, was the small harbour known as Pigeon House Basin. The South Wall was evidently extended southwards and eastwards some 200 feet here to provide space for the military buildings of the Pigeon House Fort, several of which still remain; parts of the perimeter wall or rampart on the west and south still survive. The sea originally came up to the wall at high tide, but in recent years there has been extensive land reclamation here. A large power station has been built over the eastern part of the site, replacing most of the military structures.

Entrance to the fort on the west was by means of a drawbridge, which was at the position where the present road enters the fort. Immediately to the north is a gun embrasure, the gun platform being some feet above the general ground level. South of the drawbridge were two more gun-embrasures in a length of wall now demolished; the south corner of this part of the west front ended in a triangular salient, loopholed for musketry, which no longer survives. The loops in the northern face flanked this advanced part of the west front and the drawbridge. The perimeter of

the fort ran eastwards from the musketry salient for a distance of some 40 feet, then southwards about 145 feet. This north-south length of wall survives, with two arched gun-embrasures of regular masonry in the northern section. The guns were placed on the rampart, approached by steps from the interior of the fort; like those in the advanced part of the west front at the fort entrance, they had a field of fire westwards over the approach from Dublin.

Of the south wall of the fort about half survives, a length of some 400 feet. Farther east the road crosses the site of the wall; to the east of the road a length of the south wall with three arched gun-embrasures was recently demolished in the mid-1980s (Fig.89). From this eastern end of the south wall the perimeter of the fort ran northeast and then northwards to the junction with the eastern extension of the South Wall. The entrance to the fort here was by means of a drawbridge and through the passageway of a two-storey gatehouse. North of the gatehouse on the rampart were three guns on traversing platforms, two front-pivoted and the northernmost gun rear-pivoted in a circular emplacement at the northern corner of the fort. These guns had a field of fire to the east and northeast, commanding the harbour wall and the approach of shipping sailing upstream. To the south of the gatehouse were a large magazine and stores. An element of the fort that survives is a wall forming the southern and eastern perimeter of the Pigeon House Basin, where musketry loops in the wall commanded the harbour.

In June 1804 there was a detachment of thirty-five artillerymen in a new ordnance barrack and sixty soldiers in a large house in the eastern part of the fort.[14] Another large house was occupied by officers and civilians, and there was a magazine and naval storehouses and a 'bombproof' capable of accommodating 200 soldiers in an emergency; this must have been a vaulted structure of masonry or brickwork to resist shellfire. The guns were seven 24-pounders, three on traversing platforms; one 18-pounder, three 12-pounders and one howitzer on garrison carriages; and four 12-pounders, two 6-pounders and two howitzers on field carriages. There were in addition eight mortars. A parapet had recently been added to several parts of the fort and a stable built for fourteen horses.

A plan of the Pigeon House Fort, with the addition of a much larger proposed fort, drawn to accompany a report of a committee of Royal Engineers in Ireland of November 1805, indicates the outline of the fort much as it appears on later plans.[15] The large bow-fronted house that survives today at the south-east angle of the fort is shown, with a number of other buildings, including the magazine and stores behind the east rampart.

The proposed new fort was on a much larger scale, enclosing the existing fort and extending eastwards about 1,000 feet and a similar distance southwards from the eastern part of the South Wall. The area enclosed by this new work would have been over six times the area of the Pigeon House Fort, involving expensive construction over the strand to the south and east. Two demi-bastions flanked the approach from Dublin, with entry across a ravelin sited between them. This proposed west front of the new work was some 500 feet to the west of the existing fort entrance. The size of the bastions proposed for the south and east of the fort, and the distance between them, was greater than at the new hexagonal fort on Spike Island in Cork Harbour, which was being planned at this time. The size and spacing of the bastions were comparable to the dimensions of the proposed new fortress at Killurin Hill, south of Tullamore, a plan of which was also submitted with the report of the Royal Engineers of November 1805.

While the ambitious plan to extend the Pigeon House Fort did not go ahead, it appears that work continued over the next decade to improve the defences and the accommodation. Weston St John Joyce, in *The Neighbourhood of Dublin* (1921), states that the Pigeon House Fort cost over £100,000 and that construction started in 1813; but while extensive works may have been in progress in that year the place had been a military post since 1798, and it is evident that by 1804 there were new military structures and a

Fig. 90. Richmond Fort on the Millmount, Drogheda.

defensive perimeter, including recently constructed parapets.

One of the reasons for establishing the Pigeon House Fort was that Dublin Castle was vulnerable to attack by insurgent forces. The only other defensive work near the city was the Magazine Fort in the Phoenix Park. Late eighteenth-century plans, including one of 1793, indicate a slight breastwork or parapet in advance of the drawbridge (see Fig.70).[16] It appears that the present ravelin here was constructed by 1811, when it was referred to in a report of that year. Barrack buildings provided with musket-loops take the place of a parapet and rampart; walls linking the ravelin to the fort are provided with musket-loops at the level of the dry moat, which was enlarged to include the ravelin. The armament of the fort in April 1804 was four 6-pounders, four 5 1/2-inch howitzers and two 8-inch mortars.[17]

Another work on the east coast near Dublin is the circular structure on the Millmount at Drogheda, named Richmond Fort by Lewis in his *Topographical Dictionary of Ireland* (1837). According to Lewis it was erected in 1808 and mounted two 9-pounders on traversing platforms. A low circular wall encloses the flat top of the Millmount, with two curved projections behind which were the 9-pounders on their traversing platforms. Placed in the centre is a circular tower, which accommodated a magazine, gunner's store, and soldiers' quarters. The tower is of similar proportions to a Martello, about forty feet in diameter, while the diameter of the enclosure formed by the outer retaining wall is some ninety feet (Fig.90). At the foot of the Millmount, which was a citadel to the walled town in the sev-

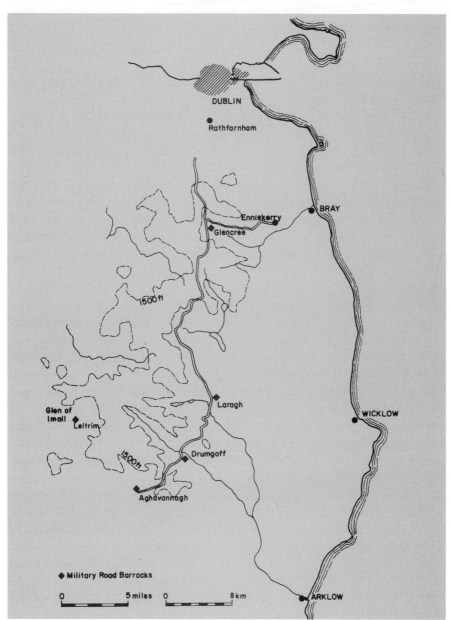

Map 14.
Wicklow Military Road
and Barracks 1800-1815.

enteenth century, is a group of barrack buildings from which there is access to the summit of the mount by means of a straight flight of stone steps. Richmond Fort—evidently named after the Duke of Richmond, who became viceroy in April 1807—must have been intended as a local strong-point for the Drogheda garrison; situated on high ground, it overlooks the southern half of the town and much of the part north of the River Boyne. The map of the Eastern Military District of 1815 gives a garrison of 340 infantry at Drogheda in permanent barracks—those adjacent to the Millmount—which may be compared with smaller garrisons at Bray, Wicklow and Arklow.[18]

In February 1800 the 'principal magistrates and gentlemen of the county of Wicklow' submitted a petition to the viceroy, Marquis Cornwallis, asking for roads to be constructed across the Wicklow Mountains to aid the troops and yeomanry in their fight against the rebels still holding out under Michael Dwyer.[19] The mountains

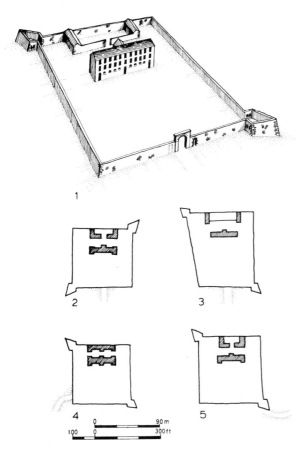

Fig. 91. Military Road Barracks, Wicklow. 1 Reconstructed view of Drumgoff; 2 Laragh; 3 Drumgoff; 4 Aghavannagh; 5 Leitrim..

who was to be employed in surveying the coast in connection with the signal towers and Martellos some four years later, was one of the engineers on the Irish establishment; the Royal Irish Engineers were disbanded following the Act of Union in 1801.

By February 1802 ten miles of the road had been completed and five miles half finished; Taylor estimated the new length of road of eighteen miles to Aghavannagh at £500 per mile, while he calculated the total cost of the road with bridges and culverts at £20,000.[20] Five barracks were constructed in connection with the road: at Glencree, Laragh, Drumgoff and Aghavannagh, and a detached barrack at Leitrim in the Glen of Imaal to the west (Map 14). In April 1802 Taylor reported that with 200 soldiers and 100 labourers the road might be completed to Seven Churches (Glendalough) during that season. Detachments of the Duke of York's Fencibles and the North Cork Militia had worked on the road, but few of the local people were inclined to work more than a few days at a time.

In April 1806 Taylor reported on the progress and expense of the Military Road. By this time the road was completed from Rathfarnham to Laragh barrack, near Glendalough, and from Laragh to Drumgoff barrack in Glenmalure, a distance of some thirty miles, including four miles from Enniskerry to Glencree. The total cost including the four miles from Drumgoff to the barrack at Aghavannagh, yet to be completed, was estimated at £39,430.[21] Taylor requested 150 soldiers to be employed by May to enable the work to be completed that summer. By April 1809 part of the road between Laragh and Drumgoff was still not completed, while the total cost was now estimated at over £41,000. The work was to be finished by October that year.[22]

Early in 1803 plots of ground were being acquired as sites for barracks along the line of the road. The road began south of Dublin near Rathfarnham and passed the new barrack at the head of Glencree; the road from Enniskerry up to Glencree also formed part of the Military Road. Barrack buildings survive at Glencree,

had been a rebel refuge since 1798, when some of the insurgent forces had retreated there after their defeat at Vinegar Hill outside Enniscorthy. In the event of another rising it was feared that rebels assembled in the Wicklow Mountains might advance on Dublin in conjunction with an insurrection in the city—this was in fact part of the plan of Robert Emmet's rising in July 1803. Dwyer held out in the mountains until he was persuaded to surrender in December 1803.

The first public reference to what became the Military Road was in the *Freeman's Journal* of 10 June 1800. Two hundred soldiers—fencibles and militia—were to be employed constructing the road, work on which started on 12 August. Captain Alexander Taylor was ordered to survey the line of the road in February 1800, but this was postponed for several months so that it could be carried out in better weather. Captain Taylor,

Life has conquered: the wind has blown away;
'Alexander, Caesar and all their power and sway;
Tara and Troy have made no longer stay;
Maybe the English too will have their day'. trans. from the (18thC) Irish by Frank O'Connor.

Paul M. Kerrigan.
20 July 1974.

Fig. 92. *Drumgoff Barracks, Military Road Wicklow. 1 Barrack building from north-east; 2 central doorway to barrack building; 3 exterior of north-west bastion musket loops; 4 interior of north-west bastion.*

but with the addition of many later structures it is not easy to determine the original layout of the perimeter walls. The other four barracks were laid out to a standard plan (Fig. 91). The road continued south over the Sally Gap—an important route across the mountains from east to west—and southwards to the second barrack at Laragh. The barrack here is in use as a residence, and most of the perimeter wall, with the two bastions at diagonally opposite corners, survives. The wall enclosed an area approximately 270 feet square, the two corner bastions being provided with musket-loops in their flanks for enfilade fire along all four walls of the perimeter. This basic plan of a square or rectangular enclosure with bastions at two of the diagonally opposite corners was used in early eighteenth-century fortified barracks in Scotland: like the Wicklow barracks, they were intended for defence by musketry, there being no provision for the use of artillery.

The Military Road continued southwards to Drumgoff in Glenmalure. Here the ruins of the barrack survive and much of the perimeter wall, with the gateway and the two corner bastions, the rectangular enclosure being somewhat larger than that at Laragh. The barrack building is approximately 125 feet long and 25 feet wide, three storeys in height, placed towards the southern side of the enclosure, with some ancillary buildings behind it (Fig.92). Some miles farther to the south-west the military road terminated at Aghavannagh, where the barrack is now a youth hostel. The enclosure is similar in dimensions to Laragh, and musket-loops survive in the barrack building on the side close to the perimeter wall.

Some miles to the north-west of here was Leitrim barrack, of the same layout as Laragh and Aghavannagh, but in a ruined condition as early as 1842; unlike the other barracks it was not on the Military Road, being in a more isolated location to the west of the mountains in the Glen of Imaal.

The *Freeman's Journal* of 3 March 1803 reported that the barracks were each to have a captain and 100 men, except for Leitrim barrack, which was to have a garrison of 200. However, in November 1805 Leitrim had a guard of an officer and 25 men, and the same numbers were to be accommodated at the other four barracks, which were evidently nearly completed.[23] Michael Dwyer had surrendered in December 1803. He had been in contact with Robert Emmet and had agreed to bring his Wicklow men into Dublin in the event of a successful rising; but the failure of Emmet's rising in July 1803, the absence of definite information concerning a French landing, and the construction of the Military Road and barracks all contributed to Dwyer's decision to surrender.

The building of the Wicklow Military Road with its defensible barracks is an example of the effectiveness of a small guerrilla band, using mountainous country as a base, forcing the authorities to maintain much larger numbers of regular soldiers to police the area. It may be argued that the existence of Dwyer's band in the Wicklow Mountains diverted a considerable number of troops away from Dublin and the defence of the coast, a factor clearly to the advantage of a possible French landing.

By February 1809 over £41,000 had been expended on the road, and with a further sum of nearly £2,000 required for completion and the expense of construction of the five barracks noted as £26,500, the overall cost was some £70,000: an amount similar to that expended during 1804-06 on the Martellos and batteries on the coast north and south of Dublin. In July 1806 Arthur Wellesley, later Duke of Wellington, visited Glencree; he remarked that it would lodge 200 men. He travelled along the Military Road to the barrack at Laragh, which he noted as being exactly the same as Glencree, which suggests that the perimeter defences were the same at Glencree as at the other four barracks. He travelled on the unfinished road from Laragh to Glenmalure, where he noted the barrack at Drumgoff; about 100 soldiers were employed on the construction of the road at the time of his inspection, which continued on as a survey of defences on the south and west coasts.[24]

Two of the barracks were later to be used in the nineteenth century as constabulary barracks—those at Glencree and Aghavannagh. The map of the Eastern Military District of 1815 notes an infantry garrison of 75 men at each of the five new barracks constructed with the Military Road; but not long after this date all or most of them ceased to be military posts.[25] Glencree is in use today as a study centre for peace and reconciliation.

4
Wexford and Waterford Harbour

Included in a list of signal stations in 1804 were signal posts at Rosslare Point and Baginbun Head. By the following year the decision had been made to construct Martello towers at these two positions instead of signal towers, and the Martellos were under construction by September 1805, with the signal masts erected nearby. They were to provide for coastal defence and also accommodate the naval signal crew. The tower at Rosslare Point or Fort Point guarded the entrance to Wexford Harbour, just over half-a-mile wide, to the north; the Martello on Baginbun Head protected the nearby anchorage to the north-east. The cost of the two towers in a list of defence expenditure of December 1805 appears as £4,600, some £2,300 each, which may be compared with the two Dublin towers at Robswall and Balcarrick in the same schedule, costing approximately £1,800 each.[1]

Wellington in his tour of inspection visited them in July 1806; it appears that they were completed by then, having been constructed by the same builder.[2] He suggested that a battery of three or four 24-pounder guns be placed on 'Strongbows Point' (presumably the promontory just to the north-east of the Baginbun tower). He noted that this tower mounted one 24-pounder carronade, and recommended it should have

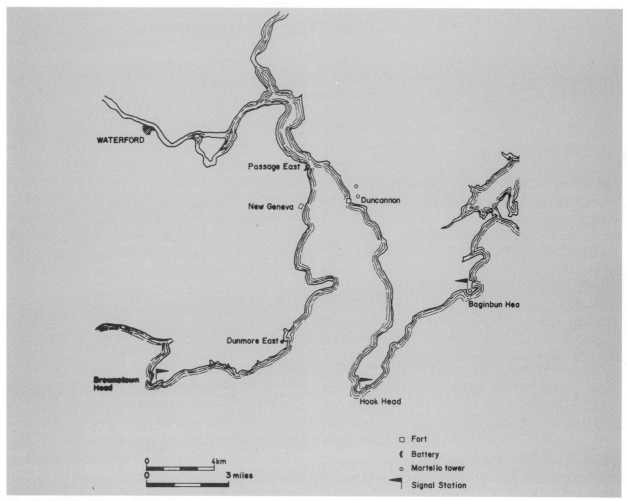

Map 15. Waterford Harbour 1793-1815.

been at least an 18-pounder gun, which would have a greater range than a carronade. The tower at Rosslare Point appears to have been the same as that at Baginbun, and with the same armament.

Baginbun Martello is unusual in having four machicolations at parapet level, unlike the typical arrangement of one machicolation over the entrance doorway. Apart from this the basic design is like that of the Dublin towers: it is constructed of regular ashlar masonry, the sides are battered, and the depth of the parapet is marked by a string course at the level of the gun platform.

The tower at Rosslare Point no longer survives; it was sited close to the seventeenth-century Rosslare Fort at the northern end of the nar-

row peninsula here. During the attack on Wexford in June 1798 by government forces the insurgents held the fort, with three 6-pounders and some 200 men, but were driven out of it by a naval attack of cutters and ships' launches armed with carronades.[3] By this time the fort must have been in a ruined condition. The site is now under water.

The principal fortification in the south-east of Ireland was Duncannon Fort, on the eastern side of Waterford Harbour (Map 15). Military reports by Roy, Townshend and Vallancey earlier in the eighteenth century had remarked on the weakness of the fort, commanded on the landward side by high ground. The author of 'Thoughts on the Defence of Ireland' of August 1796 stressed the importance of Waterford Harbour and the three river valleys of the Suir, Barrow and Nore, which provided easy access to the interior of the country and northwards towards Dublin for an invasion force.[4] The weakness of Duncannon Fort was noted, and it was recommended that the old battery at Passage should be repaired. Four 18-pounders should be mounted at New Geneva barracks overlooking the estuary on the western side and a new battery constructed upstream at the junction of the Suir and the Barrow. Transports of an invasion fleet could conveniently unload heavy stores at New Ross or Waterford, while the Barrow valley provided a good route for an enemy to advance on Dublin.

Lieutenant-Colonel Tarrant of the Royal Irish Engineers also submitted a report in 1796: 'Observations on the Harbour of Waterford, the Fort of Duncannon, of Passage and Ballyhack Point …'[5] He remarked that the sea battery in Duncannon Fort was well situated to command the channel, seven guns being placed to rake a ship approaching up the estuary, fourteen other guns bearing on her starboard bow and beam when nearer the fort, and four guns firing on her stern should she pass the fort. There were twenty-five guns in the fort, 24-pounders and 18-pounders, the same armament recorded some thirty years earlier.

Tarrant recommended a site near Ballyhack Church, upstream of Duncannon, as a good position for an additional battery for the estuary, providing a cross-fire with the Duncannon guns. At Passage the derelict battery with guns removed was noted, built some fifteen years earlier during the American war; he suggested reconstruction and repair of the gun platforms and barrack here to bring the battery into use again.

In April 1804 the ordnance in Duncannon Fort was listed as follows:[6]

Guns:	15	24-pounders
	10	18-pounders
	3	12-pounders
Carronades:	1	12-pounder
Mortars:	2	8-inch

This armament indicates no significant increase in the artillery of the fort since Tarrant's report eight years earlier. It is unlikely that Duncannon would have been a major obstacle to a determined large-scale French invasion, particularly if troops and artillery were landed to attack the fort from the high ground inland. With a following wind and a flood tide, sailing ships could pass the fort relatively quickly, to unload troops and equipment farther upstream. Smaller craft and ships' boats might pass upstream out of range of the guns of the fort by keeping close to the western side of the estuary. Guns at New Geneva Barracks directly opposite Duncannon—four 18-pounders were suggested for this position in 1796—would have covered the shallow water on the west side and provided a cross-fire with the guns of the fort situated one-and-a-half miles to the east. Passage battery was in a good position to fire on ships that had passed Duncannon Fort, ships that would only have been able to bring a few bow-chasers to bear on the battery until they were abreast of it and able to use their main broadside armament; the river at Passage, less than half-a-mile across, was completely commanded by any guns placed there. Tarrant described in 1796 the circular tower or blockhouse, built in the middle of the sixteenth century, without floors or roof, a small barrack and nine gun-embrasures, two of which directly commanded the narrow river channel; the embrasures were a few feet above high-water level.[7]

Despite the importance of Passage it appears that it was not brought back into action as a battery. Early nineteenth-century views depict the ruined blockhouse and battery; today nothing appears to survive except a small circular flanker with musket loops dating perhaps from the sixteenth or early seventeenth century.

The 1796 report on the defence of Ireland stressed the importance of repairing Duncannon Fort on the side overlooking the water, as it was in a poor condition; the fort should also be garrisoned with effective troops and no longer be used as a recruiting depot. In April 1804 an inspection report noted a shortage of artillery-

Fig. 93. Plan of Duncannon Fort 1858-1870 (based on plans of 1858 and 1867-70). A Lower battery; B Circular battery; C North battery; D Mortar battery; E Magazine; F Landface east battery; G Ditch; H Glacis; J Casemated battery; K-K approximate line of covered way on plan of 1806.

men but a good supply of $5^{1}/_{2}$-inch shells to be used from the 24-pounder guns (these were howitzer shells).[8] In October 1810 *Faulkner's Dublin Journal* carried a notice from the Officers of the Ordnance inviting estimates from contractors willing to extend the lower battery at Duncannon in accordance with plans and specifications at the Engineer's Office at the fort.

An account of Duncannon in *The Irish Tourist* by Atkinson (1815) notes thirty-one guns mounted, and adds: 'When I visited this fort, workmen were engaged in building an addition thereto, which, when complete, six or eight guns will be added to its present force, amounting in the whole to about forty pieces of heavy cannon,

beside two or three ship carronades....' Lewis in his *Topographical Dictionary of Ireland* (1837) noted that the fort was able to mount forty-two pieces of cannon and had a 'bombproof' erected in 1815; the barrack had accommodation for 10 officers and 160 men.

Duncannon is a complex of defensive elements and buildings constructed at various times over a period of several hundred years, from Elizabethan times up to the 1940s (Fig.93). A casemated battery at the east end of the south front of the fort most probably dates from the Napoleonic period, judging by the regular masonry of the two gun embrasures (Fig.94). The battery is not depicted on a small-scale plan of

Duncannon Fort of January 1806, forming part of a report of a committee of Royal Engineers in Ireland, [9] but it is shown on later plans of 1858 and 1867-70. This casemated battery protected the south front of the fort, which is built on a rocky cliff; guns or carronades at the two embrasures would have commanded this face of the fort with a field of fire to the west as far as the sea batteries commanding the deep-water channel, and the sandy beach immediately south of the fort, which is exposed at low tide. The battery is almost a detached work, approached from outside the fort by a stone staircase from the top of the counterscarp south-east of the entrance gate. Just to the west of this casemated work was a circular battery at the south end of the east-facing rampart; this evidently mounted one gun on a traversing platform, and there was a similar one-gun battery at the southern end of the upper sea battery. The guns on these batteries had a traverse of about 270 degrees; the 1804 report noted six of the 24-pounder guns with traversing carriages. A mid-nineteenth-century plan shows the two circular batteries, the lower sea battery with eight wide-splayed embrasures, the upper sea battery with six narrow-splayed embrasures, and nine embrasures in the parapet of the *tenaille trace* landward rampart. On the southern side of the fort was a mortar battery, while another battery on the north-west front mounted three guns on traversing platforms. On the north side of the fort are a magazine, ordnance store and armourer's workshop. The barrack buildings follow the line of the *tenaille trace* or zigzag of the eastern rampart on the landward front, with another barrack building behind the upper sea battery at the western end; this is noted as 'Artillery Barrack' on the 1858 plan; a date-stone of 1724 is on the façade.

The 1806 plan of Duncannon depicts three works inland of the fort. These appear to be proposals for batteries or redoubts to defend the landward approach to the fort: these works were not undertaken, but two Martello towers were built here some eight years later.

Half a mile inland from the fort is a Martello tower, with another tower about half a mile to the

Fig. 94. Gun embrasures of casemated battery, Duncannon Fort.

north; both towers are on the high ground overlooking Duncannon. These were under construction in October 1814. They are oval or elliptical in plan, unlike the other Wexford tower that survives at Baginbun, which, like the Dublin towers, is circular. They are similar in design to the tower on the north shore of Galway Bay and the tower at Banagher: built of regular masonry courses, they have no string course at the base of the parapet to mark the level of the gun platform. The doorway is as usual at first-floor level, on the side away from Waterford Harbour; but while this protected the door from gunfire from ships it was vulnerable to a landward attack. The elliptical plan of these towers with a circular gun platform resulted in a much broader parapet on the seaward side, gradually reducing to a narrower parapet on the opposite side, similar to the English south-coast towers. The Martello towers inland of Duncannon Fort were evidently sited in an attempt to improve the defences on the landward side and to prevent an enemy gaining possession of the high ground on which they stand. Atkinson describes the Martello towers in his account of Duncannon:

> The grounds beyond this village, being higher than the rock on which the fort stands, it had been deemed expedient to build two towers, on elevated positions above the village. These on which four pieces of cannon will be planted, were in progress when I visited the fort, and when complete, they will defend the approaches to the fort and village, on the

land side....

From this it appears that the towers were each to mount two guns, although it is possible they were not placed in position, as it seems that the towers were not completed until after the end of the Napoleonic Wars. The freehold deed for tower no. 1, nearest to the fort, dated from May 1811, indicates perhaps the date of the land acquisition or start of construction.

Directly across the estuary from Duncannon was the military post at New Geneva, originally intended as a settlement for craftsmen exiled from Switzerland. Some fifteen acres was allocated as the site of a new town in 1784, but the project did not materialise, and after the outbreak of war with France in 1793 the place became a barrack, occupied at first by the Waterford Militia. In June 1794 the Tyrone Militia were at New Geneva, and in the following year there were barracks there intended to accommodate 2,000 men but with bedding for only 1,200. The place was used as a temporary prison for insurgents after the battle of New Ross in 1798. In a list of barracks in Ireland in 1811, New Geneva was noted as being able to accommodate 62 officers and 1,728 men (infantry);[10] in the same list Duncannon Fort had a garrison of 7 officers and 222 men. The enclosure at New Geneva was rectangular, some 850 by 800 feet, with a bastion at each corner. Contemporary plans indicate barracks for officers and soldiers parallel to each perimeter wall, leaving an open space or parade ground in the centre; but by the time of the first edition of the Ordnance Survey the place was in ruins, only the outline of most of the barrack buildings being indicated. Much of the perimeter wall and three of the four corner bastions survive; the structural evidence suggests that the bastions were additions. As in the barracks on the Wicklow Military Road, the corner bastions were intended for use with musketry and are provided with loops for this purpose. The walls are now some nine to twelve feet high, the upper three feet or so being evidently a later addition. A two-storey building that survives in the southeast corner of the enclosure may be part of one of the barrack buildings.

5
Cork and Kinsale

Cork Harbour is perhaps the best anchorage of its size in Ireland.

It was increasingly used in the late eighteenth century, eventually replacing Kinsale both as a naval base and as a port for merchant vessels, particularly those bound across the North Atlantic and to the West Indies. It was the principal naval station in Ireland during the French Revolutionary war and the Napoleonic wars.

In 1793 the fortifications here consisted of the mid-eighteenth-century battery at Cove (Cobh), the two harbour entrance forts of Ram Head and Carlisle, and the fort on Spike Island. In addition to these three forts, constructed during the American War of Independence, batteries had been constructed at Roche's Point, at the harbour entrance south of Carlisle Fort. All of these works appear to have been neglected after 1783 and had to be brought back into use after the outbreak of war with the French Republic early in 1793.

The small fort at the east end of Spike Island was to be superseded by the construction of a much larger, regular fortification in the early years of the nineteenth century. The harbour entrance fortifications—Carlisle Fort and Ram Head Battery (renamed Fort Camden)—were modified and reconstructed to some extent over the following twenty years. The battery at Cove was brought back into service, and five Martello towers were erected at locations around the harbour in the closing years of the Napoleonic wars. On Haulbowline Island large storehouses and other naval buildings were built, while on Rocky Island powder magazines were constructed. A large new barrack was erected on the high ground to the north of Cork, while at Ballincollig gunpowder mills were established, to be followed by a new artillery barrack on an adjacent site (Map 16). At Kinsale new barracks were constructed, and some improvements carried out at Charles Fort. Extensive new barracks were

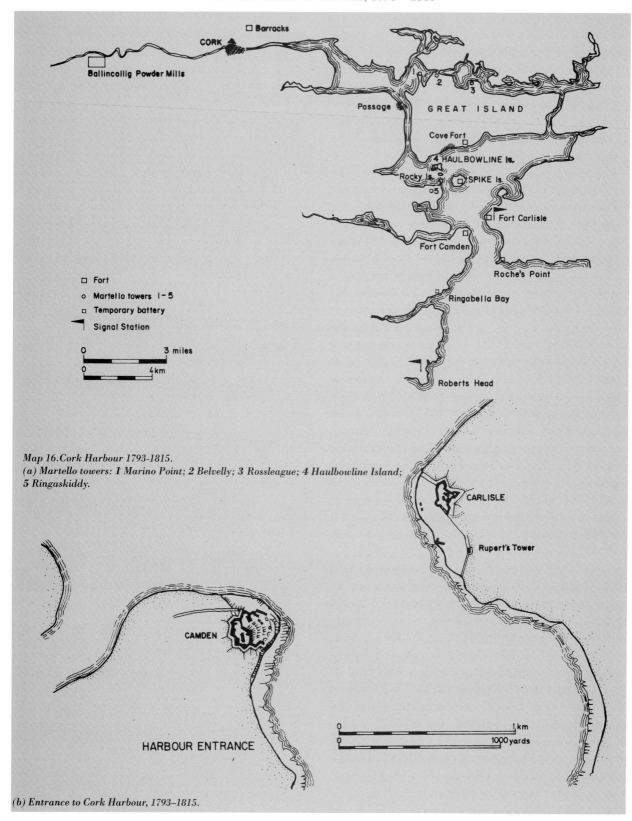

Map 16. Cork Harbour 1793-1815.
(a) Martello towers: 1 Marino Point; 2 Belvelly; 3 Rossleague; 4 Haulbowline Island;
5 Ringaskiddy.

(b) Entrance to Cork Harbour, 1793–1815.

erected at Fermoy after 1797, work continuing for the next twelve years, providing accommodation for between 2,000 and 3,000 men. Fermoy, situated north of Cork Harbour on the main crossing-point of the River Blackwater on the road to Dublin, appears to have been intended as a military post from which troops might act against an invasion force landing at Cork Harbour or farther to the west. The concentration of troops here is related to the earlier eighteenth-century proposals for assembly points for the army at Kilworth, Ardfinnan or Clonmel.

In 1805 the construction of a large fortress was proposed, thirty miles farther inland from Fermoy and some eight miles from Clonmel. Sited on high ground between Fethard and Cashel, the proposal consisted of an extensive work with eight bastions and six ravelins, having an outwork half a mile to the north on Tullamain Hill. Like the similar schemes at this time for new fortresses at Killuran Hill near Tullamore and at Cross More near Clontibret in Co. Monaghan, it was not constructed.

Fort Carlisle. Captain John Brown of the Corps of Irish Engineers, promoted lieutenant-colonel in 1800, was responsible as commanding engineer in the Southern District for works at Cork Harbour and Bantry Bay. He left Ireland in 1802 and later constructed the Royal Military Canal as part of the defences of the south coast of England, where he was not in favour of the Martello towers.

A sketch plan of Carlisle Fort by Brown 'as it stood in April 1793'—some two months after the outbreak of war with France—depicts the layout at this time.[1] The fort is shown as an irregular work with an acute-angled bastion facing east, the direction from which a landward attack might be expected. To the north is a demi-bastion, the enclosure of the work being completed by an irregular *tenaille trace* on the west and south; two barrack buildings for infantry within the fort are sited behind the ramparts flanking the bastion. A ditch links the demi-bastion to the shore down the steep hillside to the north-west. The fort is linked by an entrenchment to Rupert's Castle some three hundred yards to the

south; the castle is surrounded by an irregular work that is linked by a ditch on the steep slope on the west, to the waterside of the harbour entrance below. Along or just above the shoreline forming the eastern side of the entrance to Cork Harbour are several detached batteries, linked by a breastwork or parapet. An artillery barrack is depicted in the rear of two, two-gun batteries; farther north are a landing place, an emplacement for one gun, and another gun emplacement, and at the northern end close to the northern ditch a 'new battery' is noted, evidently intended to fire on ships that had managed to sail through the harbour entrance. It is possible that this work was constructed a few years earlier, when there was the danger of a war with Spain and when batteries were erected at Carlisle and Ram Head opposite, although when the alarm had passed they had been dismantled.

The plan by Brown may be compared with an earlier, larger-scale plan by Vallencey, 'Plan of Carlisle Fort, Cork Harbour 1781' (see Fig.74). [2] This notes the northern work with the bastion and demi-bastion as 'Howard's Redoubt'; it is depicted with the same layout as that shown on Brown's drawing, except for the absence of a defensive wall on the west, where Brown depicts a *tenaille trace*. The long entrenchment is shown linking Howard's Redoubt to the work to the south, 'Prince Rupert's Redoubt and Castle' which is somewhat different in outline on the Vallencey plan. The lower battery, along the harbour entrance near sea level, is also shown in more detail, with almost forty gun-embrasures in an irregular parapet layout following the rocky coastline.

A sketch of Carlisle Fort by Brown, which must be later than his 1793 plan, a perspective view from Rupert's Castle, indicates some changes in the northern work.[3] The southern side is depicted with a new demi-bastion and an arched gateway or sallyport in the short length of rampart linked to its west face (Fig.95). These structures survive on the site today, with most of the eastern bastion—which has lost its salient angle—the demi-bastion to the north, and their linking ramparts (Fig.96).

Fig. 95. Carlisle Fort from Rupert's Tower 1793 by John Brown (National Library of Scotland Ms 2863 f.46 v.)

Ordnance Survey plans of Carlisle of 1842 show additional works, which must have been constructed during the 1803-15 period. The two demi-bastions were linked by a rampart, which incorporates a semicircular gun platform: this replaced the *tenaille trace* wall or rampart depicted on Brown's plan of 1793. A third barrack building, of similar size to the two earlier barracks, was constructed, resulting in a triangular space between the three structures in the centre of the work. Rupert's Castle was apparently replaced with what is noted as a tower— evidently similar to the bombproof barrack or blockhouse of the Shannon Estuary batteries. A new ditch runs from this tower southwards to the water's edge of the harbour entrance, superseding the earlier entrenchment, which was constructed from Rupert's Castle to the shoreline to the west.

A report on the Cork Harbour and Kinsale defences of April 1804 lists the ordnance at Carlisle Fort.[4] A battery below the fort mounted fourteen 24-pounders and one 18-pounder—possibly a reference to the gun emplacements along the harbour entrance near sea level. The half-moon battery in the fort, forming, like the lower battery, 'a part of the marine defence of the har-

bour', mounted twelve 24-pounders. The Cockpit Battery mounted three long and two short 6-pounders; the North-East Flagstaff Battery had two short and five long 6-pounders, and five 12-pounders, for land defence. The South-West Flagstaff Battery had two 18-pounders, which flanked the harbour entrance, two long 6-pounders, one 12-pounder, and two 18-pounders. The South Gate Battery had two 18-pounders, making 'altogether 53 pieces of ordnance .... The carriages in general want repair .... Shot furnaces are provided.' The artillery detachment of five gunners was to teach the battery exercise to about 188 men of the 4th Garrison Battalion. The garrison, at about three per gun, was not enough for a 'respectable

Fig. 96. Carlisle Fort.

Fig. 97. Fort Westmoreland, Spike Island, Cork Harbour from the north-east. Ringaskiddy Martello tower is at the top right. (Irish Air Corps photo.).

defence with ordnance unaided by musketry'.

In June 1804 the lord lieutenant, the Earl of Hardwicke, in communication with London, stated that the Cork Harbour entrance forts were to be put into a state of defence and 'a work with three batteries should be erected at Roche's Tower [presumably Roche's Point] which is situated at the first entrance.'[5] This no doubt involved a reconstruction to some degree of the

batteries here, which mounted twelve 24-pounders in 1783.

Fort Camden. Ram Head Battery, constructed in 1779, was brought back into service during the French Revolutionary wars after 1793 (see Fig.73).[6] Renamed Fort Camden, after the lord lieutenant of 1795-98, the Earl of Camden, the fortification does not appear to have been substantially altered during the Napoleonic wars.

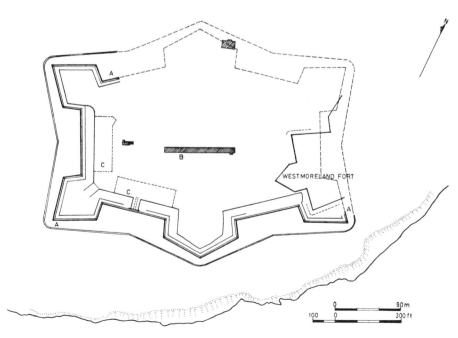

Fig. 98.
Plan of the new fortress on Spike Island, Cork Harbour (after PRO MPF 191). The line of the east front overlaps part of the earlier Fort Westmoreland. A bastions and ramparts completed or under construction May 1809; B temporary barrack; C areas excavated for barracks.

Additional barrack buildings and gun positions left the basic layout of the work unchanged: gun emplacements on two levels overlooking the harbour entrance to the east, with a landward defence on the west of a *tenaille trace* of ditch and rampart enclosing the high ground.

The inspection of April 1804 for Camden Fort noted the armament. On the lower battery were thirteen 24-pounders for marine defence, seven on truck carriages and six on traversing platforms; in the fort were mounted five 18-pounders, three 12-pounders and five 6-pounders. The traversing platforms were new and the truck carriages serviceable.[7]

Ringabella and Oyster Haven batteries. In July 1799, batteries were listed at Ringabella and Oyster Haven. At Ringabella Bay, on the north side, some two miles south-west of Fort Camden, was a battery mounting two 24-pounders and one 6-pounder. On the eastern side of the entrance to Oyster Haven, two miles east of Charles Fort, Kinsale, a battery mounted two 12-pounders. It appears that both these batteries were temporary works, still in existence in 1803.

Cannon listed at Cork Harbour and Kinsale in 1799 and evidently still in position in January 1803 included twenty-four 24-pounders at Cove Fort, six guns at Haulbowline Island, twenty-nine 24-pounders and some smaller guns and a number of mortars at the fort on Spike Island, eleven 24-pounders and a number of smaller-calibre cannon at Fort Camden, twenty-five 24-pounders, seven 18-pounders and some smaller guns and mortars at Fort Carlisle, and seventeen 24-pounders, some 12-pounders and 6-pounders and three mortars at Charles Fort, Kinsale.

The batteries at Ringabella and Oyster Haven do not appear in the inspection report of April 1804 on the forts and batteries of Cork Harbour and Kinsale, suggesting that they were not brought back into action when war was renewed in 1803 following the Peace of Amiens.

Spike Island. The fort of the American war period was sited at the eastern end of Spike Island.[8] The much larger fort that replaced it occupies the centre of the island, and the exten-sive glacis that surrounds it extends over most of the remainder of the island (Fig.97). The regular outline of the fort consists of six bastions connected by ramparts and surrounded by a broad dry ditch. In 1804 an average of £4,000 a month was being expended on the Spike Island fortifications and the works at Bantry Bay,[9] while in the same year the ordnance on Spike Island was noted as twenty-six 24-pounders (five of which were French guns), three 13-inch mortars, ten 6-pounders, and five small swivel guns. It seems probable that these were mounted in the earlier fort while work progressed on the new fortification.[10] In July 1806 the works here were inspected by Arthur Wellesley as part of his tour of military posts in the south and west of the country; the following year he was appointed chief secretary for Ireland, a post he held until 1809.[11]

A plan of the new fortress under construction on Spike Island, dated 1 May 1809, indicates that it was approximately half completed at that time (Fig.98).[12] Part of the landward outline of the much smaller eighteenth-century work noted as 'Westmoreland Fort' is depicted at the east end of the new work, overlapping the line of the east front of the new fortification. In May 1809 the north-west bastion, west front, southwest bastion, south-centre bastion, south front and south-east bastion were constructed. The northern front, north-central bastion, north-east bastion and east front are depicted only in broken line, the work on these not yet having started. Part of the dry moat and counterscarp wall surrounding the new fortress is shown, extending from in front of the north-west bastion, along the west front, and across the south front to the south-east bastion. No covered way was provided on the counterscarp; a section through the north-west bastion indicates that most of the glacis here is artificial, consisting of made-up ground. The counterscarp wall, partly constructed at this time, varied in height from six to sixteen feet, extending to a much greater depth below ground to the foundation level.

A long, narrow temporary barrack is depicted on the plan, located in the centre of the fort,

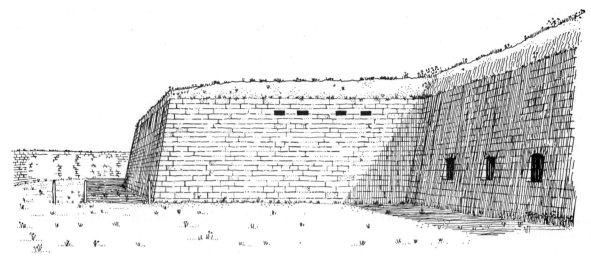

Fig. 99. Fort Westmoreland: north central bastion, with flank gallery musketry loops.

while rectangular areas behind the west and south-west ramparts are noted as excavated for the permanent barracks. Edward Wakefield, in *An Account of Ireland, Statistical and Political* (1812), noted the cost of the works on Spike Island as £1,000,000. In 1811 it was predicted that a further eight years would be needed to complete the building operations; in December 1813, Youghal bricks were being delivered to the works on Spike Island, evidently transported by sea in coastal vessels.[13] Construction work on the new fortress—which inherited the name Fort Westmoreland from its predecessor—continued until the 1860s, while from 1847 convict labour was employed, the place being used as a prison until 1883.

Fig. 100. Fort Westmoreland: entrance to flank gallery, north-west bastion.

The bastion faces are almost 200 feet in length, the flanks 75 feet, the distance along the ramparts between the bastions some 300 feet (Fig.99). In the flanks of the bastions, just below the parapet level, are galleries loop-holed for musketry (Fig.100). The absence of a covered way on the counterscarp of the dry moat (the covered way had been a feature of artillery fortification for over two hundred years) is significant, and was part of the new approach to fortification design evolving at this time. However, in most of the other features, and particularly in layout, the new Fort Westmoreland follows the typical bastion and rampart arrangement of earlier fortifications. In 1805 a fortress of similar layout and size, but with outworks and caponnières, was proposed for a site at Killurin Hill, south of Tullamore. This was one of a number of new fortifications proposed by a committee of Royal Engineers at that time.

Cove Fort. The 'Inspection Report of the Cork Harbour Forts and Batteries' of April 1804 describes Cove Fort as consisting of three batteries: the lower battery mounted six 24-pounders, the middle, thirteen, and the upper battery *en barbette*, one gun.[14] Eleven embrasures were noted as out of repair. The guns here had a field of fire over the harbour and the main channel from the harbour entrance some two miles away to the south. Close to the fort, vessels approaching upstream from the harbour entrance turn to

Fig. 101. The Cove of Cork- early nineteenth-century view of Cork Harbour; on the left Rocky Island magazine, in the middle distance the six naval storehouses and Martello tower on Haulbowline Island.

the west to follow the main channel north of Spike Island and Haulbowline Island. Most of the ramparts and parapets survive on the site, with a central archway and staircase. At the close of the Napoleonic wars the defensive function of Cove Fort appears to have ceased, and it became a hospital, as noted on the first edition of the Ordnance Survey.

Haulbowline Island. The inspection report of 1804 noted a battery of two 18-pounders on the top of the island, with two long 6-pounders dismounted.[15] Two years later the island was divided between the Admiralty and the Board of Ordnance, the Ordnance having the western part, where the Martello now stands; in the Admiralty area six large storehouses—fine examples of functional architecture—were erected at the naval victualling yard, together with other buildings and a naval hospital.[16] Wakefield noted that by 1811 over £10,000 pounds had been expended on the new works at Haulbowline.

The Cork Harbour Martello towers. Five

Martellos were constructed to add to the defence of Cork Harbour: three on the north side of Great Island—Manning Tower at Marino Point, at Belvelly, and at Rossleague, farther east—the tower on Haulbowline Island, and Ringaskiddy tower, on high ground south of Haulbowline on the west side of the harbour (Fig.101). The Marino Point tower is situated at the northern end of a long, low promontory forming the north-western extremity of Great Island. This tower was captured by 'Captain Mackay' of the Fenians in December 1867 to obtain the small arms stored there—the only known attack on a Martello tower apart from the tower in Corsica after which they are named. Just over half a mile to the east is the tower at Belvelly, built on the axis of the bridge carrying the road from Cork across from Foaty (Fota) Island (Fig.102). The bridge spans the narrow Belvelly Channel on the site of the earlier ford here. A little over a mile farther east is the Rossleague tower, sited on a promontory projecting from the north shore of Great Island. The only approach to this tower

Fig. 102. Cork Harbour: Belvelly Martello tower and Belvelly Castle, on Great Island. Belvelly Bridge, on the site of a ford, was constructed a few years before the Martello.

for building materials was by water, supplies being unloaded at a nearby quay constructed for the purpose (Fig.103). In good condition, Rossleague Martello is oval in plan, with circular-plan interior and gun platforms; a spiral stairs close to the first floor entrance leads to the ground level and up to the gun platform.

All five towers were still under construction between 1813 and 1815.[17] The contractor was to be supplied with bricks delivered from Youghal, which were to be landed at Spike Island—brickwork was used for the interiors and vaulting. In September 1814 there was correspondence concerning the construction of traversing platforms for the guns, and in the following month an instruction was issued to have the cast-iron pivots provided as soon as possible, to be made in Cork. In March 1815 the towers at Rossleague and Marino Point were still not completed.[18]

The tower on high ground at Ringaskiddy, just less than a mile south of the tower on Haulbowline, is unusual in being surrounded by a rock-cut ditch. Entry is by means of a small footbridge, and there may have been a drawbridge here originally (Fig.104). All five towers survive in a fair condition today. They are constructed of squared rubble built to courses, or more regular ashlar masonry, with brickwork interiors and vaulting. The external wall surfaces are almost vertical, resulting in a drum-shaped profile, unlike the majority of Irish towers, which have a battered wall surface, sloping inwards towards the parapet level. The Cork Harbour towers do not have a machicolation over the doorway, a characteristic they share with other towers built during the last five years of the Napoleonic wars, such as those at Galway Bay, Banagher and Duncannon. The thin wall of the machicolation would have been vulnerable to cannon-fire, compared with the much thicker wall of the tower and parapet: it is possible that this potential weakness of a tower with a machicolation when exposed to gun-fire from enemy artillery was a factor in the design of these later towers.

The three towers along the north side of Great Island were intended as a defence of the approaches to Cork Harbour from the mainland in the event of an enemy landing elsewhere on the coast and attacking from inland. While Martello towers were considered to be quite effective for coastal defence against shipping and troop landings, their value in inland situations was more doubtful: a tower was vulnerable to the concentrated fire of one or more batteries of artillery, aimed with more accuracy than was usually possible from the moving gun-deck of a ship of war.

The tower on the highest point of Haulbowline was a strong-point for the island, with a clear field of fire over parts of the harbour not visible from or within range of Fort Westmoreland on Spike Island. The Ringaskiddy tower provided for some defence of the high ground on the western side of the harbour, with a field of fire over the harbour to the east and to the north-west, the area west of Haulbowline Island. The Royal Commission on the Defence of the United Kingdom in 1859 noted that each of the five Cork Harbour towers mounted one gun; the tower at Belvelly appears to have been supported by guns in the tower-house castle a short distance to the

Fig. 103. Cork Harbour: Rossleague Martello, Great Island.

east, where there are gun-embrasures at high level that presumably date from this time. Plans of Belvelly Castle were drawn up in 1809 in case it might be converted into a defensible post. The cost of the Haulbowline Island tower was noted as somewhat over £3,000 in October 1814.[19] The Rossleague tower deed, dated 4 August 1812, indicates that the sites for the Martello towers were probably acquired about this time, although construction work was still continuing in 1815.

Fig. 104. Cork Harbour: Ringaskiddy Martello tower.

Rocky Island. On this small island south of Haulbowline Island two large magazines were constructed: building started in 1810, and by the following year over £3,000 had been expended. The magazines, a watch-house and a guard-house were still under construction in August 1814. [20] The capacity of the magazines was a total of 25,000 barrels of gunpowder, most of which was supplied by the gunpowder mills at Ballincollig. The construction of a bridge in recent years from the mainland across Rocky Island to Haulbowline has resulted in the demolition of the magazines.

Proposals for a new barrack in Cork were approved in May 1801, and it was constructed by 1805. An illustration in *A Stranger in Ireland* by John Carr (1806) depicts the barracks in the distance on the hilltop on the northern side of the city, the hillside being open space without buildings. These barracks (now Collins Barracks) superseded the smaller barrack outside the southern boundary of the city near Barrack Street. In 1778 Vallencey advocated that this high ground north of the city be the site for any new military buildings or fortifications, a commanding position overlooking Cork. The new barrack provided accommodation for almost 300 cavalry and some 3,000 infantry in 1811.[21]

At Ballincollig, some five miles west of Cork, gunpowder mills were established on a 90-acre site in 1794 by two Cork businessman, Charles Henry Leslie and John Travers. Leslie sold his interest in the mills to the Board of Ordnance in 1805 and, as Sir Henry Hardinge later explained in 1828, Ballincollig 'became one of the Ordnance Stations, both as being a convenient station for the embarcation of artillery from Cork for foreign service, as well as for the protection of the mills'. Under the administration of the Board of Ordnance the area of the manufactory was expanded to 431 acres in the period 1806-1815, which included a new cavalry barracks, administrative buildings, workers' accommodation and a greatly expanded productive capacity for the gunpowder mills. In the period 1805-1813 the Board of Ordnance invested almost £120,000 in the development of the mili-

tary-industrial complex at Ballincollig and on facilities in Cork Harbour for the storage and transportation of gunpowder. [22] The buildings occupied an area approximately $1\frac{1}{2}$ miles long by half a mile wide, along the southern bank of the River Lee; the south-east corner of the site is occupied by the artillery barrack dating from the same period. Lewis, in his *Topographical Dictionary of Ireland* (1837), notes sixteen gunpowder mills, provision for granulating and drying the powder, making charcoal, refining sulphur and saltpetre, the making of casks, small canals for communication, and the production of 16,000 barrels of powder annually. A considerable number of the buildings survive on the site, with traces of the canals and waterways.

Kinsale. At Kinsale a new barrack was constructed in the closing years of the eighteenth century, on high ground to the east of the town, superseding the small barrack built a hundred years earlier. The new barrack accommodated some 400 soldiers. At Charles Fort the inspection report of April 1804 noted a total of eighteen pieces of ordnance mounted,[23] but proposals for mounting twenty-seven 24-pounders, seven 24-pounder carronades, two 18-pounders, four 18-pounder carronades, four 12-pounders, and four 12-pounder carronades, together with other guns and mortars giving a total of sixty-six pieces of ordnance, were under way. There was also a yeomanry artillery corps attached to the fort. The accommodation was increased at about this time to provide for a garrison of 550 men.[24] Remains of stone kerbs for the iron rails for traversing platforms on the lower-level battery on the south side of the fort, commanding the approach from the harbour entrance, probably date from the programme of increasing the armament proposed in 1804. These seven front-pivoted gun positions probably mounted 24-pounders, the usual ordnance provided in coastal batteries at this time. In September 1814 building work was in progress on new quarters for artillery officers and the master-gunner.[25] The absence of new fortifications at Kinsale reflects the relative lack of importance of the harbour here compared with that of Cork, which was now the principal naval base and merchant shipping anchorage in Ireland.

6
Bantry Bay

I believe under the circumstances, it was the merriest council of war ever held.... We have not a horse to draw our four pieces of artillery . . . we have nothing but the arms in our hands, the clothes on our backs, and a good courage, but that is sufficient.... I never saw the French character better exemplified than in this morning's business. Well, at last I believe we are about to disembark ...

However, Tone and his comrades aboard the ship of the line *Indomptable* and the other vessels in Bantry Bay in December 1796 were unable to land, because of the easterly headwind, which increased to gale force over the next few days. A force of 6,000 men aboard the ships then in the bay might have been landed—the total number of troops carried by the French fleet was some 14,000. After *Indomptable* and the ships in company with her were driven from the bay at the end of December, other French ships arrived over the next few days, several anchoring close to Whiddy Island. Early in January 1797 some 4,000 men were available to form an invasion force; but the decision was made to await reinforcements, and as none arrived the ships returned to France after cruising offshore for some days.[1]

Richard White of Bantry House—Seafield in contemporary accounts—assembled his yeomanry corps and established a series of outposts around Bantry Bay. He sent the first information to General Dalrymple in Cork of the arrival of the French fleet; four days later he walked sixteen miles through the snow to Sheep's Head, where there was a detachment of his yeomanry, and observed seventeen French vessels, evidently anchored across the entrance to the bay south of Bere Island. For his efforts White was created Earl of Bantry.[2]

A contemporary account of the arrival of the French fleet pointed out that there were two roads from Bantry to Cork: one through Macroom and one by Drimoleague, Dunmanway and Bandon. Some 400 troops had been assembled in Bantry, a smaller number in Drimoleague, and 1,200 in Dunmanway, where the only artillery available was two 6-pounders. General Dalrymple, in command of the Southern District, reported in February 1797 that it was useless to construct fortifications capable of containing only small numbers of troops.[3] He listed the various harbours suitable for an enemy landing, concluding that Bantry Bay was the best, superior to Baltimore, Crookhaven and Dunmanus Bay-not a particularly original observation less than a month after the departure of the last contingent of the French fleet. He estimated that following a landing at Bantry the enemy's light troops would be in possession of Bandon after four days. Dalrymple imagined that the French would advance by two or three roads on Cork, which would capitulate immediately; the harbour and forts would be in their possession two or three days later. He recommended the formation of an army for the defence of Ireland of not less than 14,000 men, to be kept together to resist an enemy: this was the only way to oppose an invading army in a country where there were no fortifications.

Later that month Dalrymple, in communication with the commander-in-chief, Carhampton, stated that all small defence works constructed in a hurry were of little value, while it was not possible to build large-scale fortifications fast enough 'to be useful during the present war'. He thought that with the loss of Cork there was no good defensive position apart from that at Kilworth, north of Fermoy. Major le Comte de la Chaussée, on the orders of Dalrymple, surveyed the roads and strategic positions between Bantry and Cork, Macroom and Skibbereen, and between Dunmanway, Macroom and Ross Carbery, early in 1797. In April, Dalrymple was considering the construction of a line of defence, including redoubts, in west Cork, with a camp behind Dunmanway.[4] The chief secretary of

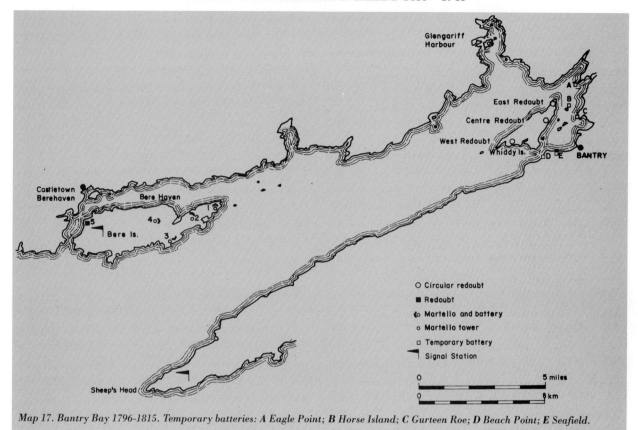

Map 17. Bantry Bay 1796-1815. Temporary batteries: A Eagle Point; B Horse Island; C Gurteen Roe; D Beach Point; E Seafield.

Ireland, Thomas Pelham, in a memorandum on
the defence of Ireland in February 1797, stressed
that Bantry Bay would now 'become the object of
public attention', and that if Berehaven was put
into a state of defence it might provide a secure
anchorage for a British fleet, or resist the
approach of an enemy, making Bantry less likely
as a landing place (Map 17).

The French fleet had avoided the Channel
Fleet of the Royal Navy on the voyage to Ireland
and on the return journey: the expedition
emphasised the risks involved in relying on naval
strength alone to defend Ireland. Some effort was
now made to provide defences at Bantry.
Temporary batteries of 24-pounders and 12-
pounders were set up at locations near Bantry
town to defend the anchorage there. Some of
these works, which were proposed in 1797, were
still in existence in 1803.

At Eagle Point, a low, rocky promontory one
mile north-east of the northern point of Whiddy
Island, the battery mounted five 24-pounders

and four 12-pounders in 1803. At Gurlenroe
(Gurteen Roe headland, east of Whiddy Island) a
battery was proposed in 1797, and in 1803 there
was a redoubt here mounting one 24-pounder
and four 12-pounders. Horse Island, a small
island east of Whiddy Island and about half a
mile north-west of Gurteen Roe, was another
location for a battery, proposed in 1797 and
mounting six 24-pounders in 1803, when the
earthwork parapets were in need of repair.[5]

Seafield battery, also proposed in 1797,
mounted one 12-pounder in 1803. The townland
of Seafield is occupied by Bantry House
demesne, and the battery was sited north of
Bantry House on high ground overlooking the
harbour. Beach Point battery was proposed in
1797 for three 24-pounders; in 1803 there were
three 24-pounders and two 12-pounders here,
the earthwork parapets in need of repair. This
was situated in the townland of Beach, perhaps
at the site of the later coastguard station opposite
the southern end of Whiddy Island, covering the

narrow southern channel to the Bantry anchorage. There were also batteries on Whiddy Island, in a dismantled state in 1803, possibly dating from 1797. A survey of Bantry in June 1797 gave a total of fifteen 24-pounders and eight 12-pounders at the batteries listed above.

It seems possible that some temporary works were also constructed at this time on Bere Island, although the first proposals to fortify the island to protect the anchorage of Berehaven appear to date from December 1803, when Rear-Admiral Calder requested protection for victual and store ships to be stationed here.[6] The vessels were to be anchored at Lawrence's Cove, ready to supply his squadron with provisions and stores. The government had already examined Bere Island with a view to the possibility of constructing defences, and Calder urged that these works be built as soon as possible. His letter was forwarded to London by the lord lieutenant, the Earl of Hardwicke, who replied to Calder in January 1804 that he agreed in principle 'as to the propriety of strengthening the works', indicating that defences in some form already existed by this date. By June, Hardwicke was reporting to London that 'works have been ordered to be erected on Berehaven Island for the protection of shipping and anchorage on that coast, under the direction of Major General Sir Eyre Coote, who commands in the District.'[7] In the following month the works and batteries on Bere Island were allocated £20,000 in a list of military expenses.

Early in February 1805, four towers, one battery with defensible guardhouse and one officers' barrack were ready for occupation, to accommodate about 300 men.[8] In March, the commander of the forces in Ireland, Lord Cathcart, was proposing to the Board of Ordnance that one or more 24-pounder carronades be provided for each tower in addition to the long 24-pounder guns mounted on them, so that the same shot or shells might apply to them. Eight carronades, 32-pounders or 18-pounders, might in the meantime be sent to Bere Island from Cork, to be replaced with an equal number of 24-pounder carronades when these were available.[9] Some time earlier

some 32-pounder carronades were lent by the navy to the commandant, Major Evans, to place the towers in a temporary state of defence before the arrival of the ordnance.

A list of works on Bere Island of January 1806 gives the following details:[10]

Casemated tower and battery
Officers' and soldiers' barracks
Hospital and store
Landing place
Roads of communication to the different
towers and batteries
Six towers and batteries
West redoubt

Four towers were noted in February 1805, which is the number shown on the first edition of the Ordnance Survey maps of the 1840s, while *A Short Account of the History and Antiquities of Bere Island* (1913) by Captain T. M. Keogh lists the four towers and their locations. From this evidence it appears that the six towers and batteries listed are an error, and that this should be four. Arthur Wellesley, in his tour of inspection of military works in the south and west of Ireland, visited Bantry Bay in July 1806 and travelled by boat from Bantry to Bere Island. In his journal he noted:

This place like Whiddy is of great extent . . . and . . . irregularity in its formation—The batteries have been constructed at great expense and which I am not sure if they would not have answered every purpose had they been formed on a less permanent plan— The towers are on very high ground and I am doubtful if they would entirely answer the purpose of completely defending the anchorage—it appeared to me that a tower is absolutely necessary on Seal Rock (Roan Carrig)as the eastern is the only passage through which a large ship would come in by. [11]

In July 1804, £20,000 had been allocated for

the work on Bere Island; by July 1806 this had increased to £22,000, and extra amounts were required for completion of works and annual repairs. The question of the cost of the works on Bere Island was raised in November 1809.[12] Between 1804 and March 1807 some £30,000 had been issued to Brigadier-General Fisher of the Royal Engineers, and an additional amount was later required—the works were nearing completion in August 1808. The correspondence of November 1809 listed the original works at some £31,000, the estimate for additional works and repairs at over £13,000 and a further sum of over £7,000 for repairs to the towers and batteries. The extra sum required was to be investigated: it was assumed that the repairs arose out of lack of supervision of the original construction work. Fisher replied in February 1810 that personal supervision at the time (presumably 1804-06) was not possible, as he was superintending the works along the Dublin coast, at Athlone and along the Shannon, and the towers at Wexford and Baginbun. He was also involved in a general inspection and survey of the country; with regard to Bere Island he remarked that there were great difficulties at the start of the works, there were no roads or paths, and most of the materials had to be sent from Cork.[13]

With the conclusion of the war with France in 1814 the Office of Ordnance was advised that it was not a good idea to spend money on temporary defence works: 'the four batteries under the protection of the towers may be dispensed with, and their guns and stores withdrawn leaving only the defences of the Western Redoubt and the towers for the defence of Bere Island and the Haven'[14] However, Berehaven continued as a base for convoys of merchant vessels bound across the Atlantic, convoys still necessary due to the war with the United States, which continued until early in 1815.

The locations of the fortifications from the east of the island moving westwards were as follows (based on the first edition of the Ordnance Survey of the 1840s):

Martello tower no. 1, battery no. 1. Ardaragh East, on the eastern promontory of the island. The battery was to the north of the tower.

Martello tower no. 2, battery no. 2. At Rerrin, approximately half a mile east of Lawrence's Cove. Battery no. 2 is not shown but presumably was close to the tower.

Martello tower no. 3, battery no. 3. Cloonaghlin West, one mile to the south-west of Lawrence's Cove. The tower is surrounded by a rock-cut ditch. The battery was sited about a quarter of a mile to the north-east of the tower.

Martello tower no. 4, battery no. 4. Ardagh, one mile to the west of Lawrence's Cove. The battery was sited just under a quarter of a mile to the north-east of the tower.

Redoubt no. 5. Derrycreeveen, at the west end of the island, overlooking the western entrance to Bere Haven, the channel here being about a quarter of a mile wide across to Dunboy Castle on the mainland opposite, somewhat narrower to the northwest. The redoubt is depicted on a mid-nineteenth-century plan as a square enclosure with a rectangular blockhouse on the landward side.[15] Four guns on traversing platforms constituted the principal armament, with two guns in addition on the gun platform of the blockhouse.

Signal tower. Sited about three-quarters of a mile south-east of no. 5, on high ground some 700 feet above sea level; only the ruins survive today.

The armament of the works in 1811 was eight 24-pounders at the four batteries, six 24-pounders at redoubt no. 5, and a further six 24-pounders at the four Martello towers. Two of the towers had two guns each, evidently nos. 1 and 2. The commissariat store and other military buildings were near the quay at Lawrence's Cove. The towers on the island were unusual in being sited on high ground, some of them several hundred feet above sea level. Tower and battery no. 1, overlooking Lonehort Point at the east end of the island, covered the principal entrance into Berehaven. Martello tower no. 2 gave some protection to Lawrence's Cove and also had a field of fire southwards over Bantry Bay. Tower and battery no. 3 were too far from the cove to render any effective protection (the range of the 24-pounder gun was a little over a mile with solid round shot); however, they commanded part of the southern shore of the island and that part of Bantry Bay to the south that was within range.

Tower and battery no. 4, sited a mile to the west of the landing place in Lawrence's Cove, was virtually out of range both of the cove and of Berehaven to the north: of all the towers this appears to be the least effectively sited. There seems to have been a preoccupation with siting the towers and batteries on high ground so they would not be commanded and vulnerable to attack by landing parties. Had they been sited nearer sea level they would have provided a better defence of Berehaven, Lawrence's Cove, and beaches suitable as landing places, such as that on the south side of the island less than half a mile south-east of the cove. Tower and battery no. 1 were well placed to cover the eastern entrance to Berehaven, which is a mile wide. Redoubt no. 5 was also well placed to command the narrower channel at the western entrance.

Towers 1 and 2, and Redoubt no. 5, were demolished at the close of the nineteenth century to make way for later defence works on their sites, which still survive. Towers 3 and 4 remain, prominent landmarks from most parts of the eastern end of the island.

Whiddy Island. In May 1804 the Office of Ordnance in Dublin Castle received three estimates for works to be constructed on Whiddy Island.[16] The estimates from Thomas Mahony—highly recommended by Mr White, the brother of Lord Bantry—were to finish three circular redoubts on hills on the island. Masonry, carpenter's work and other trades are listed; a considerable part of the deep rock-cut ditch around each redoubt was evidently completed by this time, and they were capable of defence as they were. The east redoubt was to be completed in twelve months, the west redoubt in nine months and the centre redoubt in six months; the estimated total cost was some £2,200. The east and west works were each to mount eight guns and house 100 men, the centre redoubt, twelve guns and 150 men. The fortifications were not completed in the time estimated: it was not until September 1806 that the centre redoubt was

ready to receive troops. A year later, in September 1807, the east redoubt was finished, followed by the third redoubt in November that year.[17] In March 1808 the Office of Ordnance was instructed to allocate the necessary storage space for provisions within the works, as until this was done they could not be considered to be in a state of defence.[18] An inspection of the works on Whiddy Island in 1809 found the buildings in a poor condition, the roofs leaking and likely to affect the health of the troops quartered in them.

The guns on the redoubts were 24-pounders mounted on traversing platforms, spaced at regular intervals around the perimeter, firing over the parapet; each gun could be trained through about 180 degrees. The siting of each work on a hilltop ensured an extensive all-round field of fire for the artillery and small arms of each garrison. The northern redoubt (the 'east redoubt' in contemporary documents) is some 200 yards from Whiddy Point East, the north-eastern point of the island; the distance to the water's edge to the north-west and to the east being somewhat less, all the ground here was within effective musketry range. For repelling a landing party approaching in ships' boats, the 24-pounder guns could be loaded with canister or caseshot, or the heavier grapeshot, both having a range considerably greater than the musket of the infantryman. The distance to the mainland to the north is just over a mile, to Eagle Point to the north-east a mile, so that any vessels attempting to sail through the northern channel here would have been within range of the 24-pound iron shot of the guns.

The southern channel leading to the anchorage east of Whiddy Island was similarly defended by the west redoubt, which, being sited on high ground, also protected about half the north-west coast of the island. The guns of the centre redoubt also gave some protection to the northern half of this coastline, overlapping in its field of fire with that of the other two redoubts; being closer to the east shore of the island, this hilltop work also had most of the anchorage east of the island within range.

The siting of the works allowed for all-round

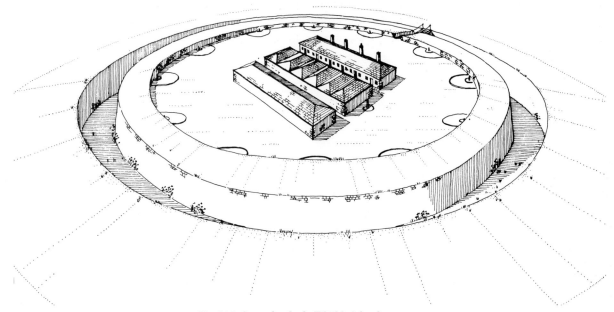

Fig. 105. Central redoubt Whiddy Island.

defence of the island and many of its beaches, although once landing parties had gained a foothold the undulating terrain— particularly the area between the west and centre redoubts— would have provided some protection from the defending artillery.

The east and west redoubts are of similar dimensions. Around each is a glacis or smooth slope of ground where the original hillside has been levelled about a hundred feet across to expose any attacking party to the gunfire and musketry of the defenders. After advancing up this steep slope their next obstacle would have been a rock-cut ditch some twenty-four feet wide surrounding the circular redoubt, which is some 210 feet in diameter. Entry across the ditch was by means of a drawbridge. The parapet of the redoubt was some twelve to fourteen feet in thickness, behind which the front-pivoted traversing carriages of the 24-pounders were placed, with a banquette or firing-step for infantry in the intervals between the guns. The east and west redoubts are now inaccessible and overgrown. Mid-nineteenth-century plans indicate three long ranges of single-storey barrack and store buildings occupying most of the central space of the east redoubt, while the west redoubt had an unusual layout of buildings: two large

semicircular-plan structures with a passageway in between on the diameter of the enclosure. In both redoubts the buildings were divided up into smaller apartments and rooms for officers' and soldiers' quarters, stores and magazines. Inside the gateway of the west redoubt was a guard-house, presumably with a loop-holed wall for defence of the gate and drawbridge. In the same position in the east redoubt was a banquette behind a traverse about twenty feet long, to defend the gate and drawbridge and protect the barrack buildings nearest to the gateway.

The centre redoubt is of larger diameter— some 250 feet—to accommodate the larger armament of twelve guns and somewhat more extensive barrack and store buildings for the larger garrison. Otherwise the layout and details were similar to those of the other redoubts, the arrangement of the barracks and stores being similar to that of the east redoubt, with three ranges of buildings accommodating officers, soldiers' quarters, magazine, ordnance stores, commissariat stores and guardhouse (Fig.105).

These buildings within the redoubts were generally casemated—vaulted in masonry or brickwork to render them 'bombproof'—to provide protection from high-angle fire from mortars or field howitzers, which fired a hollow iron shell filled with gunpowder, fused to explode, if possible, on impact. The vaulted structures were covered with slate roofs, giving the buildings a conventional appearance from the outside, as may be seen in the centre redoubt today.

The disposition of the fortifications on Whiddy Island, which is much smaller in extent than Bere Island, is generally more successful: most of the coastline of the island was within range of the 24-pounder guns, and the east and west redoubts had a field of fire over the channels leading to the anchorage to the east. If the batteries of the 1797-1803 period on the mainland, noted above, were still in use during the 1803-14 war, together with the battery on Horse Island, this part of Bantry Bay was well-defended.

Glengarriff Harbour. This harbour on the north side of Bantry Bay some three miles northwest of Whiddy Island provides a sheltered anchorage; to provide some protection the Martello tower and adjacent battery were constructed between 1804 and 1806. The tower is rather crudely built of rubble masonry when compared with the regular ashlar stonework of many other Irish Martellos. The walls are vertical rather than battered, and one gun (noted as an 8-inch howitzer in 1809) mounted on the roof gun platform had an all-round field of fire by means of a traversing platform turning on the central pivot. The battery is of unusual form, with a high wall rather than the usual broad, low parapet and is attached to the eastern side of the tower. A contemporary plan shows that the battery was originally detached from the tower, the space some 50 feet wide being later closed by two walls linking the battery to the tower, as indicated on the first edition of the Ordnance Survey. Sited on the highest point of Garinish Island in the centre of the harbour, the guns here would have covered the anchorage adequately. Gun Point at the eastern side of the harbour entrance may recall the site of a gun battery from this period or possibly earlier. In 1811 Garinish Island was noted as having an armament of three 24-pounders, Whiddy Island twenty-eight 24-pounders.

A contemporary opinion on the construction of the Bantry Bay fortifications and their effectiveness is provided by Edward Wakefield in *An Account of Ireland, Statistical and Political,* (1812), volume 2:

It is the opinion of every naval and military officer with whom I have conversed that all these works are useless.... But why should it be supposed, that the French, when they next visit Ireland, will put into Bantry Bay? .... Are there no harbours on the western coast, in which another fleet could anchor? It is admitted that no extent of coast in the world, affords so many places of equal safety; if the principle on which Bantry has been protected be proper, why not fortify the rest?

As the expense involved made this out of the question, he continued:

Since it is impossible therefore, to erect fortifications on all those parts of the coast where an enemy might land, little can be gained by fortifying one or two places, which they will never perhaps visit.

In Ireland the attempt was made to fortify the principal harbours and landing places of most advantage to the enemy. With the exception of the Shannon Estuary and Galway Bay, the west coast was not defended; the intention in the event of a landing was to hold the line of the Shannon until reinforcements were sent from Dublin or elsewhere.

7
The Shannon Estuary and Galway Bay

Following a petition from the Limerick merchants on the lack of defences to protect shipping in the Shannon Estuary in 1781, a battery of eight 24-pounders had been constructed by 1783 at Tarbert Island, but it appears that this was a temporary work, abandoned or dismantled over the following ten years. War with France early in 1793 renewed the need for defence of the estuary here, where a large number of vessels were able to anchor south-east of the island, sheltered from westerly and north-westerly winds. Two batteries were under construction between 1794 and 1795; in August 1794, ten large pieces of ordnance were landed at Tarbert. *The Ennis Chronicle* reported the following month that eight wagons carrying gunpowder and sixteen carts loaded with grapeshot and roundshot arrived at Limerick from Dublin on their way to theTarbert fortifications (two forts were under construction, supervised by Colonel James Ferrier of the Royal Irish Engineers), most of the guns being mounted on the batteries by this time. In June 1795 it was reported that the works were nearly completed, with sixteen 24-pounders and six 6-pounders to be mounted on gun platforms formed of stone slabs from Shanagolden.[1] This suggests perhaps two batteries each with eight 24-pounders commanding the river and some 6-pounders for landward defence.

Documents of the Board of Ordnance of 1804 note that a lease was entered into by the Irish Board of Ordnance in May 1797 for land at Knockayne or Massey Hill, on which a dwellinghouse, storehouse, guardroom and magazine were built, supervised by Ferrier. By 1804 these were unoccupied, as the works had been dismantled —possibly during the Peace of Amiens, from March 1802 to May 1803. Massey's Hill is on the mainland just to the south of the western point of Tarbert Island, so that it seems possible that one of the batteries was sited near here.

The Shannon Estuary was one of the three invasion areas included in the French government's instructions to Vice-Admiral Villaret de Joyeuse in October 1796 during the preparations for the expedition to Ireland. The suggested landing places in order of preference were Galway Bay, Bantry Bay, and the mouth of the Shannon. Included in the orders issued to the ships' captains of the French fleet that arrived at Bantry Bay in December 1796 was a rendezvous at the mouth of the Shannon in case of separation and failure to meet off Mizen Head. Wolfe Tone was in favour of the ships that remained in Bantry Bay attempting a landing in the Shannon Estuary. By this time small detachments of the government forces had been marched towards Bantry and were assembling between Bantry and Cork at such towns as Bandon and Mallow. The detachment of the Londonderry Militia stationed at Tarbert marched to Mallow, joining other companies of the Londonderry and the Louth and Westmeath Militia, which had all been marched from Limerick during the first days after the French fleet's arrival in Bantry Bay.[2] Consequently, a French landing near Tarbert or elsewhere on the estuary of the Shannon would have met with little opposition, the Limerick garrison being some two days' march away.

In August 1806, Arthur Wellesley visited Tarbert on his tour of the defences of the south and west coasts.[3] His journal notes the forts on Tarbert, and he advocated having four or six 24-pounder or 32-pounder long guns 'fitted on the non recoil principle' here—perhaps a reference to guns mounted on traversing platforms. He went aboard the gunboat *Trial* and with the flood tide travelled up river, noting that some guns should be placed on Foynes Island. Aughinish Point some two miles east of Foynes Island was another place 'where guns might be placed with advantage and appear absolutely necessary as this is the anchorage the furthest up the Shannon which a vessel of heavy draught of water would think of '.

General Charles Dumouriez, commander-in-chief of the French army in 1792, later deserted to the Austrians and in 1808 prepared a military memoir on the defence of Ireland for the British government.[4] In this report he examined places convenient for an enemy to land and suggested the construction of batteries at estuaries, bays and harbours. At the mouth of the Shannon, where it is some two miles wide, he proposed a battery at each side, and a battery was subsequently constructed on the north side at

Kilcredaun Point here. He also suggested a battery on Carrig Island, which is also the site of a later battery, a fort on Scattery Island, which today has a battery constructed a few years after his memoir, and a fort on 'Killanin' promontory, which appears to be Kilkerin Point, where another of the Shannon batteries was to be erected. He advocated a battery on Foynes Island, and the use of gunboats, bomb-vessels and fireships in the shallow waters of the estuary. Dumouriez does not mention Tarbert as the site for a battery or fort, presumably because of the existing defence works there in 1808 (Map 18).

Before Wellington's inspection of 1806 and the memoir by Dumouriez, plans were under way for defences on the lower Shannon as part of the general scheme of defence for Ireland. In June 1804 the lord lieutenant, the Earl of Hardwicke, reported to London that works were in progress between Loop Head and Tarbert.[5] Permanent works of any importance would presumably have been inspected by Wellington in 1806 or noted by Dumouriez in his memoir of January 1808: it seems likely that temporary batteries may have preceded the permanent works, all of which, except perhaps the battery that survived until

recently on Tarbert Island, must have been erected after 1808.

The Shannon Estuary batteries are all of a similar layout, with the exception of that at Tarbert, which resembled an obtuse-angled bastion in plan. The battery in each case is semicircular or D-shaped in plan, surrounded by a dry moat with six guns (except for the four-gun battery at Doonaha) arranged around the curved part of the perimeter, firing over the broad parapet. The rear of the battery was protected by a rectangular blockhouse or 'bombproof barrack' built in the moat at the centre of the landward side. On the roof of this structure were two guns for landward defence, either carronades or howitzers. Similar batteries are to be found at Keelogue on the Shannon above Portumna and at Rathmullan on Lough Swilly. The blockhouse or barrack was also described in contemporary accounts as a 'defensible guardhouse' capable of accommodating all or most of the garrison of a battery or redoubt, loop-holed for musketry, the roof to be arched over if possible with a terrace or platform on top.

Kilcredaun Point battery. This battery commanded the northern side of the mouth of the

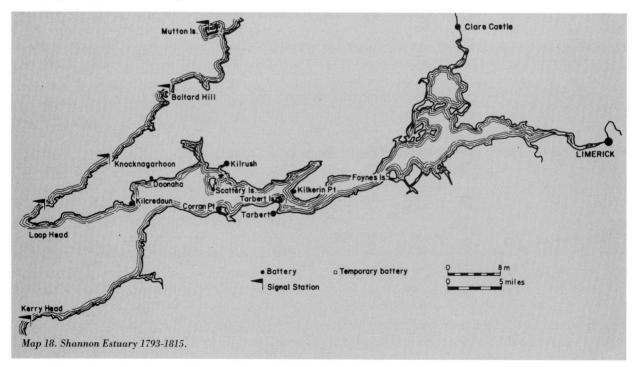

Map 18. Shannon Estuary 1793-1815.

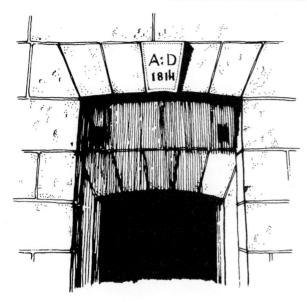

Fig. 106. The keystone over the blockhouse doorway, Kilcredaun battery, Shannon Estuary.

ters on the outer face of the wall, command the interior of the battery. Other loops are arranged on the opposite side at this level, facing the approach to the rear of the battery on the landward side—a feature only found at Kilcredaun. On the roof-level gun platform, protected by broad parapets some six feet in height, were two guns mounted on traversing platforms: howitzers or carronades for defence of the landward side of the battery. The traversing platforms, one at each end of the roof, enabled the guns to be trained through an angle of about 270 degrees, covering the ground on each flank of the battery and to the rear. The main armament of the battery consisted of six 24-pounder guns mounted on traversing platforms, each revolving on a front pivot behind the inner face of the parapet. The description of this battery and its armament is generally applicable to the other batteries, except that on Tarbert Island.

Doonaha battery. Some three miles north-east of Kilcredaun Point on the north side of the estu-

Shannon; the 24-pounders here had a range of a little over a mile, covering the deep-water channel, which is closer to the northern shore. The estuary is two miles wide at this point. The battery, forming a D-shaped enclosure in plan, has had much of the masonry facing removed from the scarp and counterscarp of the dry moat since the place was abandoned as a military post in the middle or late nineteenth century. Entrance to the battery was originally across a drawbridge over the dry ditch or moat. The defensible guardhouse is in a good state of preservation on the exterior; it was entered from within the battery by a drawbridge slightly wider than the entrance doorway, over which the keystone bears the date 1814 ((Fig.106). The guardhouse has a basement or lower ground floor, level with the base of the dry moat in which it stands. The upper floor, level with the ground level of the battery, was approached by the drawbridge; above this floor level (in this blockhouse the floor structure has collapsed) is the gun platform carried on the barrel-vaulted ceiling of the first-floor apartments (Fig.107).

Musket-loops are provided at the lower level, allowing for close defence of the moat in the manner of a caponnière. Musket-loops at the upper floor level, evidently originally fitted with shut-

Fig. 107. Kilcreduan battery, the blockhouse.

ary, this battery was similar in layout to the other batteries except that it was slightly smaller and mounted four 24-pounders instead of the usual six. The dry moat is badly eroded, though it retains more masonry and is more complete than that at Corran Point battery on the opposite shore. The bombproof barrack or defensible guardhouse is half demolished, but clearly demonstrates how strongly built these structures were, with a massive barrel-vault supporting the gun platform. The iron pivot for the centre mounting for one of the traversing platforms is visible at the western end of the roof terrace. Doonaha battery is some 200 feet wide from the outer face or scarp of the flank walls, compared with an average of 250 feet for the other batteries.

Scattery Island battery. Situated on the southern extremity of the island, close to the later lighthouse, this battery is evidently in reasonable condition and of the same layout as the other batteries. A feature that it shares with Corran Point and Kilkerin is the indented outline of the inner face of the curved parapet. This plan form reduced the thickness of the parapet immediately in front of the pivot of each traversing platform. In 1811 Scattery was noted as having eight guns, perhaps in a temporary battery that preceded the present structure.

Tarbert Island battery. Demolished during the building of the ESB power station, this battery is shown by survey plans to have been bastion-shaped in plan with two faces overlooking the estuary to the north. The main armament was arranged behind these two parapets, with three guns to each and a centrally placed gun at the salient angle, giving seven pieces of ordnance in all. The battery was some 200 feet wide and had the usual arrangement of a defensible guardhouse in the rear. Entry to the battery was through an arched gateway about seven feet wide, presumably approached originally across a drawbridge over the dry moat. The battery was sited on the highest part of Tarbert Island; it is possible that it was one of the works under construction in 1794-95 or perhaps a partial rebuilding of one of these earlier structures. The defen-

sible guardhouse was similar in dimensions and detail to those that survive in good condition at Kilcredaun and Kilkerin, suggesting a date of construction contemporary with them, between 1808 and 1814. Tarbert battery was sited about forty feet above water level, towards the southeast side of the island; a late eighteenth-century painting of the Shannon depicts a battery with embrasures close to water level on the north side of Tarbert Island, which may be the battery of 1783 or a work built by Ferrier in the 1790s. In 1811 Tarbert was recorded as having thirteen guns, suggesting that this battery at water level or another work was in use in addition to the battery and defensible guardhouse described above.

Kilkerin Point battery. Kilkerin Point is directly opposite Tarbert Island, just over a mile to the north-east. The batteries on Tarbert and Kilkerin completely commanded the river here with a cross-fire from their guns: sailing ships altering course in the bend in the river would have been well within range of the 24-pounders mounted in each battery. Kilkerin Point battery is in good condition apart from some damage to the counterscarp and at the entrance gateway (Fig. 108). The dry moat has most of the stonework of the retaining walls forming the scarp and counterscarp. The blockhouse is well preserved on the exterior (Fig. 109). At the lower level covering the dry moat are musket-loops, five at each end of the building, some of which have been blocked up at a later date. The loops have external splays and are about two feet wide by two-and-a-half feet high on the outside face of the wall. On the upper level five similar loops command the interior of the battery, with the entrance door at one end of this facade. The doorway is set within a recess in the wall face some eight inches deep to accommodate the drawbridge when raised vertically in front of the door. Iron pulleys for the drawbridge are set in the wall above the doorway, while at the cill of the door is an iron bar on which the drawbridge pivoted.

The walls of the blockhouse are battered from base to parapet level at an angle of about 1:12; the scarp walls of the battery are built to a simi-

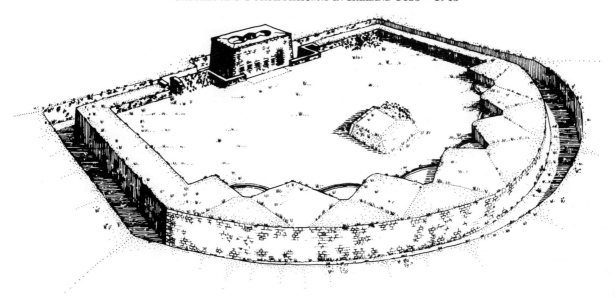

Fig. 108. Kilkerin battery from the north-east.

lar slope, which is to be found in many of the fortifications and Martello towers of this period,
both in ashlar masonry and in walls such as these
of squared rubble laid to courses. The lower level
of the blockhouse was divided into rooms for
stores and a magazine and must have been
reached by stairs or ladder from the floor above.
The upper floor provided accommodation for
officers and soldiers and is divided by a cross-
wall into a large space, 31 feet long by 18 feet
wide, with a smaller room at one end, 9 feet by
18 feet. A large window at each end of the building provided light and ventilation. In the thickness of the outer wall of the guardhouse a narrow
stone stair gives access to the gun platform
above. Here two guns were mounted on traversing platforms for the landward defence of the
battery; Lewis in his *Topographical Dictionary
of Ireland* (1837) notes two howitzers at Kilkerin,
Tarbert and Scattery in addition to the main
armament of 24-pounders, so these must have
been mounted on the guardhouse gun platform.
The use of 5½-inch howitzers would have allowed
for the use of their shells in the 24-pounder guns:
there is a reference to this practice at Duncannon
Fort in 1804.

The width of the battery at Kilkerin is just
over 250 feet from the outer face of the parapet
on each flank; the dry moat is 14 feet wide on the
flanks and on the curved front of the battery and
19 feet at the rear, where it is increased in width
to include the guardhouse. The parapet is 17 feet
wide on the flanks of the battery and 12 feet at
the rear, while the indented plan of the inner face
of the parapet at the six-gun positions results in a
thickness of about 24 feet at the front pivot of
each gun mounting and some 35 feet at the maximum thickness between each gun. This form of
parapet resulted in a form of wide-splayed shallow embrasure in front of each gun position
(Fig.110).

The Kilkerin guardhouse, some 54 feet long by
33 feet wide, is typical in its dimensions and
details; the guardhouse at Tarbert was almost
identical, which suggests that they were constructed to the same plans and at the same time
(Fig.111). Entry to the battery at Kilkerin was
originally by means of a drawbridge; iron pulleys
remain at each side of the gateway recessed into
the dressed stonework and secured by iron
straps. Within the battery enclosure on the axis
of the layout is a small semi-basement vaulted
structure covered with earth, noted on plans as
'shell filling room'. Similar structures existed at
Tarbert, Scattery and Corran Point. The land at
Kilkerrin was acquired by the government in
March 1811, the battery evidently being constructed soon after this date.

Fig. 109. Kilkerin battery, the blockhouse from the south.

Corran Point battery, Carrig Island. This battery commanded the southern part of the channel between Carrig Island and Scattery Island, a distance of about two miles, so that the passage of the river here was commanded by the two batteries. The moat and ramparts of the Corran Point battery have almost disappeared, the removal of the stonework causing the gradual collapse of the scarp and counterscarp. The guardhouse remains, the doorway having been altered and extended in recent years to form an opening at ground level. The gun platform at roof level with its positions for two guns is approached from the upper floor level by a staircase built within the wall thickness, as at Kilkerin. The inner face of the parapet and the banquette are constructed of regular ashlar masonry, the banquette having a shallow groove in the stonework for the iron rail of the traversing mount for each gun. The guardhouse has the usual battered-wall surfaces, constructed of squared rubble built to courses with regular masonry at the quoins and at the door, window and musket-loop openings. Plans indicate that the battery had the same layout as the other Shannon batteries, the curved front of the battery having the inner face of the parapet indented at each gun position, as at Kilkerin. Lewis, in his *Topographical Dictionary of Ireland* , describes the work as a battery and bombproof barrack for twenty men; by 1837 it had become a

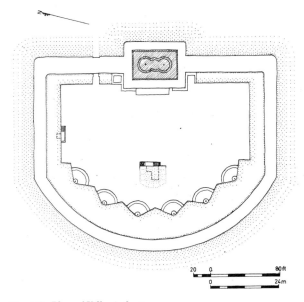

Fig. 110. Plan of Kilkerin battery.

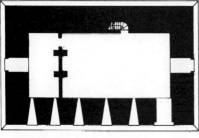

GROUND FLOOR

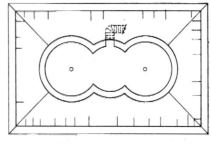

GUN PLATFORM

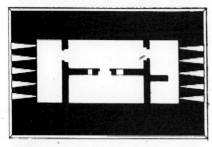

BASEMENT

Fig. 111. Plans of blockhouse of Kilkerin battery.

coastguard station. His similar descriptions of the other batteries at Scattery, Tarbert and Kilkerin also include the armament of 24-pounders and two howitzers at each place.

Foynes Island battery. Just over ten miles upstream of Tarbert a battery was placed on the western point of Foynes Island, another location suggested by Wellington and by Dumouriez. This was an earthwork battery for six 24-pounders, which would have been capable of commanding the full width of the river, which is a mile wide from Battery Point across to the Co. Clare shore to the north-west. Remains of the battery survive on the site.

The Shannon Estuary batteries were well placed to cause maximum damage to an enemy fleet sailing up the river or attempting to land an invasion force, but they would not have prevented a large-scale French landing. The batteries also provided protection for vessels anchored within range of their guns, otherwise vulnerable to attack by enemy ships of war or privateers. In 1804 the gunboat establishment in Ireland included five gun vessels in the Shannon Estuary armed with 18-pounder guns and 32-pounder

and 18-pounder carronades.[6] These small craft operating in the shallow waters of the estuary could not be pursued by deeper-draught vessels such as ships of the line or frigates.

Clare Castle. A late eighteenth-century view of Clare Castle from the west, by Beranger, shows the medieval bridge, part of the castle and the high perimeter wall surrounding the barracks. It is possible that the brick-edged musket-loops in the wall were inserted in the 1793-1815 period in an attempt to improve the defences of this important post overlooking the bridge. Clare Castle had been noted in the military reports of the later eighteenth century as a possible enemy landing place, while the bridge over the Fergus was a post of some strategic importance on the road from Limerick to Ennis and northwards to Galway. The barrack is a fine ten-bay masonry structure, three storeys in height, with brickwork reveals and flat arches to the large double-hung sash windows.

Limerick Castle. Limerick Castle, in which barracks had been erected in the middle of the eighteenth century, was partly reconstructed at this time. The gatehouse towers were rebuilt at the upper level in regular masonry with external-ly splayed gun-embrasures in the parapets to allow for the use of artillery at roof level. The masonry parapet with brick-lined musket-loops on the south-west tower most likely also dates from this period. The gun-embrasures and mus-ket-loops are similar in character to those at Athlone Castle, constructed in the early nine-teenth century as part of the programme of defence works on the middle Shannon.

In the journal of his tour of inspection in 1806, Wellington noted the strategic importance of Limerick as the left flank of the Shannon in the event of an enemy landing on the west coast in Clare or Galway. Farther north along the river, between Portumna and Athlone, fortifications were under construction after 1803 to defend crossing places at fords and bridges. In 1811 the barracks in Limerick accommodated some 1,200 regular troops, and those in temporary barracks in the city amounted to over 1,600. While this was somewhat smaller than the garrison at Cork, it was more than twice the force at Galway.[7]

The possibility of a landing by an invasion force on the west coast was a constant fear of the British government in Ireland from 1793 to as late as 1812. These fears were realised in August 1798 when General Humbert's expeditionary force of just over 1,000 men landed near Killala, Co. Mayo. In October that year a larger force arrived off the Donegal coast, to be defeated by a more powerful squadron of the Royal Navy. Two weeks later three French frigates and a corvette arrived off Killala with over 1,000 troops aboard, but learning of Humbert's defeat, they did not attempt to land and instead returned to France. Humbert's expedition emphasised the importance of the River Shannon as a line of defence and crossing points at bridges and fords were later fortified.

The west coast was difficult to patrol with naval vessels, and the rough terrain and lack of roads in the western counties added considerably to the problems of military defence. There were numerous landing places available, perhaps the best of which was Galway Bay, with several small harbours and sheltered beaches. Of even more importance, it was estimated that from Galway the advance guard of an invasion force could be in Dublin within six days of landing, the only serious obstacle being the Shannon and its lakes. Galway Bay had been the original objective dur-ing the preparations for the expedition to Ireland in 1796, the other landing places proposed being the Shannon Estuary and Bantry Bay, where the French fleet eventually arrived in December 1796. After 1803 and until 1811 French plans for the invasion of Ireland included a landing on the west coast. There was always the possibility of the French or their allies evading the patrols or blockading squadrons of the Royal Navy and sailing into the Atlantic to approach Ireland from the west.

It appears that little was done during the war with the French Republic, between 1793 and 1801, to construct defences at west-coast anchor-ages or harbours. However, with the renewal of war in 1803 coastal defence was undertaken on a large scale, with the extensive scheme to con-struct Martello towers, batteries and signal tow-ers; these were under construction the following year. The line of signal stations extended along the west coast, but apart from these and the Shannon Estuary batteries the only concentra-tion of defensive works was the building of three Martello towers at Galway Bay.

A military report of 1797-98 considered in detail the defence of Galway Bay, noting a land-ing place at the upper end of the bay near Oranmore and other landing places at Ballyvaughan Bay to the west of Finavarra Point, where one of the three Martello towers was later constructed.[8] The use of gunboats was advocated in the sheltered and shallow-water areas of the bay, co-operating with troops and field artillery on shore to prevent or delay a landing (Map 19). The report noted the impor-tance of the Aran Islands, which might provide some shelter for enemy shipping, particularly east of Inishmore, and the need to have a garri-son on the islands to prevent a landing. It was proposed to establish a garrison at the seven-

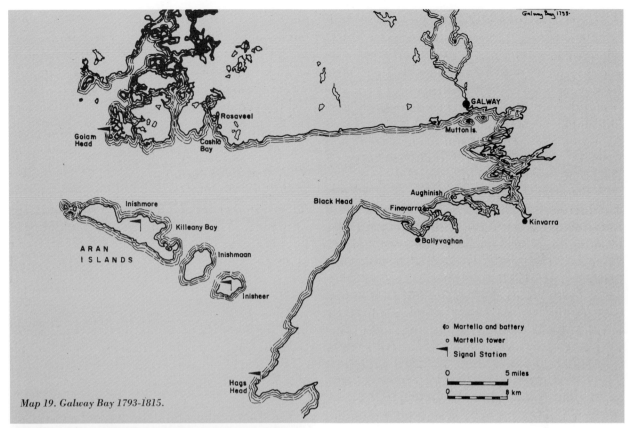

Map 19. Galway Bay 1793-1815.

Fig. 112. The 24-pounder cannon on Finavarra Martello tower, Galway Bay. Photo, Paul Gosling, Archaeological Survey of Co. Galway.

teenth-century fort of Arkin, which had been abandoned as a military post in the early eighteenth century. A line of defence was proposed around Galway, with about twenty redoubts, each to hold fifty men, with heavy guns placed on Mutton Island and Hare Island. The intention was to prolong resistance and deter an invasion force from marching inland towards Dublin or southwards towards Limerick.

In April 1804, eight 24-pounder cannon for the defence of the 'Anchoring-ground and Harbour of Galway' were listed with guns for the defence of the Shannon at Athlone.[9] It seems likely that these may have been intended for Mutton Island and Hare Island, which flank the anchorage, as proposed some years earlier. However, Arthur Wellesley on his tour of inspection in 1806 noted that 'The islands that lie off the town ... still remain in their same defenceless state....' He advocated the construction of a tower and a four-gun battery here 'to give full security to both town and vessels'.[10]

Fig. 113. Aughinish Martello tower, Galway Bay.

Finavarra tower and battery. Situated on a promontory on the south shore of Galway Bay, the guns of the Martello tower and the adjacent battery covered nearby beaches suitable as landing places. The tower is cam-shaped in plan, similar to the tower at Meelick on the Shannon and those built between 1810 and 1812 along the Essex and Suffolk coast of England. Three guns were mounted on the gun platform of the tower (Fig.112), while it is probable that the battery mounted some three or four guns. Nothing of the battery survives on the site today to indicate its size or layout, but it must have been just to the west of the tower on the low promontory. The deed for the tower, dated 21 March 1811, indicates the time of acquisition of the site or construction of the tower and battery. Mid-nineteenth-century records note a garrison at the tower of one officer and thirty-nine men, the adjacent house being for the master-gunner.

The tower has the usual entrance doorway at first-floor level, originally approached by a step ladder. Also at first-floor level are four window openings, similar to those at Meelick tower. It is constructed of ashlar masonry, the wall surfaces battered or sloping inwards towards the top. There is no string course to mark the level of the gun platform.

Aughinish tower and battery. Some three miles east of Finavarra is the tower at Aughinish, of the same design as that at Finnavarra; the battery no longer exists, but on the evidence of the first edition of the Ordnance Survey of 1842 it was situated just to the west of the tower. There was accommodation for one officer and thirty-nine men, as at the other tower, a basement water tank, a magazine, cellar and store at ground level, and the officer's and soldiers' quarters at first-floor level. It seems likely that the tower and battery here were built at the same time as those at Finavarra (Fig.113).

Rosaveel tower, Cashla Bay. Situated on the east side of Cashla Bay, this tower of elliptical plan most probably mounted one gun, or possibly two revolving about the same pivot. Cashla Bay is the nearest sheltered landing place on the north side of the bay to Galway, some twenty miles to the east. The Rosaveel tower is unusual in its profile, the battered wall surface changing to a vertical profile at the roof level without a masonry string course (Fig.114). The mid-nineteenth-century records indicate a garrison of one officer and thirty soldiers. Constructed of regular ashlar masonry like the two towers on the south shore of Galway Bay, it is in a reasonable condition except that part of the parapet has been removed.[11]

8
The Shannon: Portumna to Athlone

The military importance of the line of the Shannon had been noted in the surveys of the defences of Ireland earlier in the eighteenth century. The possibility of a French invasion following a landing on the west coast again drew the

Fig. 114. Rossaveel Martello tower, Cashla Bay.

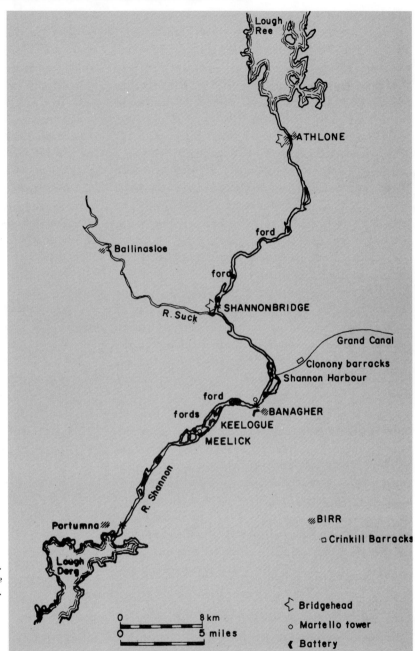

Map 20.
*The Shannon – Portumna to Athlone
1793-1815.*

attention of the British authorities in Ireland to the defence of the Shannon crossing-points. Colonel Charles Tarrant of the Royal Irish Engineers surveyed the ruined castle at Athlone in June 1793 and made recommendations to put the castle and barracks into a state of defence.

A military report on the defence of Ireland in August 1796 recommended military depots along the Shannon at Lanesborough, Athlone, Banagher and Portumna, for troops to act on this line of defence.[1] It was proposed that they be equipped with thirty field-guns, and entrenching tools for 1,000 men, evidently intended for the construction of fieldworks at crossing-points at fords or bridges. Provisions for ten days were to provide for 20,000 men and 2,000 cavalry horses. Later that year, however, there were still relatively small numbers of troops at the barracks along or near the Shannon, varying from 36 cavalry at Portumna and at Loughrea, 108 cavalry at Athlone, 72 infantry at Banagher, while farther east, the barracks at Tullamore and Phillipstown each accommodated 108 cavalry troopers.[2] This number of troops in small detachments was quite inadequate to resist an invasion force and guard the river crossing-points. By 1797 the Central District, essentially the east midlands area but including Sligo and north Roscommon and reaching as far south as Kilkenny, contained some 3,500 troops, the smallest number in the five military districts into which Ireland was divided.

General Humbert's force that landed at Killala in August 1798 crossed the Shannon at Ballintra, before he was forced to surrender at Ballinamuck in north Co. Longford. Humbert's victory at Castlebar had created panic in Athlone, and his expedition drew attention to the need to defend the crossing-places of the river. The possibility of an enemy force landing on the west coast in the vicinity of Galway Bay emphasised the importance of the River Shannon between Lough Derg and Lough Ree as a line of defence against a march on Dublin.

The renewal of war with France in May 1803 reactivated plans for defence works around the coast and along the Shannon. During the summer and autumn of 1803 plans were prepared and estimates submitted to military headquarters at the Royal Hospital, Kilmainham, providing for defence works along the Shannon at Meelick, Keelogue, Banagher, Shannonbridge, and Athlone, on the 35-mile length of the river between the two lakes.[3] By May 1804 artillery fieldworks were established at these locations: batteries or redoubts of earthwork parapets protected by ditches and timber palisades.[4] Portumna is not included in contemporary lists of the works or lists of land required for defence purposes in 1806:[5] it seems likely that the speed with which the timber bridge at Portumna could be destroyed in an emergency was the principal reason for the apparent absence of defence works at the river crossing here. The bridge had recently been constructed, being opened to traffic in March 1797 (Map 20).

Instructions in July 1803, a few days after Emmet's rising in Dublin, included provision for destroying the masonry bridge at Banagher should the need arise; the same orders gave instructions for pontoons to be provided to enable two temporary bridges to be placed across the Shannon, together with the necessary equipment such as anchors and cables.[6] Some eight miles upstream of Portumna were fords at Meelick and Keelogue. Fieldworks were constructed here by May 1804: a contemporary plan of these defences depicts the layout, while a list of 1804 notes:[7]

		12-pounders	8-inch howitzers
Keelogue:	Work A	3	1
	Work B	7	2
Meelick:		4	1

Also noted are temporary magazines, huts for accommodation of the garrison, and a spare 12-pounder gun at Keelogue, not attached to a battery. Work A remains today in an overgrown condition a short distance north of the later, permanent battery erected on the site of work B; it is an irregular quadrilateral enclosure surrounded by a ditch. South of these two fieldworks a smaller battery is shown on the contemporary plan, noted as C, an emplacement on a small island for one 12-pounder gun; [8] further downstream at Meelick a battery is indicated on Cromwell's Island (most probably the site of the seventeenth-century fort), noted as having an armament corresponding to the 1804 list. Farther south another small one-gun battery for a 12-pounder is shown on what is evidently Moran Island. The 1806 list of land required for defence notes:

Ford at Keelogue

A, B Batteries	Inniskerig Is. [Incherky Island]

Ford at Meelick

A Battery	Cromwell's Island
B Battery	Moran Island

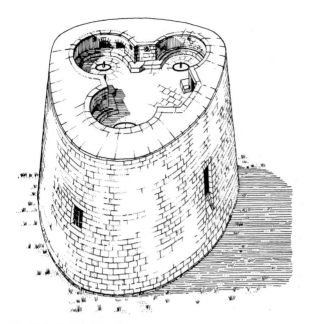

Fig. 115. Meelick Martello tower.

In the 'Remarks' column of this list it is noted that:

> the land has been proposed to be taken during the war, or for such time as the govt. may require. It will however rest with govt. to decide on the importance of these passes and whether any permanent works should be erected for their security.

These remarks are also applied to the earthworks at Banagher and Shannonbridge. Battery B at Keelogue was later rebuilt in its present form, most likely after 1810, at which time the defences at Shannonbridge and Athlone were still fieldworks. The Martello tower at Banagher was started in 1811 and it seems likely that at this time a decision was made to convert the earthwork defences along the river into permanent masonry structures.

The Martello tower at Meelick was evidently built as part of this programme, sited across the river to the south-east of the battery on Cromwell's Island. The tower may have been

intended to support the battery, or possibly it superseded the island battery, which was then abandoned. The tower is cam-shaped in plan, similar to those built in England along the Essex and Suffolk coast between 1810 and 1812, and of the same design as the two towers on the south shore of Galway Bay at Finavarra and Aughinish, which appear to have been constructed at this time. The ground level of the tower contained stores and a powder magazine, the first-floor level with its timber floor providing the living accommodation. Two staircases, symmetrically arranged in plan, are contained within the wall thickness, and lead from each side of the first-floor level to the rear of the gun platform above. The gun platform is 'trefoil' in plan, providing for three guns; the structure is supported on a central stone pier, cylindrical in shape, passing down through the tower to ground level. Each of the three guns was mounted on a traversing platform and capable of being trained through an arc of about 220 degrees (Fig.115).

Meelick Martello tower is in a reasonable condition, having its original iron-sheeted door in position at the first-floor level entrance. The gun platform retains the iron pivots for traversing platforms and the iron rails on which they were mounted (Fig.116). The ringbolts fixed to the inner face of the parapet are arranged so that they hinge back into a shallow recess cut in the regular ashlar stonework; block and tackle attached to these ringbolts assisted the gun crew in training the guns on their movable platforms. The inner face of the parapet rises to just less than six feet above the gun platform; the *banquette* or step for musketry fire on which the outer rails for the guns are mounted is nineteen inches above the gun platform and some twenty inches wide. Above the banquette are five regular courses of well-built ashlar masonry, each about nine inches high, capped by six-inch-thick coping stones. The parapet dimensions are similar to those at other Martello towers. Also at

Fig. 116. Meelick Martello gun platform and parapet.

Meelick there are arched recesses in the inner face of the parapet, some three to four feet wide and two feet high, perhaps intended for ammunition storage. The tower is approximately 60 feet wide at its largest dimension at ground level, somewhat less at parapet level, due to the battered wall surface of the exterior. The Galway Bay towers are of a similar size and shape. Two large windows, one at each side of the tower, are placed at first-floor level at the start of two staircases that lead up to the roof level.

The river navigation here and as far as Incherky Island about a mile farther upstream was changed considerably during the 1840s by the construction of a broad new channel and Victoria Lock. The river banks and islands, now extensively covered with undergrowth and trees, must have been much more open and free of obstructions when the Shannon fortifications were constructed, to provide an effective field of fire for the guns. Meelick Martello is some 400 yards north of Victoria Lock, to the west of the canal.

The fort or battery now on the site of battery B at Keelogue is similar in design to the Shannon Estuary forts built at this time. The enclosure or battery is somewhat smaller, but there is the same type of rectangular blockhouse or 'bombproof barrack' placed at the rear of the work. In the battery were seven guns mounted on traversing platforms, firing over the broad parapet to the north and west. Two howitzers or carronades were on the roof-level gun platform of the barrack, protected by a masonry parapet, as on the Shannon Estuary fortifications. The total armament of the new work was the same as that

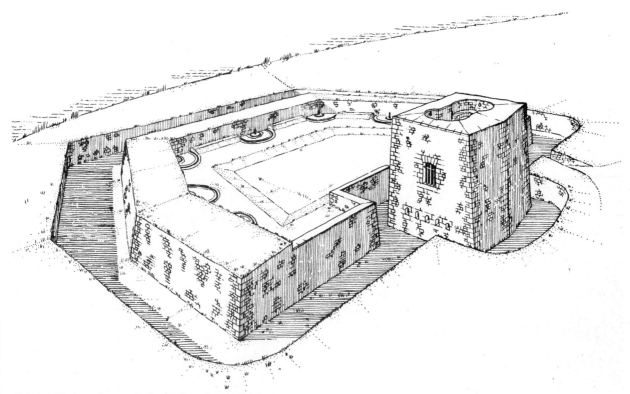

Fig. 117. Keelogue battery, Incherky, from the south-east.

of its predecessor, but it is most likely that larger-calibre 18-pounder or 24-pounder cannon on the traversing platforms replaced the earlier 12-pounder guns. The cost of the building work was noted in 1817 as somewhat less than £8,000.[9] Keelogue battery is in a reasonable state of preservation except for some damage to the entrance gateway, where entry was originally by a drawbridge across the dry moat. A smaller drawbridge or wooden gangway provided access from the battery to the doorway of the blockhouse.

The battery is some 200 feet wide (the Shannon Estuary batteries are on average about 250 feet) while the blockhouse is similar to those of the estuary except that the external wall away from the battery enclosure is formed into two splayed faces, forming an obtuse angle in plan. The front of the battery is of half-hexagon plan form, unlike the segmental or curved plan form of the estuary batteries. There are gun positions for seven front-pivoted traversing platforms

within the battery, the guns firing over the broad, earth-topped parapet some sixteen feet wide. Musket loops in each end of the blockhouse at the lowest level covered the dry moat at the rear of the battery (Fig.117). At first-floor level, on the same level as the interior of the battery, was living accommodation for the garrison; from here a staircase within the thickness of the splayed external wall leads up to the gun platform on the roof above, where the banquette and parapet dimensions are similar to those at Meelick Martello tower. Like the Meelick tower, the blockhouse at Keelogue is constructed of very precise ashlar masonry. At each end of the blockhouse at first-floor level is a large window opening similar to those at Meelick.

Four miles upstream from the ford at Keelogue was the masonry bridge at Banagher, its series of small arches similar to the present bridge at Shannonbridge. This bridge was demolished in the 1840s when extensive improvements were carried out to the Shannon navigation, being

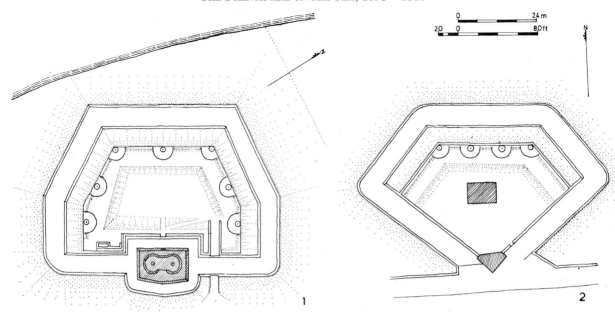

Fig. 118. Plans of Keelogue battery and Fort Eliza, Banagher.

replaced by the present bridge a short distance upstream. On the west bank of the river was a canal—now largely filled in—parallel to the river; between this canal and the river is the tower known as Cromwell's Castle, just downstream from the original bridge, the abutment of which is visible in the river bank. The 1804 defence works here were listed as:[10]

		18-pounders	12-pounders
Banagher:	Castle Battery	-	2
	Barrack Battery	-	3
	Field work	3	-

The 1806 list of land for defence works notes:[11]

Banagher:

A. Battery and store room	barrack yard	govt. ground
B. Old Tower repaired	end of bridge on canal bank	90 feet front on the canal
C. Battery	in the marsh left of the bridge	

Evidently by this time Cromwell's Castle had been modified and partly rebuilt, and is listed at B above. A brick vault was inserted to carry a gun platform for a gun on a traversing platform at roof level. Part of the interior of the building at ground level was used as a powder magazine. The castle is entered by a doorway at first-floor level, evidently inserted at this time; the upper part of the structure—about one-third of the height—was rebuilt in regular masonry, the earlier seventeenth-century stonework being generally smaller and irregular. On the roof-level gun platform is a pivot for a traversing platform; the gun here had a limited field of fire westwards along the road from Loughrea and Eyrecourt. In effect, this earlier structure was converted into something similar to a Martello tower.

The barrack battery, noted in 1804 as three 12-pounders, was later to take the form of three guns placed at high level behind a broad parapet forming part of the perimeter wall of the barracks; these guns would have been in line with the original bridge, a short distance from its eastern end. The high surrounding wall and the gun emplacement of the barracks survive. While several of the ruined overgrown buildings inside were recently demolished. Instructions were issued in 1807 to proceed with the construction of the barrack in Banagher, presumably replacing or incorporating an earlier structure on the site,

Fig. 119. Doorway to Banagher Martello tower.

and making the place defensible with the high perimeter wall and gun platform.

The fieldwork battery 'in the marsh left of the bridge' armed with three 18-pounders provided supporting fire for the defence of the bridge. The earthwork here was later rebuilt with masonry retaining walls, the gun platform lowered, stone kerbs to mount the iron rails for four traversing platforms set in position, and a magazine built in the centre of the enclosure. It seems probable that the first earthwork battery here was like those constructed at the same time—completed by 1804—at Shannonbridge, essentially a ditch, parapet, and gun platform and a timber palisade at the rear. The new permanent work was possibly undertaken in 1811-12 when the Martello tower near Cromwell's Castle was constructed. The cost of the new permanent battery was noted

as a little over £3,000 in 1817.[12] Some sources refer to it as Fort Eliza: it is so named on the first edition of the Ordnance Survey map of 1838, which notes the four guns.

It is a five-sided battery, the three sides facing the river formed of broad parapets, the other two sides meeting at the rear salient angle at a guardhouse, now ruined. A dry moat surrounds the battery, the entrance having been originally across a drawbridge to the gateway, close to the guardhouse. In the centre of the enclosure is the vaulted powder magazine; behind the front parapet are the stone kerbs for the iron rails on which the four guns on their traversing platforms were mounted (Fig.118). The guns were arranged to fire over the parapet and across the river, which is about 180 yards away; they would have provided supporting fire to the guns on Cromwell's Castle and the nearby Martello on the west bank, and to the three guns at the barracks. The battery guns also covered the river immediately downstream of the bridge, making it difficult for an attacking force to cross at this point. A ford is noted just below the battery in a military report of December 1805.[13]

To the west of the canal on the Galway side of the river a Martello tower was under construction in 1812. Work had started the previous year closer to the river bank, but this position was abandoned for the present site about 100 yards in advance of Cromwell's Castle, on the other side of the road to Eyrecourt and Loughrea. It was along this road that an enemy force could be expected to march in an attack on Banagher bridge, having landed in the vicinity of Galway Bay. The tower, known as Fanesker Tower, is elliptical or oval in plan, with an eccentric circular gun platform and interior, resulting in a much thicker parapet and wall to the north-west, the direction of expected attack, decreasing to the less vulnerable south-eastern side facing the river, where the doorway is placed. This plan form is similar to the earliest English Martello towers, constructed from 1805 onwards on the Sussex and Kent coasts. Similar towers in Ireland are the two towers inland of Duncannon Fort. As usual the entrance doorway is at first-floor level, originally approached by a step ladder; the roof-level gun platform is supported by a brick dome that forms the ceiling of the first-floor space of the tower. The circular gun platform with its central pivot allowed for the gun on the traversing platform to be trained through a full circle. The lower rooms of the tower at ground level followed the usual arrangement, being used for storage and a powder magazine.

The cost of the Martello was noted in 1817 as a little over £3,700.[14] There was a block and tackle provided for hauling up the external step ladder at the entrance, the door of which was noted as being covered with iron sheeting (Fig.119). The same documents also note barrier gates on the canal bridge. *Pigot's Directory* (1824) gives the following description of the fortifications at Banagher:

> *Near the bridge, on the Galway side, are two large towers, each planted with one 24lb traversing gun; and at the south-west of the bridge is a sod battery, mounting three 24 pound traversing guns for the purpose of protecting or destroying the bridge.... At the foot of the bridge is a barrack for two companies of foot, and apartments for three officers, with a military battery mounting three 12 pound guns, and a large magazine underneath which is bomb and waterproof.*

Three guns are noted at the battery, the same number as listed in 1804, but they were then 18-pounders; the Ordnance Survey of 1838 notes four guns, which corresponds to the four gun positions that survive on the site.

The Grand Canal was completed as far as the Shannon two miles north-east of Banagher at Shannon Harbour in 1804. A military camp was established here in 1803, possibly on or near the site of Clonony Barracks, which was under construction in that year, to be ready to receive 1,000 men in November. The first square of the barrack was completed in March 1804, described as a 'temporary barrack', possibly meaning buildings largely of timber construction.[15] In 1806 there was accommodation for 2,000 troops, with space for another 1,000 men.[16] The canal was of importance as a means of transporting troops and equipment quickly from Dublin to the Shannon. In 1798 the canal had been used for military transport as far as Tullamore—the limit of the navigation at that time—in the campaign against Humbert, while after Humbert's defeat at Ballinamuck the French prisoners of war had been taken by canal to Dublin. The site of Clonony barracks is about a mile east of Shannon Harbour, an area of over thirty-two acres being noted in 1806. The first edition of the Ordnance Survey map depicts 'Clonony Barrack, in ruins': two large, square parade grounds surrounded on each side by buildings, situated a short distance to the north of the canal. Very little remains today: part of the perimeter wall, some ruined outbuildings, and the outline of foundations in the fields. On the west side of the Shannonbridge-Cloghan road between Clonony Castle and the canal bridge is an entrance gateway and the remains of a guard-house.

Shannonbridge, some six miles north-west of Shannon Harbour, is the nearest crossing-point of the river to Galway Bay, forty-five miles to the west. It was estimated that French troops would have been able to march from Galway to Dublin in six days. In July 1803 plans and estimates for defence works on the Shannon were requested by the commander of the forces from Lieutenant-Colonel Fisher of the Royal Engineers, including a *tête-de-pont* or bridgehead at Shannonbridge. Fisher was also instructed to investigate the feasibility of a dam at Shannonbridge to destroy the ford at Seven Churches (Clonmacnoise) and another ford at an old castle three miles above Shannonbridge. An instruction to proceed with the defence works and assemble the necessary working parties followed in September.[17] By May 1804 the following works were constructed at Shannonbridge:[18]

		12-pounders	8-inch howitzers
Works:	A	3	1
	B	4	2
Batteries:	1	3	1
	2	2	–
	2	2	–

Two 12-pounders are also noted in reserve, not attached to any battery. A description of the Shannon fortifications in December 1805 notes that the stone bridge was built on a ford, so that the destruction of the bridge would not necessarily prevent an enemy force crossing the river here. Two enclosed works were built on the high ground on the west bank; the armament of these was noted at this time as four 12-pounders and one 8-inch howitzer in the work nearest to the bridge, and six 12-pounders and two 8-inch howitzers in the advanced work farther west. These redoubts had temporary guardhouses and magazines. Three batteries, one on the island north of the bridge and two on the east bank south of the bridge, also had temporary guardhouses and magazines, and were closed in the rear in each case with timber palisades (Fig.120). The expense of these works was noted as just over £2,000, with smaller sums for repairs and future maintenance work.[19]

In January 1806 these works were listed with the areas of ground acquired:[20]

Shannonbridge:

A	Two redoubts in front	
B	of the bridge	Lynch's Hill
No. 1 battery on the left flank		
[evidently an an error:		Island
should be *right* flank]		
No.2 batteries on the left flank		L'Estranges Ground
No.3		

A plan drawn up in 1810 shows these fieldworks in detail, while a section shows how redoubt A, nearest to the bridge, commanded the interior of the advanced redoubt somewhat less than 200 yards—effective maximum musketry range— to the west.[21] The two redoubts were square enclosures defended by ditches, earthwork parapets, and timber palisades; they were arranged in line on the high ground west of the bridge, the site of the masonry fortification constructed over the following years. The three batteries were on Lamb Island north of the bridge and on the east bank to the south. Of these, battery no. 1 on the island is still visible, with remains of its parapets and embrasures, while the ditch, parapet and gun-embrasures of no. 2 survive, although much eroded (Fig.121). The three batteries flanked the two redoubts on the opposite bank; that on the island had a field of fire north of the redoubts, the two batteries on the east bank flanking the south side and covering the road from Ballinasloe.

The construction of the present extensive masonry fortification on the west bank to replace the two earthwork redoubts (it must also have superseded the three fieldwork batteries) possibly started in 1811-12, at the time of the building of the Martello tower at Banagher, when it seems that the fieldworks along the river began to be superseded by permanent defences.

The Shannonbridge *tête-de-pont* is unique in Ireland or Britain, a remarkable example of artillery fortification of the Napoleonic period.[22] The fortifications are laid out on the west bank on high ground, in an almost symmetrical

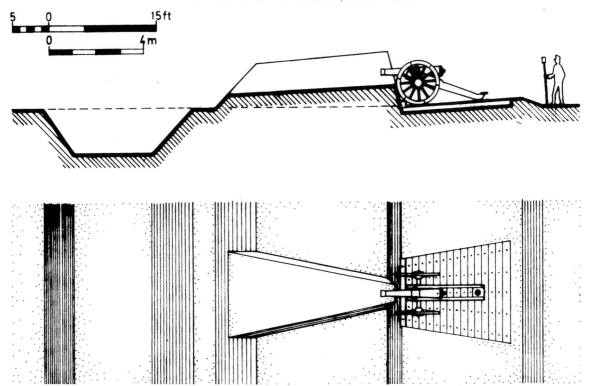

Fig. 120. Fieldwork battery: section and part plan of fieldwork battery with ditch, parapet, embrasure and gun platform (after illustration dated 1816, in C.W Pasley A Course of Elementary Fortification, 2nd ed. 1832).

arrangement on the axis of the bridge, which was completed in 1757 (Fig.122). Some 400 yards west of the river is the foot of the glacis—this was the position of the fieldwork, redoubt B, which was demolished—which slopes up to mask the west front of the advanced redoubt of the new *tête-de-pont* 200 yards to the east. The foot of the glacis was therefore within range of musketry in the advanced redoubt. The counterscarp wall supporting the end of the glacis is separated from the scarp or front wall of the redoubt by a ditch or moat, twenty feet wide. Projecting into the ditch from the redoubt is a caponnière, a 'bombproof' vaulted structure provided with musket-loops flanking the ditch. Loops in two adjacent vaulted galleries in the redoubt provided for additional defence of the ditch, and flank the caponnière north and south (Fig.124).

Above these vaulted galleries is the gun platform for four pieces of artillery on traversing platforms, probably 24-pounders like the guns

on the western salient of the Athlone batteries. These four guns had a field of fire westwards down the slope of the glacis and beyond, and could also be trained to fire to the north-west and south-west. The protected courtyard of the redoubt, from which there is access to the case-mated galleries and the caponnière, is approached by a sunken road on the centre-line of the layout. North and south of this roadway are the curtain walls linking the redoubt to the flank defences farther to the east; a small-arms battery for infantrymen armed with muskets to the north, the work to the south being a massive three-storey defensible barrack. On the flat roof of the barrack, supported by barrel-vaulted apartments below, were three guns on traversing platforms with a field of fire to the west, directly along the road from Ballinasloe. It seems probable that these were also 24-pounder guns. The front or west face of the building has two rows of musket-loops, the lower-level row being masked

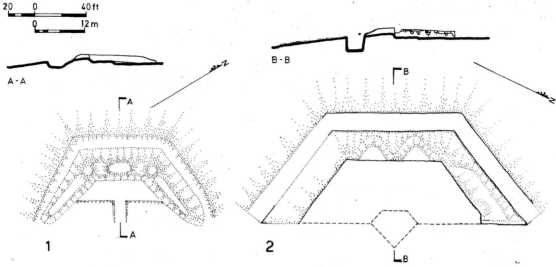

Fig. 121. Plans of Shannon batteries: 1 Battery No.2 Shannonbridge 2 guns; 2 Battery No.1 Athlone 3 guns.

by the counterscarp wall of a small glacis. Flank fire was provided along the west face of the barrack by loop-holes in the adjacent curtain wall to the north. The main road from Ballinasloe to Shannonbridge originally passed beneath an arched gateway in this curtain wall, an archway since demolished to widen the road here (see Fig.123).

The exterior of this gateway with its heavy timber doors was protected by flank fire from the rear of the advanced redoubt and from the front of the barrack. The archway opposite, in the curtain wall of the northern or right flank of the fortification, indicates the original arrangement of the road gateway, which was somewhat wider. The 'left flank building' or barrack was under construction in 1814, at which time it partly collapsed and had to be rebuilt.[23]

The eastern part of the *tête-de-pont* is bounded by a perimeter wall extending on the north and south as far as the river bank; at these corners there are half-bastions that allowed for flank fire along the river bank north and south of the bridge, which is centrally located between them. The house north of the road here originally provided accommodation for the officers of the garrison. The first edition of the Ordnance Survey map (1838) notes the casemated rooms in

the advanced redoubt as 'artillery barrack' and the left flank building as 'infantry barrack'.

On the east bank was a barrack on the south side of the main street, constructed in 1798, which is depicted on the 1810 plan. This building was demolished in 1974, but the perimeter wall of the barrack yard survives. South of this wall and about 100 yards northeast of battery no. 2 is a high-walled enclosure containing a powder magazine and two storage buildings, arranged in a symmetrical layout. The 1810 plan notes this ground as intended for the siting of a powder magazine; details of these buildings are included in documents of 1817 that cover the cost of the Shannon fortifications. The extensive bridgehead fortification at Shannonbridge, constructed after 1810 and evidently completed, like the other defence works, by 1817, indicates how seriously the possibility of an enemy landing on the west coast was taken. Shannonbridge was clearly considered a key strategic point on the Shannon in preventing an invasion force marching on Dublin.

Some twenty miles to the east of Shannonbridge and about five miles south of Tullamore, at Killurin Hill, the construction of a large-scale fortress was proposed by a committee of Royal Engineers in Ireland. A plan of

SHANNONBRIDGE

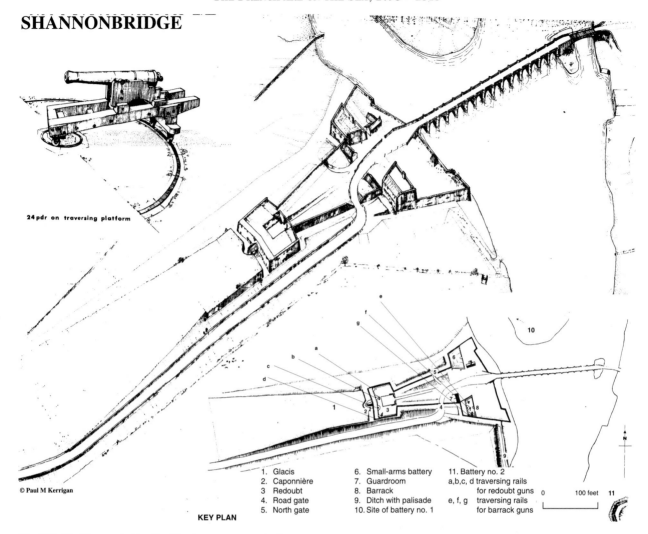

24 pdr on traversing platform

© Paul M Kerrigan

1. Glacis	6. Small-arms battery	11. Battery no. 2
2. Caponnière	7. Guardroom	a,b,c, d traversing rails
3. Redoubt	8. Barrack	for redoubt guns
4. Road gate	9. Ditch with palisade	e, f, g traversing rails
5. North gate	10. Site of battery no. 1	for barrack guns

0   100 feet

KEY PLAN

Fig. 122. The Shannonbridge Fortifications- axonometric view.

November 1805 depicts a similar plan form to the new fortress then starting construction on Spike Island in Cork Harbour, with six bastions.[24] The fortification intended for Killurin Hill was, however, somewhat larger in scale, the bastions larger and more widely spaced, with caponnières and outworks covered by an extensive glacis. This proposed work would have provided a strong-point in support of the Shannon defences and a considerable obstacle close to the most direct route to Dublin. Some four miles south of Killurin are the Slieve Bloom Mountains, extending southwards for about fifteen miles and providing a formidable obstacle for an invading

force that had crossed the Shannon and intended to march on Dublin. Such a force might either advance north of the mountains passing through Tullamore or Kilbeggan, or to the south through Roscrea.

The main roads from Portumna and Banagher to Roscrea passed through Birr. South of Birr, on high ground overlooking the road to Roscrea, a new barrack was constructed between 1809 and 1812 to accommodate 1,100 infantry. Like Clonony Barracks, this new barrack at Crinkill provided extra troops who might assist in the defence of the Shannon, in particular the crossing-points at Portumna and Banagher. The new

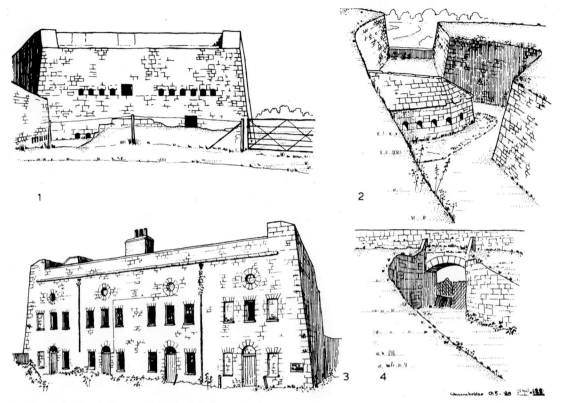

Fig. 123. Shannonbridge: **1** *Front of Left Flank Building;* **2** *Capponière from parapet of Redoubt;* **3** *rear of Left Flank Building;* **4** *Gateway in North Wall.*

garrison at Crinkill might also be deployed to prevent an enemy marching on Roscrea, from where the main road to Dublin passed to the south of the Slieve Bloom Mountains.

Extensive remains of the barrack buildings and perimeter walls survive at Crinkill. The bastion-shaped outworks at the gates appear to have been constructed later than the perimeter wall, as there is a straight joint between them. These outworks and the barrack wall near the gates are provided with loops for musketry.

Athlone is some ten miles north of Shannonbridge; the distance by river of over thirteen miles was shorter than by road to the east or west of the Shannon, and it is most likely that supplies came downstream by boat from the ordnance depot and powder magazines at Athlone for the defences at Shannonbridge, Banagher, Keelogue and Meelick. By the end of the eighteenth century the earlier fortifications

on the east side of Athlone were out of date, incomplete, and overlooked by high ground, while the works on the west had for the most part been demolished or built over by the expansion of the town in that direction.

In June 1793, Colonel Tarrant of the Royal Irish Engineers inspected the ruined castle and the approaches to Athlone on the east and west of the town.[25] He recommended that the castle be repaired to form a work defensible by musketry, emphasising that the castle commanded the barrack entrance gateway a short distance to the north. The barrack, like most of those in Ireland at this time, was surrounded by a wall with no particular defensive features—Tarrant advocated that it might be made defensible by firearms at small expense. In the years following Tarrant's inspection the houses built up against the castle were demolished to provide a clear field of fire for the garrison, and work went ahead extensive-

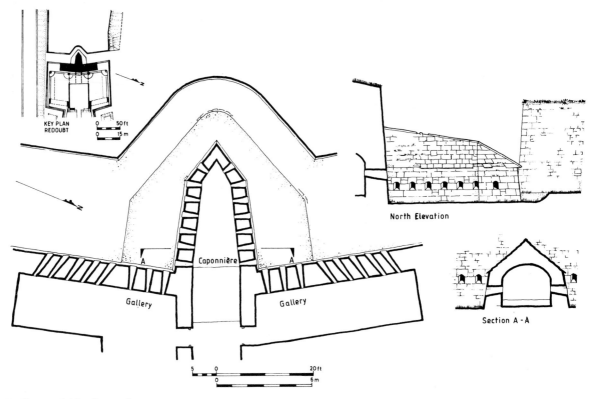

Fig. 124. Shannonbridge Capponière.

ly rebuilding the upper part of the structure with provision for gun-embrasures and musketry defence. The castle eventually became a citadel or strong-point of the town defences, in a key position immediately upstream of the old bridge.

The castle as reconstructed has at least eleven gun-embrasures, while in addition there is a traversing platform emplacement on the south-east tower overlooking the site of the bridge. The top of this tower is similar to a Martello tower. The lower slope of the entrance ramp up to the castle gateway is covered by musket-loops and by a gun-embrasure in the upper level of the north-west tower directly above. Additional musket-loops provide for the defence of the upper part of the entrance ramp and the gateway. The open space within the castle contains a large hexagonal tower, most of the upper part of which dates from the reconstruction work; it is provided with loop-holed projecting structures—similar to the machicolations on some of the Martello towers—

to allow for musketry defence. The north-east tower, overlooking the present bridge of Athlone, built in the 1840s, has two gun-embrasures in the parapet, although the limited space here suggests that there would be room for only one gun on the gun platform. The broad parapet between the northeast and southeast towers is provided with two large, widely-splayed gun-embrasures giving a field of fire over the river to the east. Just to the west of the south-east tower with its traversing gun emplacement is another gun embrasure—now blocked up—covering the open space below, depicted as 'Marketplace' on Tarrant's sketch plan. The platform of the north-west tower, approached through a barrel-vaulted passage-way, has four gun-embrasures, one of which covers the entrance ramp below. The remaining embrasures facing the north and west have each been blocked by a later wall provided with musket-loops. The western side of the castle is at a considerably higher level than the rest. At this higher level are two more gun-embrasures—now blocked up—in the high parapet wall. Guns here, firing to the west over the rooftops of the western side of Athlone, would have provided some supporting fire to the guns in the batteries beyond the canal, some 500 yards away.

Tarrant had pointed out that the high ground to the west of Athlone—Gallows Hill—commanded the town. In July 1798, temporary works of defence were erected here by Lieutenant-Colonel Buchanan of the Royal Artillery; he was, however, reprimanded early the following month by army headquarters at Kilmainham for proceeding without permission. The work was to stop, and in future, plans and estimates were to be submitted to the master-general of the ordnance for approval.[26] Three weeks later General Humbert's force landed at Killala, and after his victory at Castlebar some cavalry units of the defeated British army had retreated in panic as far as Athlone. Had Humbert advanced to Athlone defences on the high ground west of the town would have been an additional obstacle to his small army.

The plan of constructing works on Gallows Hill was revived in 1803 as part of the scheme for the defence of the line of the Shannon. In July 1803, Colonel Beckwith at Kilmainham was writing to Lieutenant-Colonel Benjamin Fisher of the Royal Engineers for plans and estimates of these works along the river, including 'a tête-de-pont to cover Athlone on the west side, including what is called the Gallows Hill....'[27] A further letter from Beckwith to Fisher refers to estimates submitted and Fisher was instructed in September to proceed with the works and lease the ground.[28] Between 1803 and 1808, land was being taken 'to enable His Majesty more effectually to provide for the defence and security of the realm during the present war....'[29] By late 1803 or early the following year, the fieldwork batteries had been erected and guns mounted at the castle. The 'Return of Ordnance attached to the different fieldworks ... of the River Shannon ... May 1804' provides details of the ordnance at the batteries west of Athlone (see Table 3).[30]

The most powerful artillery, 24-pounders, was positioned at the western salient angle of the batteries—the report of December 1805, which describes the Shannon defences, notes that these guns and the howitzers with them on batteries 3 and 4 were mounted on traversing platforms.[31] The following description in the report for Athlone is followed by a more detailed account of each battery:

The works erected for the defence of the bridge and pass over the Shannon at this place consist of eight enclosed works, connected together by lines of communication, extending from the southern to the northern extremity of the canal covering the western side of the town of Athlone.

Batteries		24-pounders	12-pounders	8-inch howitzers
	1	-	3	-
	2	-	3	-
	3	3	-	2
	4	2	-	-
	5	-	2	-
	6	-	3	-
	7	-	2	-
	8	-	2	-

Table 3. Ordnance at River Shannon fieldworks in May 1803

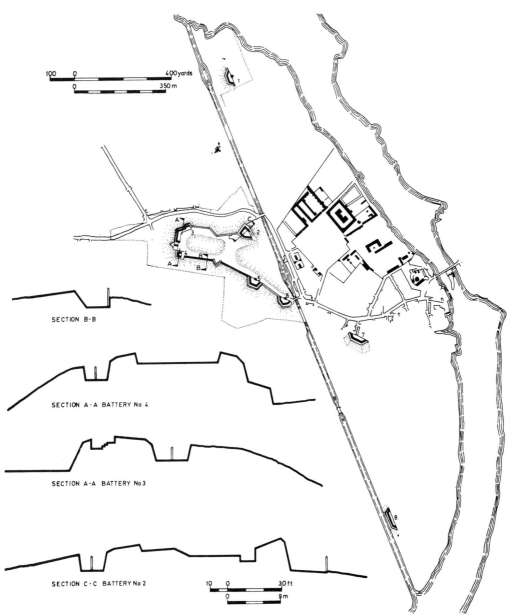

Fig. 125. The Batteries Athlone. Based on Ordnance Survey 1837, B.L. Ms 13800 (2) and PRO MR 470 (3) & (4).

Battery no. 1 was sited at the north end of the canal, between it and the river, with the canal in its front, providing for flank fire along the north of batteries 2 and 3. The 1805 report noted a loop-holed guardhouse and enclosing wall at this battery, and that it had been proposed to convert it into a redoubt—that is, that it be made capable of all-round defence—but no decision had

been taken on this. It is situated on high ground, which falls in a smooth, steep slope from the battery down to the canal bank to the west. It had a field of fire over the road from Co. Roscommon and its junction with the Galway road, some 650 yards to the south-west. It is protected by an earthwork parapet with the remains of three gun-embrasures that form broad, irregular depressions narrowing towards the inner face of the parapet. In front is a dry ditch, the scarp

Fig. 126. The Batteries Athlone, looking west along the southern lines to batteries no.3 and 4 at the western salient, c.1910. (Photo: Simmons, Athlone).

and counterscarp of which were originally faced with masonry; much of this stonework has been removed or has fallen to the bottom of the ditch, the southern half of which is largely filled in. There was a small guardhouse at the centre of the rear of the battery, a site marked today by a slight depression in the ground (see Fig.121).

Batteries 2 to 6 occupied Gallows Hill and were connected by 'lines', palisaded entrenchments or sunken pathways protected by earthwork parapets or embankments. These batteries were in advance of the canal, which also constituted a line of defence from north to south. The 1805 report noted that battery no. 2 commanded the other batteries here to the west and south—3, 4, 5, and 6; it mounted three 12-pounders, had a guardhouse and magazine and was palisaded. A line of communication connected the rear of the work to the canal to complete the enclosure of the works here (Fig.125).

A line of communication connected battery no. 2 to no. 3 some 200 yards farther west, battery no. 4 being sited just to the south of no. 3. The report of December 1805 states:

This work [no. 3] with No. 4 forms a front of five 24-pounders and two 8 inch howitzers mounted on traversing platforms—enfilading the roads of Roscommon and Ballinasloe; both these works have their guardhouses, magazines.... between them is constructed a caponier flanking their respective ditches.

From these advanced works on the western salient the line of defence ran back eastwards to batteries 5 and 6, each with its loop-holed guardhouse and magazine. At the foot of the glacis on this southern front from battery no. 4 to battery no. 6 immediately in front of the canal, the 1805 report notes an extensive bog. The report also remarked on the lines of communication linking the batteries:

The lines of communication on this front [the south front] are different from those on the opposite [north front] which are of masonry - these consist of a ditch, glacis and pal-

isades, forming a breastwork with banquettes ....(Fig. 126)

Battery no. 7 was sited on high ground in the town south of Connaught Street, some 300 yards south-east of no. 6. In 1805 the field of fire from this work was 'in part, masked by buildings the expense of purchasing which was too considerable, the removal of them was therefore deferred until the exigency of the moment.'

About 600 yards to the south, on the east bank of the canal was battery no. 8. This had been taken down by December 1805 to allow for repairing the canal lock, but had not been rebuilt at this time. The battery is not included on a plan of the fieldworks at Athlone of May 1810 and appears to have been abandoned.[32]

Lieutenant Luke Lawless of Napoleon's Irish Legion visited Ireland to obtain information on the military situation in 1811:[33] there was a plan to send 30,000 troops from France or Holland. He reported the 'Fort of Athlone' as the only fortification of any consequence in Ireland, which must be a reference to the batteries. The construction of coastal Martello towers was noted, but they were evidently not considered to be a serious obstacle to an invasion force.

A contemporary remark on the works at Athlone in 1812 was somewhat dubious about the scheme of defence along the Shannon:

Of all places of strength [in Ireland], the most important is a large fortification at Athlone, in the centre of Ireland; which was constructed, as I have been informed, for the purpose of commanding the Shannon, near which it is situated; so that an enemy landing in Connaught would be arrested in his progress, and prevented from getting into Leinster.... In the course of my tour, I remained two or three days at Athlone, and learned to my surprise, from persons not connected with the fortifications, that the

Shannon is fordable at eleven places, within eight miles of this great military station.[34]

There were a number of fords between Athlone and Portumna, which had been noted in earlier military surveys; some of these were considered of little consequence, being difficult to approach with artillery or supply wagons. Eleven fords within eight miles of Athlone must be an exaggeration; however, it is significant that, as in the report of Lieutenant Lawless, the Athlone fortifications were considered the most important in the country.

The barrack at Athlone was extensively enlarged between 1793 and 1815, being the headquarters of the Western District and the centre for the defence of the middle Shannon, with an ordnance depot for supplying the fortifications along the river. New powder magazines were erected at the western side of the barrack, near the canal and effectively in the rear of the batteries on Gallows Hill. At Mullingar, Longford and Carrick-on-Shannon, further barrack accommodation was constructed. The completion of the Royal Canal as far as Mullingar in 1806, providing for easy transport of military stores from Dublin, was perhaps a factor influencing the decision to go ahead with new military accommodation here. At Longford a new artillery barrack was built in 1808, some distance north of the earlier cavalry barrack, its perimeter taking the form of a rectangular bastioned fort. The rectangular area was some 300 by 200 feet, the bastion-shaped corner defences having flanks of some 30 feet and faces from 70 to 100 feet in length. Longford artillery barrack may be compared with the barracks on the Wicklow Military Road and with New Geneva, which had corner flankers for musketry defence. This form of defensible barrack reappears some twenty years later at Beggars' Bush in Dublin, at Nenagh and at smaller barracks such as that at Trim and Maryborough.

North of Athlone there does not appear to have been the same concern to defend the crossing-points of the Shannon as there was along the river to the south to Portumna. Barracks to the west of the river at Roscommon, Tulsk, Elphin and Boyle provided accommodation in 1811 for over 800 troops, available if necessary to defend the Shannon crossing-points between Lanesborough and Jamestown. By April 1804 the barrack at Carrick-on-Shannon had been enlarged and repaired. North of Carrick, Lough Allen and the nearby mountainous terrain were obstacles to an invasion force moving eastwards; to the north-east some twenty miles distant from Lough Allen is Enniskillen, which was an important fortified military post between 1796 and 1815, a key position between Upper and Lower Lough Erne. A similar distance north of Lough Allen were other bridgehead defences, at Belleek and Ballyshannon on the River Erne.

9
The North

The northern part of Ireland was of particular concern to the military authorities in the 1790s, as the United Irishmen were well organised in Ulster, drawing much of their strength from the Presbyterian community there—the society had been founded in Belfast in October 1791. In 1797, General Lake had under his command in the Northern District some 11,000 troops, the largest force in the five military districts into which Ireland was divided. The people were disarmed and large quantities of small arms and pikes were surrendered or seized by military search parties.

Ulster remained quiet until the risings in Antrim and Down in 1798. In October that year a French squadron with some 3,000 troops on board, evidently heading for Lough Swilly, was intercepted off the Donegal coast by a more powerful detachment of the Royal Navy. Following the defeat of the French in this naval action, their flagship, *Hoche*, was brought into Lough Swilly, and some of her heavy guns were taken ashore to be used in temporary batteries there.[1] These batteries appear to be the first coastal defence works to be set up in the north of Ireland during the French Revolutionary war; the only other coast defence in Ulster was provided by the guns of Carrickfergus Castle, overlooking Belfast Lough.

To the south and west of Lough Swilly, at crossing-points of the River Erne at Enniskillen, Belleek and Ballyshannon, defence works were constructed between 1796 and 1798. At Enniskillen a square redoubt was built about 1796, serving as a western defence to the town. This work is sited on high ground overlooking the bridge leading to the town approximately a 100 yards to the east. The redoubt is 140 feet square, surrounded by a dry moat or ditch, 15 feet wide. At each corner was a gun mounted on a traversing carriage; the pivots for these remain on the site today.

On high ground on the east side of the town the seventeenth-century, rectangular bastioned fort was brought back into use as a fortification at this time. This earthwork is noted on the Ordnance Survey map of 1834 as 'East Battery', while the redoubt overlooking the western bridge is 'West Battery' and 'Military Hospital', the hospital being the two-storey building in the redoubt. Enniskillen was an important strategic position on the route between Ulster and the west, and the centre of the defence was the castle, where, in 1796, the sum of £7,000 was expended in restoring it as the Castle Barracks with new buildings, while the keep was extensively reconstructed as barracks. Southwards to Belturbet, Upper Lough Erne formed a barrier of some twenty miles to an invasion force attempting to move from the west into Ulster. To the north-west of Enniskillen, Lower Lough Erne extends somewhat less than twenty miles to where

Fig. 127. Barrier and Redoubt at Belleek 1798 by Captain William Smith. TCD Ms 942/2/113.

it flows into the River Erne a short distance east of Belleek.

At Belleek, the junction of several roads linking Sligo, Enniskillen and Donegal, a fortification was built on high ground overlooking the bridge; rather less than half of this work survives on the site today. Contemporary sketches by Captain Sir William Smith of the Royal Engineers show this redoubt to the south-west of the bridge, which is depicted with a double palisade or barrier built across it, also constructed by Smith.[2] The front of the redoubt overlooking the bridge was an indented trace or zigzag in plan, provided with several gun-embrasures, while the flanks and rear of the work were loop-holed for musketry (Fig.127). A semi-circular outwork protected the entrance to the redoubt in the side farthest from the bridge—the west side—indicating that the work was principally intended as a defence against an attack from across the river to the east and north-east. The foundations of the semi-circular outwork may be identified on the site, while the western wall north of the outwork, the northern wall with modern alterations, and part of the eastern front, also survive. Two arched gun-embrasures at the eastern end of the north wall, in a position to command the bridge, are some eight to nine feet wide on the outer face of the wall; these embrasures are now blocked up. A mid nineteenth-century plan of Belleek redoubt[3] depicts a symmetrical layout on approximately an east-west axis (Fig.128). The east front with a central triangular projection or redan was 100 feet wide, the overall dimension from the salient of the redan to the outer face of the semi-circular outwork being somewhat over 160 feet. Accommodation and stores for the garrison were arranged along the north, west and south sides of the redoubt, leaving an open space or courtyard in the centre. The sketches of Belleek by Captain Smith date from 1798; the work had been planned early that year and had been provided with guns by the end of September.

Ballyshannon, four miles west of Belleek, was another important crossing-point of the Erne, and a possible landing place for an invasion force at the estuary just to the west of the bridge and town. Drawings by Smith of Ballyshannon, dated 1797 and 1798, depict a defence work south of the bridge, evidently just to the south of the cavalry barracks here.[4] It is shown as a loop-holed wall for musketry defence with a semicircular projection, presumably covering the entrance as

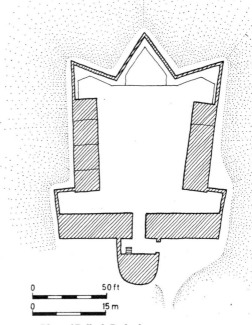

Fig. 128. Plan of Belleek Redoubt.

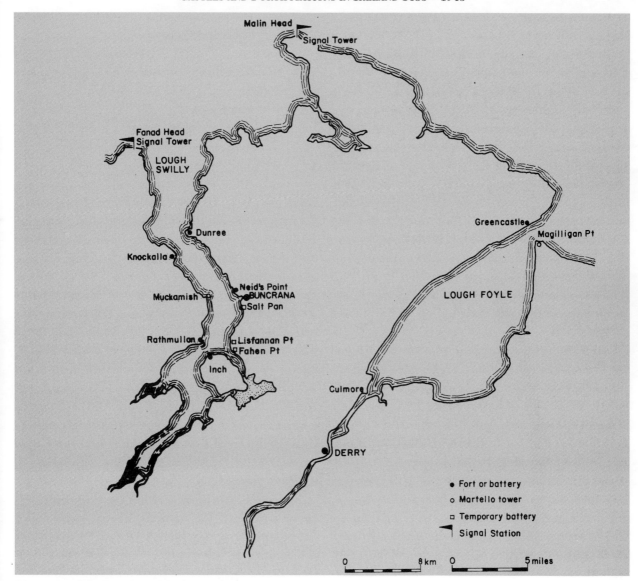

Map 21. Lough Swilly and Lough Foyle 1798-1815.

at the Belleek redoubt. This bridgehead defence work protected the bridge from attack from the south; north of the bridge is the military barracks constructed in 1700, while a short distance to the north-west is Ballyshannon Church, next to which Captain Smith established a military post, as noted on one of his sketches of 1797, which has the bridgehead fortification in the foreground. The first edition of the Ordnance Survey map of 1836 indicates the horse barracks near the south end of the bridge, but does not seem to show any defence work here at that time.

A reference to a battery at Ballyshannon in December 1803 may refer to the defences at the bridge:

Half a brigade of artillery should be quartered at Ballyshannon.... It has become necessary to cause that proportion of the barrack accommodation situated in the battery there to be given up to the Board of Ordnance for the purpose of accommodating the half brigade [5]

235

A 'light brigade' of field artillery at this time consisted of three 6-pounders and one 5½-inch howitzer, with the appropriate ammunition caissons and complement of artillerymen. The fortifications along the Erne at Enniskillen, Belleek and Ballyshannon provided bridgehead defences at these crossing-places, strengthening the line of Upper Lough Erne, Lower Lough Erne and the river from Belleek to Ballyshannon, a natural obstacle of some forty-five miles from Belturbet to the estuary. In 1811, garrisons in permanent and temporary barracks along the Erne were: 180 men at Belturbet, some 750 at Enniskillen, 50 at Belleek redoubt and some 300 in temporary barracks at Belleek, and over 750 troops at Ballyshannon, with more than half of this number in temporary barracks.[6]

Lough Swilly. In November 1798, guns from the French ship of the line *Hoche* were in use at temporary batteries in Lough Swilly.[7] Captain Smith depicts these works at Rathmullan, Muckamish and Knockalla, on the west side of the lough, and at Inch, Saltpan Hill, Neids Point and Dunree, on the east shore (Map 21).[8] At all of these locations, except Saltpan Hill, permanent works were constructed in the early years of the nineteenth century. A manuscript map of Lough Swilly evidently depicts the earliest batteries of late 1798 or early 1799—it is undated, but the watermark of the paper is 1794.[9] These batteries were:

A West Fort (Knockalla)
B East Fort (Dunree)

No.		Guns
1	Rathmullan	2
2	Inch	2
3	Fahan Point	1
4	Lisfannan Point	1
5	Salt Pans	1
6	Signal Point	1

Two of these batteries, Fahan Point and Lisfannan Point, on the east shore south of Buncrana, are not included in Smith's sketches, and were perhaps abandoned before his involvement in the Lough Swilly defences. Not shown on the map is Muckamish on the west side of the lough, which Smith depicts as a temporary battery. The map also includes proposed troop positions between Buncrana and Derry, and a 'moveable corps' at Newtown Cunningham. Anchorages are indicated between Buncrana and Rathmullan, the distance between forts A and B being given as 2,780 yards; the distance between Rathmullan battery and that on Inch as 1,850 yards. Signal Point battery appears to be what was later named Neds Point or Neids Point.

In July 1799, E. B. Littlehales, the military secretary to the Lord Lieutenant and Commander of the Forces, Lord Cornwallis, informed the Master-General and Board of Ordnance that it was considered that 'a sum not exceeding £300 will effectually complete the works at Lough Swilly,' indicating that temporary batteries only were contemplated at that time.[10] A report of 1804 remarked on the shortage of artillerymen at Lough Swilly:

> *The ordnance and ammunition is in good condition though the means of using them is inadequate from the scanty number of artillerymen—due to reduced numbers the brigades are of twenty gunners instead of the establishment figure of thirty-four.*[11]

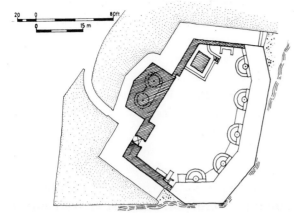

Fig. 129. Plan of Rathmullan Battery, Lough Swilly.

Also included is a list of ordnance at Lough Swilly, April 1804:[12]

	42 pdrs	8
Iron Ordnance with	24 pdrs	1
standing carriages	18 pdrs	11
	9 pdrs	2
	1 pdrs	2
Traversing platforms		
	42 pdrs	6

The 42-pounders were French guns from the *Hoche*; five of the 18-pounders were mounted at Dunree, six at Knockalla.

Rathmullan. Smith's sketch of Rathmullan in 1800 is a distant one, noting the work on the point at Rathmullan with two 42-pounders on traversing platforms. It seems probable that these guns, with some form of earthwork parapet to protect them, were on the site of the present masonry battery. The battery was evidently built in 1813 and is similar to those in the Shannon Estuary built at about the same time. Rathmullan is not so regular in plan as the Shannon batteries, having an approximately D-shaped battery with a blockhouse or 'bombproof barrack' at the rear or landward side (Fig.129). There were five 24-pounders on traversing platforms mounted behind the broad parapet overlooking the sea, the guns having a field of fire eastwards across the estuary to Down Fort on Inch, one mile away (Fig.130). These two works protected the channel between them, which led up to Ramelton and to the other part of the lough up to Letterkenny. Their guns also covered the anchorage to the north to some degree. On the blockhouse at Rathmullan were two guns, noted on a mid nineteenth-century plan as $5\frac{1}{2}$-inch howitzers, the same calibre as the 24-pounders in the battery.

At the northern landward corner of the battery was a powder magazine; there was another magazine at the lower level of the blockhouse, while near the centre of the battery was a shot furnace. The battery and blockhouse survive in reasonable condition, defended on the landward side by a glacis and dry moat; a sunken roadway, curved in plan, gives access to the moat near the southern side of the blockhouse and almost opposite the entrance to the battery, which is an arched gateway flanked by musket-loops and by loops in the lower level of the blockhouse (Fig.131). Rathmullan battery has recently been

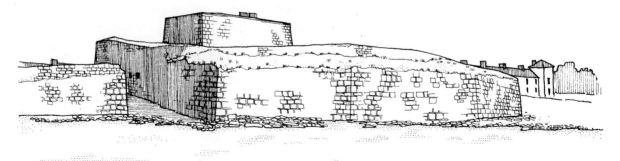

Fig. 130. Rathmullan Battery.

Fig. 131. Rathmullan blockhouse and entrance.

restored and the blockhouse has a small museum and exhibition area.

Muckamish Martello and battery. Situated on the west side of Lough Swilly some three miles north of Rathmullan, on a narrow promontory, Muckamish Martello tower defends the landward side while seaward of the tower is the three-gun battery. Sir William Smith's sketch of this site indicates in a distant view a gun on a traversing platform, protected by a parapet, dated 1799. This temporary work was superseded by the permanent fortification of the Martello tower and battery, presumably in 1812-13, when the other Lough Swilly permanent works were under construction. An early plan for Muckamish depicts a tower and a three-gun battery, dated 1801:[13] this must have been a proposal—the earliest for a Martello tower in Ireland—as the present layout is different. The deed for Muckamish is noted as 21 December 1810 on a mid nineteenth-century plan, which shows the three traversing mounts for 24-pounders, that on the salient angle of the battery with a centre pivot and a circular track or rail, the other two, one on each side, having a front pivot and a semicircular rail. The same plan notes the tower as mounting two 24-pounder guns on traversing platforms, working from the

same central pivot (Fig.132). The tower is circular in plan, with a machicolation above the entrance doorway on the first-floor level. The tower is of a different character from those elsewhere in Ireland, except perhaps the one at Magilligan Point at the entrance to Lough Foyle. Muckamish battery was also provided with a shot furnace, and closer to the tower was a powder magazine. Approach to the battery was by means of a drawbridge which was overlooked by the tower.

Some two miles east across Lough Swilly is the battery at Neids Point; the distance is noted as 3,333 yards on the mid nineteenth-century plan, so that 24-pounders at these two locations would have completely commanded the approach up to Buncrana or Rathmullan and anchorages between them a short distance to the south. Muckamish is now a private holiday residence.

Knockalla Fort. The third coast defence work on the west shore of Lough Swilly is Knockalla fort or battery, some three miles north of Muckamish. Several sketches by Captain Smith of this site indicate gun emplacements for guns on traversing platforms - three are depicted on one drawing, with a barrack building on higher ground at the rear. In this sketch of 1799 the battery does not appear to be completely enclosed on the landward side. The site was extensively remodelled, possibly retaining the earlier barrack and to some extent the parapet on the sea-

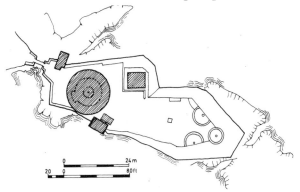

Fig. 132. Plan of Muckamish Martello tower and battery.

238

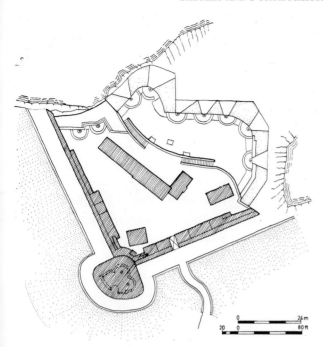

Fig. 133. Plan of Knockalla Fort, Lough Swilly.

ward side. The plan of the fort may be compared with an open fan, a tower on the landward salient angle forming the hinge or pivot. From the tower the two landward walls of the fort lead down to the edge of steep rocky cliffs, the walls protected by a dry moat some twenty feet wide (Fig.133). Backing onto these walls are casemated soldiers' quarters. The fort is approached, as is Rathmullan battery, by means of a sunken roadway, curved in plan, through the glacis on the southern flank. This roadway leads to the moat and the arched entrance gateway, which is flanked by musket-loops and also defended by loops in the lower level of the tower fifty feet away (Figs.134 and 135). These loops enfiladed the dry moat on this side.

The enclosure of the battery area is at two levels, the lower, nearer the sea, having seven wide-splayed embrasures in the parapet for guns on traversing platforms. The upper level of the battery contains the barracks, magazine, casemates and entrance gateway. Entrance to the tower was from the level of the wall walk; two guns on traversing platforms were sited at the northern side

of the upper battery, and two guns mounted on the gun platform of the tower. A mid nineteenth-century plan notes the armament of the fort, most probably the same as the original armament of the Napoleonic period: the lower seven-gun battery of 42-pounders, the upper level two-gun battery of 24-pounders and on the tower on rear-pivoted traversing platforms one 24-pounder gun to the north and a $5\frac{1}{2}$-inch howitzer to the south. The 24-pounder on the tower had a field of fire essentially over the fort to seaward, the howitzer evidently intended principally for landward defence to the east and south. A glacis surrounds the fort on the south and west, but the land rises steeply inland, making the fort vulnerable to landward attack by a force equipped with artillery. Like the other Lough Swilly defences, Knockalla was primarily a sea battery. Across Lough Swilly just a mile to the north-east is Dunree Fort, so that these two works effectively commanded the entrance to the lough with their guns.

A sketch by Smith shows the tower partly collapsed in 1815, with a note placing the blame for this on the builder: 'infamous work made therein by the contractor this fall having been foretold by Captain Sir Wm. Smith Assistant Engineer prior to the same in 1815.' The unusual crenellations or battlements here built on to the parapet of the tower must therefore date from the reconstruction after 1815. They provided extra protec-

Fig. 134. South ditch, tower and entrance, Knockalla Fort.

Fig. 135. Entrance to Knockalla Fort.

tion for the gun crews on the tower from fire from the high ground inland. In its present form there is only room for two guns on the tower, the space where a third gun might have been sited being occupied by the attractive stone turret with a conical roof that gives access to the roof from the spiral staircase (Fig.136). This staircase rises from the basement level of the tower enclosed in a tall cylindrical structure. The tower might be described as quadrant-shaped in plan, the two straight walls flanking the two dry moats of the fort, the quadrant wall front facing inland; the corners of the tower are rounded off. The pivots for the traversing platforms on the tower gun platform are quite elaborate, each with four supporting curved brackets: there are similar pivots for the two guns on the blockhouse at Rathmullan (Fig.137). There was accommodation for four officers and sixty-four soldiers in the middle of the nineteenth century, most probably the same as when the fort was first constructed. Smith gives the name 'West Fort or Battery' to Knockalla on some of his sketches of 1799, which depict the fortification not completely enclosed: the present structure, incorporating perhaps some of the earlier defences and buildings, must date from about 1812-15. Like Muckamish, Knockalla is now a private residence and is used as a holiday home: it has been extensively

restored and repaired and is in good condition (Fig.138).

Down Fort, Inch. This battery on the north of Inch is situated about one mile south-east of Rathmullan battery on the west shore. The plan is similar to Knockalla: a tower at the landward salient with two walls radiating down to the waterside. The dry moat or ditch in front of the walls does not extend around the landward face of the tower, which is quadrant-shaped in plan, similar to that at Knockalla. The battery was extensively altered in the late nineteenth century to mount more modern armament, but a mid nineteenth-century plan depicts a parapet of irregular plan on the waterfront behind which are six gun emplacements for traversing platforms—these were most probably 24-pounders.[14] Three 5½-inch howitzers were on the gun plat-

Fig. 136. Stairhead turret on tower platform, Knockalla Fort.

Fig. 137. Gun pivot on Knockalla Fort.

form of the tower, resulting in a 'trefoil' plan for the roof area within the parapet. As at Knockalla, accommodation and store-rooms were arranged along the inside of the two flank walls of the battery, which was approached along a sunken road cutting through the glacis. This

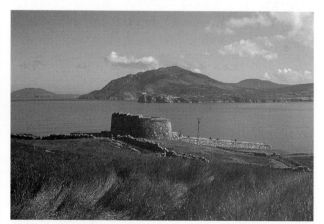

Fig. 138. Knockalla Fort from the west with Dunree Fort in the distance across Lough Swilly.

roadway entered the moat opposite the entrance gateway, which was flanked by a guardroom (Fig.139).

Sketches by Captain Smith in 1799 indicate only two guns on traversing platforms at the site, with some protection provided by an earthwork or masonry parapet. Lewis, in his *Topographical Dictionary of Ireland* (1837), gives 1813 as the date for the permanent work on Inch described above, while 1815 is on a date-stone on the landward side.

Saltpan Hill battery. Situated on the east side of Lough Swilly approximately half a mile southwest of Buncrana, Saltpan Hill battery mounted one gun on a traversing platform. Sketches by Smith in 1799 indicate a front-pivoted platform and gun protected by a parapet on the seaward side. When the six other temporary works on Lough Swilly illustrated by Smith - Rathmullan, Muckamish, Knockalla, Inch, Neids Point and

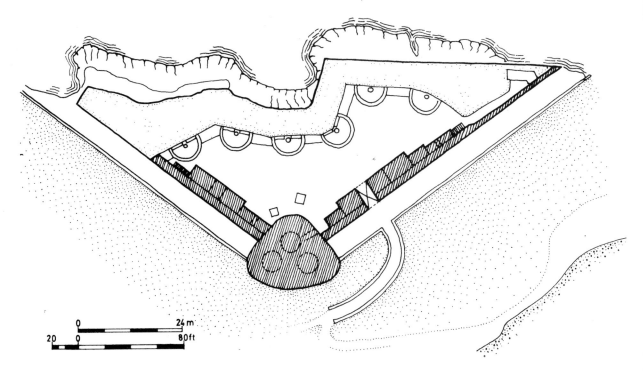

Fig. 139. Plan of Down Fort, Inch, Lough Swilly.

Dunree—were reconstructed as permanent fortifications in the early nineteenth century, it seems that no work was carried out at Saltpan Hill, and the one-gun battery here was abandoned. No defence work is indicated here on the Ordnance Survey map of 1836.

Neids Point battery. Located on a rocky headland one mile north of Saltpan Hill and a mile north-west of Buncrana, the battery here provided a cross-fire with that at Muckamish on the opposite shore. Smith's illustrations of 1799 and 1800 depict a battery with a traversing gun and parapet similar to the arrangement at Saltpan Hill. This small work was replaced by the much larger masonry battery some twelve years later—the site was acquired by Smith in December 1810, as were Muckamish, Knockalla, Rathmullan and Greencastle on Lough Foyle, by which time plans must have been drawn up for permanent works at these sites. At the landward salient with its angle of 90 degrees is a rectangular blockhouse or tower providing enfilade fire along the two landward walls and their ditches.

The battery is five-sided, with casemates against the interior of the landward walls, the three sides facing seawards forming a scarp wall and parapet behind which the original armament must have been placed. This armament was presumably mounted on traversing platforms, but the interior of the battery was reconstructed in the late nineteenth century with mountings for two 6-inch breech-loaders. The entrance gateway with the date 1812 on the keystone is in the eastern landward wall, approached by a sunken roadway, curved in plan, which is cut through the glacis.

The tower, reduced in height to the level of the adjacent walls evidently as part of the reconstruction after 1895, is similar in plan to those at Rathmullan and at Keelogue on the Shannon below Banagher, and of similar dimensions. It is unlike them in being joined to the walls of the battery where these meet at a right angle at the landward salient angle: this follows the general arrangement at Knockalla, Inch and Greencastle, where the towers are quadrant-

Fig. 140. Sketch of the East Fort or Battery on Lough Swilly, looking over to the West Fort or Battery, by Captain William Smith, 1800. The East Fort is Dunree, the West Fort Knockalla. TCD Ms 942/2/143.

shaped or elliptical in plan. The long wall of the tower facing the dry ditch is formed into two faces, making an obtuse angle in plan, as at Rathmullan and Keelogue. A few feet above the level of the ditch are angled musket-loops, set out to allow for diagonal fire across or along the ditch; similar loops are in the adjacent battery walls at this level and in the parapet.

Dunree Fort. Five miles north of Neids Point

is Dunree, on a high rocky promontory, shown on sketches by Captain Smith of 1800 and 1802 as approached by a narrow drawbridge (Fig.140). A circular or semicircular battery was sited at the higher level of the small fort, with guns projecting over the parapet on the land-ward side. At a lower level are barrack buildings, and on a sketch dated 1800 there is a loop-holed wall for musketry defence on the southern side and a counterbalanced drawbridge. The fortifi-

Fig. 141. View of the Tower at Magilligan Point and the New Work and Old Castle at Greencastle by Sir William Smith, 1817. The New Work is Greencastle Fort. TCD Ms 942/2/192.

cations are noted by Smith as 'erected for a temporary expedient', and described as the East Fort on some of the illustrations. The fort is smaller than Knockalla on the opposite shore of Lough Swilly, confined to the top of an irregular promontory with steep cliffs. The interior of the fort has been altered in the late nineteenth century in such a way that it is not possible to determine the original layout when the place was reconstructed in 1812-13. The perimeter masonry wall of squared rubble survives, acting as a retaining wall; the entrance today is in the same place as depicted on Smith's sketches, approached by a drawbridge. To the south of the entrance is an irregularly shaped flanking structure with musket-loops at a lower level; the upper level of this structure, level with the interior of the fort, now houses a reception area for the Dunree Fort Museum. In the centre of the fort is a new building with displays on the history of Dunree and the Lough Swilly defences. The Ordnance Survey map of 1836 indicates an 'ordnance ground' or military area inland of the fort; this was later extended in the late nineteenth century to include Dunree Hill, on which gun emplacements and a polygonal redoubt were erected.

Lough Foyle. Defence works at Lough Swilly defended anchorages and landing places there and protected routes leading to Derry. The more direct route to Derry, through Lough Foyle, also required defences, and the defence of the two estuaries, to be effective, had to be considered together. A detailed report on the defence of Ireland of 1796 noted that:

> in the report made to government early in 1793 it was recommended to construct a small battery at the entrance of Lough Foyle, it would be highly useful for the protection of the port of Derry if a favourable situation can be found: but Lough Swilly would afford shelter to the largest fleet.[15]

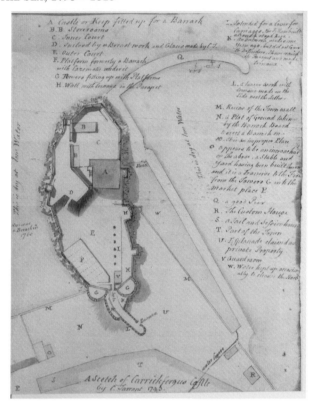

Fig. 142. A Sketch of Carrigfergus Castle by Colonel Tarrant, 1793, National Library of Ireland, 15 b 1 (19).

The report gives no proposals for defence works at Lough Swilly, although there was easy access to Derry some eight miles to the southeast.

A report of the Office of Ordnance of 1804, while listing the guns then at Lough Swilly, does not include Lough Foyle. At Derry there was a small number of artillerymen with four 6-pounder field-guns and one howitzer. There seems to be no evidence for defences at Lough Foyle at this time, and sketches of Magilligan Point by Captain Sir William Smith in 1806 do not show defence works or the Martello tower.

Greencastle Fort. Sketches of Greencastle of 1817 by Smith note it as the 'New work or fortification', possibly implying that it replaced some form of temporary defence work. The site was acquired by Smith in December 1810, and presumably the present structure was built in 1812-

13, when the Lough Swilly defences were being rebuilt. It is similar in plan to Down Fort on Inch, and Knockalla, with a tower on the landward salient angle from which two walls radiate down to the water's edge. These walls are joined along the waterfront by a retaining wall and broad parapet, behind which were five 24-pounder guns on traversing platforms. The interior of the battery is at two levels, the lower level with the five-gun battery and a magazine, the upper level at the rear adjacent to the tower. Casemated accommodation and stores back onto the two landward walls, which radiate from the tower. Entry to the fort was through a sunken roadway cutting through the glacis on the north side, across the ditch to the gateway flanked by a guardroom and close to the tower. The tower is an irregular oval in plan, approximately sixty-five feet by somewhat less than fifty feet on the minor axis. On the gun platform of the tower a mid nineteenth-century plan indicates two 5 1/2-inch howitzers on traversing platforms, resulting in a gun platform outline within the parapet similar in shape to that at the Rathmullan blockhouse and those of the Shannon Estuary. [16] The plan notes accommodation for three officers and fifty-four men. A ditch some twenty feet wide separates the glacis from the fort on the northern landward front. Directly opposite, across the narrow entrance to Lough Foyle, is Magilligan Point one mile to the south-east.

Magilligan Point Martello tower. Captain Smith includes a sketch of Magilligan Martello tower of 1817; it was evidently constructed in 1812 (Fig.141). It is basically similar to the towers near Dublin in that it is circular in plan, with a machicolation over the entrance doorway; however, it is of a somewhat plainer character, without the string course at the level of the gun platform, the battered wall surface extending from ground level to parapet. The circular gun platform thirty-one feet in diameter, larger than average, mounted an armament of two 24-

pounder guns on traversing platforms operating from the central pivot, as at the Martello at Muckamish, which is of similar size, somewhat over fifty feet in overall diameter. Magilligan may be compared to the two-gun tower on Dalkey Island, Co. Dublin, with a gun platform thirty-four feet in diameter.

Magilligan Martello tower and Greencastle Fort completely commanded the entrance to Lough Foyle with a cross-fire from their guns; there does not appear to be any evidence for any other defence works between the entrance and Derry, some twenty miles to the south-west. The seventeenth-century ramparts and bastions of Derry were largely intact in the early nineteenth century, and no effort appears to have been made to strengthen them or to erect new works here at this time.

The report on the defence of Ireland of August 1796 commented that 'from Lough Foyle to the Bay of Carrickfergus [Belfast Lough] the coast holds out no inducement for a landing to an enemy in great force.' In 1812 Coleraine was noted as 'capable of admitting only vessels of small burden at the time of high water ... From Ballycastle to Carrickfergus there is no harbour whatever ... (except a very small harbour at Portrush) . . . Belfast stands at the extremity of an extensive bay, and has the advantage of a large and commodious harbour, capable of affording excellent shelter...' [17]

The principal harbours or anchorages on the north coast were Lough Swilly, Lough Foyle, giving access to the port of Derry, and Belfast Lough. The guns of Carrickfergus Castle on the north-western shore of Belfast Lough provided a limited degree of coastal defence. The castle had fallen into disrepair by 1760 when the French squadron under the command of Thurot landed some 600 men and captured it; at that time there was a fifty-foot breach in the curtain wall. After the outbreak of war with the French Republic in 1793, Lieutenant-Colonel Tarrant of the Royal

Irish Engineers carried out repairs, as depicted on his sketch plan of the castle that year (Fig.142).[18] He built a breastwork and glacis at the eastern end of the outer courtyard, to give extra protection to the approach to the inner courtyard and keep, should the gatehouse at the landward end of the castle be taken by an attacking force. The two towers of the gatehouse were, according to Tarrant's plan, being fitted with platforms—presumably to mount artillery - while the outwork outside the gatehouse was improved by raising the parapet and forming musket-loops.

Sketches by Captain Sir William Smith, the engineer responsible for the works at Lough Swilly and Lough Foyle, depict the castle from various viewpoints, including several of the gatehouse and outwork in 1800—most of the outwork has since been demolished.[19] A plan of 1811 shows the addition of two artillery barracks in the outer courtyard and the entrance outwork of a different form when compared with the 1793 plan.[20] In 1804, fourteen iron 12-pounders, two 6-pounders and six 4-pounders are listed for Carrickfergus,[21] and it seems probable that some larger guns were soon mounted at the castle, such as 18-pounders or 24-pounders, to defend the anchorage. The 1811 plan does not show the emplacements for guns on traversing platforms that are located on the south-east side of the castle, and it appears that these date from the Crimean War period. A number of the gun-embrasures are for guns mounted on garrison carriages, and many of the musket loops evidently date from the 1793-1815 period.

Early lists of Martello towers to defend the Irish coast include two towers for Belfast Lough. However, it appears that in this instance this was only a proposal, and a search of maps and contemporary documents has so far failed to provide any evidence for their construction. On the west side of Belfast Lough is a site noted on the Ordnance Survey map of 1830 as 'Macedon Battery'; the high ground here projects into the sea, and is a good position for a gun battery. An inspection of the site today does not reveal any features such as a gun platform or parapet, although it is possible that a temporary earthwork battery was constructed here and was removed by the time of the first Ordnance Survey. No other evidence is known for a battery at Belfast Lough for the period of the French Revolutionary and Napoleonic wars. It seems strange that when considerable effort and expense were put into defending Lough Swilly and Lough Foyle, Belfast Lough depended on the limited amount of coastal defence provided by the artillery mounted at Carrickfergus Castle.

Inland in Ulster the principal military post was Charlemont Fort, little changed since the late seventeenth century; by the late eighteenth century it appears to have been more important as an artillery depot and barrack than as a fortification. During the period 1793-1800 from one to three brigades of the Royal Irish Artillery were stationed at Charlemont while smaller detachments were at Belfast, Omagh, Coleraine, Ballymena, Dundalk, Downpatrick, Enniskillen, Derry, Strabane and Carrickfergus. In 1804 there were nine 6-pounders and ten $5\frac{1}{2}$-inch howitzers at Charlemont Fort, which continued as a military post until 1858.

Proposals for new fortresses included a new work at Omagh in 1802 and at Cross More near Castle Shane in Co. Monaghan, south-east of Clontibret, in 1805 and 1806.[22] The Marquis of Cornwallis, lord lieutenant and commander of the forces in Ireland between 1798 and 1801, was in favour of inland fortresses, and a report in 1802 suggested extensive works at Omagh, at Tullamore—presumably the site at Killurin Hill—and a fortress to the west of Cork. Sir Arthur Wellesley, chief secretary in Ireland from 1807 to 1809, proposed the construction of five inland fortresses in 1807, one each in Ulster, Connacht and Munster, and two in Leinster near the Shannon. None of these large-scale proposals was carried out.

Apart from the small works at Enniskillen and Belleek, no inland fortifications appear to have been erected in Ulster between 1793 and 1815. There were barracks at twelve towns in the Northern District in 1796, while new barracks were constructed at Belfast in 1798, Omagh in 1804, and Charlemont in 1806. The government relied very much on the local yeomanry for internal security in Ulster after 1803.

From Belfast Lough southwards along the coast to north Co. Dublin there appears to have been little concern for coastal defence. A limited degree of protection was provided by the sea fencibles based at Carrickfergus, covering the coast from Larne to Donaghadee: in 1804 the command included two gun vessels as well as a large number of smaller craft. At Malahide, Co. Dublin, another sea fencible district had been set up by 1806—apparently the last district to be established—responsible for the coast from Balbriggan to Howth. The absence of signal stations along the coast from Malin Head to Dublin also reflected the opinion of the military and naval authorities that invasion was unlikely on the north-east and along the east coast from Belfast to Drogheda.

Chapter 6
Iron and Concrete: 1815-1945

WITH RELATIVELY LITTLE CHANGE in ordnance in the first half of the nineteenth century, defence works in Ireland remained largely unaltered between 1815 and the Crimean War of 1854-56. After that time rapid developments in artillery and small arms, and the introduction of iron-clad steam-powered warships, were reflected in changes in the design and construction of fortifications, changes often soon rendered ineffective by the continuing developments in the range and effectiveness of artillery. France launched the first armoured warship, *La Gloire*, in 1859, and Britain responded with *Warrior* in 1860, constructed of iron with iron armour-plating amidships. The *Army and Navy Gazette* of July 1878 remarked on the competition between new ordnance and armour:

> *The battle between guns and armour, which made its first mark in naval construction by producing the* Warrior *in our own navy and* La Gloire *in the French navy, has been steadily advancing during the interval that has elapsed, sometimes scoring a success for some monster gun, sometimes throwing guns into the shade ... in the manufacture of new plates.... From the 4^1/$_2$ inch plates of the* Warrior *we have progressed ... through 8 inch, 9 inch, 12 inch and 14 inch until at last we have reached the 24 inch plates of the* Inflexible ....

The Armstrong breech-loading gun—a long-range rifled gun—was introduced in the British services in 1859, but problems led to a reversion to the muzzle-loader, the new rifled muzzle-loading or RML gun, in the 1860s. Large numbers of existing smoothbore guns were also converted into RML guns. The range of artillery was now increased from just over a mile to about five miles—some 8,000 to 9,000 yards—rendering many of the features of fortifications redundant. Outlying forts surrounding cities and naval bases now had to be constructed much farther out to provide protection against bombardment. The effectiveness of the new rifled guns was demonstrated in the American Civil War and the Franco-Prussian War. The much-increased range of the muzzle-loaded rifle with which the infantry of the American Civil War were equipped demonstrated the effectiveness of the defensive fire-power of troops in temporary field-works or rapidly constructed shelter trenches. By the end of the war breech-loading carbines and rifles were in use, and the Gatling gun, the first effective machine-gun, was introduced. The American Civil War witnessed the first engagement between steam-powered iron-clad warships, which marked the end of the wooden sailing warship with its broadside armament of smooth-bore cannon. The advent of the armoured battleship equipped with the new long-range rifled guns resulted in radical changes in the design and construction of harbour defence works, with detached iron-clad sea forts, and batteries consisting of masonry casemates with iron shields protecting each gun emplacement. The considerable expense of these casemates was a factor in the development of the 'disappearing carriage', where the gun was placed in a circular or semi-circular pit some ten feet deep. The gun fired over the parapet in the raised position and returned to the lower level to be loaded. Captain Moncrieff of the Edinburgh Militia Artillery developed this design of gun carriage, and it was approved for service in 1871 with a 7-inch RML gun. A new pattern with an eleven-foot pit was approved in 1875. Casemates with iron shields, and Moncrieff emplacements, are to be found at the Cork Harbour entrance forts, Camden and Carlisle.

The RML gun was replaced at the end of the century with more efficient breech-loading ordnance, resulting in new emplacements in forts and batteries. Developments in fortification from the 1860s onwards included the use of concrete and the increasing reliance on large-scale earthworks forming ramparts and traverses, and for the protection of masonry casemates and magazines. In layout and design the 'polygonal' system, with straight lines of rampart depending for close defence on deep ditches with caponnières and counterscarp galleries, superseded the bastioned trace, which had survived in various forms since the sixteenth century. The naval base at Cork Harbour was strengthened with new works at Fort Camden and Fort Carlisle, while new batteries were constructed to protect the fleet anchorages at Berehaven and Lough Swilly. Belfast Lough was also defended by batteries, while the Pigeon House Fort provided some protection for the port of Dublin (Map 22).

Fear of the possible intentions of France under Napoleon III and the introduction of iron-clad warships into the French navy resulted, in 1860, in the *Report of the Commissioners Appointed to Consider the Defences of the United Kingdom*. The proposals included the construction of a ring of forts at the naval bases at Portsmouth and Plymouth and elsewhere, which were subsequently under construction over the next decade. For works at Cork Harbour a sum of £120,000 was allocated, most of which was expended on new landward defences and sea batteries at Camden and Carlisle.

In 1842, battery no. 12 at Glasthule, Co. Dublin, near the new East Pier of Kingstown Harbour, was regarded as redundant by the Board of Works:

As this battery is in a state of complete dilapidation…from its position…it is clear that it will never be used again as a means of defence while such very superior situations are available on either side, as the heads of the piers and Sandy Cove Point….[1]

Part of the site of the battery was required for a roadway alongside the proposed new railway to Dalkey. However, the response from the commanding officer of the Royal Engineers in Ireland was that this would involve the destruction of the magazine at the rear of the battery. The Board of Ordnance was not prepared to dispose of the battery and its supporting tower no. 12 unless a site for another battery was provided to the south for a work of equal strength. New batteries were evidently intended at the pier heads of Kingstown Harbour at this time, and these batteries and that at Sandycove 'would be better supported from such a battery than they can from battery no. 12 in its present position.' The engineers stated that there was no foundation for the allegation of complete dilapidation of battery no. 12. Finally, early in 1843, the Board of Ordnance stated that they had no objection to giving up the land on which the battery stood 'provided the Board of Works erected adequate defence or defences on the piers of the harbour of Kingstown.' Tower no. 12, just inland of the battery, was to be retained. The battery was evidently removed later or at least partly demolished on the landward side, to allow for the construction of the railway and the adjacent road. The other tower here, no. 13, had been demolished when the railway from Dublin to Kingstown was constructed some years earlier.

A pier-head battery was eventually constructed by 1857 on the East Pier, armed with nine guns. A contemporary plan, 'East Pier,

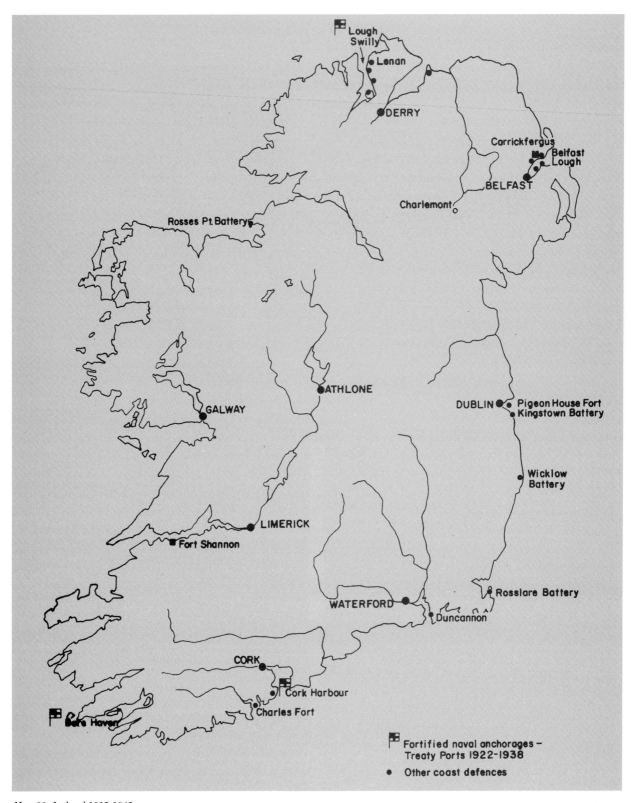

Map 22. Ireland 1815-1945.

Fig. 143. East Pier Battery, Kingstown (Dún Laoghaire).

Kingstown, New Battery, 1860', notes the armament:[2]

3 68-pounders	upper battery
3 32-pounders	lower battery
2 32-pounders	ground battery

A casemate with an arched gun-embrasure situated below the upper battery now has the embrasure blocked up; although this is indicated on the plan, no armament is given for this element of the defence. The upper battery and the casemated gun had a field of fire out to sea, while the lower battery—at an intermediate level—covered the harbour entrance and Dublin bay to the north. These upper and lower battery guns were on traversing platforms, each sited in a semicircular emplacement within the thickness of the broad parapet. The ground battery, on the level of the pier walkway, is provided with two arched gun-embrasures in the parapet with a field of fire over the harbour. The parapet of the ground battery is also provided with musket loops between and on each side of the two gun-embrasures, all executed in precise ashlar masonry. The pier-head battery is almost circular in plan, with the lighthouse in the centre; it is entered through an arched gateway from the pier (Fig. 143).

In the Dublin area, several of the towers had guns of somewhat larger calibre in 1859-61 when compared with their original armament. Dalkey Island tower was equipped with two 64-pounders, the battery having three 64-pounders, in place of the original 24-pounders; at some time after 1868 the entrance to the tower at parapet level was replaced by the present doorway a few feet above ground level. Tower no. 3 at Cork Abbey and no. 10 at Bullock each mounted a 32-pounder. By 1859 the guns at no. 6 battery at Loughlinstown had been removed. Sandycove battery—no. 11—was altered and some of the buildings rebuilt or improved after 1860. Tower no. 1 at Bray was demolished towards the turn of the century, as were towers 3 and 4 farther north. Battery no. 8 on Killiney Bay was removed in 1868 to provide the site for the first Killiney railway station. By 1859 the battery at tower no. 2 at Bray was dismantled, the guns and traversing platforms being removed.

Duncannon Fort. In September 1860 it was reported that additions and alterations here had recently been completed:

Captain Synge, commanding Royal Engineers at the Curragh Camp, together with Lieutenant Price, R.E., from Kilkenny, inspected the works . . . carried out by Mr Abraham Stephens. The sea face of the fort is now prepared for mounting 68-pounder Armstrong guns, on traversing platforms, capable of throwing shot and shell six miles to the entrance of the harbour. There has also been erected two extra magazines and five shell rooms for the storage of shot and shell for the use of those large guns, with four banquettes for riflemen. [3]

It seems probable that the Armstrong guns may not have been installed: in 1867 only smooth-bore guns and carronades are listed at Duncannon. In 1861 it was noted that Duncannon Fort was commanded by high ground inland, repeating the remarks made in earlier centuries; however, the sea battery was well placed to cover the approach of shipping. In 1867 there were twenty-three guns and two carronades as armament; by 1881 four of the guns had been converted into RMLs, and four RML guns were noted in 1895. The fort was used by local militia artillery for training and does not appear to have been considered important enough to merit an up-to-date armament, possibly because of the poor position of the fort. Waterford Harbour was not considered to be as important as Cork and the later fleet anchorages of Berehaven and Lough Swilly, and as a result no attempt was made to provide adequate coastal defence here in the closing years of the century.

Cork Harbour. The Royal Commission report of 1860 noted the existing defences of Cork Harbour, including the Martello towers. Forts Camden and Carlisle in the commanding positions on the entrance headlands were to have their landward defences remodelled and additional sea batteries constructed to cover the approach to the harbour and the entrance channel. A line of casemates then under construction in the large bastioned fortress on Spike Island was to be completed, and the remains of the earlier Fort Westmoreland on the eastern end of the island were to be removed. Additional guns should be mounted on the southern face of the fortress bearing on the harbour and harbour entrance.

It was recommended that Corkbeg Island be occupied with a small work to prevent its occupation by an enemy force and to provide an improved cross-fire of the harbour. Remains of a small polygonal fort on the south-west of Corkbeg may be this work proposed in 1860. The battery at Queenstown (Cove Fort), which was at this time dismantled, should be remodelled and armed with one tier of heavy guns. The position of this battery was noted as well situated over the approach to the upper part of the harbour and would support the Spike Island fortress if it was attacked on the eastern front. A battery was also recommended for White Point, on Great Island north-west of Haulbowline Island, a location noted as Battery Point in the eighteenth century.

The report noted the Martello towers around Cork Harbour, and it was evidently intended that they be retained as defence works; it was also proposed that an additional four towers be constructed, three at Ballycotton Bay and one at Ringabella Cove to the south-west of the harbour entrance. The defence of Kinsale by Charles Fort was apparently considered adequate, and a small work with four or five guns was proposed for the defence of Youghal Harbour. The possession of the anchorage of Cork Harbour could not be obtained without the reduction of Spike Island and the harbour entrance forts, and the proposals in the Royal Commission report reflected the importance of Cork as a naval base.

The estimate for carrying out the commissioners' proposals at Cork was approximately

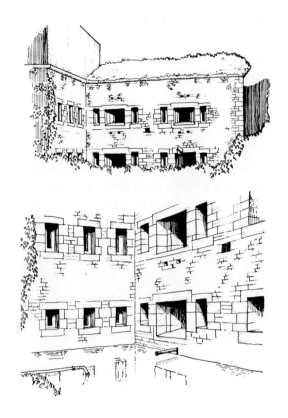

Fig. 144. The Capponnière, Fort Camden, Cork Harbour.

£120,000, on the basis that a great proportion of the work would be done by the convicts imprisoned on Spike Island. A garrison of about 2,500 men would be required for the defence of Cork Harbour. On the evidence of the works that survive, it appears that most of the expenditure must have been on Forts Camden and Carlisle.

Fort Camden. Following the recommendations of the Royal Commission, the new land front was started in 1862, including casemated barracks on the north flank, completed in 1864. The landward front was half completed by 1868. The landward defences, consisting of a deep rock-cut ditch, a caponnière and a rampart, replaced the earlier *tenaille trace* here. The ditch is extended down to sea level on the north side of the fort, following the steep slope of the hillside overlooking the entrance to Crosshaven. On the south flank of the fort the ditch is taken down nearly to

sea level at the harbour entrance. Here the scarp and counterscarp are of concrete.

The caponnière is situated at the south-western salient of the fort at the junction of the western and southern ditches. It is a massive two-storey structure in the ditch, fronted by a small wet moat. On the flanks are two levels of gun-embrasures and musketry-loops, supported by flanking loops in adjacent scarp galleries. The caponnière has regular masonry quoins and ashlar stonework at the gun-embrasures and loops, all very precisely executed. The external wall surface generally is of squared rubble laid to courses. The gun-embrasures on ground and first-floor level are each flanked by adjacent musketry-loops. The scarp gallery has three loops for small arms at ground and at first-floor level. The front of the caponnière has arched embrasures at the lower level, smaller rectangular openings on the upper level (Fig.144).

Access to the caponnière from within the fort is no longer possible, as the passageway has been blocked up. The use of the deep ditch and caponnière as elements of fortification for close defence are typical of the polygonal system then being applied to the design of forts such as those surrounding the naval bases at Portsmouth and Plymouth. The caponnière is similar to those

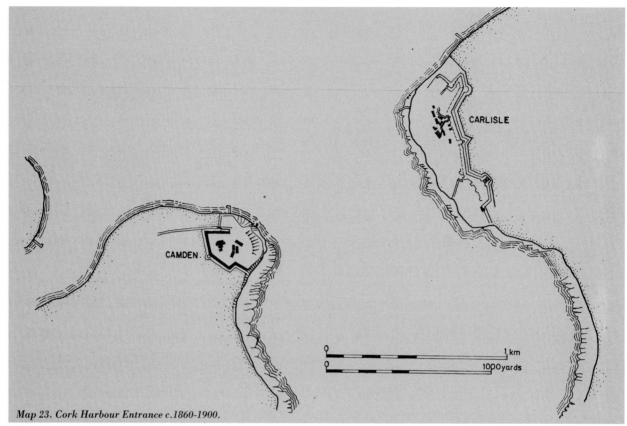

Map 23. Cork Harbour Entrance c.1860-1900.

constructed at this time at the Drop Redoubt on the Western Heights at Dover.

New batteries were constructed overlooking the harbour entrance channel, some at high level and a casemated four-gun battery with iron shields near water level, which mounted four 10-inch RMLs in 1873. Elsewhere in the sea batteries there were three more 10-inch RML guns, six 7-inch RMLs and some smaller guns. Three of the 7-inch RML guns were on Moncrieff disappearing carriages.

The *Irish Builder* of September 1870 describes the work under way at Camden and Carlisle:

The outer defences of Camden and Carlisle Forts which command the entrance to the magnificent harbour of Queenstown are being pushed forward rapidly. Several companies of the 43rd Regiment have arrived, and are encamped on the heights. They are daily employed in sinking the new trenches,

and carrying out other works, some of which are upon a stupendous scale. Each fort is now virtually cut off from the mainland by a wide ditch fully forty feet deep. Besides this, means are provided for working under cover large batteries of heavy guns that, completely hidden from view, can, whenever required, open a destructive fire upon approaching vessels, and annihilate a hostile fleet before it could pass through the channel between the two lines of fortification. The convict labour is being turned to account upon the new Government Dockyard works at Haulbowline which are, however, but slowly progressing.

Convict labour was employed on the Spike Island fortress, which had become a prison in 1847. Smaller numbers of prisoners were located at Camden and Carlisle; in 1883, Spike Island convicts were removed to other prisons and the

Fig. 145. Casemate gun emplacement with iron shield, Fort Camden.

place became a military post without the additional role of prison and labour camp.

Some £32,000 had been expended at Camden out of an estimate of over £68,000 by 1868. In the last decade of the century there was a mixed armament typical of many forts of the period, and the older guns were soon to be superseded by the new breech-loaders. The two upper batteries overlooking the harbour entrance mounted RML guns, the right or seaward battery three 10-inch, the left battery three 7-inch guns. The casemated battery near the water level mounted, as before, four 10-inch RMLs. There were three 7-inch RMLs in the left lower battery and four 32-pounder guns in the caponnière, for defence of the ditches. There were also three 6-pounder quick-firer guns (QFs) and a number of the new rifled breech-loading guns, including four 40-pounders on the ramparts.[4] By the early years of the following century the RML guns began to be superseded by breech-loaders, supported by the quick-firing guns and machine-guns.

An important feature of the fort is the Brennan torpedo installation at water level facing the entrance channel. The system was patented in 1884 and acquired by the British government the following year. The torpedo system was suitable for the narrow harbour entrance—about a 1,000 yards across (Map 23). The torpedo was controlled by two reels of wire that governed the range and controlled the direction of the weapon. The torpedo store, boiler-room and engine-room and a staircase leading up to the ground level above survive. Support brackets also remain that originally carried the launching-way down into the water at a gradual slope. A drawing of 1887 depicts the layout. The Brennan torpedo system became obsolete by the end of the century, having been installed in great secrecy at a small number of forts at estuaries or harbours, including Cliffe Fort in the Thames Estuary, at Garrison Point at the entrance to the Medway, and at Fort Albert on the Isle of Wight overlooking the Needles Passage.[5] Close to the Brennan torpedo installation at Camden is a small harbour connected with submarine mining of the harbour entrance areas; rails for transporting the mines survive on the quayside

A short distance to the south, the casemated battery survives, each gun emplacement fronted by a rusticated masonry wall with a segmental arch, the opening below closed with an iron shield containing at its centre the rectangular gun-port. The shields are some two feet thick, in a form of sandwich construction made up of several layers of iron plates and other material (Figs.145 and 146). Inside the casemates some of the equipment remains that supported the mantlet, a thick curtain of rope behind the shield. This was to protect the interior of the gun emplacement from small arms fire and from fragments of metal or masonry from the exterior of the casemate entering the gun-port as a result of being struck by enemy shot.

Fort Carlisle. The works at Carlisle that started in 1861 considerably extended the fortified area. On the landward side a rock-cut ditch was excavated some distance to the east of the earlier fortifications. On the north it runs down the steep slope to sea level, crossed by the bridge at the fort entrance. The new landward ditch and rampart, the ditch defended by caponnières, extends for a distance of more than a 1,000 yards, with several re-entrant and salient angles, from north to south, finally following the slope down to the water level. The earlier bastioned work of Fort Carlisle survives within these later defences. As at Fort Camden opposite, there are batteries and gun emplacements at high level and close to sea level; these vary in date from the early casemates with iron shields and Moncrieff disappearing carriage emplacements of the 1870s to the later positions for breech-loading guns. By 1868 nearly £28,000 had been expended out of a total estimate of some £87,000.

The armament of the fort in the last decade of the century was, again as at Fort Camden opposite, a mixture of older guns such as the RMLs with the new breech-loaders and quick-firers.

Fig. 146. Iron shield of casemate, Fort Camden.

The RML guns included eight 7-inch guns placed in two four-gun batteries; two 10-inch, three 11-inch and two 12-inch; and three 6-pounder QFs. On the ramparts were three 40-pounder breech-loaders and other smaller guns and machine-guns. Moncrieff disappearing carriages were evidently provided for the 7-inch RML guns, four on the 1871 model and four on the Mark II model of 1875.[6]

The centre caponnière is approached by a long ramp from the interior of the fort and is provided with gun-embrasures and musketry-loops. On the western edge of the hill top on which the fort stands are batteries and gun positions with a field of fire over the harbour entrance and southwards over the approach to the harbour. Some of these emplacements that originally mounted RML guns were remodelled for breech-loaders. Concrete predominates as a building material here, with some cement rendering and brickwork of ancillary structures, in place of the careful masonry craftsmanship of the earlier nineteenth century. Near the water level below are casemated gun-emplacements, similar to those at Camden opposite but without the rusticated stonework. The segmental arches of carefully dressed *voussoirs* span the embrasure openings with their iron shields (Fig.147). Also at this level just above the rocky shoreline is a line of semi-circular concrete emplacements for disappearing carriages, evidently the Moncrieff carriages of the

Fig. 147. Casemate gun emplacement with iron shield, Fort Carlisle, Cork Harbour.

1870s, protected on the seaward side by a broad grass-covered earth embankment.

Fort Westmoreland, Spike Island. The hexagonal bastioned fort of the Napoleonic period, on which work continued well into the middle of the nineteenth century, was not extensively remodelled like the harbour entrance forts of Camden and Carlisle. The fort itself must have been substantially completed by 1860, apart perhaps from work continuing on the extensive glacis occupying a large part of the area of the island. The Royal Commission report advocated some remodelling of the fort for heavier ordnance, particularly to cover the harbour entrance and the harbour generally, guns to be casemated behind shields or on Moncrieff carriages. Towards the end of the century there was a variety of RML guns mounted at the bastions of the fort. The three northern bastions each had one 7-inch RML, the south-western bastion or no. 2, one 11-inch, the central southern or no. 3 bastion, three 12-inch, and the south-eastern or no. 4 bastion, two 11-inch RMLs.[7] The heaviest guns fired southwards over the harbour and towards the entrance (Fig.148). The platforms of the bastions were modified with emplacements for these guns. At some locations, principally on the northern bastions, the mountings for the earlier traversing platforms for smooth-bore cannon may be identified. Close defence of the broad dry moat was provided for to some extent by the galleries with musketry loops in the flanks of the bastions. As at the other harbour forts, the RML guns were soon to be superseded by the new breech-loaders in the early years of the following century.

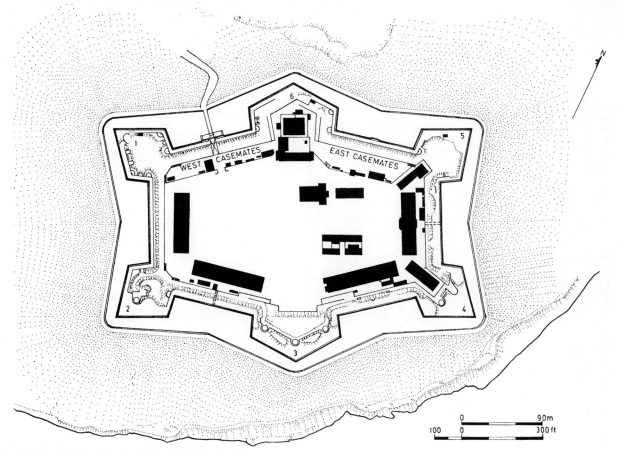

Fig. 148. Plan of Fort Westmoreland, Spike Island, Cork Harbour

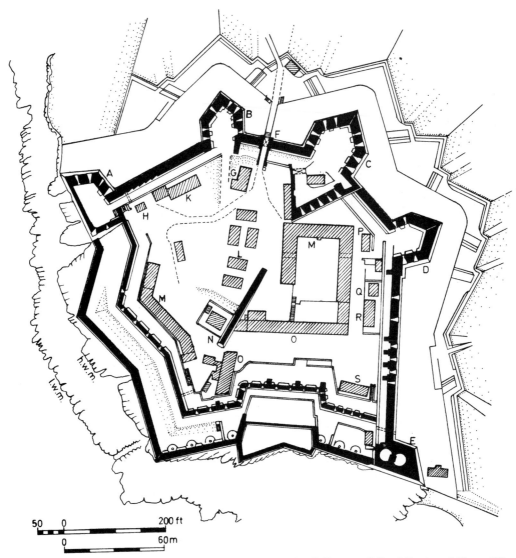

Fig. 149. Plan of Charles Fort, Kinsale, 1870, after Ordnance Survey plan. *A Devil's Bastion; **B** North Bastion; **C** Flagstaff Bastion; **D** East Bastion; **E** Charles Bastion; **F** Gateway; **G** Guard Room; **H** Engine House; **K** Barrack Stores; **L** Wooden Huts; **M** Soldiers' Quarters; **N** Magazine; **O** Officers' Quarters; **P** Cookhouse; **Q** Royal Engineers stores; **R** Hospital; **S** Officers' and Master Gunner's Quarters. By 1870 most of the embrasures on the sea batteries were blocked up.*

Much less was expended at Spike Island than at either of the two harbour entrance forts of Camden and Carlisle. By 1869, just over £4,000 had been spent out of an estimate of some £17,000.

Bantry Bay does not appear to have been considered to be of any great naval or military importance by those planning the new fortifications following the Royal Commission report of 1860. Ordnance Survey plans of 1867-69 give no armament for the three circular redoubts on Whiddy Island and suggest that the towers and the square redoubt on Bere Island were not armed at this time.[8] It was not until some thirty years later that the importance of Berehaven as a fleet anchorage resulted in the construction of new batteries and redoubts on Bere Island, at which time no attempt was made to defend Whiddy Island with modern works.

The Shannon Estuary batteries were gar-

Fig. 150. Gun on rear-pivoted traversing platform, Carrickfergus Castle.

risoned in 1844 by detachments of the Royal Marines, eleven or twelve men at each battery. They are listed at Kilcredaun, Scattery Island, Doonaha, Carrig Island, Tarbert and Kilkerin Point.[9] There appears to be no evidence to indicate any attempt to improve the armament of these defences after this time; the structural condition and layout of the batteries today suggest that they were not altered in any significant way since their construction. The Limerick City Militia Artillery trained at Tarbert battery before 1887, when the location for their annual training was changed to one of the Cork Harbour forts. Earlier fortifications such as Duncannon Fort and Charles Fort at Kinsale were used by militia artillery units for practice, often with guns that were rapidly becoming obsolete (Fig.149).

Inland on the Shannon between Portumna and Athlone the fortifications at the crossing-points of the river continued as military posts. In 1828 the guns were still mounted at Meelick tower, Keelogue battery, Banagher, Shannonbridge, the Athlone batteries and Athlone Castle. *The Parliamentary Gazetteer of Ireland* (1844) noted Banagher, Shannonbridge and Athlone as 'fortified passes still maintained upon the Shannon'. The artillery was removed from Keelogue in 1863, but the guns were still in position at Shannonbridge the following year.

The Shannonbridge fortifications and the Athlone batteries would have provided very limited resistance to the powerful rifled ordnance that came into use in the 1860s. However, the American Civil War and later conflicts in Europe demonstrated the effectiveness of the defensive fire-power of infantry in temporary fieldworks or shelter trenches. It seems probable that troops armed with the much more effective rifles of this period, occupying the Athlone batteries and their connecting entrenchments, would have been able to repulse a large-scale infantry attack . At Athlone Castle, the iron rails that carried the traversing platform for a gun on the south-east tower are dated 1861, indicating a new mounting here, and possibly a reconstruction of the parapet here was also carried out at this time. The circular emplacement is protected by a parapet of regular masonry, similar to that of a Martello tower. A plan of War Department property at Athlone of 1862, corrected 1866, includes the castle and the batteries.[10] Control of the river crossing-points must also have been considered of importance for the internal security of the country, and the presence of military garrisons provided a reinforcement for the police should the need arise.

An indication that some of the Shannon defences were still considered to be of military importance towards the end of the century may

Fig. 151. Gun on front-pivoted traversing platform, Carrickfergus Castle.

be seen in the Ordnance Survey maps of 1886-91. The Shannonbridge defences and the Athlone batteries, castle and barracks are omitted from the maps, the areas occupied by these works being left blank. In contrast, Meelick tower and Keelogue battery are depicted in some detail, evidently no longer considered of any defensive value. By this time, some concern for security in the Ordnance Survey maps is evident, increasing the difficulties of those attempting to locate and identify later fortifications and military installations.

Record plans of the three Galway Bay Martello towers at Finavarra, Aughinish and Cashla Bay of 1866, while noting the accommodation and other details, do not make any reference to the guns, and it seems probable that they were no longer armed at this time. No batteries are indicated at Finavarra or Aughinish in 1866, and although they are noted on the Ordnance Survey of 1842 it is not possible to make out any detail of the layout from the maps or from an inspection of the sites today.

An Ordnance Survey plan of Belleek redoubt, noted as 'Belleek Barracks', 1860, also notes the accommodation in some detail but does not refer to the guns, so it appears that these were removed by this time.[11] At Enniskillen the stone facing of the East Fort was removed in 1823 and used in construction work in the town. It seems probable that the West Fort or redoubt also ceased to have a military role as a defence work about this time: the Ordnance Survey of 1834 notes the building within the redoubt as 'Military Hospital'.

At Lough Swilly, in 1859 the towers and batteries were still evidently equipped with the same armament as when they were constructed before 1815. Rathmullan mounted two $5\frac{1}{2}$ inch howitzers on the blockhouse and five 24-pounders in the battery; at Muckamish there were five 24-pounders; at Knockalla there were two 24-pounders and seven 42-pounders in the battery

with a howitzer and a 24-pounder on the tower. On the opposite shore, Down Fort on Inch had three $5\frac{1}{2}$-inch howitzers on the tower, but the six-gun battery appears to have had no guns mounted at this time. At the entrance to Lough Foyle Greencastle Fort mounted two howitzers on the tower and five 24-pounders in the battery; on the opposite headland Magilligan tower mounted two 24-pounder guns.

At Carrickfergus Castle, which became the headquarters of the Antrim Militia Artillery in 1855, the east battery was reconstructed for 64-pounder rifled guns mounted on traversing platforms, which still survive (Figs.150 and 151). The parapet was rebuilt with regular granite masonry, three of the guns placed at wide double-splayed embrasures, with the rear-pivoted southern gun mounted *en barbette* in a semicircular emplacement. The traversing platforms and gun carriages are similar to those at Plymouth Citadel. The armament at Carrickfergus in 1857 was six 24-pounders, seven 32-pounders, six 64-pounders and a mortar.

Other defence works on Belfast Lough were batteries at Holywood on the south-eastern shore and at Woodburn on the opposite side, presumably near Woodburn Abbey, not far to the west of Carrickfergus. At Holywood in 1887, 9-inch RML guns replaced earlier ordnance and 6-inch breech-loaders replaced 64-pounder RMLs. In the same year it was recommended that 10-inch RMLs at Woodburn be replaced with heavier guns.[12] These two batteries were proposed in 1882, when it was noted that the only defence work was Carrickfergus Castle.

Other batteries were established towards the end of the century at Wicklow, Rosslare, and Rosses Point, Co. Sligo. The *Army and Navy Gazette* in January 1878 reported:

Fig. 152. Nine-inch RML gun from the Black Castle Battery, Wicklow.

The War Office has purchased the Marine Hotel, on the Morrough, Wicklow, for the purpose of a barracks for the [Wicklow Artillery] regiment. Negotiations are in progress for the purchase of the Black Castle for artillery practice.

The Ordnance Survey (town map of 1911) depicts the Castle Battery on the coast south of the ruins of the castle: a line of four gun-emplacements with a magazine in their rear. The location of the two northern emplacements may be identified on the site today. The two positions farther south have the remains of gun mountings, front pivots and two iron rails at each emplacement, the rear rail incorporating a toothed track, with an arc of 106 degrees. The barrel of a 6-inch breech-loader lies at one of these gun positions; there is no evidence today of any form of parapet protecting these emplacements.

A short distance to the north of these emplacements are three smaller rectangular gun platforms, on the south side of the Black Castle promontory, probably intended for use with muzzle-loaders on garrison carriages. Two 9-inch RML guns associated with the battery are now displayed on stone plinths some distance farther north, overlooking Wicklow Harbour; they date from 1865-72 (Figs.152 and 153). The battery appears to have been primarily a practice bat-

tery for the Wicklow Militia Artillery between 1878 and the turn of the century.

At Rosslare, Co. Wexford, a battery was established towards the end of the nineteenth century. Local information refers to two guns, a muzzle-loader and a breech-loader. These were evidently dumped on the beach nearby when the battery became redundant, and one of the guns, which is visible in the sand from time to time, is evidently an RML gun. Ancillary buildings, a barrack and a drill hall were associated with the battery. There is documentary evidence concerning the arrival of a ship to supply the battery with ammunition around 1906. Like the Wicklow battery, this one may have functioned as a practice battery for militia artillery, and also in providing some protection for Rosslare Harbour.[13]

The Sligo Militia Artillery trained at Rosses Point, where there are some remains of the battery. The site is at Bomore Point, just north-west of the village of Rosses Point. Training is recorded between 1896 and 1908, and two 9-inch RML guns with their carriages and traversing platforms arrived at the battery in 1898. In 1902 and subsequent years there are references to a breech-loading gun here.

Two RML guns at the Corrib Rowing Club at Galway were purchased from the Admiralty in May 1906, following changes in the naval reserve at Renmore, according to the *Galway Observer,*

Fig. 153. Nine-inch RML gun from the Black Castle Battery, Wicklow.

and these are now on their carriages and traversing platforms outside the club. It appears that they formed part of a naval reserve practice battery at Renmore, the extensive barrack complex east of Galway, established in 1880.

A portion of the property at Renmore that had been acquired by the War Department in 1852 was to be handed over to the Admiralty for a Royal Naval Reserve battery; a drill shed, magazine and two platforms are recorded, and the battery was to be available for use by the military if required.

There was evidently a policy during the beginning and middle of the nineteenth century that the military barracks in Ireland should be defensible. Most of those constructed during the Napoleonic wars were provided with musketry-loops in the perimeter walls, where possible to allow for flanking fire and to protect the gateways (Fig.154).

The plan of a rectangular enclosure with musketry bastions at the corners, such as the artillery barrack at Longford of 1808, is found again in the layout of the Maryborough (Portlaoise) barrack of 1830. The main enclosure is some 250 feet by 160 feet wide, with bastion-shaped projections loop-holed for musketry at the corners. There is a barrack of about the same date, similar in size and layout, at Trim.

A much more elaborate layout, with the perimeter walls following the outline of an artillery fort with eight bastions, is that at Beggars' Bush Barracks in Dublin, covering an area about four times larger than Maryborough or Trim. Beggars' Bush, constructed in 1827, is provided with musket-loops in the bastions and curtain walls. The large bastions—the faces are about 125 feet in length—and the scale of the work give the place much of the character of a fortress or citadel. The large number of barracks elsewhere in Dublin and throughout the country emphasised the military dimension of the government of Ireland. At Nenagh, Co. Tipperary, the

infantry barrack is surrounded by a wall taking the form of a five-sided bastioned fort with two demi-bastions flanking the entrance, evidently dating from 1830.

The bastion-shaped outworks at Crinkill Barracks appear to be later in date than the perimeter wall. These loop-holed works defending the gates and providing for flanking fire are joined to the perimeter wall with a straight joint. The barrack was built between 1809 and 1812, and these outworks may have been added during the next thirty or forty years to improve the defence of the perimeter. At Longford Barracks, established towards the end of the eighteenth century, loop-holes for musketry were being inserted in the perimeter wall in 1843. At Athlone Barracks in 1852 a new gateway and an adjacent outwork termed a caponnière were under construction. The caponnière was a semicircular-ended structure with musket loops covering the market square and the approaches to the gateway from the streets to the east and west. This structure was taken down and rebuilt in the form of two quadrant-shaped walls flanking a new barrack entrance constructed on the river front in 1931, the present entrance.[14]

Other defensible buildings in nineteenth-cen-

Fig. 154. Board of Ordnance boundary stone, Boyle Barracks, Co. Roscommon. The early eighteenth-century house, unusual for its vaulted structure, later became a barracks, with a perimeter wall loopholed for musketry.

tury Ireland were coastguard stations and police barracks. Provision was made at some of these for defence by firearms, loop-holes being located at appropriate positions. The coastguard had its origins in 1831 and came under the customs service until 1857, when it was transferred to the Admiralty. The many duties of the coastguard service included reporting on the movement of foreign warships and shipping generally, patrolling the coast, and the prevention of smuggling. The coastguard between 1858 and 1867 was organised in three districts to cover the coast of Ireland: the total of some 200 coastguard stations along the coast was grouped within each district into divisions, each with a divisional headquarters.[15] Many of the stations consisted of a long, narrow block of accommodation, single-storey or two-storey in height, with a square or rectangular tower at one end. The tower, which housed a watch-room or look-out post on the upper floor, was often arranged to enable a limited degree of flank fire from loop-holes in its walls to cover one or both long faces of the main building. Some of the earlier coastguard buildings of this plan form do not have these defensive features. It is possible that after the service came under the Admiralty, or following the Fenian Rising of 1867, more attention was paid to defence of the coastguard stations. The station at Knockadoon in east Cork was captured by the Fenians in March 1867, the arms taken and the coastguards taken prisoner. The coastguard was an armed force, and the stations were vulnerable to attack by insurgents hoping to seize arms and ammunition. Within the buildings were racks for muskets or rifles, bayonets, pistols and cutlasses.

Ringsend coastguard station of 1874 has two bay windows at first-floor level in the tower at the east end of the building. These windows are each provided with loopholes for firearms in their flanks, allowing for defence of the east and north front of the station. Another bay window on the south front was also fitted with loop-holes, while there were openings in the base of the bay windows to allow for firing downwards between the stone corbels. Greystones coastguard station is also provided with musketry loop-holes. Other stations had a small number of loop-holes in the tower at ground and first-floor level and in some other positions to provide a limited degree of defence.

A number of military barracks became police barracks during the nineteenth century; two of those on the Wicklow Military Road, Glencree and Aghavannagh, were constabulary barracks by 1839-42. Like the coastguard, the police (later to become the Royal Irish Constabulary) was an armed force. A number of police barracks were attacked by the Fenians in 1867; perhaps partly as a response to these attacks the RIC barrack at Naas of 1870-71 is provided with a large number of loop-holes for firearms. These are in the oriel or bay windows, which also had openings to permit firing downwards between the supporting corbels.

In November 1904, the *Irish Builder* reported the completion of the new electricity generating works at the former Pigeon House Fort on the South Wall of Dublin Harbour. The fort, purchased from the War Department by Dublin Corporation for £60,000, had been used until a short time previously as a barrack for an artillery detachment and for training the Dublin Militia Artillery. The Pigeon House was not regarded by the military authorities as being of any strength or importance during the second half of the nineteenth century. No attempt appears to have been made to provide an adequate armament here to defend the port of Dublin: a limited number of small-calibre RML guns, some quick-firer guns and machine-guns are noted as armament in 1895. A few years earlier a battery of four 9.2-inch breech-loaders had been proposed for Poolbeg, the eastern end of the South Wall, at the harbour entrance.[16] The site intended may have been the earlier Half-

Moon Battery, midway between the Pigeon House and Poolbeg.

The Magazine Fort in the Phoenix Park has additional structures built on top of the demi-bastions, increasing their height. These loop-holed works may date from the Napoleonic period or somewhat later—they appear to be shown on the 1837 Ordnance Survey. In the last decade of the century there were ten 12-pounder guns mounted at the fort, which continued as a British military post until 1922.

The introduction of breech-loading ordnance in the last decade of the nineteenth century resulted in these guns replacing the earlier rifled muzzle-loaders at the coastal forts and batteries. For closer defence and for rapid response to the possibility of attack by torpedo boats, quick-firing guns were mounted at appropriate positions. Breech-loading guns were installed at Cork Harbour, Berehaven, Lough Swilly and Belfast Lough at the turn of the century, the RML guns were superseded and within a few years withdrawn from service.

Cork Harbour. In 1902 there were two 6-inch breech-loaders at Fort Camden, a number of 6-pounder and 12-pounder quick-firers, and a variety of other guns, including three 10-inch RMLs and some Maxim machine-guns.[17] The three RML guns were dismounted in 1903; by 1908 there were five 12-pounder QFs, and two 6-inch BLs as decoy guns. Movable armament included a number of QF guns. In 1912 the armament was basically the same as four years earlier, and in 1913 the five 12-pounder QFs were still in position.

A new work, Templebreedy Battery, was constructed just over a mile to the south of Camden, overlooking the approach to the harbour entrance. Two 9.2-inch BLs were approved for this site in 1906; the same armament was recorded in 1912-13 and continued in position here until after the Second World War.

At Fort Carlisle, the South Battery also mounted 9.2-inch BL guns in 1906, and 6-inch BLs are recorded at the fort in 1908. In 1912-13 the North Battery and Rupert's Tower Battery each mounted two 6-inch BLs, the South Battery two 9.2-inch BLs and three 12-pounder quick-firers.[18] The concrete gun emplacements and their associated magazines survive at Camden and Carlisle, in each fort sited on high ground, some 200 to 250 feet above sea level.

At Spike Island in 1906 there were five 6-inch BL guns proposed or in position on the bastions of Fort Westmoreland. Two of these guns were at no. 3 bastion, the central southern bastion overlooking the harbour and harbour entrance. In 1913 two 9.2-inch BL guns were mounted at Spike Island.

The defences at Cork Harbour emphasised the importance of the dockyard facilities and naval anchorage in the years before 1914, an importance that was demonstrated during the First World War, when Cork Harbour, then known as Queenstown, was the headquarters of the Royal Navy command in Ireland.

Berehaven. A number of new batteries and redoubts were constructed on Bere Island to protect the anchorage of Berehaven, the entrances at east and west and Bantry Bay to the south. These works were divided into two command areas:

Berehaven Eastern Fire Command: East Entrance	Berehaven Western Fire Command: West Entrance
Batteries	*Batteries*
Ardaragh	Ardnakinna
Lonehort	Derrycreeveen
Rerrin	Reenduff
Redoubts	
Leaherns Neck	
South of Neck	
Rerrin	

The Martello tower no. 2 at Rerrin was demolished to provide a space in the centre of Rerrin

Redoubt, and tower no. 1 was replaced by Lonehort Battery. The new defences were under consideration in 1895, when breech-loaders, quick-firers and machine-guns were approved for both entrances. The principal defence was at Lonehort Point at the eastern entrance to Berehaven, and by 1906 both entrances had batteries of 12-pounder QF guns as a defence against torpedo boats as well as emplacements for larger ordnance.

The armament at the batteries between 1906 and 1913 was: Lonehort, one 9.2-inch BL and two 6-inch guns; Ardaragh, four 12-pounder QFs; Rerrin, one 9.2-inch BL and, noted in 1906 only, two 6-inch guns. At Ardnakinna were four 12-pounder QFs; Derycreeveen had two 6-inch guns and Reenduff two 4.7-inch quick-firers.[19] No armament is listed for the redoubts, and it appears that these were works intended to be defended by infantry.

Rerrin Redoubt is sited on high ground overlooking Berehaven to the north and Bantry Bay to the south. It is now in the form of three-quarters of a circle in plan, the missing quadrant at the north occupied by a rectangular barrack block. On the outer edge of the flat roof of the barrack is a brick parapet wall loop-holed for musketry. The redoubt is surrounded by a steep glacis or embankment sloping up to a narrow firing-platform. Protected and covered by the glacis are casemates on each side of the central open space. It seems that by 1906 the redoubt was intended for infantry defence only, possibly aided by some movable armament or machine-guns. The redoubt was built at the same time as Martello no. 2, masking the lower part of the tower in the centre of the redoubt.

The original layout at Martello no. 2 on this site is depicted on a plan of the 1860s. It was flanked by casemated soldiers' quarters on each side with a casemated magazine to the south, protected by a glacis around most of the perimeter. The internal form of the present redoubt closely follows the original line of the casemates and retaining wall of the glacis, which surrounded the Martello. The redoubt has been formed by retaining the casemates, retaining wall and glacis, remodelled to some extent into the present work, while the demolition of the tower has resulted in the open space in the centre.

Lonehort Battery is located at the eastern promontory of the island, covering the eastern entrance to Berehaven. It is of irregular plan form, the perimeter defended by a ditch of which the scarp and counterscarp are of concrete. In addition to the armament of breech-loaders and quick-firers, both entrances to Bere Haven were covered by search-lights. The anchorage was considered to be important for merchant vessels passing to the south of Ireland, and was fortified to resist attack by warships.

Contemporary plans indicate the layouts and locations of the Bere Island Batteries. Lonehort Battery plans and sections depict four concrete caponnières and a scarp gallery at a re-entrant angle, provided with musketry-loops for defence of the ditch. The three emplacements are sited from north to south on the centre-line of the work, the 9.2-inch gun at the south overlooking Bantry Bay. Infantry trenches are located within the battery around the perimeter; in the centre is an open space with a guardhouse and other buildings.

Ardaragh Battery, sited a short distance north-west of Lonehort, overlooking Berehaven, has a symmetrical layout consisting of a line of four gun-emplacements. At the western end of Bere Island, Ardnakinna Battery, with a similar layout to Ardaragh for four 12-pounder QFs, covered the western channel into Berehaven. Derrycreeveen Battery or Upper West Battery, sited farther north overlooking the western channel, is a concrete emplacement for two guns with basement cartridge and shell stores. Some 350 yards north-west of Derrycreeveen Battery is Reenduff Battery—Lower West Battery—nearer to the water level and built on the site of the Napoleonic period redoubt no. 5. The two gun-emplacements of Reenduff are 150 feet apart, the 4.7-inch guns covering the western channel and part of the western end of Berehaven anchorage. Concrete, steel joists and asphalt in the gun-emplacements and ancillary buildings reflect the changes in construction methods and materials of the early years of the twentieth century.

At Ardnakinna Point a joint naval and military war signal station was established; drawings of June 1914 depict separate naval and military watch-rooms and living accommodation, with a semaphore mast on top of the two-storey building.

Lough Swilly. In 1894 a plan for the defence of Lough Swilly was drawn up, using only the fortifications on the east side at Dunree, Neids Point and Inch. In the following year work started on a new work at Dunree, on the hilltop inland of the old fort, to be known as Dunree Hill Battery. The new fort or redoubt constructed at this time is an irregular seven-sided work, with flanking projections at four of the salient angles, occupying the hilltop some 300 feet above sea level. A record plan of 1899 indicates the layout, with two gun-emplacements on the west slope of the hillside some distance below the redoubt, overlooking Lough Swilly to the west and north.

The concrete scarp wall of the redoubt is some fourteen feet high from the base of the ditch, inclined almost three feet to give a battered wall face at a slope of 1:5. The flat-bottomed ditch surrounding the redoubt is about six feet wide, the counterscarp being in the form of a slope at an angle of some 40 degrees, the crest of which is some six feet above the bottom of the ditch. Entry to the redoubt is at the level of the ditch at the north end of the west front, through a pair of iron-sheeted doors.

The gun-emplacements are on the slope of the hill west of the redoubt. The battery appears to have been enclosed at some distance by an iron fence or spiked palisade, which connected with the redoubt on the south-west and north: in effect the redoubt defended the landward side of the battery. The perimeter palisade extended up the hillside on the south-west and on the north side, in each case being sited in the centre of a rock-cut ditch of similar dimensions to that surrounding the redoubt. The iron palisade remains in these ditches and originally connected to the scarp wall of the redoubt, crossing the redoubt ditch.

The two 6-inch breech-loaders were in position on the gun-emplacements by October 1897; these are recorded as the main armament in 1906, with one 4.7 inch QF gun at the old fort. In 1907, two 4.7-inch guns were mounted at Dunree. In 1912, mark VII 6-inch guns replaced those installed fifteen years earlier, constituting the principal armament at Dunree until 1945.

In 1895, a new battery at Lenan just over three miles north of Dunree was to be armed with three 9.2-inch BL guns, two 6-pounder QFs, and some machine-guns.[20] However, by 1909-14 only two of the 9.2-inch guns were in position at Lenan Head Battery, with the addition of three machine-guns. These large-calibre BL guns extended the defence of Lough Swilly over the sea approaches to the north and north-west, well past Malin Head and Fanad Head.

At the earlier battery at Neids Point, two 6-inch BLs and two 64-pounder RML guns for drill purposes were approved in 1895: by 1906 the two BL guns were recorded as being in position.[21] The interior of the battery was extensively modified by the construction of the two emplacements for the 6-inch breech-loaders, with a basement magazine between them, replacing the original layout here and removing any evidence on site of the number and position of the earlier armament. A wing battery survives outside the earlier battery enclosure, sited just to the north of the blockhouse. This line of six gun-emplacements presumably dates from this period of reconstruction. The four northern emplacements have front pivots and iron rails or tracks similar to those at the two gun positions at the south of the battery at the Black Castle, Wicklow, described above. The two southern emplacements at Neids Point wing battery each have a central pivot and a circular track, presumably to allow for a field of fire southwards towards Buncrana as well as north and west across Lough Swilly. The blockhouse or rectangular tower of the 1812 battery has been reduced in height to the level of the parapets of the adjacent landward walls; this may have been done to give the guns in the wing battery, particularly the two nearest guns with the centre pivot mountings, a clear field of fire to the south and south-west. Another reason for reducing the height of the blockhouse may have been to make the battery a less prominent target for ships at the entrance to Lough Swilly. No armament is listed at Neids Point in 1913, and the garrison appears to have been withdrawn by the following year.

The original fort on Inch was also reconstructed after 1895, when two 6-inch BL guns were approved as armament, and the interior remodelled with two emplacements similar to the arrangement at Neids Point.[22] A small caponnière at one angle of the reconstructed battery flanks a concrete scarp and narrow ditch, the counterscarp of which is formed by a sloping earth bank. The tower on the landward salient has been reduced in height, to the general level of the landward walls. By 1906, two 6-inch BLs were mounted here, but in 1913, no armament is listed and the garrison was evidently withdrawn before the First World War.

The much-increased range of the guns now allowed for defence of Lough Swilly from the works on one shore only, resulting in the three fortifications on the west side being abandoned. The four batteries on the east shore described above were further reduced to two, those at Lenan and Dunree, before 1914. Lough Swilly

constituted a defended port for merchant shipping of the American trade passing north of Ireland, and a fortified anchorage for the Royal Navy, which was to be an important naval base with headquarters at Buncrana between 1914 and 1918.

Belfast Lough. In November 1904, the *Irish Builder* reported on proposals for batteries to be constructed at Grey Point and Kilroot:

The fortification of Belfast Lough, so long projected and so often postponed, has at length taken shape. Over fifty years the project dates back, and one cannot wonder if the fortification of today will be so obsolete half a century later as that of fifty years ago is today. The points selected for the batteries are at Grey Point, on the Co. Down side, with a range from the inner channel entrance to the Copelands; and at Kilroot ... on the Antrim side. Land for both batteries has been acquired, and work has been commenced at Grey Point by Messrs. W. J. Campbell and Son, building contractors, Ravenhill Road, Belfast, who secured the contract against unusually large competition. The contract is a measurement one, based on the district schedule of the War Dept. The Grey Point Battery is expected to cost about £10,000. The Messrs. Campbell carried out several of the recently completed Lough Swilly forts, hence they are experienced in the class of work required.... The Kilroot Battery is not expected to mature until the completion of that at Grey Point.

The implication of this report is that the batteries noted at Holywood and Woodburn in 1887 were relatively insignificant works, or no longer in existence in 1904. Proposals for Grey Point and Kilroot dated back to 1895, when three 6-inch breech-loaders were proposed for each site.

By 1907, each battery was equipped with two 6-inch breech-loaders and three Maxim machine-guns.[23] The 6-inch BL guns were in position at Grey Point and Kilroot until after the Second World War. The guns covered the approach to Belfast Lough from the north and east—the Copeland Islands are eight miles east of Grey Point—and the channel up to Belfast.

The importance of Cork Harbour, Berehaven and Lough Swilly was emphasised during the 1914-18 war: towards the end of the war, ships of the United States Navy made use of these anchorages, and facilities were provided for naval air stations or seaplane bases.

The Anglo-Irish Treaty of December 1921 included the retention of these three fortified harbours by Britain, subsequently to be known as the 'Treaty Ports'. Belfast Lough harbour defences were also included in the Treaty—indicating perhaps some doubt concerning the permanence of the partition of the country. The Irish Free State was to provide port facilities for the Royal Navy, and the British army remained in occupation of the forts and batteries that protected them. At Cork Harbour these were Fort Westmoreland on Spike Island, Fort Camden, Templebreedy Battery and Carlisle Fort. On Bere Island the batteries and redoubts continued to be garrisoned by British forces, as were Dunree Fort and Lenan Battery at Lough Swilly.[24]

The ports were divided into two coast defence areas. North Irish Coast Defences, with headquarters at Belfast, comprised Belfast Lough, with batteries at Kilroot and Grey Point, and Lough Swilly. South Irish Coast Defences, with headquarters at Queenstown (Cobh), consisted of the Cork Harbour forts and Berehaven, protected by the works on Bere Island. The port facilities remained available to the Royal Navy, and the fortifications were under British control until the Anglo-Irish Agreement of 1938, when they were handed over to the Irish government.

Detachments of the Irish army replaced the British garrisons. The transfer included the fortifications, buildings, armament, ammunition and equipment, and was to take place before the end of 1938. The Cork Harbour transfer took place in July 1938, that at Berehaven in September, and Dunree and Lenan at Lough Swilly in October.

The armament of the Treaty Port fortifications at the transfer in 1938 was essentially the same as it was during the 1914-18 war. One of the 9.2-inch guns at Templebreedy was defective and was replaced by the War Office. It appears that in reaching the decision to hand over the ports, the British government was acting on naval and military advice that the cost of bringing the defences up to date, and the complications of supplying the ports in time of war, made their retention of doubtful value. The importance of the ports as naval bases and for merchant shipping in the context of future submarine warfare in the North Atlantic seems to have been disregarded or overruled. The retention of the Treaty Ports by Britain would have made it difficult for Ireland to remain neutral, which was the policy adopted a year later on the outbreak of war in 1939.

The increasing effectiveness of aerial bombardment was demonstrated during the Spanish Civil War, and in this regard the ports were vulnerable and their fortifications equipped with very little in the way of effective anti-aircraft weapons. The only provision for defence against aerial attack at Cork Harbour between 1920 and 1937 appears to have been a limited number of machine-guns at Camden and Carlisle. In 1940, three anti-aircraft positions were constructed at Dunree Hill Battery and one anti-aircraft post in the old Dunree Fort. In December1942, work started on new gun positions for the two 6-inch breech-loaders which were removed from No. 3 Bastion of Fort Westmoreland in Cork Harbour and sited in new emplacements in casemates in July-August 1943, providing additional protec-

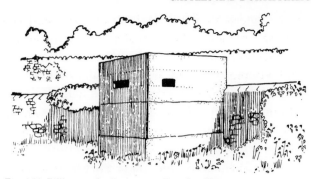

Fig. 156. Pillbox on the Boyne near Beaulieu House.

tion, particularly from aerial attack. Four 40mm Bofors anti-aircraft guns were mounted at Fort Westmoreland in June 1942, which could also be used against landing parties and naval vessels. There were also Hotchkiss and Lewis guns for defence against low-flying aircraft.

The most important new work carried out by the Corps of Engineers of the Irish army was Fort Shannon, on the south side of the Shannon Estuary west of Tarbert Island at Ardmore Point. There were two gun-emplacements for 6-inch breech-loaders, magazines, search-light positions, engine-room, electricity supply station, and living accommodation. This work, carried out in 1942, included the provision of water supply and approach roads. Each 6-inch gun mounting was anchored to a reinforced concrete foundation some six feet deep.

On a much smaller scale were the pillboxes or machine-gun posts at various locations around the country. One of these is sited at the northern end of the bridge over the River Barrow at Monasterevan (Fig.155). This concrete structure is partly incorporated in the masonry parapet of the bridge, and has horizontal openings, one covering the bridge to the south and the other the roadway to the west. On the north side of the estuary of the River Boyne some two miles downstream of Drogheda is another concrete pillbox. It is sited on the river bank at a road junction between the riverside road and one leading northward to Beaulieu House, built up against the stone wall on the river bank. Only about three feet of the structure projects above the

wall; one of the gun apertures covers the road to the north, the other two openings, the river to the east and south. From the landward side the pillbox is largely hidden by the riverside wall (Fig.156). Other pillboxes sited on Bere Island have iron shutters in the horizontal gun slits. On the demi-bastions of the Magazine Fort in the Phoenix Park, Dublin, are concrete machine-gun posts constructed on top of the earlier loop-holed structures. Duncannon Fort overlooking Waterford Harbour was also occupied between 1939 and 1945 and has some small structures built at this time; at Forts Camden and Carlisle there are some concrete works loop-holed for musketry, observation posts and some light gun-emplacements.

Another element of coastal defence was the establishment of a line of coast watching posts, first proposed early in 1939. The Coast Watching Service set up later that year was part of the Marine Service until 1942, and operated separately until October 1945, when it was disbanded. A number of the look-out posts were sited close to the signal towers of 1804-06; they extended from Co. Louth around the coast southwards and up the west coast to Donegal, the last two posts being east of Malin Head. Bray Head signal tower on Valentia Island was converted into a

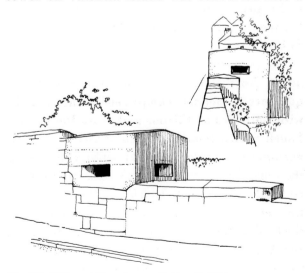

Fig. 155. Pillbox at Monasterevan Bridge, Co Kildare.

coast watch station and the tower reduced in height; it had formerly been used as an Admiralty signal station in 1907. Sybil Head tower was also reconstructed in 1907 with a flat roof and concrete first floor supported on steel joists, to serve as an Admiralty signal station; it was occupied as a coast watching post as part of the line set up in 1939. During the 1914-18 war the signal towers at Roberts Head and Mizen Head on the Cork coast were also in use as Admiralty signal stations, when Queenstown was the headquarters of the Royal Navy in Ireland. It seems probable that other towers were also in use at that time as observation or signal posts; the Martello tower at Rush in north Co. Dublin was in use as an Admiralty signal station between 1909 and 1920.

Over eighty look-out posts were set up after 1939, at most of which small concrete observation buildings were constructed. On the seaward side of Ballylinchy signal tower at Kedge Point, near Baltimore, are the remains of a small concrete structure that appears to have been one of these look-out posts. They were equipped with telephone, semaphore and morse code equipment, and the movements of ships and aircraft were recorded by the observers.

In September 1939, anti-aircraft batteries were established at Dublin, Dublin Airport, Rineanna (later to become Shannon Airport), and at Cork Harbour. In Dublin, guns were sited at Clontarf, Alexandra Basin, Ringsend Park (where there were four guns) and Booterstown. There were also anti-aircraft guns in the Phoenix Park, at Baldonnel airfield and several other locations.[25] In April and May 1941, several of these batteries were in action, firing on German aircraft over Dublin. Search-light posts were established at Howth, Blackrock Park, Dalkey, and other sites.

In Northern Ireland, there were twenty heavy anti-aircraft guns, most of which were in Belfast, and twelve light anti-aircraft guns. The defences were concentrated at Belfast and Derry; after the bombing of Belfast in April 1941 the anti-aircraft defences of the city were doubled, but these had little effect during the next bombing raid by the Luftwaffe the following month. On Belfast Lough, the batteries at Grey Point and Kilroot were in commission, with another battery at Larne armed with two 6-inch guns in operation between 1943 and 1944. There were also batteries with 6-inch guns at Orlock on the north coast of Co. Down and at Magilligan.

Grey Point Battery continued in operation until the disbandment of the Coast Artillery in 1956. Concrete structures originally built on top of Magilligan Martello tower at the entrance to Lough Foyle were constructed during the 1939-45 period, while nearby, close to the water level, are concrete pillboxes overlooking the shipping channel leading up Lough Foyle to Derry.

The garrisons were removed from Fort Shannon, Carlisle Fort and Templebreedy in 1946, and in the following year the forts on Bere Island were closed down. The Lough Swilly forts, Dunree and Lenan, ceased to have a regular garrison in 1952, but a maintenance staff was retained at Dunree.[26]

Artillery fortifications, introduced into Ireland in the middle of the sixteenth century, no longer had an active role in local or national defence after some four hundred years of development. The architecture of the earlier fortifications from the seventeenth to early nineteenth century, often of a monumental character with carefully constructed masonry, gave way by the beginning of this century to open concrete gun-emplacements, backed by small ancillary structures, often with little or no defensive features. The attempt was subsequently made to provide some protection against aerial attack, in some instances involving major construction by installing the guns in casemates. The history of artillery fortification in Ireland comes to an end with these reinforced concrete emplacements.

Chapter 7
Conservation and Restoration

CONSERVATION WORK AND SOME restoration has been carried out in recent years at a number of fortifications falling within the period covered by this book. These include some of the later castles that have early gun-embrasures, some fortified houses and bawns of the early seventeenth century, and a small number of artillery forts and batteries ranging in date from the seventeenth century through the Napoleonic period to the early years of this century.

Several of the castles with early gun-loops or gun-embrasures are in State Care as national monuments, including Aughnanure, Cahir Castle and the Black Castle at Leighlinbridge. In Northern Ireland, examples of these castles under the care of the Department of the Environment include Narrow Water Castle, Kilclief Castle and other castles in Co. Down. At Carrickfergus Castle, the large brick gun-embrasures of the middle of the sixteenth century survive with later artillery emplacements of the nineteenth century.

A number of the plantation bawns and castles of the early seventeenth century are also in state care in Northern Ireland; Park's Castle, Co. Leitrim, is a plantation house and bawn that is a national monument in the Republic. The fortified houses of Kanturk, Portumna and Burncourt are also national monuments, Kanturk and Portumna having had extensive conservation work carried out. Parts of the town walls and bastions of Carrickfergus survive, while the circuit of ramparts and bastions enclosing the city of Derry make it the outstanding example of artillery fortification of the early seventeenth century in Ireland. Hillsborough, Co. Down, is an example of a mid-seventeenth-century square bastioned fort—with later alterations and additions— in State Care.

The most extensive programme of conservation work, under the supervision of the National Parks and Monuments Branch of the Office of Public Works, is that under way at Charles Fort, Kinsale, the most important artillery fort of the late seventeenth century in the country (Figs. 157 and 158). The earlier artillery fort at Kinsale, Castle Park (now generally known as James Fort), is also in State Care as a national monument, including the blockhouse at water level.

The early eighteenth-century Magazine Fort in the Phoenix Park, Dublin, with a number of additional structures from the nineteenth century and from the 1939-45 period, may in future be open to the public: proposals that the fort

Fig. 157. Devil's Bastion Charles Fort before restoration.

Fig. 158. Devil's Bastion Charles Fort after restoration.

Fig. 159. Student workcamp at Charles Fort in 1972.

become a military museum may result in much-needed conservation work here.

Lough Swilly has been the centre of much recent conservation effort, including work on the batteries at Rathmullan and Neids Point, and the more extensive programme at Dunree Fort. At Dunree, the fort of the Napoleonic period on the headland is now a museum, opened in July 1986, with a new exhibition building mounting displays illustrating the history of Dunree and the Lough Swilly defences over a period of almost 150 years. Knockalla Fort opposite Dunree has also been extensively repaired and restored over a number of years by the owners. The Martello tower and battery some distance to the south at Muckamish, also in use as a holiday residence, is well maintained and in good condition. At the entrance to Lough Foyle, Magilligan Martello tower is now under the care of the Department of the Environment for Northern Ireland, and conservation and restoration work has taken place, including the removal of the Second World War

structures built on top of the tower (Figs.160 and 161). The Martello at Sandycove on Dublin Bay now forms part of the James Joyce Museum, but the emphasis here is naturally on Joyce and his work rather than on the Martello tower as a military structure. The opportunity remains for one of the Dublin towers, or possibly one of those at Cork Harbour or elsewhere in Ireland, to be restored as a small military museum with perhaps a reconstruction of a traversing platform and gun on the roof gun platform. In the context of what has been achieved at Dunree Fort, this would not be a difficult undertaking. Rossleague Martello tower at Cork Harbour has been partially restored by Cork County Council and is in good condition.

Work is now complete at Grey Point Battery on Belfast Lough, where it is hoped in future to restore the original armament of two 6-inch guns as part of the material displayed. After a long period of neglect, artillery fortifications in Ireland are now receiving some of the attention that has been given for many years to the medieval castles. With Grey Point, opened in May 1987, the museum at Dunree Fort, and conservation work at the batteries at Neids Point and Rathmullan, a good start has been made on displaying examples of these fortifications to the general public. The ramparts and bastions of Derry and of Charles Fort, Kinsale, now open to the public, provide a good impression of larger-scale seventeenth-century fortifications.

Local enterprise and employment schemes with the aid of Government funds and professional supervision might give rise to conservation work on a number of fortifications, following the example of what has been done at Lough Swilly. Student work-camps at Charles Fort, Kinsale, in the summers of 1972 and 1973 played an important part in subsequent developments there, leading to an extensive programme of conservation and restoration work, which is still continuing (Fig. 159). Such local efforts on a number of smaller fortifications may help to develop an awareness of these largely neglected structures and perhaps assist in their preservation generally. The remote location of some of them, such as the Shannon estuary batteries and the Martello towers on Galway Bay, has helped in their preservation to some degree. At one of the Shannon Estuary batteries, Kilkerin Co. Clare, the blockhouse has undergone restoration in recent years: similar plans for Rosaveel Martello on Galway Bay have not yet materialised.

The much larger-scale Shannonbridge fortification is one of the few artillery fortifications in Ireland on which there is a preservation order under the National Monuments Acts; another artillery fortification on which a preservation order has been made is the earthwork Green Fort at Sligo. There must be many more earthwork forts, and fieldworks constructed during the warfare of the seventeenth century, awaiting discovery, some of which may best be identified by aerial photography. The walls and towers at Waterford, including the Watch Tower with its early gun-loops, are to be preserved as part of the planning scheme for the city; further information on the defences has been provided by recent archaeological excavations at a number of locations on the line of the walls here. At Drimnagh, some three miles to the west of the

Fig. 160. Magilligan Martello tower before restoration. (Historic Monuments & Buildings Branch, Department of the Environment, Northern Ireland).

Fig. 161. Magilligan Martello tower after restoration. (Historic Monuments & Buildings Branch, Department of the Environment, Northern Ireland).

Fig. 162. Fort Camden, Cork Harbour, from the south-east (Courtesy Dr. Daphne Pochin Mould).

centre of Dublin, the moated castle, including some seventeenth-century buildings, has been undergoing restoration under professional supervision for the past seven years and is now open to the public. Also open to the public is Rathfarnham Castle, the fortified house some three miles south-east of Drimnagh; a national monument in State Care since 1986. Extensive conservation and restoration work has been carried out here. The Barry family castle at Barryscourt, near Carrigtohill, Co. Cork, is undergoing large-scale restoration/conservation

Fig. 163. Reconstruction work on 19th-century gunpowder incorporating mill at Ballincollig Gunpowder Mills, Co. Cork in 1995 (Photo: Dr. Colin Rynne).

work by the Barryscourt Trust and the Office of Public Works. Barryscourt Castle is now in State Care and was opened to the public since 1994.

While a fair number of the Martello towers and batteries of the Napoleonic period survive, the case may still be made for preservation orders to protect a representative selection of these from demolition or alteration. A visit to the Pigeon House Fort on the South Wall of Dublin Harbour revealed the destruction of a length of the southern perimeter wall, which incorporated several arched gun-embrasures, an act of official vandalism that must have taken place late in 1985 or during the first part of 1986. Cork County Council has now taken over responsibility for Fort Camden from the Irish Department of Defence (Fig.162). Plans include opening the fort to the public, with exhibits and display areas on the history of the fort and its armament. In 1993 Cork County Council opened an interpretative centre at Ballincollig Gunpowder Mills to accompany its complete working restoration of a mid-nineteenth century gunpowder incorporating mill on the site (Fig.163). This is, at the time of writing, the only operational mill of its type in these islands.

The future of artillery fortifications in Ireland depends ultimately on public awareness and on the involvement of local and State agencies in their preservation, conservation and restoration. They are part of the history and heritage of Ireland.

Appendix: Irish Signal Towers

APPENDIX: SIGNAL TOWERS: This list is based on information compiled from PRO HO 100/121, f.130-134, Military Affairs, Ireland, July-December 1804; HO 100/127, f.90-92, Military Affairs, Ireland, August-December 1805; and HO 100/133, f.25-26, Military Affairs, Ireland, May-June 1806.

1. Pigeon House: Signal post erected 1804, officers and signal crew to be accommodated in the fort.

2. Dalkey: Tower finished by September 1805, signal lieutenant appointed May 1805. Signal crew of midshipman and two signalmen.

3. Ballygannon: Not started by September 1804, as there was the possibility of building a Martello here; walls built by September 1805. By April 1806 work continuing and signal mast erected.

4. Wicklow Head: Officer and crew to have accommodation in the lighthouse; by September 1805 signal mast erected.

5. Mizen Head: In September 1804 the tower was soon to be completed; the signal mast was erected by this time. By September 1805 the signal lieutenant was appointed and the tower reported as completed.

6. Kilmichael Point: In September 1804 the tower was to be finished in about a month, and the signal mast was erected. In September 1805 still under construction; walls completed and some carpentry work but no workmen on site. Still not completed by April 1806.

7. Cahore Point: In September 1804 the tower was to be finished in about a month; a year later it was reported as completed and signal mast erected.

8. Blackwater: In September 1804 the tower was to be finished in about a month; a year later it was reported as completed and signal mast erected.

9. Fort Point: Report of September 1804 notes that a tower was begun but stopped as there was the possibility of erecting a Martello here. A year later the Martello was under construction to defend the harbour and also to accommodate the signal crew; the signal mast was erected. Martello still under construction in 1806.

10. Hill Castle: Tower complete in September 1804 but no furniture for the rooms. A year later tower reported as complete except for plastering and painting; signal mast erected.

11. Cross Faranogue (Forlorn Point, west of Kilmore): Tower complete but no furniture for the rooms in September 1804. Reported as complete except for plastering and painting a year later; signal mast erected.

12. Baginbun Head: Tower not begun in September 1804; possibility of a Martello tower here. Martello under construction a year later. Report in 1806 remarks that the tower was to defend the anchorage and house the signal crew. Signal mast erected by September 1805.

13. Hook: Officer and signal crew to be housed in the lighthouse tower; rooms not ready in September 1804. Signal mast erected by September 1805.

14. Brownstone Head: The walls of the tower built and signal mast erected by September 1804; completed but damp a year later. Signal lieutenant appointed February 1806.

15. Island of Kane (Townland of Islandkane South) Tower not yet started but contracted for in September 1804; not completed a year later, by which time the signal mast was erected. Signal lieutenant appointed February 1806.

16. Burnmahon (Bunmahon): Walls built and signal mast erected by September 1804; tower completed but damp a year later. Signal lieutenant appointed January 1806.

17. Ballyvoil Head (Ballyvoyle): Tower not yet begun in September 1804, but contracted for; nearly completed a year later, by which time the signal mast was erected. Signal lieutenant appointed January 1806.

18. Ballymona (possibly Mine Head, Ballynamona townland): Walls built and signal mast erected by September 1804; completed by 1806. Signal lieutenant appointed January 1806.

19. Ardmore: Walls built and signal mast erected by September 1804; completed by 1806. Signal lieutenant appointed October 1805.

20. Knockadoon: In September 1804 this tower was complete and the officer and crew in residence. Signal lieutenant appointed November 1805.

21. Ballynacotta (probably situated in Ballymacotter townland, between Ballycotton and Roche's Point): In September 1804 this tower was complete and officer and crew in residence. Signal lieutenant appointed May 1804.

22. Carlisle Fort: Officer and signal crew to be lodged in the fort in September 1804, signal mast erected by September 1805. Signal lieutenant appointed December 1804.

23. Robert's Head: In September 1804 the tower was completed and officer and crew in residence. Signal lieutenant appointed May 1804.

24. Barry's Head: Tower nearly completed in September 1804; a year later noted as badly finished and damp, by which time the signal mast was erected. Signal lieutenant appointed May 1804.

25. Old Head of Kinsale: Tower nearly completed in September 1804; a year later noted as finished but very damp, by which time the signal mast was erected. Signal lieutenant appointed May 1804.

26. Seven Heads: In September 1804 the tower was nearly completed and officer and crew in residence; a year later noted as finished but damp in wet weather. Signal lieutenant appointed in June 1804. In need of repair in 1806.

27. Galley Head: Tower nearly completed in September 1804; finished and signal mast erected by September 1805, by which time there was a signal crew and military guard here.

28. Glandore: In September 1804 the tower was half built and the signal mast erected; completed by September 1805. Signal lieutenant appointed September 1804.

29. Toe Head: In September 1804 the tower was more than half built and the signal mast erected; a year later the tower was finished and weather-slated. Signal lieutenant appointed August 1805.

30. Kedge Point (Ballylinchy signal tower): In September 1804 the tower was one-third built and the signal mast erected; a year later the tower was finished and weather-slated. Signal lieutenant appointed September 1805.

31. Cape Clear: The walls of the tower built to two feet above ground in September 1804; finished and weather-slated a year later, by which time the signal mast was erected. Signal lieutenant appointed September 1805 (Lighthouse and ancillary buildings were subsequently built within the signal tower enclosure.)

32. Lamcon (Leamcon, two miles west of Schull): In September 1804 the tower was half built; finished and weather-slated a year later, by which time the signal mast was erected. Signal lieutenant appointed September 1805.

33. Brow Head: In September 1804 the tower was half built; nearly finished and weather-slated a year later, by which time the signal mast was erected. Signal lieutenant appointed September 1805.

34. Mizen Head: In September 1804 the tower was half built; nearly finished and weather-slated a year later, by which time the signal mast was erected. Signal lieutenant appointed October 1805.

35. Sheep's Head: Work expected to begin September 1804; signal mast erected by September 1805, by which time it was expected that the tower would be completed the following month. Signal lieutenant appointed November 1805.

36. Bere Island: As no. 35.

37. Black Ball Head: As no. 35.

38. Dursey Island: As no 35, apart from appointment of signal lieutenant.

39. Hog Island: Not yet begun in 1804; not contracted for in 1805, and not begun in 1806. This may be identified on 1804 map of signal towers as Scariff Island; not indicated on first edition of Ordnance Survey 6-inch map, and it seems possible that a signal tower was not constructed here. With the omission of this signal station, Dursey Island station would have to communicate directly with that on Bolus Head fourteen miles distant.

40. Bolus Head: In September 1804 the materials were on site but work had not yet begun; a year later the walls were built to a height of sixteen feet. Nearly finished in April 1806. It appears that this tower was at Bolus Point, where only the foundations survive today. Half a mile south-east is an enclosure with four square corner flankers noted as 'Bolus Signal Tower' on the first edition of the Ordnance Survey 6-inch map. However, the estimate for this tower and those at Bray Head, Great Blasket and Sybil Head were all the same, at £720 1s 4d, an average cost, indicating that the standard signal tower was built here. The larger enclosure nearer to Bolus Head is presumably a later structure.

41. Bray Head, Valentia Island: Foundations excavated by September 1804; built but requiring weather-slating, and signal mast erected, by September 1805.

42. Great Blasket Island: Foundations excavated by September 1804; built but requiring weather-

slating, and mast taken down, by September 1805. Completed and signal mast erected by 1806.

43. Sybil Head: In September 1804 construction just begun, to be finished in about seven weeks; a year later the tower was completed but required weather-slating. Signal mast erected.

44. Brandon Head (Ballydavid Head: Ballydavid signal tower): As for no. 43.

45. Kerry Head: No report September 1804; a year later the tower was finished but required weather-slating or rough-cast finish externally, to prevent water penetration in wet weather. Signal lieutenant appointed October 1805.

46. Loop Head (sited over a mile north-east of Loop Head): As for no. 45, except that signal lieutenants are recorded as being appointed in March and November 1805.

47. Knocknagarhoon: As for no. 45, except for signal lieutenant appointment.

48. Baltard Hill (Ballard townland, at Ballard Bay): As for no. 45, except for signal lieutenant appointment.

49. Mutton Island: Not in signal tower list for September 1804. Tower completed but requiring weather-slating or rough-cast finish by September 1805.

50. Hag's Head: As for no. 45, except for signal lieutenant appointment.

51. South Isle of Arran (Inisheer): Just begun in September 1804; nearly finished a year later but no workmen employed at this time. By April 1806 tower reported as nearly built but no workmen employed for some time.

52. Great Isle of Arran (Inishmore): As for no. 51.

53. Lettertmullan Island (Golam Head): Tower begun September 1804, to be completed by the end of December; by September 1805 the tower was being roofed. Masonry work completed by April 1806.

54 Ard Castle Hill: Tower begun September 1804, to be completed by the end of December;

by September 1805 the walls were nearly completed. Masonry work finished by April 1806.

55. *Bunowen Hill over Slyne Head:* As for no. 54.

56. *Cleggan Hill over Dog's Nose:* As for no. 54.

57. *Inishturk:* In September 1804 not yet contracted for; mast landed and step fixed. A year later the foundations were excavated but no materials on site. Partly built by April 1806.

58. *Shivel Head, Clare Island:* In September 1804 not yet contracted for; mast landed and step fixed. A year later walls nearly built. Slating finished by April 1806.

59. *Saddle Hill, Achill Island:* In September 1804 not yet contracted for; mast landed and step fixed. A year later foundations were excavated but no materials on site. Walls built to officer's room by April 1806.

60. *Tarmon Hill* (Termon Hill: Glash signal tower): No report in September 1804. A year later the tower was roofed and signal mast erected. Noted as slated by April 1806.

61. *Slievemore Hill* (Tower Hill): No report in September 1804. A year later the tower was ready for roofing and the signal mast erected. Ready for slating by April 1806.

62. *Benwee:* Not in September 1804 list of signal stations; appears in September 1805 list as Benmore, built up to officer's room; mast not erected. Ready for slating by April 1806.

63. *Glensky* (Glinsk): No report in September 1804. A year later the tower was built up to officer's room; no signal mast supplied. Ready for slating by April 1806.

64. *Creevagh:* Tower nearly completed in September 1804; almost finished and signal mast erected a year later. In need of repairs in 1806; signal lieutenant appointed July 1805.

65. *Rathlee:* Tower built to second floor by September 1804; almost finished and signal mast erected a year later. In need of repairs in 1806; signal lieutenant appointed July 1805.

66. *Carrowmabla Hill* (Carrowmably): Tower built to second floor by September 1804; nearly finished and signal mast erected a year later.

67. *Knocklane Hill:* Tower built to second floor by September 1804; almost finished and signal mast erected a year later.

68. *Stridagh* (Streedagh): Tower built to second floor by September 1804; nearly finished and signal mast erected a year later.

69. *Killcologue Point* (Mullaghmore): Tower built to second floor by September 1804; almost finished and signal mast erected a year later.

70. *John's Point:* Construction of tower just begun in September 1804; nearly finished and signal mast erected one year later. Completed by 1806; signal lieutenant appointed November 1805.

71. *Carrigan Head:* As for no. 70, except that signal lieutenant appointed February 1806.

72. *Malin Beg:* As for no. 70, except for appointment of signal lieutenant.

73. *Glen Head:* As for no. 70, except for appointment of signal lieutenant.

74. *Dauras Head* (Dawros Head): Tower not begun in September 1804; a year later the tower was to be completed in about a fortnight; no signal mast erected. Completed but no approach road built by April 1806; signal mast erected.

75. *Croye Head* (Crohy Head): Tower built to first floor and soon to be finished, with materials and mast on site in September 1804. A year later the tower was to be completed in about a fortnight; signal mast erected. Completed but no approach road built by April 1806. Signal lieutenant appointed February 1804.

76. *Mullaghderg Hill:* Tower in a similar state to no. 75 in September 1804 but mast not on site; a year later tower completed except for painting and the signal mast was erected. Completed but no approach road built by April 1806.

77. *Bloody Foreland:* Excavations under way for foundations in September 1804 but mast not on site; a year later tower completed except for

painting; signal mast not erected. Completed with signal mast erected but no approach road built April 1806.

78. Horn Head: Tower built about four feet above surface in September 1804, when it was intended to be completed by November, a year later there were alterations being carried out on the roof and the signal mast was not yet erected.

79. Melmore Head: As for no. 78. Signal lieutenant appointed February 1806.

80. Fannat Point (Fanad): One storey of tower built by September 1804, when it was intended to be completed by November; a year later there were alterations being carried out on the roof. Signal mast erected. Signal lieutenant appointed January 1806.

81. Malin Head: Walls of tower nearly completed in September 1804, when it was intended to be completed by November; a year later there were alterations being carried out on the roof. Signal mast erected. Signal lieutenant appointed February 1806.

Glossary

Approaches
Trenches excavated by a beseiging force towards a fortress.

Assault
An attack or storm against a fortification.

Banquette
An infantry fire step behind the parapet.

Barbette
Breastwork of a battery without embrasures. *En Barbette* - the arrangement of artillery to fire over the parpapet of a defensive work.

Bastion
Projecting work, generally level with the ramparts, for mounting artillery to provide for flank fire: the early rounded or semi-circular form was gradually replaced by the four-sided Italian-style angle bastion from the early sixteenth century onwards.

Battlement
A parapet wall with alternating embrasures or crenels, and raised portions or merlons.

Bawn
Defensive walled enclosure - also the courtyard or defensive enclosure of a tower house or fortified house.

Breach
An opening made in the rampart, wall or bastion by artillery bombardment or mining.

Bulwark
Sixteenth and early seventeenth-century term for a bastion, gun emplacement or blockhouse.

Capponière
A covered passage way in the dry ditch from the fortress to an outwork, or a casemated work projecting into the ditch for flank defence at low level, provided with musketry loops or artillery embrasures.

Casemate
A vaulted chamber of masonry or brickwork within the ramparts or bastions, for living quarters, storage or as a defensive casemate when provided with musketry loops or artillery embrasures.

Citadel
Fort within or on the perimeter of a town's fortifications, defensible both against external attack and from within the town.

Counterfort
Interior buttress built against retaining walls of the scarp or counterscarp.

Counterguard
Outwork of two faces forming salient angle, in front of a bastion.

Counterscarp
Sloped earthwork face or retaining wall on the outer side of the ditch.

Covered Way
Chemin Couvert. Pathway on the outer edge or counterscarp of the ditch, in which the defenders were protected by the parapet of the glacis

Crannóg
An artificial island formed in a lake with a defensive palisade or breastwork around its perimeter.

Crownwork
Outwork consisting of a bastion flanked by demi-bastions at each side, linked by ramparts.

Curtain
The length of wall or rampart between towers or bastions forming the principle defensive line.

Demi-bastion
Half bastion formed with one face and one flank.

Demi-lune
Half moon. An outwork in advance of the curtain. In the seventeenth century the term sometimes appears to be interchangeable with *Ravelin.*

Embrasure
Opening in a parapet or wall for artillery.

Enfilade
Flank fire along the length of a fortification.

Face
The two sides of a bastion or other work towards the field.

Flank
The two sides of a bastion linking the faces to the adjacent curtains.

Flanker
A gun emplacement recessed into the flank of a bastion. Sixteenth and seventeenth-century term for a bastion or corner tower flanking the rampart or curtain wall of a fortification.

Glacis
A broad gentle slope extending from the retaining wall or parapet fronting the covered way, or extending from the counterscarp of a fortification.

Guérite
Sentry box projecting from the angle of a bastion or salient angle of a fortification at parapet level.

Hornwork
Outwork composed of two demi-bastions linked by a rampart.

Orillon
A rounded or square-ended projection of the bastion face, resulting in a retired or recessed flank to the bastion.

Parapet
Wall or breastwork of masonry, brickwork or earthwork usually thick enough to resist cannon fire, on the forward edge of the top of the rampart.

Place of Arms
An enlargement of the covered way at salient or re-entrant angles as assembly points for the garrison to defend the outworks or to sortie.

Rampart
Earthwork or reveted embankment forming the main line of defence of a fortification.

Ravelin
A triangular outwork in front of the curtain between two bastions, often sited to protect a gateway in the fortification.

Redoubt

1. A small enclosed work, without bastions or flank defence either in the form of an earthen fieldwork or as a permanent fortification.

2. An outwork generally of triangular form used in conjunction with works such as crownworks or hornworks in the late seventeenth and eighteenth centuries.

3. In the context of early eighteenth-century Ireland, a small defensible barrack, sometimes sited in a small fort or redoubt of the previous century.

Re-entrant

Angle facing inwards as opposed to a salient angle, such as the junction of bastion flank and adjacent curtain.

Revetment

Retaining wall of fortification or ditch.

Salient

A projecting angle in a line of defence.

Sap

Siege trench excavated towards the fortress under attack, usually zigzag in form to protect the sappers and soldiers of the beseiging force.

Sconce

Detached earthwork fort, seventeenth century.

Scarp

The sloping front of the rampart rising from the bottom of the ditch to the base of the parapet, either an earthwork slope or or a masonry or brickwork revetment.

Tenaille trace

Line of defence or rampart in a succession of re-entrant and salient angles forming a zigzag plan.

Terreplain

The broad fighting platform on the rampart protected by the parapet.

Tête-de-pont

Bridgehead fortification. sometimes quite extensive in area, defending the end of a bridge.

Traverse

An earthwork or reveted structure to obstruct enfilade fire from the beseigers; traverses in the covered way provided protection to the defenders and were a form of parapet when provided with a banquette or firing step. Traverses in the mid- or late nineteenth century forts were often of very large dimensions to provide protection for troop accommodation or magazines.

The above list does not include all the elements of bastioned fortification which in the late seventeenth century became very complex. Fortifications in Ireland did not generally have the extensive outworks which were a feature of the larger European fortresses.

ARTILLERY

The muzzle-loading guns of bronze or iron of the sixteenth and seventeenth century were only gradually standardised with regard to type and calibre. The names by which the guns were known were replaced by the eighteenth century by the classification of the gun-weight of its cast-iron shot. Contemporary accounts of artillery of the earlier period vary in details of guns, calibre, weight of shot and range; the list below is an outline only of approximate dimensions and weights. Other guns classified by weight of shot were 8pdr, 12pdr and the 24pdr. The point blank range of the falcon and saker was just over 300yds, that of the demi-culverin and culverin 400 and 460yds respectively. The range of these guns at 10° elevation varied from some 1,900 yards for the Falcon and 2,650 yards for the culverin.

Seventeenth Century Artillery

NAME OF GUN	Length in feet	Weight in lbs	Bore in inches	Weight of shot in lbs
Robinet	5	160	$1\,^1/_4$	$^3/_4$
Falconet	4-6	500	2	$1\,^1/_4$
Falcon	6	700	$2\,^1/_4$	$2\,^1/_4$
Minion	6-8	1200	3	4
Saker	8-9	1500	$3\,^1/_2$	$5\,^1/_4$
Demi-culverin	9-10	3000	$4\,^1/_2$	9
Culverin	9-11	4000	5	18
Demi-cannon	10-12	6000	6	32
Cannon of 7	8-10	7000	7	42
Cannon of 8	-	8000	8	68

Notes

NOTES
Abbreviations used in notes

BL	British Library
Cal. Carew MSS	*Calendar of the Carew Manuscripts*
Cal. S. P. Ire.	*Calendar of the State Papers of Ireland*
f.	folio
Ir. Sword	*Irish Sword*
JCHAS	*Journal of the Cork Historical and Archaeological Society*
JGAHS	*Journal of the Galway Archaeological and Historical Society*
JKAS	*Journal of the Kildare Archaeological Society*
JOAS	*Journal of the Old Athlone Society*
MOD	Ministry of Defence Library (London)
ms.	manuscript
NLI	National Library of Ireland
NLS	National Library of Scotland
NMM	National Maritime Museum (London)
Ormonde MSS	*Ormonde Manuscripts*
PRO	Public Record Office
PROI	Public Record Office Ireland
PRONI	Public Record Office Northern Ireland
RIA	Royal Irish Academy
SPO	State Paper Office
TCD	Trinity College, Dublin
UJA	*Ulster Journal of Archaeology*
vol.	volume

CHAPTER 1
Artillery Fortifications in Europe and Ireland

1 E. Viollet-le-Duc, *An Essay on the Military Architecture of the Middle Ages* (1860), translated from the French by M. Macdermott illustrates several of these transitional works.

2 Iain MacIvor, 'Artillery and major places of strength in the Lothians and the East Border, 1513-1542', in *Scottish Weapons and Fortifications, 1100-1800*, edited by D.H.Caldwell (1981), 94-152. This includes several sketches of conjectural arrangements for mounting iron breech-loading guns in the casemates.

3 T.E.McNeill, *Carrickfergus Castle* (1981).

4 G. A. Hayes-McCoy, *Irish Battles* (1969), for the battles of the Yellow Ford and Kinsale. Sean O' Faolain, *The Great O'Neill* (1942), captures the atmosphere of the period in a unique way.

5 G. A. Hayes-McCoy, *Ulster and Other Irish Maps c. 1600* (1964), illustrates a number of these forts with contemporary pictorial maps.

6 C.Duffy, *Siege Warfare: the Fortress in the Early Modern World, 1494-1660* (1979).

7 Rolf Loeber, 'Irish country houses and castles of the late Caroline period: an unremembered past recaptured', in *Irish Georgian Society Bulletin*, vol. 16 (January-June 1973), 1-70, provides the first detailed study of the architecture of this period in Ireland. See also the same author's pioneering work *A Biographical Dictionary of Architects in Ireland,1600-1720* (1981); much of this first appeared as 'Biographical dictionary of engineers in Ireland, 1600-1730' in *Ir. Sword*, vol. 1, (1977-79), 30-44, 106-122, 230-255, 282-314. Many of these architects and engineers were involved in the design and construction of fortifications.

8 Paul M. Kerrigan, 'Charles Fort, Kinsale', in

Ir. Sword, vol. 13 (1977-79), 323-338.

9 NLI ms. 3137.

10 R.Blomfield, *Sebastien le Prestre de Vauban, 1633-1707* (1938, reprinted 1971).

11 E. H. Stuart Jones, *An Invasion That Failed: the French Expedition to Ireland, 1796* (1950), gives a detailed account of this event.

12 J. G. Coad and P. N. Lewis, 'The later fortifications of Dover', in *Post-Medieval Archaeology*, vol. 16 (1982), 141-200.

CHAPTER 2
Castle to Fort: Tudor Ireland, 1485-1603

1 G. A. Hayes-McCoy, 'The early history of guns in Ireland', in *JGAHS*, vol. 18 (1938), 43-65. This is still the best account of the introduction of firearms and cannon into Ireland and their increasing use during the sixteenth century. See also S. de hOir, 'Guns in Medieval and Tudor Ireland' in *Ir. Sword*, vol. 15 (1982), 76-88.

2 D. B. Quinn and K. W. Nicholls, 'Ireland in 1534', in *A New History of Ireland*, vol. 3: *Early Modern Ireland*, 1534-1691 (1976), 1-38, include a description and map of the lordships into which Ireland was divided in the early sixteenth century.

3 D. Bryan, *The Great Earl of Kildare* (1933), 71, 83. Kildare's expeditions to attack various castles are detailed.

4 Correspondence from Skeffington and the Council of Ireland to the King, 26 March 1535, quoted in *JKAS*, vol. 1 (1894), 229.

5 Hayes-McCoy, *Ulster Maps*, plate VI.

6 Hayes-McCoy, 'Early history of guns in Ireland', 56.

7 Harold G. Leask, 'The ancient walls of Limerick', in *North Munster Antiquarian Journal*, vol. 2 (1941), 99.

8 These Waterford loops were brought to my attention by the late Stan Carroll who, with Ben Murtagh, provided details of the Watch Tower loops. The internal splayed embrasures of these loops have sockets in the walls at cill level, presumably to take a wooden rail or beam on which the gun barrel rested; it is too far back from the opening to have provided a socket for a pivot.

9 TCD ms. 1209 (10).

10 PRO MPF 277.

11 *Cal. S. P. Ire.*, 1509-73,110-12, *Cal Carew MSS*, 1515-74, 230.

12 *UJA*, series 1, vol 3 (1855), 77.

13 Peter Harbison, 'P.Burke's painting of Youghal', in *JCHAS*, vol. 78 (1973), 66-79.

14 *An Archaeological Survey of Co. Down* (1966), 228-230.

15 Hayes-McCoy, *Ulster Maps*, plate 1.

16 PRO MPF 85, 'Plan of the Fort of Corkbeg', c.1571.

17 Iain MacIvor has drawn my attention to the similarity of Corkbeg to the fort at Dunglass, and states that the date of c. 1551 is quite likely for the plan form and details of Corkbeg.

18 *Cal S.P.Ire.*, 1509-73, 135.

19 *Cal. Carew MSS, 1515-74*: instructions to the Earl of Sussex, May 1560 (item 25).

20 McNeill, *Carrickfergus Castle*, 21

21 TCD ms. 1209 (64), by Francis Jobson, 1591, which also shows Duncannon and Waterford. NLI ms. 3137 (11) is a view of Passage by Phillips, 1685.

22 Richard Caulfield (ed.), *Council Book of Kinsale* (1879), xix, xxii.

23 E.M. Jope, 'Fortification to architecture in the north of Ireland', in *UJA*, series 3, vol.23 (1960), 116

24 TCD ms. 1209 (26).

25 PRO MPF 95 'A draught of the towne and castle of Roscommon', probably by Sir Nicholas Malby, July 1581.

26 Contemporary plans include F.M. Jones, 'The plan of the Golden Fort at Smerwick, 1580', in *Ir.Sword*, vol 2 (1954), plate 5 (from the Spanish Nunciature Papers in the Vatican Archives); NMM Dartmouth Collection of Irish Maps, no.31, 'Plan of the Battle of Smerwick', and a plan with dimensions in Alfred O'Rahilly, 'The massacre at Smerwick, 1580', in *JCHAS*, vol 42 (1937), plate 1.

27 *Cal. Carew MSS*, 1575-78, 285.

28 A plan of Fiddaun is reproduced in *JGHAS*, vol 4 (1905-06), 81. See also Maurice Craig, *The Architecture of Ireland from the Earliest Times to 1880* (1982) for plan, 62.

29 A plan of Mashanaglas is in H Webb Gilman, 'Castlemore and connected castles in Muskerry, Co. Cork', in *JCHAS*, vol.1 (1892), 234. The castle probably dates from before 1585.

30 P.H. Hore, *History of the Town and County of Wexford* (1900-06), vol 1, 263.

31 Hore ibid. vol 4, 8. Chapters 1-14 detail the history of Duncannon Fort up to the middle of the nineteenth century.

32 *Cal. S.P. Ire.*, 1588-92, 284-307

33 TCD ms. 1209 (64).

34 *Cal. Carew MSS, 1589-1600*, 128-131.

35 TCD ms.4877 (2).

36 *Cal.S. P. Ire., 1588-92*, 369. For Yorke's involvement in the fortifications see 311, 319, 347, 348.

37 TCD ms.1209 (46).

38 TCD ms. 1209 (58).

39 Caulfield, *Council Book of Kinsale*, xxii.

40 PRO MPF 82, plan of Newry; MPF 83 and 84, castle. Reproduced in *Archaeological Survey of Co. Down*. The drawings are attributed to Lythe: see J.H. Andrews, 'The Irish surveys of Robert Lythe', in *Imago Mundi*, vol.19 (1965), 22-31.

41 TCD ms.1209 (34).

42 TCD ms.1209 (14) includes three small-scale plans: the early fortified settlement at Derry, Dunalong and Lifford, reproduced as fig.25.

43 Harold G. Leask, *Irish Castles* (1941, revised and reprinted 1964) reproduces this drawing of Burt (fig.72, 109).

44 TCD ms. 1209 (55).

45 TCD ms. 1209 (52).

46 TCD ms. 1209 (46).

47 TCD ms. 1209 (71).

CHAPTER 3
Cannon and Musket, 1603-1691

[1] *Plantation, new towns, forts and fortified houses, 1603-1641.*

1 J. Buckley, 'Report of Sir Josias Bodley on some Ulster fortresses in 1608', in *UJA*, series 2, vol.16 (1910), 61-64.

2 *Cal. Carew MSS*, 1603-25, 214-217.

3 TCD ms.1209 (30).

4 *Cal. Carew MSS*, 1603-25, 215.

5 *Cal. Carew MSS*, 1603-25, 216.

6 *Cal. Carew MSS*, 1603-25, 216-17.

7 TCD ms. 1209 (65).

8 TCD ms. 1209 (48).

9 A. Rowan, *The Buildings of Ireland: North-West Ulster* (1979), 436.

10 Leask, *Irish Castles*, 131.

11 Leask, *Irish Castles*, fig.92; Maurice Craig, *The Architecture of Ireland from the Earliest Times to 1880* (1982), 124, plan 127.

12 E.M.Jope (ed.), *Studies in Building History* (1961), includes 'Early seventeenth-century houses in Ireland' by Harold Leask, and 'Some Irish seventeenth-century houses and their architectural ancestry', with a plan of Killincarrig House, by D.Waterman.

13 T.W.Moody, *The Londonderry Plantation, 1609-41* (1939).

14 TCD ms.1209 (33).

15 Jope 'Fortification to architecture', 97-106.

16 Rowan, *Buildings of Ireland*, 187, 359, 421-422; E.M. Jope, 'Scottish influence in the north of Ireland: castles with Scottish features, 1580-1640', in *UJA*, series 3, vol.14 (1951), 32-47.

17 TCD ms.1209 (29).

18 D.Waterman, 'Castle Archdale', in *UJA*, series 3, vol. 22 (1959), 119.

19 D.Waterman, 'Sir John Davies and his Ulster buildings', in *UJA*, series 3, vol.23 (1960), 89-96.

20 Jope, 'Fortification to architecture', 97-106 for illustrations of these bawns.

21 NLI ms. 3137 (42).

22 TCD ms. 1209 (24)

23 Moody, *Londonderry Plantation*, for details and plans of Derry, Coleraine, and Culmore

24 Rowan, *Buildings of Ireland*, 364, 373-376.

25 TCD ms. 1209 (39).

26 TCD ms. 1209 (41, 42).

27 Rolf Loeber, 'A gate to Connaught: the building of the fortified town of Jamestown, Co. Leitrim, in the era of plantation', in *Ir. Sword*, vol. 15 (1983),149-152, plate 16, for a plan of Jamestown of 1730.

28 Paul M. Kerrigan, 'Seventeenth-century fortifications, forts and garrisons in Ireland: a preliminary list', in *Ir.Sword*, vol. 14 (1980-82),145,

and plate 16 for a plan of Monaghan, which is a reproduction of TCD ms. 1209 (32).

29 *Cal. S. P. Ire.*, 1633-47 ,180-181

30 BL add. ms. 24200.

31 Kerrigan, 'Seventeenth-century fortifications', 151; Paul M. Kerrigan, 'The fortifications of Waterford, Passage and Duncannon, 1495 to 1690', in *Decies*, vol. 29 (1985), 12-23.

32 This map is reproduced in H.Murtagh (ed.), *Irish Midland Studies* (1980), plate 23; Pynnar's drawing of the fort is reproduced in plate 24.

33 TCD ms. 1209 (50).

34 TCD ms. 1209 (66).

35 TCD ms. 1209 (72).

36 Richard Caulfield (ed.), *Council Book of Youghal* (1878), 121,135.

37 Hayes-McCoy, *Ulster Maps*, plate 22, reproduces this plan of Castle Park. PRO S.P. 63, vol. 242, f. 549, identifies the parts noted on the plan as A to P.

38 *Cal. S. P. Ire.*, 1633-47, 166, 173.

39 *Cal. S. P. Ire.*, 1633-47, 199.

[2] *The Confederate Wars and the Cromwellian conquest, 1641-60.*

1 Loeber, 'Biographical dictionary of engineers', *Ir. Sword*, vol. 13 (1979) 304-305.

2 Loeber, 'Biographical dictionary of engineers', 106.

3 J. R. Powell, 'Operations of the Parliamentary Squadron at the Siege of Duncannon in 1645', in *Ir. Sword*, vol. 2 (1954), 17-21, plate 1.

4 J.R.Powell, 'Penn's expedition to Bunratty in 1646', in *Mariner's Mirror*, vol. 40, 4-20.

5 D. Bryan, 'Ballyshannon Fort, Co. Kildare, 1642-50', in *Ir. Sword*, vol. 4 (1959-60), 93-98. The contemporary plan is BL add. ms. 21427.

6 Hore, *History of Wexford*, vol. 5, 254.

7 Hore, loc.cit. 254.

8 NMM, Dartmouth Collection of Irish Maps, 1 (16), 'A description of Kinsale' by Johannie Mansell.

9 M. D. O'Sullivan, 'The fortifications of Galway', in *JGAHS, vol.* 16 (1934-35), 1-47.

10 TCD ms. 1209 (73).

11 NLI ms. 3137 (28).

12 T.J.Westropp, 'Clare Island survey, history and archaeology', in *Proc. Royal Irish Academy* vol. 31 (1911-15). P. Walsh 'Cromwell's Barracks, a commonwealth garrison fort on Inishbofin, Co. Galway', *JGAHS* 42 (1989-90), 30-71.

13 *Cal. S.P.Ire.*,1647-60, 687-688.

14 H. Murtagh, 'The town wall fortifications of Athlone', in *Irish Midland Studies* (1980), 96-97.

15 For details and documentary references to these and other fortifications see Kerrigan, 'Seventeenth-century fortifications', 3-24,135-156.

16 D. Bryan, 'Colonel Richard Grace, 1651-52', in *Ir. Sword*, vol. 4, 43-51.

17 BL Lansdowne ms. 821, f.150.

18 BL Lansdowne ms. 821, f.160.

19 *Cal. S. P. Ire.*, 1647-60, 687-688.

20 *Archaeological Survey of Co. Down*, 408-410.

21 *Cal. S. P. Ire.*, 1660-62, 283.

22 NLI ms. 3137 (23).

23 M. Gowan, 'Dunboy Castle, Co. Cork', in *JCHAS*, vol. 83 (1978), 1-49.

24 B. L. Townsend, 'History of "Bryan's Fort", Castletownshend', in *JCHAS*, vol. 42 (1937-38), 1-49, and 55 for plan.

25 *Cal. S. P. Ire.*, 1647-60, 623-625, 803, 815-816. A photocopy of the estate map, 'The estate of Sir John Freke in the County of Cork' by Thomas Sherrard, 1787, is in NLI 21 F 105 (17).

26 R. Dunlop, *Ireland Under the Commonwealth* (1913), contains information on forts and garrisons of this period, including those in Connacht and along the Shannon and the fortifications of Athlone. An unusual Cromwellian-period castle, with two acute-angled redans (similar to Mashanaglas) is Ireton's Castle, see C. Cairns, 'Guns and Castles in Tipperary', *Ir. Sword*, vol.16 (1985), 111-116, plan 115, plate 13.

27 Dunlop, *Ireland Under the Commonwealth*, 666.

28 Hore, *History of Wexford*, vol. 1, 260, 263-266.

[3] The Restoration and the Jacobite War, 1660-1691.

1 *Ormonde MSS*, new series, vol. 3, 25-26.
2 NLI ms. 2274.
3 *Calendar of State Papers (Domestic)*, 1672, 239.
4 *Cal. S. P. Ire.*, 1666-67, 318, NLI 21F 55 (1), reproduced in Loeber, 'Irish country houses',17.
5 *Cal. S. P. Ire.*, 1666-67, 96.
6 *Cal. S. P. Ire.*, 1666-67, 441-443.
7 NMM, Dartmouth Collection of Irish Maps, viii, 10-12, for de Gomme's proposal.
8 NLI ms.3137 (2, 4).
9 Caulfield, *Council Book of Kinsale, xlix, liv.*
10 Caulfield, *Council Book of Kinsale, xliv.*
11 Kerrigan, 'Charles Fort', 323-338.
12 BL add. ms. 28085.
13 NLI l5B 22 (1).
14 Staffordshire County Library, D 1778/v/3.
15 *Ormonde MSS*, new series, vol. 6, !64-165.
16 *Ormonde MSS*, new series, vol.6, 537-538.
17 NLI ms. 3137 and 2557; *Ormonde MSS*, vol. 2, 309-335.
18 National Gallery of Ireland, no. 7533.
19 Loeber, 'Irish country houses'. The plan of Rathcline is in NLI ms. 8646 (6).
20 J. G. Simms, 'Sligo in the Jacobite War, 1687-91', in *Ir. Sword*, vol. 7 (1965), 124-135, includes a plan of the defences.
21 NLI ms. 2742.
22 Murtagh, 'Town wall fortifications of Athlone', 101-106.
23 G. Story, *A Continuation of the Impartial History of the Wars of Ireland* (1693).
24 H. Murtagh, 'Ballymore and the Jacobite War', in *JOAS* vol. 1 (1974-75), 242-246.
25 NLI ms. 3137 (26).
26 NLI ms. 2742.
27 S. Mulloy, 'French engineers with the Jacobite army in Ireland, 1689-91', in *Ir. Sword*, vol. 15 (1983), 222-232, includes a contemporary map of Kinsale and plans of Athlone and the Irish Town, Limerick.
28 Jope, 'Fortification to architecture', 115, for a plan of the East Fort.
29 B. B. Williams, 'An artillery fort on Trannish Island, Co. Fermanagh', in *Clogher Record*, vol. 9 (1977), 295-296.
30 H. Mangan, 'Sarsfield's defence of the Shannon, 1690-91', in *Ir. Sword*, vol. 1 (1949-51), 24-32.
31 Worcester College, Oxford, ms. YC 20 ccvi, reproduced in Loeber, 'Biographical dictionary of engineers', plate 28.
32 NLI ms. 2742.

CHAPTER 4
A Century of Neglect, 1691-1793.

1 R. Wyse Jackson, 'Queen Anne's Irish army establishment in 1704', in *Ir. Sword* vol. 1 (1949-52), 133-135. For the midlands see Paul M. Kerrigan, 'Garrisons and barracks in the Irish midlands, 1704-1828', in *JOAS* vol 2 (1985), 100-108.
2 Harold G. Leask, 'Redoubts occupied by the Royal Scots in Ireland in the eighteenth century', in *Ir. Sword* vol. 1 (1949-53), 188-190.
3 G. Stell, 'Highland garrisons, 1717-23: Bernera Barracks', in *Post-Medieval Archaeology*, vol. 7, (1973), 20-30.
4 Hore, *History of Wexford*, vol. 1, 384-386.
5 Details of works to fortifications and barracks and the engineers responsible are in Loeber, 'Biographical dictionary of engineers'.
6 NLI 15 B 14 (11).
7 BL Egerton ms.917.
8 NLI 16 G 17 (38), map of the Phoenix Park, 1789; NLI 16 G 17 (42), plan of the Magazine Fort, 1793.
9 James Hardiman, *The History of the Town and County of Galway* (1829).
10 A copy of this plan is in the Architectural Archive, Merrion Square, Dublin, with a location map indicating that the site was to have been at Dunboy Castle.
11 Caulfield, *Council Book of Youghal*, 437, 473.
12 *Commons Journal, Ireland*, vol. 5 (1749-56), Ixviii.
13 Roy's report is in RIA ms. G I 2 and in NLI ms. 14, 306.
14 NLI ms. 14, 306.
15 NLI ms. 14, 306.

16 NLI ms.14,306.

17 NLI ms. 14,306.

18 PRO MPF 159 (3), plan of Ram-Head Battery, constructed 1779.

19 J.J.Crooks, *History of the Royal Irish Regiment of Artillery* (1914), 227.

20 PRO MPF 159 (4), plan of Carlisle Fort, Cork Harbour, 1781.

21 Crooks, *Royal Irish Artillery*, 227.

22 NLI 15 B 22 (54) and PRO MPF 159 (6) are plans of this fort.

23 Crooks, *Royal Irish Artillery*, 227.

24 Crooks, loc.cit.

CHAPTER 5.
The French are on the sea, 1793-1815

[1] *Historical background*

1 SPO OP (1796) 23/9.

2 Stuart Jones, *An Invasion That Failed.*

3 F. W. Ryan, 'A projected invasion of Ireland in 1811', in *Ir. Sword*, vol. 1 (1949-53), 136-141.

[2] *The signal towers*

1 G. Wilson, *The Old Telegraphs* (1976).

2 PRO HO 100/121, f.89-90; NLI, Kilmainham Papers, ms. 1119, f 368-369.

3 PRO HO 100/120, f.47-49.

4 PRO HO 100/121, f.7.

5 PRO HO 100/121, f.121-125.

6 BL add. ms. 35719, f.158.

7 NLI 15 B 13.

8 NLI, Kilmainham Papers, ms. 1122, f.311.

9 SPO OP 530/219/4.

10 NLI ms. 4707.

11 NLI, Kilmainham Papers, ms. 1122, f.380.

12 NLI, Kilmainham Papers, ms. 1123, f.6.

13 SPO OP 530/230.

14 TCD ms. 942/1/15-16, 18-20, 22-24, TCD ms. 942/2/2.

15 Information on this site and other Kerry signal towers kindly supplied by Mr Tom Shortt of Caherciveen.

16 Information kindly provided by Tim Robinson of Roundstone, Co. Galway.

17 NLI ms. 8182, 1-12; SPO OP 526/174/18.

18 SPO OP (1809) 283/61.

19 Paul M. Kerrigan, 'Gunboats and sea fencibles in Ireland, 1804', in *Ir. Sword*, vol. 14 (1980-82), 188-191.

20 PRO HO 100/133, f.23, for 1806 list, HO 100/120, f.309, for 1804 list.

[3] *Dublin and Wicklow*

1 J.T.Gilbert (ed.), *Documents Relating to Ireland, 1794-1804* (1893, reprinted 1970), 91-98.

2 SPO OP (1796) 23/9.

3 NLI ms. 809.

4 Paul M. Kerrigan, 'Minorca and Ireland, an architectural connection: the Martello towers of Dublin Bay', in *Ir. Sword*, vol. 15 (1983), 192-196; plate 20 for a reproduction of a contemporary plan of the tower at Adaya.

5 PRONI, T3465/164-168.

6 PRO HO 100/132, f.39-41, list of towers and batteries for the defence of the coast in the vicinity of Dublin, 24 December 1805.

7 PRO HO 100/132, f.39-41.

8 Ordnance Survey (Dublin), collection of plans of barracks and defence works, Ordnance Survey plan, 1859.

9 TCD ms. 2182.

10 NLI, Kilmainham Papers, ms. 1122, f.333.

11 NLI, Kilmainham Papers, ms. 1122, f.334-336.

12 NLI, Kilmainham Papers, ms. 1122, f.374, 378.

13 PRO HO 100/132, f.29-49.

14 NLI ms. 175, f. 272, inspection report of Dublin district, correspondence of Office of Ordnance, April-September 1804.

15 PRO MPHH 84.

16 NLI 16 G 17 (42).

17 NLI ms. 175, f.479.

18 Paul M.Kerrigan, 'A return of barracks in Ireland, 1811', in *Ir. Sword*, vol.15 (1983), 277-283, transcribed from NLI ms. 10217, details the garrisons in 1811.

19 SPO OP 293/1 (3).

20 SPO OP 293/1 (11).

21 SPO OP 293/1 (12).
22 SPO OP 293/1 (18).
23 NLI, Kilmainham Papers, ms. 1122, f.375.
24 NLI ms. 4707.
25 TCD ms. 2182.

[4] *Wexford and Waterford Harbour.*

1 PRO HO 100/132, f.47.
2 NLI ms. 4707.
3 Paul M. Kerrigan, 'The naval attack on Wexford in June 1798', in *Ir. Sword*, vol. 15 (1983), 198-199, from BL add. ms. 21142.
4 SPO OP (1796) 23/9.
5 Hore, *History of Wexford, vol.* 4, 253-254.
6 NLI ms. f.175, f. 498.
7 J. C. Walton, 'Aspects of Passage East: part 2', in *Decies*, vol. 11 (1979), 22.
8 NLI ms. 175, f.290.
9 PRO MPHH 84.
10 Kerrigan, 'Barracks in Ireland', 277-283.

[5] *Cork and Kinsale*

1 NLS ms. 3268, f.3lv and 32, sketches and note-books of Major-General J. Brown.
2 PRO MPF 159 (4).
3 NLS ms. 2863, f.46v.
4 NLI ms. 175, f.297.
5 PRO HO 100/120, f.304.
6 PRO MPF 159 (3).
7 NLI ms. 175, f. 298. In 1813 three ranges of infantry barracks were under construction at Camden, the contractor being James Mahony: NLI ms. 5194, letter book, Office of Ordnance, Ireland 1813-15.
8 NLI 15 B 22 (54) and PRO MPF 159 (6) for plans of this fort.
9 NLI ms. 175, f.321.
10 NLI ms. 175, f.298.
11 NLI ms. 4707.
12 PRO MPH 191.
13 NLI ms. 5194, f.52.
14 NLI ms. 175, f.296.
15 NLI ms. 175, f.298.
16 Niall Brunicardi, *Haulbowline, Spike and Rocky Islands* (1982).

17 NLI ms. 5194.
18 NLI ms. 5194, f.253, 269, 353.
19 NLI ms. 5194, f.316.
20 NLI ms. 5194, f.l95, 303.
21 Kerrigan, 'Barracks in Ireland', 277-283.
22 NLI ms. 175. 350 barrels of gunpowder were to be ready for delivery to the Board of Ordnance by 1 May 1804, part of a contract for 1,000 barrels. For the most recent account of the development of Ballincollig Gunpowdermills see George D. Kelleher *Gunpowder to Ballistic Missiles- Ireland's War Industries.* Belfast 1992
23 NLI ms. 175, f.300.
24 NLI, Kilmainham Papers, ms. 1122, f.246.
25 NLI ms. 5194, f.237.

[6] *Bantry Bay*

1 Stuart Jones, *An Invasion That Failed*, gives a detailed account of Bantry Bay and of the French and British naval forces.
2 Lady Ardilaun, *Tales of a Grandfather* (1914), contains a collection of documents and information relating to the Bantry Bay episode.
3 NLI ms. 809.
4 NLI ms. 809.
5 PRO MPHH 11; PRO WO 55/831.
6 PRO HO 100/120, f.9-10, 11-14.
7 PRO HO 100/120, f.303-304.
8 NLI, Kilmainham Papers, ms. 1122, f.327-328.
9 NLI, Kilmainham Papers, ms. 1120, f. 11.
10 SPO OP 230/2.
11 NLI ms. 4707.
12 PRO HO 100/155, f.69.
13 PRO HO 100/155, f.81-86.
14 NLI ms. 5194, f.198-199.
15 Ordnance Survey (Dublin), collection of maps and plans of Bere Island.
16 NLI ms. 175, 19 May l804.
17 NLI, Kilmainham Papers,ms. 1122, f.409; ms. 1123, f.13, 19.
18 NLI, Kilmainham Papers, ms. 1120, f.81 .

[7] *The Shannon Estuary and Galway Bay*

1 A. Dillon, 'The fort at Tarbert, Co. Kerry', in *Irish Sword, vol.* 3 (1959-60), 286.

2 Sir H. McNally, *The Irish Militia, 1793-1816* (1949), 97-98.

3 NLI ms. 4707.

4 J.A.MacCauley, 'General Dumouriez and Irish Defence', in *Ir. Sword*, vol. 10 (1969-70), 98-108, 165-173, is a translation of this memoir.

5 PRO HO 100/120, f.301-302.

6 Kerrigan, 'Gunboats and sea fencibles', 188-191.

7 Kerrigan, 'Barracks in Ireland', 277-283.

8 Oireachtas Library, ms. 8H 21.

9 NLI ms. 175, f.592.

10 NLI ms. 4707.

11 P. Gosling, 'Silent guns; two pieces of early 19th century ordnance on the shores of Galway Bay', in *JGAHS* vol 42 (1989-90), 139-143.

[8] *The Shannon:Portumna to Athlone*

1 SPO OP (1796) 23/9, f.14-15.

2 Paul M.Kerrigan, 'A military map of Ireland of the 1790s', in *Ir.Sword*, vol. 12 (1976), 247-251.

3 NLI, Kilmainham Papers, ms. 1199, f.352, 364-365.

4 NLI ms. 175, f.280-289.

5 SPO OP (1806) 230/2.

6 NLI, Kilmainham Papers, ms. 1119, f.353.

7 NLI ms. 175, f.287, lists guns and ammunition from Meelick to Athlone.

8 BL add. ms. 36278 (extracts), plan of the River Shannon between Co. Galway and King's Co.

9 PROI, Bryan Bolger Papers, 2B, Board of Ordnance. These papers give details, measurements and costs of the Shannon fortifications in May 1817, by which time the works were evidently complete.

10 NLI ms.175, f.287.

11 SPO OP (1806) 230/2.

12 PRO, Bryan Bolger Papers, 2B. See Paul M. Kerrigan, 'The defences of the Shannon; Portumna to Athlone 1793-1815', in *Irish Midland Studies*, edited by H. Murtagh (1980),168-192, for more precise details of costs, and documentary references.

13 PRO HO 100/132, f.37, report of December 1805, notes the ford, as does PRONI, T 3465/168, which also details Lord Cathcart's tour of

the Shannon defences and part of the west coast and Shannon estuary, December 1804.

14 PROI, Bryan Bolger Papers, 2B.

15 NLI, Kilmainham Papers, ms.1122, f.207-208, 227, 263.

16 SPO OP (1806), 230/2.

17 NLI, Kilmainham Papers, ms.s1119, f.352, 364-365.

18 NLI ms. 175, f.287.

19 PRO HO 100/132, f.46-47.

20 SPO OP (1806), 230/2.

21 PRO MR 470, map of fieldworks at Shannonbridge and section through the works, referred to in Brigadier-General Fisher's letter of 23 May 1810.

22 Paul M. Kerrigan, 'The Shannonbridge fortifications', in *Ir. Sword*, vol. 11 (1974), 234-245

23 PROI, Bryan Bolger Papers.

24 PRO MPHH 84.

25 NLI ms. 10207, the report and plan were reproduced in *Ir. Sword*, vol. 4 (1960), 180-181.

26 NLI, Kilmainham Papers, ms. 1116, f.138-139.

27 NLI, Kilmainham Papers, ms. 1119, f.352-353.

28 NLI, Kilmainham Papers, ms. 1119, f.364-365.

29 PROI lA/30/29 rev. exch. docs., no. 45-73, papers relevant to compensation for lands taken for defence works, 1803-08; TCD ms. 5808, maps of plots of land on Gallows Hill taken for the public service, surveyed by J. Hampton.

30 NLI ms. 175, f.287; this includes eleven 6-pounders on garrison carriages mounted at the castle.

31 PRO HO 100/132, f.29-38.

32 PRO MR 470 (3, 4), map of the fieldworks at Athlone, 1810, referred to in Brigadier-General Fisher's letter of 23 May 1810. See also Paul M. Kerrigan, 'The batteries, Athlone', in *JOAS* vol. 1 (1974-75), 264-270, and 'The batteries: some additional notes', in *JOAS* vol. 2 (1978), 24-25, which discusses this map and the following plans: BL ms. 13380 (2): an early plan that must date from 1803-04, including battery no. 8, which had been removed by December 1805. PRO MPHH 85 (5); plan of the works at Athlone, with pro-

posed alterations, 1805. This depicts proposed additions to batteries 1, 2, 5 and 6 to make them capable of all-round defence turning them into redoubts. A detached outwork is shown in advance of batteries 3 and 4: these proposals were not carried out. PRO MR 1399 : plan and section of battery no . 1,1837 .

33 F.W.Ryan, 'A projected invasion of Ireland', in *Ir. Sword*, vol. 1 (1949-52), 136-141.

34 E. Wakefield, *An Account of Ireland, Statistical and Political* (1812), vol. 2, 815.

[9] *The North*

1 Paul M. Kerrigan, 'The capture of the *Hoche* in 1798', in *Ir. Sword*,vol. 13 (1977-79), 123-127.

2 TCD ms. 942/2,112-114, 116-120.

3 Ordnance Survey (Dublin), collection of maps and plans of barracks and defence works.

4 TCD ms. 942/2, 101, 102, 105, 111.

5 NLI, Kilmainham Papers, ms. 1122, f.232.

6 Kerrigan, "Barracks in Ireland", 227-283.

7 NLI, Kilmainham Papers, ms. 1116, f.252.

8 TCD ms. 942/1 and 942/2.

9 NLI ms. 22023.

10 NLI, Kilmainham Papers, ms. 1117, f.130-131.

11 NLI ms. 175.

12 NLI ms. 175 , f. 494.

13 Rowan, *Buildings of Ireland*, plate 91, reproduces this plan.

14 This plan of Inch battery, and those of Rathmullan, Muckamish, and Knockalla, are in the Ordnance Survey (Dublin) collection of maps and plans of barracks and defence works.

15 SPO OP (1796) 23/9, f.16.

16 Ordnance Survey plan: see note 14.

17 Wakefield, *An Account of Ireland*, vol. 1.

18 NLI 15 B 1 (19).

19 TCD ms. 942/2,149-153.

20 McNeill, *Carrickfergus Castle*, plate 29, reproduces this plan.

21 NLI ms. 175, f.491.

22 Plans of the proposed fortress at Cross More near Castle Shane include PRO MPHH 84 (3), 1805; MR 570 (4), 1805; MPHH 84 (11), 1806; and MR570 (6), 1806.

CHAPTER 6.
Iron and concrete, 1815-1945

1 *Parliamentary Papers*, vol. 50 (1843), reports and correspondence relative to Dublin and Kingstown Railway.

2 Ordnance Survey (Dublin), collection of maps and plans of barracks and defence works.

3 *Irish Builder,* vol. 2 (1860), 326.

4 MOD, RA-RE Works Committee, 1895.

5 I.V.Hogg, *Coast Defences of England and Wales, 1856-1956* (1974), 97-98, 108, 152.

6 MOD, RA-RE Works Committee, 1895.

7 MOD, RA-RE Works Committee, 1895.

8 Ordnance Survey (Dublin), collection of maps and plans of barracks and defence works.

9 'Limerick District: return of troops and barracks accommodation, 1844', in *Ir. Sword*, vol. 3 (1957-60), 128-129.

10 Army Archives, Dublin.

11 Ordnance Survey (Dublin), collection of maps and plans of barracks and defence works.

12 PRO WO 33/47.

13 Information kindly provided by Dr J. B. Swan, Wexford.

14 M.K.Hanley, *The Story of Custume Barracks, Athlone,1697-1974* (1974).

15 Paul M. Kerrigan, 'Irish coastguard stations', in *Ir. Sword*, vol. 14 (1980-82),103-105.

16 PRO WO 33/47.

17 PRO WO 192/32.

18 PRO WO 33/604.

19 PRO WO 33/605.

20 MOD, RA-RE Works Committee, 1895.

21 MOD, RA-RE Works Committee, 1895.

22 MOD, RA-RE Works Committee, 1895.

23 PRO WO 33/47.

24 J. Buttimer, 'The Treaty Ports', in *An Cosantóir*, vol. 38 July 1978, 195-199.

25 *An Cosantoir*, vol. 33, November 1973 (Artillery Corps issue).

26 J.E.Dawson and C. Lawlor, 'Coast defence artillery', in *An Cosantóir*, vol. 33 November 1973, 391-396.

Bibliography

Andrews, J.H. 'The Irish surveys of Robert Lythe', *Imago Mundi*, vol.19 (1965), 22-31.

Ardilaun, Lady *Tales of a Grandfather*. 1914.

Blomfield, R. *Sebastien le Prestre de Vauban, 1633-1707*. 1938 (reprinted 1971).

Brunicardi, Niall *Haulbowline, Spike and Rocky Islands*. 1982.

Bryan, D *The Great Earl of Kildare*. 1933.

Bryan, Dan 'Colonel Richard Grace, 1651-52', *Ir. Sword*, vol. 4, (1959-60), 43-51.

'Ballyshannon Fort, Co. Kildare, 1642-50', *Ir. Sword*, vol. 4 (1959-60), 93-98.

Buckley, J 'Report of Sir Josias Bodley on some Ulster fortresses in 1608', *UJA*, series 2, vol.16 (1910), 61-64.

Buttimer, J 'The Treaty Ports', *An Cosantóir*, vol. 38, July 1978, 195-199.

Cairns, C 'Guns and Castles in Tipperary', *Ir. Sword*, vol.16 (1985), 111-116.

Caldwell, David *Scottish Weapons and Fortifications 1100-1800*. 1981.

Caulfield, Richard (ed.) *Council Book of Youghal*.1878.

Council Book of Kinsale. 1879.

Coad, J. G. and Lewis, P. N 'The later fortifications of Dover', *Post-Medieval Archaeology*, vol. 16 (1982), 141-200.

Craig, Maurice *The Architecture of Ireland from the Earliest Times to 1880*. 1982.

Crooks, J.J. *History of the Royal Irish Regiment of Artillery*. 1914.

Dawson, J.E. and Lawlor, C. 'Coast defence artillery', *An Cosantóir*, vol. 33 November 1973, 391-396.

Dillon, A 'The fort at Tarbert, Co. Kerry', *Irish Sword*, vol. 3 (1959-60), 286.

Duffy, C *Fire and Stone: The Science of Fortress Warfare 1660-1860*. 1975.

Siege Warfare: the Fortress in the Early Modern World, 1494-1660. 1979.

The Fortress in the Age of Vauban and Frederick the Great 1660-1789. 1985.

Dunlop, R *Ireland Under the Commonwealth*. 1913.

Gilbert, J.T. (ed.), *Documents Relating to Ireland, 1794-1804*. 1893, (reprinted 1970).

Webb Gilman, H 'Castlemore and connected castles in Muskerry, Co. Cork', *JCHAS*, vol.1 (1892)

Gosling, P 'Silent guns; two pieces of early 19th century ordnance on the shores of Galway Bay', *JGAHS* vol 42 (1989-90), 139-143.

Gowan, M 'Dunboy Castle, Co. Cork', *JCHAS*, vol. 83 (1978), 1-49.

Hale, John R. 'The Early Development of the Bastion- An Italian Chronology, c.1450-1534' in

Hale J.R., Highfield, H and Smalley, B. (eds.) *Europe in the late Middle Ages*. 1965.

Renaissance Fortification: Art or Engineering. 1977.

Hanley, M.K. *The Story of Custume Barracks Athlone , 1697-1974* . 1974.

Harbison, Peter 'P. Burke's painting of Youghal', *JCHAS*, vol. 78 (1973), 66-79.

Guide to the National Monuments of Ireland. 1992.

Hardiman, James *The History of the Town and County of Galway*. 1829.

Hayes-McCoy, G. A. 'The early history of guns in Ireland', *JGAHS*, vol. 18 (1938), 43-65.

Ulster and Other Irish Maps c. 1600 (1964).

Irish Battles (1969).

HMSO Belfast *Historic Monuments of Northern Ireland, An Introduction and Guide*. 1983.

de hOir, S. 'Guns in Medieval and Tudor Ireland' *Ir. Sword*, vol. 15 (1982), 76-88.

Hogg, I.V. *Coast Defences of England and Wales, 1856-1956*. 1974.

Hore, P.H. (ed.) *History of the Town and County of Wexford*. 6 vols 1900-11.

Hughes, B.P. *British Smooth-bore Artillery- The Muzzle Loading Artillery of the 18th and 19th Centuries*. 1969.

Hughes, Quentin *Military Architecture*. 1974 (revised ed. 1991).

Stuart Jones, E. H. *An Invasion That Failed: the French Expedition to Ireland,1796.* 1950.

Jackson, R. Wyse 'Queen Anne's Irish army establishment in 1704', *Ir. Sword* vol. 1 (1949-52), 133-135.

Jones, F.M. 'The plan of the Golden Fort at Smerwick, 1580', *Ir.Sword*, vol 2 (1954), 41-42.

Jope, E.M. 'Scottish influence in the north of Ireland: castles with Scottish features, 1580-1640', *UJA*, series 3, vol.14 (1951), 32-47.

'Moyry, Charlemont, Castleraw and Richhill: fortification to architecture in the north of Ireland', *UJA*, series 3, vol.23 (1960), 97-123.

Jope, E.M. ed. *An Archaeological Survey of Co. Down* (1966).

Jope, E.M. ed. *Studies in Building History.* 1961

Kelleher, George D. *Gunpowder to Ballistic Missiles- Ireland's War Industries.* 1992.

Kenyon, John R. *Castles, town defences and artillery fortifications in Britain and Ireland: a bibliography.* Council for British Archaeology, Res Rep. no.53, 1983 and Res.Rep. no.72, 1990.

Kerrigan, Paul M. 'The Shannonbridge fortifications', *Ir. Sword*, vol. 11 (1974), 234-245.

'The batteries, Athlone', *JOAS* vol. 1 (1974-75), 264-270.

'A military map of Ireland of the 1790's', *Ir.Sword* vol. 12 (1976), 247-251.

'Charles Fort, Kinsale', *Ir. Sword*, vol. 13 (1977-79), 323-338.

'The capture of the *Hoche* in 1798', *Ir. Sword*, vol. 13 (1977-79), 123-127.

'The batteries: some additional notes', *JOAS* vol. 2 (1978), 24-25

'The defences of the Shannon; Portumna to Athlone 1793-1815', in *Irish Midland Studies*, edited by H. Murtagh (1980), 168-192

'Seventeenth-century fortifications, forts and garrisons in Ireland: a preliminary list', *Ir.Sword* vol. 14 (1980-82). 3-24, 135-56.

'Gunboats and sea fencibles in Ireland, 1804', *Ir. Sword*, vol. 14 (1980-82), 188-191.

'Irish coastguard stations 1858-67', *Ir. Sword*, vol. 14 (1980-82), 103-105.

'The naval attack on Wexford in June 1798', *Ir. Sword*, vol. 15 (1983), 198-199,

'A return of barracks in Ireland, 1811', *Ir. Sword* vol.15 (1983), 277-283.

'Minorca and Ireland, an architectural connection: the Martello towers of Dublin Bay', *Ir. Sword*, vol. 15 (1983), 192-196.

'The fortifications of Waterford, Passage and Duncannon, 1495 to 1690', *Decies*, vol. 29 (1985), 12-23.

'Garrisons and barracks in the Irish midlands, 1704-1828', *JOAS* vol 2 (1985), 100-108.

'Fortifications in Tudor Ireland 1547-1603', *Fortress*, no.7, November 1990, 27-39.

Leask, Harold G. 'The ancient walls of Limerick', *North Munster Antiquarian Journal*, vol. 2 (1941), 99.

Irish Castles and Castellated Houses (1941, revised and reprinted 1964).

'Redoubts occupied by the Royal Scots in Ireland in the eighteenth century', *Ir. Sword* vol. 1 (1949-52), 188-190.

Litchfield, Norman E.H. *The Militia Artillery 1852-1909.* 1987.

Loeber, Rolf 'Irish country houses and castles of the late Caroline period: an unremembered past recaptured', *Irish Georgian Society Bulletin*, vol. 16 (January-June 1973), 1-70

A Biographical Dictionary of Architects in Ireland, 1600-1720. 1981.

'Biographical dictionary of engineers in Ireland, 1600-1730' *Ir. Sword*, vol. 1, (1977-79), 30-44, 106-122, 230-255, 282-314

'A gate to Connaught: the building of the fortified town of Jamestown, County Leitrim, in the era of plantation', *Ir. Sword*, vol. 15 (1983), 149-152.

'The lost architecture of the Wexford plantation' in Whelan, K (ed.) *Wexford: History and Society.* 1987.

'Operations of the Parliamentary Squadron at the Siege of Duncannon in 1645', *Ir. Sword*, vol. 2 (1954), 17-21.

Mallory, Keith and Ottar, Arvid *Architecture of Aggression: a history of military architecture in north west Europe 1900-1945.* 1973.

Mangan, H 'Sarsfield's defence of the Shannon, 1690-91', *Ir. Sword*, vol. 1 (1949-53), 24-32.

MacCauley, J.A. 'General Dumouriez and Irish Defence', *Ir. Sword*, vol. 9 (1969-70), 98-108, 165-173.

MacIvor, Iain 'Artillery and major places of strength in the Lothians and the East Border, 1513-1542', in *Scottish Weapons and Fortifications, 1100-1800*, edited by D.H.Caldwell 1981, 94-152.

McNally, Sir H. *The Irish Militia, 1793-1816* (1949)

McNeill, T.E. *Carrickfergus Castle* (1981)

Moody, T.W. *The Londonderry Plantation, 1609-41* 1939.

Moody, T.W., Martin, F.X., and Byrne, F.J. *A New History of Ireland: Vol. III, Early Modern Ireland 1534-1691.* 1976.

Mulcahy, M., McNamara, T.F. and O'Brien, B. 'Elizabeth Fort, Cork', *Ir. Sword*, vol 4 (1959-60), 127-134.

Mulloy, S. 'French engineers with the Jacobite army in Ireland, 1689-91', *Ir. Sword*, vol. 15 (1983), 222-232.

Murtagh, H. 'Ballymore and the Jacobite War', *JOAS* vol. 1 (1974-75), 242-246.
'The town wall fortifications of Athlone', in Murtagh H (ed.) *Irish Midland Studies*. 1980, 89-106.

O' Faolain, Sean *The Great O'Neill a Biography of Hugh O'Neill Earl of Tyrone 1550-1616*. 1942.

O'Neil, B.H. St. J *Castles and Cannon: a Study of Early Artillery Fortifications in England*. 1960.

O'Rahilly, Alfred 'The massacre at Smerwick, 1580', in *JCHAS*, vol 42 (1937).

O'Sullivan, M.D. 'The fortifications of Galway', *JGAHS*, *vol.* 16 (1934-35), 1-47.

Powell, J.R. 'Penn's expedition to Bunratty in 1646', *Mariner's Mirror*, vol. 40, 4-20.

Quinn, D. B. and Nicholls, K. W. 'Ireland in 1534', in *A New History of Ireland*, vol. III: *Early Modern Ireland, 1534-1691* (1976), 1-38.

Rolf, Rudi and Saal, Peter *Fortress Europe*. 1986 (English language ed. 1988).

Rowan, A *The Buildings of Ireland: North-West Ulster* . 1979.

Rowan, A and Casey, Christine *The Buildings of Ireland: North Leinster*. 1993.

Ryan, F. W. 'A projected invasion of Ireland in 1811', *Ir. Sword*, vol. 1 (1949-53), 136-141.

Salter, M *Castles and Stronghouses of Ireland*. 1993

Saunders, Andrew *Fortress Britain - Artillery Fortification in the British Isles and Ireland*. 1989.

Simms, J. G. 'Sligo in the Jacobite War, 1687-91', *Ir. Sword*, vol. 7 (1965), 124-135.

Jacobite Ireland 1685-91. 1969.

Shelby, L.R. *John Rogers, Tudor Military Engineer*. 1967.

Stell, G. 'Highland garrisons, 1717-23: Bernera Barracks', *Post-Medieval Archaeology*, vol. 7, (1973), 20-30.

Stevenson, Ian 'Ireland- Two Treaty Ports and the one that Never Was', *Fortress*, no.12, February 1992, 51-60, no.13 , May 1993, 34-45.

Story, G. *A Continuation of the Impartial History of the Wars of Ireland*. 1693.

Thomas, Avril *The Walled Towns of Ireland*. 2 vols, 1992.

Townsend, B. L. 'History of "Bryan's Fort", Castletownshend', *JCHAS*, vol. 42 (1937-38), 1-49.

Viollet-le-Duc, E *An Essay on the Military Architecture of the Middle Ages*. 1860, translated from the French by M. Macdermott

Wakefield, E *An Account of Ireland, Statistical and Political*. 1812.

Walsh, P 'Cromwell's Barracks, a commonwealth garrison fort on Inishbofin, Co. Galway', *JGAHS* 42 (1989-90), 30-71.

Walton, J. C. 'Aspects of Passage East: part 2', *Decies*, vol. 11 (1979).

Waterman, D 'Castle Archdale', *UJA*, series 3, vol. 22 (1959).

'Sir John Davies and his Ulster buildings', *UJA*, series 3, vol.23 (1960), 89-96.

Williams, B. B. 'An artillery fort on Trannish Island, Co. Fermanagh', *Clogher Record*, vol. 9 (1977), 295-296.

Wills, Henry *Pillboxes: A study of U.K.Defences, 1940*. 1985

Wilson, G *The Old Telegraphs*. 1976.

Index